TACITUS

ANNALS I

TACITUS

ANNALS I

Edited by

N.P. Miller

Bristol Classical Press

This impression 2007
This edition published in 1992 by
Bristol Classical Press
an imprint of
Gerald Duckworth & Co. Ltd.
90-93 Cowcross Street, London EC1M 6BF
Tel: 020 7490 7300
Fax: 020 7490 0080
inquiries@duckworth-publishers.co.uk
www.ducknet.co.uk

First published by Methuen in 1959
Published by Bradda Books Ltd, 1965
Published by Basil Blackwell Ltd, 1984

©1959, 1992 by N.P. Miller

A catalogue record for this book is available
from the British Library

ISBN 978 1 85399 358 9

Printed and bound in Great Britain by
CPI Antony Rowe, Chippenham

PREFACE

It is the aim of this series that the book should be, if necessary, self-supporting. I have accordingly tried, in Introduction, Commentary and Vocabulary, to provide the minimum amount of information necessary for an understanding of the text. But I should like to emphasize that these are not intended to be substitutes for dictionaries, grammar-books and special studies on points of literary or historical interest, and that it is hoped that the student will pursue the references to such works. Where possible, the gist of important foreign publications, which might not be readily accessible, has been given.

The text here printed differs in some fifteen places from the Oxford Text; none of these changes is an original emendation, but a choice from alternatives already suggested. The reading of the Oxford Text is given in each place in a footnote, and the reasons for preferring another reading are discussed in the Commentary. The line-numbering of the Oxford Text has been replaced by the more convenient sub-sections of the Teubner edition.

Tacitus provides a good basic training in scholarship; the text is in a reasonably good condition, but presents some interesting problems which still merit discussion; the linguistic and literary value of his work is considerable, and important for the understanding of Latin as a whole; and there are countless historical problems raised by his narrative, over whose value historians are still arguing. I cannot pretend to have dealt adequately with all these points, but I hope that I have indicated what the difficulties are.

v

In preparing this edition I have consulted the editions of Furneaux (Oxford, 1896), Nipperdey/Andresen (Berlin, 1892), Jacob Gronovius (Utrecht, 1721) and Orelli (Zurich, 1859). Of more general works of reference I have used Gerber and Greef, *Lexicon Taciteum* (Leipzig, 1903) and Kühner-Stegmann, *Lateinische Grammatik* (Leverkusen, 1955). Other books and periodicals used are acknowledged in the Commentary. Professor Syme's important study, *Tacitus* (Oxford, 1958), appeared too late for me to use it here. The translation of various phrases which is given in the Commentary, may be that of Michael Grant (Penguin Books, 1956), Church and Brodribb (Macmillan, 1891), or my own.

I should like to record my most grateful thanks to Professor W. S. Maguinness, General Editor of this series, for much help and encouragement; to Professor W. H. McCrea of Royal Holloway College and Mr D. H. Sadler, O.B.E., Superintendent of H. M. Nautical Almanac Office, Herstmonceux, for answering my questions about Eclipses; to Professor D. M. Jones of Westfield College, for advice on a philological point; to Mrs V. Way, for allowing me to use some valuable notes on *Annals* I made by her husband, the late J. A. H. Way, Lecturer in Humanity in the University of Glasgow; to Professor R. G. Austin of Liverpool University and Professor H. Tredennick of Royal Holloway College, for patiently reading parts of the Introduction and Commentary and making many helpful criticisms and suggestions thereon; and to Miss A. Woodward, for much help in reading proofs. For the errors that remain I regret that I am alone responsible.

One debt I cannot now repay. Mr J. W. Pirie, late Senior Lecturer in Humanity in the University of Glasgow, first showed me the fascination of the study of Tacitus, and by his own shrewd scholarship indicated the method such a study should follow. If this edition has any merit, it owes much to him, to whose memory it is affectionately dedicated.

N. P. M.

Royal Holloway College,
June 1958

CONTENTS

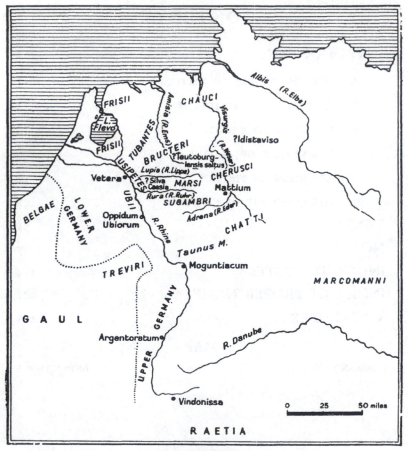

GERMANY

To illustrate Chapters 31–71

INTRODUCTION

I

THE LIFE AND WORKS OF TACITUS

We know singularly little of the life of Tacitus, and that little
has been pieced together mainly from casual references in his
own writings and in the letters of the Younger Pliny. Cornelius Tacitus [1] must have been born about A.D. 55 (Pliny, in
Ep. VII, 20, 3–4, indicates that Tacitus was a few years older
than Pliny himself, who was born in A.D. 61/2), and was
perhaps of Celtic stock, from N. Italy or S. Gaul.[2] That he
was not a Roman is clear from the story in Pliny, *Ep.* IX, 23,
when he was asked *Italicus es an prouincialis?* And this is
supported by his circle of friends at Rome—Agricola, Pliny,
Julius Secundus and others—men who came, not from the
Roman aristocracy, but from good Italian or Romanized
Gallic stock. The Cornelius Tacitus mentioned by the Elder
Pliny (*H.N.* VII, 76) as an *eques Romanus* and procurator of
Gallia Belgica, is probably the father of the historian; dates,
and identity of a not very common name make this likely,
and a father who was an *eques* would provide a plausible
background for what we know of Tacitus, and would belong
to the kind of circle where Tacitus continued to find his
friends.

His public career, he explains in *Hist.* I, 1, began under
Vespasian and was advanced by Titus and Domitian. We

---

[1] The *praenomen* is not certain. A writer of A.D. C 5 calls him Gaius: but Publius
(from the superscription to *Ann.* I in M) seems on the whole more likely.

[2] M. L. Gordon in *J.R.S.* 1936, pp. 145 sq. examines the evidence of the
name Tacitus, which may be Celtic in origin, and is most commonly found
in the north.

know that under Domitian, in A.D. 88, he was praetor (*Ann.* XI, 11), but precisely what the earlier offices were is uncertain. It seems likely, however, that he was given the *latus clauus*, the mark of Senatorial rank, by Vespasian, and he may have held the quaestorship under Titus. Early in his career (A.D. 77) he married the daughter of the great general Agricola (*Ag.* 9), and with her he was absent from Rome between A.D. 89 and 93 (*Ag.* 45), almost certainly governing a province, which may have been one of the Gauls. He returned to Rome in 93 and lived through the last three years of Domitian's Reign of Terror, an experience which embittered him and coloured his interpretation of earlier reigns.

In 97, under Nerva, he held the consulship (Plin. *Ep.* II, 1, 6) and in the next few years we hear of his appearance as counsel in court and his eloquence there (Plin. *Ep.* II, 11). About A.D. 113 he was proconsul of Asia, and his name is recorded on an inscription from Caria. The last datable reference we have is in *Ann.* II, 61, where the Eastern boundary of the Roman world is described in terms valid only between A.D. 115–117. Tacitus probably lived to see the end of Trajan's reign in 117, but died shortly afterwards.

He was thus not only a man of letters, but a man who followed a public career, and a noted orator. His literary works are as follows:

(*a*) *Dialogus de Oratoribus*. This is now generally accepted as being by Tacitus. It is a discussion in dialogue form on the reasons for the decline of oratory, and is a pleasant piece of writing in a style rather like Cicero's. The characters are well drawn and the writing is lively. It is probably contemporaneous with the *Agricola* and *Germania*: its very different style is due to its different *genre*.

(*b*) *Agricola*, a biography of his father-in-law, was published in A.D. 98, after the death of Domitian. It is not a critical appreciation in the modern sense of biography, but more in the nature of a panegyric. Much of the book deals with Agricola's campaigns in Britain, which are treated in a way which foreshadows the future historian. The style is much more recognizably 'Tacitean' than that of the *Dialogus*, showing compression and variety and barbed *sententiae*.

(c) *Germania*, published later in the same year, treats *De origine et situ Germanorum*. It belongs to a recognized literary genre, describing the country, peoples and customs of a race. Much of it must have been based on literary sources, but the work gives an impression of care and accuracy. Tacitus may have learned something of the Germans from his father (if the procurator of Belgica was his father), and may himself have served from 89–93 in one of the provinces near to Germany. The style of the *Germania* is, as would be expected from its date, very like that of the *Agricola*.

(d) The *Histories*,[1] his first major historical work proper, appear to have been completely published by A.D. 109. (They are mentioned in Pliny, *Ep.* VI and VII, which were probably written between A.D. 104 and 108.) This work covered the period from the death of Nero to the death of Domitian (*Ann.* XI, 11) i.e. A.D. 68–96, but only Books I–IV and part of V have survived. The Annals and Histories together formed thirty books,[2] of which the Annals probably accounted for eighteen, leaving twelve for the Histories. In the Histories Tacitus is writing of his own times, and he must have used primary sources for most of the period. His individual style is here fully developed.

(e) The *Annals* (*Ab excessu diui Augusti*) are his latest and most impressive work. They consisted (probably, see above) of eighteen books, covering the period from the death of

---

[1] Title in Plin. *Ep.* VII, 33, 1.
[2] Jerome, *Comm. in Zach.* 3, 14 (in Migne, *Pat. Lat.* 25, 1522).

Augustus to the death of Nero (A.D. 14–68), but of these VII–X are completely lost, and V, VI, XI and XVI are mutilated. Books I–VI, dealing with the reign of Tiberius, about which Tacitus felt strongly, show the most marked eccentricities of style; XI–XVI, though still unmistakably 'Tacitean,' are less peculiar and intense.

II

TACITUS AS AN HISTORIAN

The reputation of Tacitus the Historian has been a curious one. He has at different times been accused of being a Renaissance forgery, a pathological liar striving only for effect, a rhetorician who sees the truth only from the standpoint of his own case, and a stylist who follows slavishly a single literary source and turns it into Tacitean Latin.[1] No one now believes in the theory of forgery because, apart from its intrinsic improbability, coins and inscriptions discovered after the manuscripts of Tacitus confirm facts for which he is the only other source; no Renaissance forger could have known them. Nor are the other theories now held in their extreme form. But doubts remain, and they are important, because for much of the period Tacitus is the best (sometimes the only) literary source, and we must know how far he is to be trusted.

The doubts arise, not from the facts he records (for most of these continue to be triumphantly confirmed by later discoveries), but from his interpretation of them. His picture of the reign of Tiberius in *Annals* I–VI is no longer accepted as the whole truth; his interpretation of motives is not always convincing; his villains tend to be too villainous and his view of human nature over-cynical. Now an historian cannot be

---

[1] Cf. Ross, *Tacitus and Bracciolini. The Annals forged in the fifteenth century*. Bacha, *Le Génie de Tacite*. Jerome, *Aspects of the study of Roman History*. Fabia, *Les Sources de Tacite*.

denied the right to put forward his interpretation of the events he is recording; it is part of his job, and the part which distinguishes him from a simple chronicler. Nor can it be denied that in his judgment there will be a certain subjective element; he is an individual, with an individual's mind, and on many matters his honest decision will be different from another man's. The essential point is that it should be honest, and based on a careful and skilled attempt to establish the facts. Tacitus has, it is generally agreed, sometimes produced an interpretation which distorts the facts; what has to be decided (and the decisions of modern historians on Tacitus differ much as Tacitus and Velleius differed about Tiberius) is whether he is an honest and capable but sometimes mistaken historian, or a careless and unreliable historical novelist.

Methods of composition are important here, and there are some points which tell significantly in Tacitus' favour. To begin with, the general impression given by his work is that it is serious in intention and in production bears the mark of the integrity of a great mind. Artistic integrity, no less than any other kind, is almost impossible to counterfeit, and deliberate deceit leaves a taste which is indefinable but unmistakable. From this taste the works of Tacitus are entirely free. That being so, what he himself tells us of his aim and methods in writing history need not be dismissed as a formal protestation of disinterestedness, but may be taken at its face value. The aim [1] is not the aim of a modern historian, and the methods of critical research could be carried much farther, and to that extent the value of Tacitus' work is depreciated: but for an ancient historian the aim and methods show considerable enlightenment. For the ancient historian depended

[1] His aim is a moral one, to record the good and to deter men from evil words and deeds by the knowledge that posterity will hear of them (*Ann.* III, 65).

much more on literary sources than does his modern successor, and was much less critical in his use of them. Tacitus professes careful collation of previous histories (e.g. *Ann*. IV, 10 and 57; XIII, 20) and says that where they agree he will follow that account, where there is a discrepancy he will record it under the author's name. This is not quite so haphazard a proceeding as it sounds: for his authorities had such differing backgrounds and prejudices, that an incident about which they all agree might reasonably be accepted as a true account: and the relatively small number of specific references to discrepancies can be accounted for, if we take it that Tacitus meant he would so record them only when he could not himself feel certain which was correct. There is plenty of evidence for careful consideration and shrewd judgment of sources (e.g. his comment on Fabius in *Ann*. XIII, 20) and for independent researches made in an attempt to settle a difficult point (e.g. *Ann*. III, 3; IV, 53).

His literary sources for the early books of the Annals were probably the histories of Aufidius Bassus, Servilius Nonianus and possibly the Elder Seneca: but none of these is mentioned by name. On specific points he consulted 'specialist' works, such as the Elder Pliny's 'German Wars' (*Ann*. I, 69) and the Memoirs of the Younger Agrippina (*Ann*. IV, 53); his account of the legionary mutiny in Germany (*Ann*. I, 31–49) must owe much to Pliny. And the Pannonian revolt too is presented in such detail that Tacitus must have had a first-hand source for it, perhaps a work by one of the officers present. He no doubt elaborates the episodes, but his knowledge of names like Percennius (16) and the centurion Lucilius' nickname (23) seems to indicate a detailed source. Frequently he indicates a number of authorities by such phrases as *tradunt plerique* (*Ann*. I, 13, 29, 53). He obviously knew the speeches of Tiberius (*Ann*. I, 81), and may have found them in the *acta senatus* (the

Roman Hansard); his only specific reference to the *acta* is in
Ann. XV, 74, but his detailed reporting of senatorial proceedings indicates that he may have used them more frequently
than the single reference implies. For much of the Histories
he must have used primary sources, because no literary accounts
existed of contemporary history; and a letter of Pliny's to
Tacitus, giving first-hand and detailed information about an
incident which Tacitus wished to incorporate in his Histories,
shows that he did trouble to collect accurate information.
It is improbable that, having begun his historical writings on
this method, he would in his later work ignore the primary
sources entirely.[1]

Tacitus can thus be vindicated as an honest and careful
historian. But the discrepancy between fact and interpretation
remains. There are several reasons for it.[2] Tacitus, writing of
the reign of Tiberius some seventy years after its end, would
inevitably be faced with conflicting accounts of it. Velleius,
e.g. and Aufidius Bassus favoured Tiberius; any writer connected with the elder Agrippina would be strongly biased
against him; and between Tiberius and Tacitus came the
Flavian dynasty, who constantly played down the whole
Julio-Claudian house as an effete aristocracy. Much of the
material which would have helped to settle this problem was
in the imperial archives and inaccessible. Tacitus saw the
explanation of his conflicting sources in the hypocrisy of
Tiberius—an explanation almost certainly wrong, but not
completely impossible and foolish. Once he had come to that
decision, and had seen in Tiberius' reign the seeds of Domitian's Reign of Terror, the beginning of the treason trials and
of the servility of the Senate, his own experiences coloured

---

[1] For a good account of Tacitus' use of his sources, see Marsh, *The Reign of Tiberius*, pp. 233 sq.
[2] Walker, *The Annals of Tacitus*, pp. 138 sq., discusses them at length.

his interpretation of the earlier period, and he uses the full force of his style to emphasize what seems to him a very dreadful thing. The motives he sees as likely ones for an action are nearly always discreditable—the hypocrisy of Tiberius, e.g. suggested in *Ann.* I, 7, 3; 77, 3; 81, 2; the suggestion (10, 7) that Augustus wanted Tiberius as a foil for his own more brilliant qualities; while the reasons offered to explain (80, 2) an aspect of Tiberius' provincial policy are none of them to his credit, and none takes account of the possibility that Tiberius had legitimate and statesmanlike reasons for that policy. If alternative motives are suggested, one at least is usually discreditable (as in *Ann.* I, 3, 3; 5, 2; 10, 2; 11, 4; 62, 2). Note that Tacitus the historian does not commit himself to the statement that that *was* the reason. But he cannot resist quoting one which fits so well his own gloomy picture of the early Empire: and the damage is done by the mere mention. As Cicero makes his point neatly by listing all the topics he is not going to mention (*praetereo, omitto*, etc.), so Tacitus insinuates the doubt about motive into the reader's mind.

He uses tradition and rumour in much the same way. The whole story about Livia in *Ann.* I, 5 (*rumor incesserat*) is almost certainly a pure fabrication of anti-Caesarian gossip,[1] and Tacitus does not present it as fact. But it does damage, as does the quoted rumour about Tiberius' motives in 76, 4: the seed has been planted, even though he starts with *non crediderim*. This is perhaps most clearly seen in his treatment of cc. 9–10 of *Ann.* I. These purport to be a balanced summing up of the

---

[1] The parallelism of this story with the account of Claudius' death and the accession of Nero (*Ann.* XII, 68) has been noted. The comparison was probably drawn not by Tacitus, but by one of his sources. But he is not unaware of the value of the better-authenticated story about Nero in bolstering the weaker case against Tiberius. For a full discussion of the passages see *C.Q.* 1955, pp. 123 sq.

reign of Augustus, 9 presenting the case in his favour, 10 the criticisms made against him. But 10 is the longer chapter, its criticisms are detailed and so more emphatic than the general considerations dealt with in 9, and §§ 1–3 are a contemptuous twisting of Augustus' own statements in *Res Gestae* 1.[1] There is no doubt which view of Augustus Tacitus finds most to his liking; but he does not in fact commit himself to either— both are presented as the traditions they undoubtedly were.

A similar connexion of style and interpretation can be seen both in short phrases, where a slight change of style or construction throws the emphasis where Tacitus wants it (e.g. *Ann.* I, 10, 2, *arma quae in Antonium acceperit contra rempublicam uersa;* the change to *contra* is not only to avoid monotony) and in longer sections, as in cc. 72–4 where all the brilliance of his style is used to emphasize the enormity of the renewed treason trials, or the rather romantic style which marks the whole story of Germanicus' handling of the legionary revolt.

All this is sufficiently disturbing. Yet it can be taken too seriously. Tacitus was neither a rogue nor a fool, and we must not imagine him as maliciously distorting the truth or as having no care for it. The motives he suggests are often wrong, but the important thing is that Tacitus *records the fact* they are intended to explain. A dishonest historian need only have suppressed it; a bad historian might not have thought it worth recording; as it is, we have the paradox of Tacitus' interpretation of Tiberius' reign being called in question by the facts which he himself records.

His bias against Tiberius has the great merit of being obvious, so that it can be taken into account and countered. All historians, being human, have some bias, and the really dangerous ones are those who do not immediately reveal it. Also,

[1] See *J.R.S.* 1912, p. 197.

his picture of Tiberius, though biased, is by no means without value. 'Rehabilitation' of that Emperor can go too far, and it is desirable that Tacitus should remind us that the treason trials under Tiberius are important, and that all was not well with his reign.

The writings of Tacitus are an incomparable literary production, but they are more than that. He has not the analytical mind of Thucydides, nor the degree of detachment to which that historian attained; Tacitus is too emotionally involved to be an historian of that calibre. But he can grasp and handle his material, and his methods and judgments shine in comparison with those of most other Roman historians. He sees the tragedy of man portrayed in the history of the Roman Principate, and he presents that tragedy as he sees it, dramatically and with passionate conviction. His work remains one of the great achievements of ancient historiography.

III

THE STYLE OF TACITUS

Two things in particular influence a writer's style—the intellectual climate of the age in which he lives, and his own character. The literary prose of the Silver Age was very different from the measured cadences and smooth structure of the full-dress Ciceronian style. The difference between prose and poetry had become less marked, and prose now borrowed much of the vocabulary and syntax of poetry, and also its shorter sentence. Rhetoric was a dominating influence and it was a rhetoric artificial and remote from life, which aimed at entertaining a sophisticated and easily bored generation. A speaker had to be witty, incisive and novel if he was to hold his audience.[1] It is not easy to be witty or incisive in a

[1] See Tacitus, *Dial.* 19-20.

Ciceronian period, and so the short, abrupt sentence came into favour—a sentence-form which is admirably suited to raising and holding the audience's interest for a short time, and which gives scope for wit and epigram, brilliance of display and novelty of expression; but which can irritate and jar when sustained in a work of any length.

Most of these elements appear in the style of Tacitus. But the artificiality and affectation which often accompany them in other writers are not apparent, because Tacitus really has something to *say*; he is not making elegant statements about nothing in particular, but quite properly using his mastery of language to emphasize his point.

It is worth while to examine in some detail the structure of Tacitean prose, and to compare it with the classical norm, because it is perhaps here that Tacitus is most original and most effective. To take first a series of short sentences: all Latin writers make use of the short sentence, especially in rapid narrative, but the technique of Tacitus is not that of, e.g. Cicero.

Cic. *Verr.* II, 1, 66. *Rubrius istius comites inuitat; eos omnis Verres certiores facit quid opus esset. mature ueniunt, discumbitur. fit sermo inter eos, et inuitatio ut Graeco more biberetur; hortatur hospes, poscunt maioribus poculis, celebratur omnium sermone laetitiaque conuiuium.* These sentences are short, but complete, and the logical connexion between them is clearly marked; *comites* is picked up by *eos* and in turn becomes the subject of *ueniunt;* the placing of the verb at the beginning of successive clauses (*fit, hortatur, celebratur*) helps to define the structure and to make the progression clear. The pattern is not that of a periodic sentence, but the process is still recognizably weaving. The hist. present tense produces a vivid picture of the incident described. Variety is obtained by different placing of similar words (contrast the positions of *Rubrius* and *Verres*, and *mature ueniunt* with *fit sermo inter eos*), by change of subject (*Rubrius, Verres, comites, sermo*), by alternation of personal and impersonal verbs (*ueniunt, discumbitur, biberetur, hortatur*) and by a slight admixture of abstract nouns used in the normal way. The whole basis of the passage is personal and verbal—note the emphasis on the verbs from *fit* to the end.

Tac. *Ann.* I, 49, 1–2. *clamor uulnera sanguis palam, causa in occulto; cetera fors regit. et quidam bonorum caesi, postquam intellecto in quos saeuiretur pessimi quoque arma rapuerant. neque legatus aut tribunus moderator adfuit: permissa uulgo licentia atque ultio et satietas.* This is, in essentials, a similar piece of rapid narrative, delivered in short sentences. But this time the impression is not only of rapidity, but of deliberate brevity and compression. The sentences are not all in themselves complete, as were Cicero's; the verb 'to be' is omitted and there is no attempt to weave the sentences into a composite fabric—instead, the passage is deliberately disjointed, the sentences gaining their effect from contrast with each other. Variety in this passage comes from a lack of exact verbal balance in balancing phrases (*palam, in occulto: legatus, uulgo: clamor uulnera sanguis, licentia atque ultio et satietas*), from an alternation of personal and abstract nouns (*fors, quidam, legatus, licentia*) and of purely abstract and more material nouns (*clamor, uulnera, sanguis, causa*) and from a varying construction (*clamor* &c. with the verb understood, *fors* personified as the subject of *regit, quidam* with a finite verb, *licentia* &c. as the subjects of their clause). The effect is founded on nouns, not verbs; there is a great concatenation of abstract nouns, vivid and striking in their use, and the omission of the verb 'to be' throws greater emphasis on them. The total effect is obtained by bald statements of the essential qualities of the situation, statements which gain colour and point from their juxtaposition.

The same general characteristics are to be seen in the periodic sentences. For this, comparison may more usefully be made with Livy than with Cicero. The rhetorical style of Tacitus, as shown in the speeches, is much nearer the teaching of the rhetorical schools of his day and therefore less individual than his narrative style. The Livian period may perhaps be taken as the classical norm of that sentence-structure as used in historical narrative.

Livy XXX, 4, 1–3. *cum legatis, quos mitteret ad Syphacem, calonum loco primos ordines spectatae uirtutis atque prudentiae seruili habitu mittebat, qui, dum in colloquio legati essent, uagi per castra, alius alia aditus exitusque omnes, situm formamque et uniuersorum castrorum et partium, qua Poeni qua Numidae haberent, quantum interualli inter Hasdrubalis ac regia castra esset, specularentur moremque simul noscerent stationum uigiliarumque, nocte an interdiu opportuniores insidianti essent et inter crebra colloquia alii atque alii de industria, quo pluribus omnia nota essent mittebantur.* The impression produced by this is of something not unlike the Ciceronian rhetorical period; the structure is organic, and the subordinate clauses and phrases are woven into the fabric of the whole (note especially the clauses between *qui* and *specularentur* and the way in which dependent phrases are firmly inserted in the parent clause—between *calonum . . . mittebat*, e.g. and *alii . . . mittebantur*). There is a logical connexion between clauses, similar to the one which was noticeable in the narrative style of Cicero: *legatis*, e.g. is carried on by *quos*, and stands in obvious contrast to *calonum*, which in turn is connected with *ordines*, and that is picked up by *qui* and subdivided by *alius*; one main statement (*mittebat*) stands near the beginning of the sentence, and the second (*mittebantur*—the echo is surely not accidental) at the end, rounding off the period. Certain words, phrases and clauses stand in obvious balance with one another (*aditus, exitus*;

situm, formam; et uniuersorum, et partium; qua Poeni, qua Numidae; specularentur, noscerent); while variation of noun with noun clause (*aditus, quantum . . . esset, morem*), of temporal clause with adj. (*dum . . . essent, uagi*) and of position of clauses (*nocte an interdiu* elaborates *morem* instead of being directly dependent on *noscerent* as *quantum . . . esset* is on *specularentur*) —all such devices help to avoid any monotony which over-rigid balance might produce. Abstract nouns (*uirtutis, prudentiae, situm, formam, morem*) are used sparingly and, on the whole, in the orthodox manner; and, as in Cicero, the foundation of the sentence is verbal and personal.

Tac. *Ann.* I, 2, 1. *postquam Bruto et Cassio caesis nulla iam publica arma, Pompeius apud Siciliam oppressus exutoque Lepido, interfecto Antonio ne Iulianis quidem partibus nisi Caesar dux reliquus, posito triumuiri nomine consulem se ferens et ad tuendam plebem tribunicio iure contentum, ubi militem donis, populum annona, cunctos dulcedine otii pellexit, insurgere paulatim, munia senatus magistratuum legum in se trahere, nullo aduersante, cum ferocissimi per acies aut proscriptione cecidissent, ceteri nobilium, quanto quis seruitio promptior, opibus et honoribus extollerentur ac nouis ex rebus aucti tuta et praesentia quam uetera et periculosa mallent.* This is a much jerkier and more abrupt sentence, and its components are of a somewhat different kind. There is no clearly marked connexion between clauses, either organically or chronologically—the impression is almost of contrast rather than connexion. It starts harmlessly and deceptively with the *postquam* clause, which lasts until *reliquus* and appears to contain, very properly, three statements depending on *postquam* and three abl. abs. in subordination to them; but *postquam* lacks a verb, the abl. abs. are not evenly distributed, and *Pompeius . . . oppressus* has not the logical importance of *nulla publica arma* and *Caesar dux reliquus*, though it balances them in construction; the subject of the main verb (*Caesar*) is not given the structural importance one might expect, but appears as one third of the subject of the *postquam* clause, and only its skilful placing within that clause makes its real position clear. There follows an abl. abs., grammatically subordinate to *ferens* but logically parallel to it, and within these phrases the ideas (but not the constructions) of *triumuiri*, *consulem* and *tribunicio iure* are balanced. The *ubi* clause is normal, except for the lack of parallelism introduced by *dulcedine*; for *donis* and *annona* are material things, *dulcedine* is not, so that one's attention is arrested by the unusual phrase—the technique is that of the writer who described an old man seen 'digging with great energy and a tablespoon'. Then comes the main statement of the sentence, expressed by two clauses which complement each other and whose verbs are historic infins. There we might have expected the sentence to end: but Tacitus adds another and connected main statement— this time expressed in an abl. abs.—and on it depend two causal clauses, whose balance is again out of joint, *nobilium* being postponed to the second clause so that it stands in close and marked contrast with *seruitio*, and the elaboration of *ceteri* sq. showing which clause Tacitus wished especially to emphasize. *mallent* is logically the consequence of *extollerentur* but is simply joined to it by *ac* and left to make its own effect, and the sentence ends on a bitter and cynical note, but without giving any impression of a rounded structural whole. It is emphatically a sentence whose effect depends on nouns, not verbs; it contains very few verbs of any kind, and its main statement is expressed by hist. infins., which form is as near as a verb can get to being a noun.

The effect of a sentence such as this is not that of the smoothly rounded period. Tacitus makes his point more by line than by decoration; he uses as few words as possible and packs them full of meaning—their own meaning and the

colour they get from their context. One may compare *Ann.*
I, 13, 1 where he describes Tiberius' mistrust of Arruntius
(*diuitem, promptum, artibus egregiis et pari fama publice, suspectabat*); here every word counts, and the full meaning
comes from the careful placing of the words in relation to one
another, and the finishing of a catalogue of virtues by the
significant verb *suspectabat*. Again, he quite deliberately avoids
exact balance and antithesis, a device which is extraordinarily
effective and which requires for its effect a knowledge in the
reader of what the normal balanced phrase would be. The
basic principle of the stylistic device is in fact that of the
famous limerick:

> *There was an old man of Dunoon,*
> *Who always ate soup with a fork,*
> *For he said, 'As I eat*
> *Neither fish, fowl nor flesh,*
> *I should finish my dinner too quick.'*

Tacitus' aim is not simply entertainment or parody, but he
too wishes to surprise his reader into attention and so to make
his point; and his phrases such as *per acies aut proscriptione*
(*Ann.* I, 2, 1): *incertum metu an per inuidiam* (11, 4): *deliguntur
legiones, quinta dextro lateri, unetuicesima in laeuum, primani
ducendum ad agmen, uicesimanus aduersum secuturos* (64, 5) are
intended to be noticeably different from the normal anti-
thetical arrangement and so to attract interest and attention.

Tacitean sentences are not woven as the Ciceronian or
Livian period is woven, but the phrases are laid on as a painter
lays on colours, so that each is effective not only in itself, but
enhances the neighbouring one and is enhanced by it. Colour
and dignity too, are given to the prose by the avoidance of
common terms (occasionally carried to extremes, as in the
'agricultural implements' of *Ann.* I, 65, 7) and by the use of

archaic and poetic words (e.g. in *Ann*. I, *quis* for *quibus* (8, 3) *occipere* (39, 3), *lymphatus* (32, 1), *fragmen* (61, 3), *peruigil* (65, 1)) and of phrases which echo the poets, especially Virgil. *tantae molis capacem* (11, 1), e.g. is an obvious reminiscence of *Aen.* I, 33, *tantae molis erat Romanam condere gentem:* and *immotum . . . fixumque* (47, 1) recalls *Aen.* IV, 15, *fixum immotumque.* Here again the device is not purely formal and stylistic, but is designed to emphasize a statement or bring a word into prominence. Tacitus is a master of the significant word, whether it gains its significance by being a poetical word used in a prose context (as in the exx. above), or by being a new invention (see *regnatrix*, 4, 4 and note there), or simply by being an ordinary word whose context deepens its emotional content (see *dominatio* used of Augustus in 3, 1 after being used of Sulla in 1, 1; *procumbere* (12, 1), *simulacra* (77, 3), *imago* (81, 2)). The language of Tacitus is highly metaphorical (*exuere*, 2, 1; 4, 1; 75, 2: *imago*, 10, 3; 81, 2: *grauescere*, 5, 1: *exardescere*, 74, 4 and many others), and he uses personified abstract nouns freely (e.g. *nox*, 28, 1; 49, 1; 50, 4; 64, 3: *uaecordia*, 32, 1: *cupido*, 49, 3; 61, 1). There are many epigrammatic statements, used especially to end a sentence or close a chapter (note the closing phrases of cc. 6, 8, 55, 69, 73, and 81, and such statements as 80, 2, *ut callidum eius ingenium, ita anxium iudicium*). These *sententiae*, though having much in common with the standard rhetorical device of the age, are not merely clever phrases, but spring from a profound and often tragic experience of life; they are neatly turned, but they have something of importance to say—something which may be bitter and cynical, but will never be artificial or affected.

The style, in fact, reflects not only the age but the man. Tacitus was an embittered soul, resigned to the worst being true, inclined to see always the possible base explanation and, merely by stating it, to make the reader see it too. In his

tortuous sentences can be seen not only his striving after
variety, but the intensity of his thought and the bitterness
of his feelings. The historical prose of Tacitus owes something
to Sallust, who knew how to use short sentences, archaisms
and poetic words to startle and impress; but it goes far beyond
him, and the brooding thoughtful mind, working on the,
terse epigrammatic style of the day, has produced a controlled,
compressed prose which is unique in Latin literature.

IV

THE SYNTAX OF TACITUS

(In this section, and in the Commentary, the term 'classical'
is employed as a convenient method of reference to the stricter
usage of the age of Cicero and Caesar.)

There are few things in Tacitean syntax which cannot in
themselves be paralleled from the works of other writers,
especially the poets and Silver Latin authors. But the use
which he makes of them in combination is so distinctive,
and his fondness for certain constructions so characteristic,
that it seems desirable to give a separate account of his syn-
tactical usage and to show, if possible, how such constructions developed within the developing Latin language. The
history of a construction before the classical period is often
very illuminating for the Tacitean usage; Tacitus often twists
a construction for his own special purposes, but it is nearly
always to make it do a duty of which it is inherently capable
—as we recognize, once Tacitus has demonstrated its proper-
ties to us.

THE CASES

1. *Accusative.* In general terms, the acc. defines and limits the
verb's action.

(i) A limitation of this kind is provided by the simple *acc. of the goal*, used after verbs of motion—a construction confined in classical Latin prose to names of towns, *domus*, *rus*, &c. The poets, however, made much freer use of this acc., especially with compound verbs, where the compounding preposition helped to support the case; this freedom Tacitus imitates. Cf. *Ann.* I, 13, 6, *genua aduolueretur*; 16, 1, *legiones seditio incessit* (cf. 61, 1, *incedunt maestos locos*) and similar exx. with *inuolare* (49, 3), *adsultare*, *incurrere* (51, 3) and *inuadere* (61, 1); *animum penetrauit* (69, 3) is simple acc. of goal, without any support from a compounding preposition. The acc. found with *egredi* (30, 2), *euadere* (51, 4) and *elabi* (61, 4)—verbs which we should normally expect to be followed by an abl.—is developed from the acc. of the goal by analogy; either the analogy of opposites, because *ingredi*, *inuadere*, &c., take an acc., or because verbs of kindred meaning (*relinquere*, *uitare*, e.g.) are used with an acc.

(ii) A similar development, producing an acc. with verbs originally intransitive, is seen in the acc. which becomes increasingly common with *verbs expressing emotion*. The acc. defines and limits the action, and so *flere aliquem* means 'to weep, as far as someone is concerned', i.e. 'to weep for someone'. Certain verbs (*flere* and *dolere*, e.g.) have developed this acc. by the time of Cicero; others are not so used until a later period. *pauescere* (*Ann.* I, 4, 2, *bellum pauescere*) is first used transitively in Silver Latin. Cf. 59, 5 *ne inperitum adulescentulum . . . pauescerent*.

(iii) With many verbs, the action is limited by some external thing which, expressed in the acc., becomes the direct object of the verb. This is one of the commonest ways of defining the verbal action, and needs no further comment. But it is possible also to define that action by reference to something inherently connected with the action itself (*internal acc.*): 'I strike a man' is direct (external) acc., but 'I strike a blow' is internal. One branch of this acc. is the use of neuter pronouns and adjs. (*id, multum, aliquid, nihil,* &c.), which limit and define the action by meaning 'in respect of', 'to the extent of'. Cf. Plaut. *Rud.* 397, *id misera maestast; Ann.* I, 70, 3, *nihil strenuus ab ignauo differre.*

(iv) The *acc. in apposition* to a whole phrase amplifies the phrase or expresses its aim; it is thus a branch of the internal acc. and is dependent on the action implied by the phrase. Cf. *Ann.* I, 3, 1, *subsidia dominationi Claudium . . . extulit*; 27, 1, *manus intentantes, causam discordiae*; also 30, 1; 49, 3; 74, 3; 81, 2. It is a brief, pointed usage, employed by poets both Greek and Roman (cf. Eur. *Or.* 1105, ʹΕλένην κτάνωμεν, Μενέλεῳ λύπην πικράν ' Let us kill Helen (an action which will be) a bitter grief to Menelaus'), brought into prose by Sallust, and used by all the historians, especially Tacitus.

(v) The *acc. of Respect,* used with adjs. and participles, is a poetical construction, imitated from the Greek (πόδας ὠκὺς ʹΑχιλλεύς -'Achilles swift of foot'). Latin had two usages which helped to make this imitation possible: firstly, the use of neuter pronouns and adjs. mentioned in § (iii), and secondly, the use of the acc. of the part of the body after verbs like *exui* (*exuta pedem* 'with foot bared' easily becomes *nuda pedem* 'bare as regards the foot'). The Augustan poets took this basis and on it built a much wider and bolder and deliberate imitation of the Greek construction. This acc. is very commonly used of parts of the body (*flaua comas,* Ovid, *Met.* VI, 118: *os umerosque deo similis,* Virg. *Aen.* I, 589), but is by no means confined to them (cf. *Cynthia uerba leuis,* Prop. II, v. 28). Tacitus was the first author to use it in literary prose, See *Ann.* I, 50, 1, *frontem ac tergum uallo, latera concaedibus munitus; Hist.* IV, 20, *frontem tergaque ac latus tuti; Ann.* XV, 64, *frigidus iam artus.*

2. *Genitive*. The gen. case defines the sphere of reference of a noun, adj. or verb. This can be done in many ways, some of which are specific enough to become sub-sections and be described by names of their own. A word can, e.g. be defined by being described as belonging to someone (*domus Ciceronis* —possessive gen.), or as forming part of a larger class (*aliquid boni*—partitive gen.). These and other uses of the gen. extend and overlap, until it is often difficult to label a particular ex. with complete certainty.

(i) *Gen. of Reference*. According to the definition given above, all gens. are gens. of reference, some merely being more specific in their reference than others. But the term is usually reserved for the wide general category ('as regards', 'in respect of') which is not definite enough to be more specifically labelled. This gen. is already well established in early Latin, especially in legal contexts (*capitis damnare* 'to condemn in respect of his life') and is greatly extended by the poets and later writers. See § (ii). Tacitus uses the gen. of reference not only with such verbs, but also loosely attached to nouns; cf. *Ann.* I, 16, 1, *licentiam turbarum* ('licence as regards rioting'); 59, 4, *sacerdotium hominum* ('a priesthood with reference to men'); 59, 6, *gloriae . . . ducem* ('a leader connected with glory'); 75, 3, *ueniam ordinis* ('indulgence as regards his rank'). These gens. with nouns may often be explained as objective defining gens. (§ iv), but it seems better to reserve that term for the narrower category of more exact definition, and treat them as simple gens. of reference.

The gen. of reference first becomes common with adjs. in the Augustan poets, and comes from there into Silver Latin prose. It is an extension of the normal use of the gen. with adjs.—adjs. expressing desire and knowledge, fullness or emptiness, partition or sharing are naturally followed by a gen. The classical gen. in, e.g. *ignarus consilii* is easily extended

to other adjs. of kindred meaning; *incertus consilii* is an easy
step, but the further extension to *ambiguus consilii* produces a
gen. which is quite recognizably one of reference, and not
objective. This construction also offers a concise form of
expression, a point which both poets and Silver writers would
appreciate. Exx. in *Ann.* I are 32, 2, *animi ferox;* 46, 2, *seueritatis
et munificentiae summum;* 62, 2, *formidolosiorem hostium;* 69, 1,
ingens animi; and, with the further extension to the gen. of
the gerund 7, 3, *ambiguus imperandi;* 29, 1, *rudis dicendi.* Some
of these exx. stand nearer to the original objective gen. than
others, but they all show considerable extension of the classical
usage.

(ii) The *'Legal'* Gen. is a special extension of the gen. of
reference in legal contexts. Its use with verbs of accusing
and condemning, and their kindred adjs., is classical (see § (i)
and cf. *Ann.* I, 21, 3, *rerum capitalium damnatos*). The Silver
Latin writers extend it to express 'charge' or 'sentence' with
words much more loosely connected with accusation and
prosecution. Cf. *Ann.* I, 3, 4, *flagitii conpertum* 'proved guilty
of crime'; 74, 1, *maiestatis postulauit.*

(iii) *Partitive Gen.* One of the ways in which the classical
language uses this gen. is after the nom. and acc. only of
neuter sing. adjs. and pronouns expressing quantity—*tantum
ciuium, quid noui.* Tacitus and the later writers extend this
usage and we find: (*a*) cases other than the nom. or acc. e.g.
61, 1, *umido paludum;* 61, 2, *medio campi;* 65, 5, *lubrico paludum;*
(*b*) the adj. or pronoun governed by a preposition—53, 5, *in
prominenti litoris;* (*c*) the neuter plural of the adj. or pronoun—
9, 2, *alia honorum;* 17, 3, *inculta montium;* 50, 3, *obstantia
siluarum;* 61, 1, *occulta saltuum;* 65, 1, *subiecta uallium.* Some
of these last exx. come near to being gens. of definition—
see § (iv). Classical Latin also uses a partitive gen. after
masc. or fem. superlative adjs.; this is later extended to

positive adjs.—in *Ann.* I, cf. 2, 1, *ceteri nobilium;* 51, 2, *ceteri sociorum.*

(iv) The *Gen. of Definition or Content* is frequently used instead of a noun or adj. in apposition. *uligines paludum (Ann.* I, 17, 3) = 'swampiness consisting of marshes' and so 'marshy swamps'. Cf. 78, 2, *sedecim stipendiorum finem;* 76, 1 (with the gerundive), *remedium coercendi fluminis.* The classical writers use this gen. to a limited extent (Cic. *Mur.* 23, *uirtutibus continentiae, grauitatis, iustitiae*), the poets and post-Augustan writers much more, extending it even to *urbs,* &c. Cf. Virg. *Aen.* I, 247, *urbem Pataui; Ann.* VI, 50, *promunturium Miseni.* They also use it with *nomen (Hist.* IV, 18, *castra quibus Veterum nomen est*); in *Ann.* I, cf. 2, 1, *triumuiri nomine;* 9, 2, *nomen inperatoris.*

(v) *Gen. of Gerundive (Purpose).* It is notoriously difficult to define and explain exactly the uses of this gen. Broadly speaking, it defines the sphere or range within which an action holds, and can therefore define that action's goal or purpose; e.g. *abolendae infamiae* in *Ann.* I, 3, 6 means (if it is a gen. and not a dat.) 'a war *consisting in* (or *concerned with*) the wiping out of the disgrace' and therefore 'to wipe out the disgrace'. It is a use of the gen. which has obvious affinities with the Greek use of τοῦ and the infin. to express purpose (cf. Thuc. II, 22, ἐκκλησίαν τε οὐκ ἐποίει αὐτῶν . . . τοῦ μὴ ὀργῇ τι μᾶλλον ἢ γνώμῃ ξυνελθόντας ἐξαμαρτεῖν, 'to prevent their making a mistake'), but it is a genuine Latin construction and not a mere Graecism. It is found (a) attached to a noun— *Ann.* III, 27, *multa populus parauit tuendae libertatis;* (b) used predicatively—Cic. *Leg.* II, 59, *cetera in XII minuendi luctus sunt;* (c) defining a whole phrase—*Ann.* II, 59, *Aegyptum proficiscitur cognoscendae antiquitatis.* Cicero shows isolated exx. of this gen., Sallust and Livy rather more, Tacitus uses it fairly frequently.

3. *Dative.* This case indicates basically the person interested
in or emotionally concerned with an action. As with the gen.,
many of its functions have become sufficiently clear-cut to be
labelled as separate sub-sections: and one of them has become
so important as to give the case its name (the 'giving' case,
from its use with *dare*). But the proper meaning of the Dative
is 'for', not 'to', and on that meaning all its functions ultimately depend.

(i) All dats. are therefore dats. of *Interest*, but the term is
usually applied by grammarians to those exx. where the
person concerned stands to gain or lose something, when the
action is to his *advantage or disadvantage*; e.g. *praedia aliis coluit,
non sibi* (Cic.), *ferrum atque arma adimi militibus* (Livy). In *Ann.*
I, cf. 11, 2, *nitenti . . . (uerba) implicabantur*; 59, 3, *sibi tres
legiones . . . procubuisse*; 71, 3, *cunctos . . . sibi firmabat.*

(ii) Used with *esse* this dat. indicates *possession*; *illi duae
fuere filiae* (Plaut.), *huic homini spes nulla salutis esset* (Cic.).
The possessive dat., as one would expect, draws attention to
the possessor rather than the thing possessed; *est patri meo
domus* tells us something about 'my father'—that he has a
house—while *domus est patris mei* is a description of the house.
In *Ann.* I, cf. 11, 2, *Tiberio . . . (erant) suspensa uerba*; 13, 1,
Tiberio nulla . . . ira; 29, 4, *promptum . . . ingenium Druso erat*;
50, 3, *festam eam Germanis noctem*; 53, 1, *nec alia . . . Tiberio
causa.* This dat. is sometimes found attached directly to a noun;
see 24, 2 *rector iuueni* and note there. In 69, 2 *principium ponti*
it is extended from persons to things.

(iii) A less specialized interest in the action is conveyed by
the ethic dat. (*ecce tibi est exortus Isocrates* means 'then (you will
be interested in this) Isocrates appeared'). When the person's
interest is that of a spectator, and is described by a participle,
we have the category which may be called the *Dat. of the Point
of View.* The construction is a development of the Latin dat.

in imitation of a common Greek construction, and the point of view may be either literal and local (the earlier construction) or mental. E.g. *Gomphos peruenit, quod est oppidum primum Thessaliae uenientibus ab Epiro* (Caes. B.C. III, 80, 1); or *uere aestimanti Aetolium magis bellum fuit* (Livy, XXXVII, 58, 8). Cf. *Ann.* I, 32, 3, *altius coniectantibus*.

Here too belongs another imitation of a Greek construction —see 59, 1, *quibusque bellum . . . cupientibus erat* and the note there.

(iv) In certain contexts the person concerned with the action is also the *agent* by whom it must be accomplished. *faciendum est mihi illud* means 'that, as far as I am concerned, must be done', and so 'I must do that'. The usage, first confined to gerundives, was soon extended to perfect participles passive (*mihi cognitum*, &c.) and then to finite forms of the verb (cf. Cic. N.D. II, 123, *dissimillimis bestiolis communiter cibus quaeritur*). But the connexion with the dat. of interest remains firm, and it is probably not until Livy that the dat. is found as agent pure and simple—cf. Livy, V, 6, 14, *auctores signa relinquendi . . . non uni aut alteri militi, sed uniuersis exercitibus audiuntur.* This dat. is common in Livy and Tacitus. In *Ann.* I, cf. 1, 2, *claris scriptoribus*; 10, 2, *ne ipsis quidem . . . laudatas*; 17, 6, *sibi . . . hostem aspici*; 42, 2, *quibus . . . proiecta*; 57, 1, *barbaris . . . habetur*; 62, 2, *Tiberio . . . probatum.*

(v) When the dat. of interest refers not to a person, but to a thing, the interest of the thing is considered to lie in the action's being fulfilled, i.e. in the purpose of the action. This *Dat. of Purpose* is found early in Latin, and in the classical period, but only within certain limits; it is confined mainly to single nouns used (*a*) predicatively—*praesidio est*; cf. *Ann.* I, 57, 5, *praedae data*; (*b*) with certain adjs. of suitability and fitness—*id aptum est tempori et personae* (Cic.); cf. *Ann.* I, 2, 1, *seruitio promptior*; 48, 3, *seditioni promptum*; (*c*) with verbs of

'considering', 'imputing', 'choosing' and kindred terms—
hunc sibi domicilio locum delegerunt (Caes.); cf. *Ann*. I, 10, 1,
obtentui sumpta; also, by an extension, with verbs of motion
like *mittere* and *uenire*—*auxilio mittere* and *subsidio uenire* are
common. Tacitus uses this dat. with verbs more freely; cf.
Ann. I, 23, 5, *centurionem . . . morti deposcit*; 29, 4, *corpora extra
uallum abiecta ostentui*; 51, 2, *incessitque itineri et proelio*; (*d*)
attached to a noun—in classical prose only in the phrase
receptui signum; the poets greatly extended this dat. (*causam
lacrimis*, Virg. *Aen*. III, 305) and Livy brought it into prose.
In *Ann*. I see 3, 1, *subsidia dominationi*; 22, 1, *seditioni duces*;
24, 2, *rector iuueni* (and note).

In the gerundive construction, its use in classical prose is
confined to a few legal formulae, defining the duties of certain
officials—*quindecimuiri sacris faciundis, decemuiri stlitibus iudi-
candis*, &c. Livy and Tacitus extend this usage, Tacitus especially employing it frequently. He uses it in many of the
constructions listed under (*a*)—(*d*) above (cf. *Ann*. I, 23, 4,
perferendis . . . mandatis idoneus; 31, 2, *agendo . . . censui intentum*;
54, 1, *retinendis . . . sacris instituerat*; 60, 2, *distrahendo hosti
mittit*; 62, 1, *primum extruendo tumulo caespitem*) and often
independently, as the equivalent of a Final clause; cf. *Ann*.
I, 26, 2, *cur uenisset neque augendis militum stipendiis neque
adleuandis laboribus*.

(vi) The *Dat. expressing motion towards a Goal* is a further
extension of the dat. of purpose. *leto datus* is still recognizably
a predicative dat., but *leto missus* can be interpreted as motion
towards a goal. The poets found this brief expression more
useful than a prepositional phrase, and extended its use greatly
(cf. Virg. *Aen*. V, 451, *it clamor caelo*) and post-Augustan
writers followed their example. This dat. is therefore a legitimate development of Latin usage, but it is also influenced by
such Greek phrases as ἀνατείνας οὐρανῷ χεῖρας 'raising his

hands to Heaven'. Cf. *Ann.* I, 19, 1, *pectori usque adcreuerat;* 23, 1, *pedibus aduolutus;* 41, 1, *externae fidei;* 74, 2, *saeuitiae principis adrepit.*

4. *Ablative.* The Latin abl. has to carry the functions of three original Indo-European cases—the pure abl., the instrumental-sociative and the locative. Although there are, naturally, cross-influences from each of these to the others, the origin of most ablatival usages remains fairly clear, and the Tacitean abl. may therefore be considered within these basic categories.

(i) The pure abl. denotes origin or separation—'from'. The simple *abl. of source, without a preposition,* is used in classical Latin prose to express 'place from which' only within certain limits (*Roma, domo,* &c.) and its more extensive use is condemned by Quintilian (I, 5, 39) as a solecism. But the poets found it convenient, and from Livy on it is common in prose; cf. Vell. I, 4, *profecti Graecia.* Exx. in *Ann.* I are 3, 3, *remeantem Armenia;* 41, 1, *progrediuntur contuberniis.* The usage should be distinguished from such exx. as 65, 2, *paludibus emersum; Ann.* II, 69, *abire Syria,* where the abl. depends on the preposition compounded with the verb.

(ii) The instrumental-sociative case expresses means or accompaniment, both in the widest sense.

(a) The means may be local, expressing *route by which.* Instrumentals such as *terra marique, publica uia* are common, and the extension of this useful abl. to express route began early in Latin. Cf. Cic. *De Or.* III, 133, *transuerso ambulantem foro;* Livy, III, 51, 10, *porta Collina urbem intrauere.* In *Ann.* I see 8, 3, *porta triumphali;* 60, 2, *finibus;* 63, 3, *litore Oceani.*

(b) Or the means may be that *in respect of which* a statement is true. See *Ann.* I, 16, 3, *procax lingua* and note there.

(c) Accompaniment is expressed in many ways, from personal accompaniment to the circumstances surrounding an event.

This latter *abl. of attendant circumstances* is seen in phrases such as *Ann.* I, 8, 6, *longa potentia*; 26, 2, *nulla . . . licentia*; 38, 1, *bono magis exemplo quam concesso iure*. From it develops the more specialized abl. of quality.

(*d*) *Abl. of Quality. uir bono animo progreditur* easily becomes *uir bono animo est*, where the abl. has been detached from the verb and attached to the noun. In *Ann.* I, cf. 46, 2, *principem longa experientia*; 64, 2, *locus uligine profunda*. This abl., in classical Latin, normally qualifies not a proper name or noun of special reference, but a generic noun (*uir, mulier*) standing in apposition to the name (Caes. *B.C.* III, 91, *Crastinus . . . uir singulari uirtute*). But Tacitus uses it attached directly to the name, a shorter and more striking expression; see 13, 1 (*Arruntium*) *artibus egregiis*; 24, 2, *Seianus . . . magna apud Tiberium auctoritate*; 60, 1, *Inguiomerus . . . uetere apud Romanos auctoritate*. In some exx. the connexion is so loose that it is difficult to tell whether the abl. is one of quality or of attendant circumstances—e.g. 4, 5, *accedere matrem muliebri inpotentia*.

The abl. of quality is invariably, until late in Latin, qualified by an adj. One can say *uir summa prudentia* but not *uir prudentia*. Occasionally a qualifying gen. takes the place of the adj.; cf. Cic. *N.D.* I, 91, *ut homines deorum forma nascerentur*; *Ann.* I, 57, 4, *filia Segestis, mariti magis quam parentis animo*.

(*e*) The *instrumental abl. of the gerund* is used by the poets and post-Augustan writers to express attendant circumstances. The instrumental force is considerably weakened, and the meaning of the gerund so used is indistinguishable from that of a present participle agreeing with the subject (which is what it has become in modern Italian—cf. *mandando, credendo*, &c.). The two are in fact often combined; cf. *Ann.* XV, 38, *in edita assurgens et rursus inferiora populando*. Livy is the first writer to make any considerable use of this gerund, and it is characteristic of the style of Tacitus. In *Ann.* I, cf. 10, 7, *excusando*.

(iii) The locative abl. expresses both 'place where' and 'time when'.

(a) In classical Latin prose the use of this abl. without *in* to express *place* is limited—*locus, regio* and a few other such words are alone found in this construction. See *Ann.* I, 25, 1 and note there. But the poets and post-Augustan writers use it much more freely. Cf. Virg. *Aen.* III, 110, *habitabant uallibus imis*; and in *Ann.* I, 61, 2, *semiruto uallo, humili fossa*; 61, 3, *lucis*; 64, 4, *medio*; 65, 1, *tentoriis*.

(b) The abl. *expressing extent of time* is in origin a local abl. expressing 'time within which'. Duration of time can be expressed in two ways, according to the point of view: either 'how long did the battle go on?' (answer *est pugnatum horas quinque*) or 'within what limits of time did the battle take place?' (answer *est pugnatum horis quinque*, as in Caesar, *B.C.* I, 46). The first is by far the commoner method used in the classical period, but there are exx. of the abl. in Cicero and Caesar, and it becomes common in Livy and Tacitus. It also becomes looser in usage, and often indicates simple duration of time instead of completed action within definite limits, which is its classical use. In *Ann.* I, cf. 53, 4, *quattuordecim annis exilium tolerauit*.

(iv) *Abl. absolute.* The interlocking of the three main ablatival functions is very clearly seen in the abl. abs., which can express time, manner, cause, &c., and, quite generally, attendant circumstances (see *Ann.* I, 77, 1, *occisis . . . militibus* and note there). The extensive use of the abl. abs. is one of the marks of Tacitus' style, and he uses it to express many things, including an additional major statement (as in *Ann.* I, 15, 1). One usage may be specially mentioned—the *impersonal abl. abs.* The neuter past participle, used impersonally in the abl. abs., is found at all periods of Latin—cf. Ter. *And.* 807, *haud auspicato* 'without taking the auspices', Livy, XXXV,

35, 14, *uelut imperato* 'as if an order had been given'. Its use with a subordinate clause depending on it is a later development, found occasionally in Cicero (e.g. *Inv.* II, 34, *cur praetereatur demonstrato*) and quite commonly in the historians. In *Ann.* I, cf. 35, 5, *addito acutiorem esse*; 46, 1, *nondum cognito qui fuisset exitus*; 49, 1, *intellecto in quos saeuiretur*; 66, 2, *comperto uanam esse formidinem*; 75, 3, *conperto paternas ei angustias esse*.

THE VERB

5. *The Subjunctive.* Tacitus uses the independent subj., in main clauses, very much as the classical writers do. The potential subj. (e.g. 28, 5, *recipias*; 43, 1, *cecidissem*; 76, 4, *crediderim*) is common, and these and other subjs. are noted in the commentary. In subordinate clauses, several Tacitean usages are sufficiently notable and characteristic to require special mention.

(i) *Repeated Action.* After such words as 'whoever' and 'whenever' classical Latin regularly uses the perf. and plup. indic.; *cum uenit* 'whenever he comes', *cum uenerat* 'whenever he came'. The use of the subj. to express repeated action is a development especially characteristic of Latin prose in and after Livy, though its origins lie in the classical period. The usage appears to start with *si* and *cum* (cf. *Ann.* I, 7, 5, *cum . . . loqueretur*), but in Livy and Tacitus it is common with other temporal conjunctions also (cf. *Ann.* I, 27, 1, *ut quis . . . occurreret*; 44, 5, *ubi . . . obiectauissent*) and with the indefinite and relative pronouns (15, 3, *cui . . . euenisset*). Its origin is disputed, but its development must have been encouraged by, e.g. the use of the subj. with circumstantial *cum* (e.g. Cic. *Verr.* IV, 48, *cum in conuiuium uenisset*, where the context provides a frequentative meaning), the influence of the Greek frequentative construction, the Roman liking for the generic subj. (*cum* being regarded as = 'on such occasions as') and the natural desire of a maturing language for definition of expression; 'whenever' is not simple isolated fact, and the Romans began to feel that it should not be expressed by the indic. The subj. did not, however, oust the indic. entirely: Tacitus uses both constructions (in *Ann.* I, 44, 5 they are found together): and the indic. remains the normal construction with primary tenses. But the common use of the frequentative subj. is a mark of Silver Latin style.

(ii) *Temporal clauses* show one major extension of the use of the subj. In classical prose a subj. verb after the conjunctions 'before' and 'until' indicates intention on the part of the subject of the main verb—*exspectabam dum rediret*, 'I waited until he should return'. But the use of the subj. to express nothing more than subordination was growing, and from Livy on it is found, especially with *donec*, to express what is simply a temporal relationship between the clauses. In *Ann.* I, cf. 1, 2, *donec deterrerentur;* 13, 6, *donec . . . oraret*; 32, 2, *donec . . . dederetur.*

(iii) The subj. used with *tamquam* and *quasi* also shows an extension of the classical usage. Classical Latin uses this subj. to express an unreal comparison—e.g. Cic. *Fam.* XII, 9, 1, *tamquam enim clausa sit Asia, sic nihil perfertur ad nos praeter rumores* 'as though Asia were closed'. But the Silver Latin writers use it to mean 'on the ground that', the subj. expressing no longer unreality, but being the virtual oblique of the charge made; cf. *Ann.* I, 12, 4, *pridem inuisus, tamquam. . . plus quam ciuilia agitaret* 'he had long been disliked, on the ground that (for Tiberius felt that) he aspired to be more than a citizen'. This use is again extended until the *tamquam* clause expresses cause or explanation, much as an acc. and infin. clause would do in classical Latin—*Hist.* II, 63, *id ei obiecit, tamquam ducem se uictis partibus ostentasset* 'he made the charge that . . .'.

(iv) *Repraesentatio*. By the practice known to grammarians as *repraesentatio* Tacitus, in many subordinate clauses in *Oratio Obliqua*, reverts to the tense of the vivid direct, while preserving the subj. mood of the indirect speech. Cicero normally keeps strictly to Historic sequence after an historic principal verb. But the historians, who had in the nature of things to present much longer passages of indirect speech depending on a secondary verb, adopted this system, which not only provides welcome variety but also, by emphasizing the original tense, makes clear subtleties of meaning which are obscured by the normal rule of sequence; for according to that, an original present indic., imperf. indic., fut. indic. and present subj. might all be represented by an imperf. subj. *Repraesentatio* tends to be used especially when the original tense can be absolutely retained (e.g. present/perf. indic. becoming present/perf. subj.). When a further change is necessary, as when the original verb is fut. indic. or imperative, the normal secondary sequence is usually followed. Cf. cc. 4, 9, 10 and reported speeches *passim*. For a study of Tacitus' use of *repraesentatio* see *C.R.* 1951, pp. 144–6.

6. *The Infinitive.* (i) The Latin infin. is in origin the locative or dative case of the verbal noun, and many of its functions depend on that origin. Some of its uses stress the original case, and others that it is a verbal noun. As a noun, it can be used either as the subject or object of a verb—e.g. *decet facere* 'the doing is proper', *uolo facere*, 'I wish the doing'. Once such expressions were established and such verbs accepted as being 'followed' by an infin., verbs of similar meaning were naturally used with similar infins., and the construction spread by analogy. Many verbs of will and propriety are used with the infin. in classical prose, but not all. Many are still followed by a subordinate clause (usually *ut* and the subj.). But poetry

and the spoken language made much greater use of the infin.; both prefer a shorter and more pointed construction, and the poets especially were influenced by the more extensive use of the infin. in Greek. Here, as often, the Silver Latin prose writers (especially Tacitus) draw on poetic syntax, which has many of the qualities they most admire, e.g. brevity, novelty and colour. For such infins. in *Ann.* I, cf. those that follow *agitare* (18, 2) and *animus est* (56, 5).

The dat. case can express purpose (see § 3 (v)) and the infin., being a dat., can also have this function. This is particularly noticeable when it is used with verbs of striving and effort, compelling and persuading; *iubeo facere* means 'I give orders for the doing' and so 'I order to do'. Here again classical prose prefers the subj. with many of these verbs, but they are found in the poets and later prose writers with the infin. For exx. in *Ann.* I see 19, 3 (with *tendere*); 39, 3 (*subigere*); 63, 1 (*monere*); 64, 1 (*niti*).

(ii) The original verbal noun is very prominent also in the *Historic Infin.*, which is used in rapid narrative in a sense resembling that of the hist. present tense or the narrative imperf. The subject, when expressed, stands in the nominative. It is common to find hist. infins. in series; cf. *Ag.* 38, *Britanni trahere uulneratos, uocare integros, deserere domos.* Quintilian's explanation (IX, 3, 58) that *coepit* is understood with such infins., cannot be accepted, not least because the hist. infin. does not imply action beginning but action in progress. It is best explained as the simplest and quickest form of the required verbal notion, the bare statement of the essential meaning without any trimmings of person or tense, both of which can be deduced from the context. It thus makes a vivid impression (the vividness helped by the fact that the infin. is a noun, and nouns are more striking than verbs) and is much used in swift narrative by all the historians, especially Sallust and Tacitus. Cf. *Ann*. I, 4, 2, *pauci . . . disserere, plures . . . pauescere, alii cupere*; 16, 2, *lasciuire miles, discordare*; and many other exx. Tacitus uses this infin. in subordinate clauses also, but there are no exx. in *Ann*. I; see *Ann*. II, 4, *ubi minitari Artabanus*; *Ann*. III, 26, *postquam exui aequalitas*.

7. *The Participles*. These are verbal adjs., in some of which the adjectival function is originally more prominent, while others show an opposite development, from verbal use to adjectival.

(i) The *Present participle* is strongly adjectival in its early uses, and to some extent remains so throughout its history. This is clearly seen in, e.g. its use with the gen. of reference (*rerum sciens*, *Ann*. I, 64, 4, and note) and the exx. where, with the verb *esse*, it forms a periphrastic tense (*praesens erat*, *Ann*. I, 14, 3 and note). It was not until the age of Cicero and Caesar that the verbal possibilities of the present part. were appreciated and its use with an object fully developed. It denotes accompanying circumstances rather than time, but the classical writers tended to restrict its use to the description of events contemporaneous with the main verb. Later writers, however, found in its native timelessness a good substitute for the perf. part. active which Latin does not possess, and they use it quite frequently to describe past time. Cf. Virg. *Aen*. I, 305, *at pius Aeneas per noctem plurima uoluens, ut primum lux alma datast, exire* ('*having* meditated through the night, he went out at dawn'); *Ann*. XII, 48, *Quadratus cognoscens proditum Mithridaten, uocat consilium* ('*having* discovered . . . he summoned'). There is no certain ex. in *Ann*. I, though *relabentem* (76, 1) has been taken to be one. See note there.

(ii) The difficulties about the origin of the *Future participle* are unresolved, but it seems most likely that it was in origin an adj. meaning 'likely to'. The fact that it developed only late its independent adjectival and participial functions is not an insuperable objection to this view; the history of the present participle is in many ways very similar, and there is no doubt about its origin. In the classical period the fut. part. is used almost exclusively as a periphrastic tense with *esse* (*scripturus sum* 'I am about to write'; *sensurus es* 'you are likely to feel'); only *futurus* is at all commonly used as an attributive adj. (*res futurae* &c.). But by Sallust, Livy and the Augustan poets it is used with increasing frequency without *esse*, to express:

(*a*) Future action, cf. Livy, XXI, 1, 4, *cum . . . exercitum eo traiecturus sacrificaret.*

(*b*) Intention or fate—'sure to', 'likely to'; cf. Virg. *Aen.* II, 511, *fertur moriturus in hostes*; *Ann.* I, 31, 1, *tracturis*; 79, 3, *erupturum.* By a further development this use can be made precise enough to express purpose (*Ann.* I, 24, 1, *consulturum*) —a development obviously influenced by the similar use of the Greek fut. part.

(*c*) Both fut. action and intention, but with the part. taking the place of an hypothetical clause, especially in a conditional sentence. Cf. Livy IX, 29, 4, *quieturus haud dubie, nisi ultro arma Etrusci inferrent*; in *Ann.* I, 36, 2, *si omitteretur ripa, inuasurus hostis* (see note there); 45, 2, *si imperium detrectetur, bello certaturus* (= *constituit se bello certaturum esse*); 46, 2, *cessuris . . . ubi uidissent* (= *eis qui cessuri fuissent*).

(iii) The *Perfect participle* originally indicated not past time but present state; but as present state frequently results from past action, it was easily extended to cover that—which is, in fact, its most common classical use. But the original element remains in the 'circumstantial' participle, describing a state of things contemporaneous with the main verb. In *Ann.* I see 65, 3, *capto . . . campo*; 77, 1, *occisis . . . militibus.* This use of the perf. part. is found in classical Latin (cf. Cic. *Verr.* V, 77, *ut his per triumphum ductis pulcherrimum spectaculum populus*

Romanus percipere possit), but it is especially common in Livy and Tacitus.

(iv) All three participles are used, with a noun, in a construction which gives the sense of an abstract noun with a gen., or of a clause beginning 'the fact that'; e.g. *interfectus Caesar* 'the death of Caesar'. The perf. part. is much the commonest in this construction—see *Ann.* I, 8, 6, *occisus* . . . *Caesar* and note there. But the others are found; e.g. Cic. *Att.* VII, 11, 4, *fugiens Pompeius mirabiliter homines mouet* ('the flight of Pompey'); cf. *Ann.* IV, 34, *id perniciabile reo et Caesar truci uultu defensionem accipiens* ('the fact that Caesar'). The fut. part. is first so used by Livy e.g. I, 25, 3, *seruitium obuersatur animo futuraque ea deinde patriae fortuna quam ipsi fecissent* ('and the fact that their country's destiny would be . . .'); in *Ann.* I, cf. 36, 2, *augebat metum* . . . *inuasurus hostis* 'the fact that the enemy was certain to invade'. Tacitus makes great use of this participial construction.

V

THE REIGN OF TIBERIUS

The Emperor Tiberius is no longer considered the monster he once was held to be, but his reign and his character remain a puzzle, part of which may be resolved by a consideration of his early years. He was born in 42 B.C., the elder son of Livia and the ardent Republican Ti. Claudius Nero. When he was three years old, his mother was divorced by Nero to enable Octavian to marry her, and from that time Tiberius and his younger brother Drusus were brought up in Octavian's household. As stepson of Augustus, he had honours and privileges conferred upon him—he took part, e.g. in the triumph of 29 B.C., and was allowed to stand for office five years before the legal age—but they tended to turn sour on

him. Drusus, though younger, had a more pleasing personality
and was preferred to him, and Tiberius found himself being
used rather unscrupulously in the service of the state and to
further Augustus' dynastic plans. Between 28 and 8 B.C. he
served in Spain, settled Armenia (temporarily at least), and
conquered tribes in Germany and Pannonia—military service
which he probably enjoyed and which he appears to have
done well, but for which he was not allowed the full triumphs
voted to him. In 11 B.C. he was forced to divorce his wife
Vipsania and to marry Julia, daughter of Augustus, in order
to act as guardian of her sons by Agrippa, who would eventually supplant him. By 6 B.C., when Gaius and Lucius were
old enough to enter public life, he had tired of his position,
and in spite of *tribunicia potestas* and a request to settle Armenia, he retired to Rhodes and scholarly seclusion for eight
years. He was probably glad, too, to get away from Julia,
life with whom was becoming insupportable.

He returned from Rhodes in A.D. 2, at his mother's request,
and two years later both Gaius and Lucius were dead and he
was again in favour as the only possible successor to Augustus.
He was formally adopted by Augustus in that year, being
himself forced to adopt Germanicus, son of his dead brother
Drusus. This was no doubt only caution on Augustus' part
(*quo pluribus munimentis insisteret*, *Ann.* I, 3), but to Tiberius
it must have seemed yet another slight, for he had a son of his
own, named Drusus. Now began one of the busiest, and
perhaps the happiest, periods of his life. His tribunician power
was renewed and he was sent to Germany, where he campaigned successfully from A.D. 4–6, and again from 10–12,
being called away from 6–9 to settle the great revolt in
Illyricum. Tiberius was a successful general, and seemed to
have on the field the self-confidence and ability to deal with
men which he so fatally lacked in civil affairs. But for his own

sake and for Rome's, what he ought to have been doing during these years was learning to be a Princeps; even in A.D. 13, when he was at last granted a co-regency, he immediately set off for Illyricum, and was recalled only by the news that Augustus was dying. Real training in civil administration he had none—a fact for which Augustus must take responsibility —and that aggravated his naturally diffident character and caused much of the difficulty in years to come.

In September A.D. 14, after a debate in the Senate (*Ann.* I, 11–13), he accepted the principate reluctantly. His personal reluctance was probably genuine enough, for he knew that he did not shine in public life. But he was a sufficient realist to recognize that a Princeps was necessary and that he alone had anything like the necessary qualifications; the difficulty was to get formal and official recognition of that fact, because the principate was not automatically hereditary. The debate was probably designed to produce from the Senate a clear statement of the position, but it was not so well managed as it might have been (see ch. 12).

Even Tacitus is forced to recognize that the first years of Tiberius' reign showed good and competent, if not inspired, government. He co-operated with the Senate, showing it open deference and granting it privileges and honours (the right to control elections, e.g. *Ann.* I, 15). He refused special honours and titles for himself (*Ann.* I, 14, 72) and showed himself willing to please. The situation was none too easy; the legions of Pannonia and the Rhine were in revolt (*Ann.* I, 16 sq., 31 sq.) and had to be dealt with; and once again Tiberius found another man, with less ability but more charm, more popular than himself. Germanicus was the popular hero of Rome, and there was some real danger that an effort might be made to make him Princeps. Personal considerations apart, this was a thing to be avoided; Germanicus might be popular but he had no great ability. He himself, however, was loyal, and Tiberius allowed him to have his way in Germany until A.D. 17, by which time he was becoming too expensive a luxury there and was needed in the East. To the East, after a triumph, he went, with Cn. Piso appointed legate of Syria to keep an eye on him. He accomplished a certain amount there, but with his genius for doing the wrong thing he irritated Tiberius by wintering in Egypt, which he should not have done without special permission. He returned to Syria in A.D. 19, to find his work undone by Piso, with whom he quarrelled, and he died there shortly afterwards, probably of a fever, but believing that he had been poisoned by Piso. His wife Agrippina brought his body back to Rome, and Tiberius gained her implacable hatred, and general unpopularity, by failing to attend the funeral and by deprecating excesses of mourning. No doubt there was reason in his attitude, but it showed lack of tact and no knowledge of human nature to behave in this way. Piso was brought to trial and committed suicide, not because of the poisoning charge, but because Tiberius was obviously not going to tolerate insubordination of the kind Piso had been practising in Syria.

For the next few years Tiberius trained his own son Drusus to succeed him, and he seemed to be shaping well; so that his death in 23 was an especially hard blow. From it Tiberius never quite recovered, and it is from this year that the deterioration of his reign can be dated. Tiberius lost heart, and began to lean more and more on his friend Sejanus (for whom see *Ann.* I, 24), whose influence, with Drusus dead and the children of Germanicus too young to count, gradually became paramount. He saw a chance of himself succeeding to the throne if he could get rid of Germanicus' family, and he used the treason trials and the relative carelessness produced by

Tiberius' grief, to accomplish this. Agrippina's friends and supporters were systematically removed, and eventually Agrippina herself and Nero, her eldest son, were banished on a charge of conspiracy, while Drusus, the second son, was imprisoned in Rome. All this was made easier by Tiberius' withdrawal to Capri in 26, which left Sejanus virtually in control of the capital. But he overstepped himself, and news of his ultimate intention was conveyed secretly to Tiberius. He hesitated long before taking action, but in October A.D. 31 he appointed Macro Prefect of Praetorians in place of Sejanus, and sent him to the Senate with a dispatch denouncing Sejanus. Sejanus was executed and there followed a crop of trials of his supporters on charges of treason.

From 31 until he died in 37 Tiberius, now *senex et solus* (Suet *Tib*. 65), remained away from Rome, in Capri or Campania. He continued to conduct public business, but signs of the bitterness and shock produced by the death of his son (now thought to have been murdered at the instigation of Sejanus) and his betrayal by his friend, were now apparent. He could not bring himself to return to Rome, he showed a new lack of moderation in prosecuting the supporters of Sejanus, he failed to settle the question of the succession. Nero and Drusus were dead, there remained only Gaius, the youngest son of Germanicus, and Tiberius Gemellus, the young son of Drusus. Gaius was the more obvious candidate, and so Tiberius seemed to find him. But he made no formal indication of his views, and failed completely to provide any training for the young man—a failure the more reprehensible in view of his own difficulties resulting from Augustus' failure to train *him*. He died at Misenum in March 37, and such was his unpopularity that the news was received with joy in Rome.

It is easy to see the faults which made Tiberius unpopular

and which marred his reign. His personality (ability combined with ironical humour, diffidence and lack of tact) not only made him personally disliked, but produced more serious consequences. The people of Ilium, realizing very late that they had not sent a mission of consolation on the death of Drusus, hastily did so, and Tiberius in turn begged to condole with them on the death of their fellow-citizen Hector. One feels some sympathy for Tiberius, to whose grief such an embassy must have been very trying: but petty humiliations of this kind lead to bitter hatred which will ultimately do the state no good. A different man, too, might have dealt more successfully with Agrippina and her following, and one less diffident might have seen through Sejanus more quickly. His retiral from Rome in 26 was a bad mistake. No doubt Tiberius the man craved privacy and a small circle of congenial friends (the stories of his unnatural excesses are a late invention, probably of the time of Domitian, and may be ignored); no doubt also he continued ably to direct business. But that very fact emphasized the complete autocracy of the Princeps, which Augustus had tried so hard to keep veiled; and his absence from Rome meant loss of prestige for himself and unnatural influence for Sejanus. However much Sejanus is to blame for the treason trials (and much of the blame is his), Tiberius cannot be completely freed from responsibility, for he was Princeps and Sejanus was his minister.

Yet Tiberius was not a bad Emperor. He administered the Empire carefully and well, and did not neglect business even in retirement. He improved communications and consequently trade, he left the imperial finances in a sound state, he chose his provincial governors with care and refused to tolerate maladministration or extortion on their part. He provided money generously to relieve distress, whether of individuals or cities. Probably his military service had shown him the needs of the provinces and raised his interest in their problems. Certainly he was much happier in his dealings with them than in those with the Senate in Rome. He followed the Augustan pattern of administration very carefully, which was in itself a sign of good intention but also of weakness. For the second Principate could not be the same as the first, and for its guide required a man of more comprehensive imagination and suavity of character than Tiberius possessed. The key to the reign is the character of the man, and although Tacitus' reading of that character is wrong, he is right in emphasizing that the problem of Tiberius is a problem in psychology.

VI

THE CONQUEST OF GERMANY

'The provinces of Gaul and Spain, and likewise Germany,' says Augustus,[1] 'from Cadiz to the Elbe, I pacified'. A misleading statement: for Germany was not a province and its state was seldom pacific. It was not until 12 B.C. that Augustus turned his attention to the country beyond the Rhine. Julius Caesar had established the Rhine as the boundary of the Empire, and ensured its safety by settling friendly Germans on its left bank, by massacring barbarian German tribes who tried to cross it, and by making punitive raids beyond its left bank. The effect of Caesar's demonstrations had not worn off; spasmodic raiding there might be, but the left bank was accepted as Roman territory and there was no danger of full-scale invasion from Germans who were not a nation, but a collection of separate and often mutually hostile tribes. The Roman invasion of 12 B.C. was not therefore punitive or precautionary, nor was it inspired by a desire to have an

[1] R.G. 26.

easy conquest or a rich reward. The country was wild and
had no riches to offer, and its undeveloped state made transport and communications difficult for an invading general.
The Roman legions moved forward in 12 because Augustus,
with Gaul now formally organized into regular provinces
(he himself spent 16–13 B.C. there), was continuing his policy
of making the Empire safe and workable and easily defensible,
and was attempting to shorten the frontier between Gaul and
the Danube. If he could reach the Elbe, he would have, in
the Elbe-Danube line, one more easily held than the present
one of Rhine-Danube. Drusus, accordingly, moved across
the river to make a preliminary survey of the country.

He moved north and east, against the Frisii and the Chauci,
and probably during this campaign constructed the famous
fossa Drusiana (*Ann.* II, 8), a canal connecting the Rhine with
what is now the Ijsselmeer, and so with the Ocean. In the
following year, starting from Vetera, he bridged the Lippe
and marched without opposition eastwards to the Weser;
he was almost trapped by the Sugambri on his way back,
but managed to defeat them through their own over-confi-
dence and consequent carelessness, and established two forts,
one at the junction of the Lippe and the Aliso, and the other
in the territory of the Chatti (*Ann.* I, 56). For his campaign of
10 B.C., Drusus changed his base to Mainz, and from there
invaded the territory of the Chatti; from there too in 9 he
struck through the lands of the Chatti and Cherusci, crossed
the Weser and reached the Elbe. On his return journey he fell
ill, and died in the summer camp. Tiberius, having escorted
his brother's body to Rome, returned to Germany and continued raiding expeditions across the Rhine. He 'almost
reduced Germany to the state of a tributary province' [1] and
returned to Rome to celebrate a triumph. Velleius' praise is

[1] Vell. II, 97.

exaggerated: but for the moment the Romans abandoned serious operations in Germany, and for the next ten years there was comparative peace. About A.D. 1 we hear of L. Domitius Ahenobarbus on the Rhine, and it was presumably about this time that he built his causeway (*pontes longi, Ann.* I, 63) over the marshy country between the Ems and the Rhine. Then the tribes became troublesome again and Tiberius, now returned from exile in Rhodes, came back to Germany in A.D. 4 to deal with the trouble.

He advanced to and crossed the Weser, and received the submission of tribes between there and the Ocean; he did not take his legions back to the Rhine for the winter, but established his winter camp near the upper waters of the Lippe. His exploits in A.D. 5 rouse Velleius to lyricism. He overran 'the whole of Germany', conquered all the most ferocious tribes and made a combined military and naval expedition to the Elbe. Having thus brought most of the German tribes into temporary control, he planned a great joint expedition from Rhine and Danube against Maroboduus and his Marcomanni in Bohemia. This had almost reached its objective when the great revolt broke out in Illyricum, and for the next three years Tiberius was fully occupied there. Germany appears to have been quite unaffected by the rising in Illyricum, which supports the view that there was no organized national resistance to the Romans, and no mass desire to invade Gaul. If there had been, a time when the Roman crack armies and generals were fully occupied elsewhere would have been the time to attack. The Rhine legions continued to do some not very serious summer raiding, and nothing of importance was accomplished by either side.

Then came disaster. In A.D. 9 the legate Quintilius Varus was tricked into moving out from his summer camp with three legions, and then treacherously attacked in difficult

country by Arminius, the young prince of the Cherusci (*Ann.*
I, 55). Varus lost his head and committed suicide, and most
of the soldiers not killed in battle were massacred after
capitulation. It was a long time since the Romans had suffered
such disaster at the hands of a foreigner, and it made a profound impression on them, producing from Augustus the
cry, *Quintili Vare, legiones redde.*[1] Tacitus describes the scene
of the carnage in *Ann.* I, 61-2. The blow to Rome's material
strength and prestige was great; but again, significantly, no
national uprising or invasion of Gaul followed. Again the
trusted and experienced Tiberius was called upon to retrieve
the disaster (*abolendae infamiae ob amissum cum Quintilio Varo
exercitum, Ann.* I, 3). From A.D. 10-12, with the assistance of
Germanicus, he concentrated on strengthening the Roman
position on the Rhine, and it was during this time that the
military districts of Upper and Lower Germany (*Ann.* I, 31,
2 n.) were established and probably acquired their four legions
each (3, 5 n.). Assaults on German territory were little more
than raids and did not go far beyond the Rhine. In 13, when
Tiberius was sent to Illyricum, Augustus despatched Germanicus 'to finish the war'[2] in Germany, and from 14-16 there
was again great activity beyond the Rhine. The campaigns
of 14 and 15 are recorded by Tacitus in *Ann.* I (50-71), and
that of 16 in *Ann.* II (5-26). After the mutiny for better pay
and conditions (*Ann.* I, 31 sq.), the repentant soldiers begged
for action against the enemy (*Ann.* I, 44), and Germanicus
led them into the territory of the Marsi (*Ann.* I, 50), where
they burned and plundered. In 15 he went farther: he burned
the capital of the Chatti, rescued Segestes and obtained the
wife of Arminius as a hostage (55-8). Then he made a joint
expedition by land and sea to the Ems, defeated the Bructeri
and devastated the country between the Ems and the Lippe

[1] Suet. *Aug.* 23.   [2] Vell. II, 123.

(60). This brought him close to the scene of Varus' defeat, and he stopped to pay last rites to the dead (61-2). He continued to pursue Arminius eastwards, into wild country, and fought a battle which was almost disastrous; then his army returned, meeting considerable difficulties and dangers on the way (63-70).

For the campaign of 16 he laid great plans. In an attempt to avoid the perennial difficulty of transport and communications, he took his army in ships by way of his father's *fossa* and by sea to the Ems, and thence marched to the Weser. He fought against Arminius at Idistaviso (on the eastern side of the river), and again rather to the north of that point. These battles were claimed as Roman victories, but they do not seem to have been decisive ones. Germanicus returned to the Rhine as he had come, by sea, and as he sailed along the coast had his fleet scattered by a storm. The loss was ultimately not so great as was at first feared, but it served to emphasize the difficulties which the Romans faced in making an attack on Germany, and Tiberius decided to abandon the attempt at conquest, and recalled Germanicus. This had to be done tactfully, for it would not be good policy for Tiberius to make a martyr of the man who was his heir and who was much more popular than he himself. So Germanicus was congratulated on his successes, granted a triumph, and asked to go as special imperial legate to the East (where indeed he was badly needed).

But the fact remained that Germany had been abandoned. It had been for some time becoming obvious that Augustus' policy of finding a better frontier by incorporating Germany was not going to work. Many successful expeditions had been made and many German tribes defeated in battle, but there had been no serious attempt at occupation and settlement, without which the country would never become a province.

Systematically to subdue a country without roads or cities, whose population was much more mobile (and therefore less easily cornered and decisively conquered) than the Gauls, required a much larger army than Rome could at any time in the early Principate spare. The Romans had their victories, but they failed to consolidate them, and their great expeditions were in the end no more than a series of glorified raids. Rome could not afford either the men or the money to continue these indefinitely. The Illyrian revolt had shown the inadequacy of the army, and the disaster of Varus had deprived it of three whole legions; the Romans were having difficulty in keeping the legions up to strength and many of the recruits were of poor quality (*Ann*. I, 31); and there was not enough money in the military chest even to pay off legionaries at the stipulated time (*Ann*. I, 78). It was becoming plain, too, that not only were the German expeditions extravagant and from the point of view of defence unnecessary, but that if continued for too long they might become positively dangerous. A common and persistent foe might unite the German tribes into a nation, which would be much more dangerous than the present sum of its parts. Finally, the campaigns of Germanicus, though showy, had accomplished little of lasting value. He was not a very competent general, and Tiberius reckoned he had had his pleasure long enough in Germany. Augustus had urged that the Empire be expanded no farther (*consilium coercendi intra terminos imperii, Ann*. I, 11) and Tiberius' own good sense and personal experience of Germany urged him to the same course. The northern frontier, as far as Germany was concerned, was quite safe; as long as the Germans were kept busy fighting one another (and a little diplomacy would from time to time ensure this) they would not trouble Rome. Roman prestige had been sufficiently re-established after the defeat of Varus, and both

Germanicus and his soldiers could be better employed on other tasks.

Within two years Tiberius was proved to be right. Arminius and Maroboduus, the two most dangerous German leaders, came to blows; Maroboduus was driven into exile (*Ann.* II, 63) and Arminius treacherously slain (*Ann.* II, 88). Gaul and the Rhine frontier continued to be adequately protected by the legions of the two Germanies, and the conquest of Germany beyond the Rhine was abandoned, to the satisfaction of Germans and Romans alike.

THE JULIO - CLAUDIANS

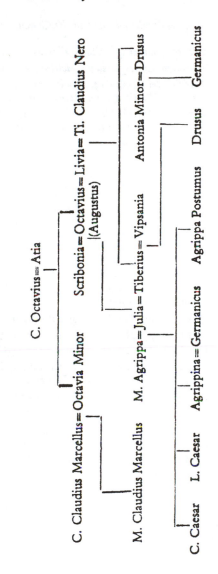

Abbreviations used in the Commentary

A.J.P.   *American Journal of Philology* (Baltimore).

B.C.H.   *Bulletin de Correspondance Hellénique* (Paris).

B.P.E.C.   *Bollettino del Comitato per la Preparazione dell' Edizione nazionale dei Classici greci e latini* (Rome).

C.A.H.   *Cambridge Ancient History* (Cambridge, 1934).

C.P.   *Classical Philology* (University of Chicago Press).

C.Q.   *Classical Quarterly* (O.U.P.).

C.R.   *Classical Review* (O.U.P.).

E. and J.   V. Ehrenberg and A. H. M. Jones, *Documents illustrating the Reigns of Augustus and Tiberius* (Oxford, 1955).

Eriksson   Nils Eriksson, *Studien zu den Annalen des Tacitus* (Lund, 1934).

I.L.S.   Dessau, *Inscriptiones Latinae Selectae* (Berlin, 1892).

J.R.S.   *Journal of Roman Studies* (London).

L.E.C.   *Les Études Classiques* (Namur).

Löfstedt   E. Löfstedt, *Syntactica* (I, Lund, 1942; II, Lund, 1933).

M.   *Mediceus primus (Laur.* 68, 1), the ninth-century manuscript containing *Annals* I-VI.

Marsh   F. B. Marsh, *The Reign of Tiberius* (Oxford, 1931).

Matt.   H. Mattingly, *Roman Coins* (London, 1928).

Parker   H. M. D. Parker, *The Roman Legions* (Oxford, 1928).

P.I.R.   *Prosopographia Imperii Romani saec.* I, II, III (Berlin, 1897: new edition, Berlin and Leipzig, 1933 *in progress*).

R.G.   *Res Gestae Diui Augusti* (*in* Ehrenberg and Jones).

R.I.C.   H. Mattingly and E. A. Sydenham, *Roman Imperial Coinage* (London, 1923).

R.I.L.   *Rendiconti dell' Istituto Lombardo* (Milan).

Sörbom   G. Sörbom, *Variatio sermonis Tacitei* (Uppsala, 1935).

T.A.P.A.   Transactions and Proceedings of the American Philological Association (Oxford, Blackwell).

Walker   B. Walker, *The Annals of Tacitus* (Manchester, 1952).

W.K.Ph.   *Wochenschrift für Klassische Philologie* (Leipzig).

The works of Tacitus are referred to thus (*Dial., Ag., Germ., Hist. Ann.*), without the author's name.

CORNELII TACITI

AB EXCESSV DIVI AVGVSTI
ANNALIVM

LIBER I

1. VRBEM Romam a principio reges habuere; libertatem et consulatum L. Brutus instituit. dictaturae ad tempus sumebantur; neque decemuiralis potestas ultra biennium, neque tribunorum militum consulare ius diu ualuit. non Cinnae, non Sullae longa dominatio; et Pompei Crassique potentia cito in Caesarem, Lepidi atque Antonii arma in Augustum cessere, qui cuncta discordiis ciuilibus fessa nomine principis
2 sub imperium accepit. sed ueteris populi Romani prospera uel aduersa claris scriptoribus memorata sunt; temporibusque Augusti dicendis non defuere decora ingenia, donec gliscente adulatione deterrerentur. Tiberii Gaique et Claudii ac Neronis res florentibus ipsis ob metum falsae, postquam
3 occiderant recentibus odiis compositae sunt. inde consilium mihi pauca de Augusto et extrema tradere, mox Tiberii principatum et cetera, sine ira et studio, quorum causas procul habeo.

2. Postquam Bruto et Cassio caesis nulla iam publica arma, Pompeius apud Siciliam oppressus exutoque Lepido, interfecto Antonio ne Iulianis quidem partibus nisi Caesar dux reliquus, posito triumuiri nomine consulem se ferens et ad tuendam plebem tribunicio iure contentum, ubi militem donis, populum annona, cunctos dulcedine otii pellexit, insurgere paulatim, munia senatus magistratuum legum in se trahere, nullo aduersante, cum ferocissimi per acies aut

proscriptione cecidissent, ceteri nobilium, quanto quis seruitio promptior, opibus et honoribus extollerentur ac nouis
ex rebus aucti tuta et praesentia quam uetera et periculosa
2 mallent. neque prouinciae illum rerum statum abnuebant,
suspecto senatus populique imperio ob certamina potentium
et auaritiam magistratuum, inualido legum auxilio quae ui
ambitu postremo pecunia turbabantur.

3. Ceterum Augustus subsidia dominationi Claudium
Marcellum sororis filium admodum adulescentem pontificatu
et curuli aedilitate, M. Agrippam, ignobilem loco, bonum
militia et uictoriae socium, geminatis consulatibus extulit,
mox defuncto Marcello generum sumpsit; Tiberium Neronem et Claudium Drusum priuignos imperatoriis nomini-
2 bus auxit, integra etiam tum domo sua. nam genitos Agrippa
Gaium ac Lucium in familiam Caesarum induxerat, necdum
posita puerili praetexta principes iuuentutis appellari,
destinari consules specie recusantis flagrantissime cupi-
3 uerat. ut Agrippa uita concessit, Lucium Caesarem euntem
ad Hispaniensis exercitus, Gaium remeantem Armenia et
uulnere inualidum mors fato propera uel nouercae Liuiae
dolus abstulit, Drusoque pridem extincto Nero solus e
priuignis erat, illuc cuncta uergere: filius, collega imperii,
consors tribuniciae potestatis adsumitur omnisque per exercitus ostentatur, non obscuris, ut antea, matris artibus, sed
4 palam hortatu. nam senem Augustum deuinxerat adeo,
uti nepotem unicum, Agrippam Postumum, in insulam
Planasiam proiecerit, rudem sane bonarum artium et robore
corporis stolide ferocem, nullius tamen flagitii conpertum.
5 at hercule Germanicum Druso ortum octo apud Rhenum
legionibus inposuit adscirique per adoptionem a Tiberio
iussit, quamquam esset in domo Tiberii filius iuuenis, sed
6 quo pluribus munimentis insisteret. bellum ea tempestate
nullum nisi aduersus Germanos supererat, abolendae magis

infamiae ob amissum cum Quintilio Varo exercitum quam
7 cupidine proferendi imperii aut dignum ob praemium. domi
res tranquillae, eadem magistratuum uocabula; iuniores post
Actiacam uictoriam, etiam senes plerique inter bella ciuium
nati: quotus quisque reliquus qui rem publicam uidisset?

4. Igitur uerso ciuitatis statu nihil usquam prisci et integri
moris: omnes exuta aequalitate iussa principis aspectare,
nulla in praesens formidine, dum Augustus aetate ualidus
2 seque et domum et pacem sustentauit. postquam prouecta
iam senectus aegro et corpore fatigabatur aderatque finis
et spes nouae, pauci bona libertatis in cassum disserere,
plures bellum pauescere, alii cupere. pars multo maxima
3 inminentis dominos uariis rumoribus differebant: trucem
Agrippam et ignominia accensum non aetate neque rerum
experientia tantae moli parem, Tiberium Neronem matu-
rum annis, spectatum bello, sed uetere atque insita Claudiae
familiae superbia, multaque indicia saeuitiae, quamquam
4 premantur, erumpere. hunc et prima ab infantia eductum
in domo regnatrice; congestos iuueni consulatus, triumphos;
ne iis quidem annis quibus Rhodi specie secessus exulem [1]
egerit aliquid [2] quam iram et simulationem et secretas libi-
5 dines meditatum. accedere matrem muliebri inpotentia:
seruiendum feminae duobusque insuper adulescentibus qui
rem publicam interim premant quandoque distrahant.

5. Haec atque talia agitantibus grauescere ualetudo Augusti,
et quidam scelus uxoris suspectabant. quippe rumor incesserat paucos ante mensis Augustum, electis consciis et comite
uno Fabio Maximo, Planasiam uectum ad uisendum Agrippam; multas illic utrimque lacrimas et signa caritatis spem-
2 que ex eo fore ut iuuenis penatibus aui redderetur: quod
Maximum uxori Marciae aperuisse, illam Liuiae. gnarum
id Caesari; neque multo post extincto Maximo, dubium an

[1] exul *O.T.*   [2] aliud *O.T.*

quaesita morte, auditos in funere eius Marciae gemitus
3 semet incusantis quod causa exitii marito fuisset. utcumque
se ea res habuit, uixdum ingressus Illyricum Tiberius pro-
peris matris litteris accitur; neque satis conpertum est
spirantem adhuc Augustum apud urbem Nolam an exani-
4 mem reppererit. acribus namque custodiis domum et uias
saepserat Liuia, laetique interdum nuntii uulgabantur, donec
prouisis quae tempus monebat simul excessisse Augustum
et rerum potiri Neronem fama eadem tulit.

6. Primum facinus noui principatus fuit Postumi Agrippae
caedes, quem ignarum inermumque quamuis firmatus animo
centurio aegre confecit. nihil de ea re Tiberius apud senatum
disseruit: patris iussa simulabat, quibus praescripsisset tribuno
custodiae adposito ne cunctaretur Agrippam morte adficere
2 quandoque ipse supremum diem expleuisset. multa sine
dubio saeuaque Augustus de moribus adulescentis questus,
ut exilium eius senatus consulto sanciretur perfecerat:
ceterum in nullius umquam suorum necem durauit, neque
mortem nepoti pro securitate priuigni inlatam credibile
erat. propius uero Tiberium ac Liuiam, illum metu, hanc
nouercalibus odiis, suspecti et inuisi iuuenis caedem festi-
3 nauisse. nuntianti centurioni, ut mos militiae, factum esse
quod imperasset, neque imperasse sese et rationem facti
reddendam apud senatum respondit. quod postquam Sallustius Crispus particeps secretorum (is ad tribunum miserat
codicillos) comperit, metuens ne reus subderetur, iuxta
periculoso ficta seu uera promeret monuit Liuiam ne arcana
domus, ne consilia amicorum, ministeria militum uulgar-
entur, neue Tiberius uim principatus resolueret cuncta ad
senatum uocando: eam condicionem esse imperandi ut non
aliter ratio constet quam si uni reddatur.

7. At Romae ruere in seruitium consules, patres, eques.
quanto quis inlustrior, tanto magis falsi ac festinantes,

uultuque composito ne laeti excessu principis neu tristiores primordio, lacrimas gaudium, questus adulationem misce-

2 bant. Sex. Pompeius et Sex. Appuleius consules primi in uerba Tiberii Caesaris iurauere, aputque eos Seius Strabo et C. Turranius, ille praetoriarum cohortium praefectus, hic

3 annonae; mox senatus milesque et populus. nam Tiberius cuncta per consules incipiebat tamquam uetere re publica et ambiguus imperandi: ne edictum quidem, quo patres in curiam uocabat, nisi tribuniciae potestatis praescriptione

4 posuit sub Augusto acceptae. uerba edicti fuere pauca et sensu permodesto: de honoribus parentis consulturum, neque abscedere a corpore idque unum ex publicis muneribus

5 usurpare. sed defuncto Augusto signum praetoriis cohortibus ut imperator dederat; excubiae, arma, cetera aulae; miles in forum, miles in curiam comitabatur. litteras ad exercitus tamquam adepto principatu misit, nusquam cuncta-

6 bundus nisi cum in senatu loqueretur. causa praecipua ex formidine ne Germanicus, in cuius manu tot legiones, immensa sociorum auxilia, mirus apud populum fauor,

7 habere imperium quam exspectare mallet. dabat et famae ut uocatus electusque potius a re publica uideretur quam per uxorium ambitum et senili adoptione inrepsisse. postea cognitum est ad introspiciendas etiam procerum uoluntates inductam dubitationem: nam uerba uultus in crimen detorquens recondebat.

8. Nihil primo senatus die agi passus[1] nisi de supremis Augusti, cuius testamentum inlatum per uirgines Vestae Tiberium et Liuiam heredes habuit. Liuia in familiam Iuliam nomenque Augustum adsumebatur; in spem secundam nepotes pronepotesque, tertio gradu primores ciuitatis scripserat, plerosque inuisos sibi sed iactantia gloriaque ad

2 posteros. legata non ultra ciuilem modum, nisi quod populo

---

[1] passus *est* O.T.

et plebi quadringenties tricies quinquies, praetoriarum cohortium militibus singula nummum milia, *urbanis quingenos*, legionariis aut cohortibus ciuium Romanorum trecenos

3 nummos uiritim dedit. tum consultatum de honoribus; ex quis *qui* maxime insignes uisi, ut porta triumphali duceretur funus Gallus Asinius, ut legum latarum tituli, victarum ab eo gentium uocabula anteferrentur L. Arruntius cen-

4 suere. addebat Messala Valerius renouandum per annos sacramentum in nomen Tiberii; interrogatusque a Tiberio num se mandante eam sententiam prompsisset, sponte dixisse respondit, neque in iis quae ad rem publicam pertinerent consilio nisi suo usurum uel cum periculo offensionis:

5 ea sola species adulandi supererat. conclamant patres corpus ad rogum umeris senatorum ferendum. remisit Caesar adroganti moderatione, populumque edicto monuit ne, ut quondam nimiis studiis funus diui Iulii turbassent, ita Augustum in foro potius quam in campo Martis, sede

6 destinata, cremari uellent. die funeris milites uelut praesidio stetere, multum inridentibus qui ipsi uiderant quique a parentibus acceperant diem illum crudi adhuc seruitii et libertatis inprospere repetitae, cum occisus dictator Caesar aliis pessimum aliis pulcherrimum facinus uideretur: nunc senem principem, longa potentia, prouisis etiam heredum in rem publicam opibus, auxilio scilicet militari tuendum, ut sepultura eius quieta foret.

9. Multus hinc ipso de Augusto sermo, plerisque uana mirantibus quod idem dies accepti quondam imperii princeps et uitae supremus, quod Nolae in domo et cubiculo in

2 quo pater eius Octauius uitam finiuisset. numerus etiam consulatuum celebrabatur, quo Valerium Coruum et C. Marium simul aequauerat; continuata per septem et triginta annos tribunicia potestas, nomen inperatoris semel atque

3 uicies partum aliaque honorum multiplicata aut noua. at

apud prudentis uita eius uarie extollebatur arguebaturue. hi
pietate erga parentem et necessitudine rei publicae, in qua
nullus tunc legibus locus, ad arma ciuilia actum quae neque
4 parari possent neque haberi per bonas artis. multa Antonio,
dum interfectores patris ulcisceretur, multa Lepido conces-
sisse. postquam hic socordia senuerit, ille per libidines pessum
datus sit, non aliud discordantis patriae remedium fuisse
5 quam *ut* ab uno regeretur. non regno tamen neque dictatura
sed principis nomine constitutam rem publicam; mari
Oceano aut amnibus longinquis saeptum imperium; legiones,
prouincias, classis, cuncta inter se conexa; ius apud ciuis,
modestiam apud socios; urbem ipsam magnifico ornatu;
pauca admodum ui tractata quo ceteris quies esset.

10. Dicebatur contra: pietatem erga parentem et tempora
rei publicae obtentui sumpta: ceterum cupidine dominandi
concitos per largitionem ueteranos, paratum ab adulescente
priuato exercitum, corruptas consulis legiones, simulatam
2 Pompeianarum gratiam partium; mox ubi decreto patrum
fascis et ius praetoris inuaserit, caesis Hirtio et Pansa, siue
hostis illos, seu Pansam uenenum uulneri adfusum, sui
milites Hirtium (et machinator doli Caesar abstulerat)
utriusque copias occupauisse; extortum inuito senatu
consulatum, armaque quae in Antonium acceperit contra
rem publicam uersa; proscriptionem ciuium, diuisiones
3 agrorum ne ipsis quidem qui fecere laudatas. sane Cassii
et Brutorum exitus paternis inimicitiis datos, quamquam
fas sit priuata odia publicis utilitatibus remittere: sed Pompeium imagine pacis, sed Lepidum specie amicitiae deceptos;
post Antonium, Tarentino Brundisinoque foedere et nuptiis
sororis inlectum, subdolae adfinitatis poenas morte ex-
4 soluisse. pacem sine dubio post haec, uerum cruentam:
Lollianas Varianasque cladis, interfectos Romae Varrones,
5 Egnatios, Iullos. nec domesticis abstinebatur: abducta Neroni

uxor et consulti per ludibrium pontifices an concepto
necdum edito partu rite nuberet; † que tedii et † Vedii Pollionis luxus; postremo Liuia grauis in rem publicam mater,
6 grauis domui Caesarum nouerca. nihil deorum honoribus
relictum cum se templis et effigie numinum per flamines
7 et sacerdotes coli uellet. ne Tiberium quidem caritate aut
rei publicae cura successorem adscitum, sed quoniam
adrogantiam saeuitiamque eius introspexerit, comparatione deterrima sibi gloriam quaesiuisse. etenim
Augustus paucis ante annis, cum Tiberio tribuniciam
potestatem a patribus rursum postularet, quamquam honora
oratione, quaedam de habitu cultuque et institutis eius
8 iecerat quae uelut excusando exprobraret. ceterum
sepultura more perfecta templum et caelestes religiones
decernuntur.

   11. Versae inde ad Tiberium preces. et ille uarie disserebat
de magnitudine imperii sua modestia. solam diui Augusti
mentem tantae molis capacem: se in partem curarum ab
illo uocatum experiendo didicisse quam arduum, quam
subiectum fortunae regendi cuncta onus. proinde in ciuitate
tot inlustribus uiris subnixa non ad unum omnia deferrent:
plures facilius munia rei publicae sociatis laboribus exsecu-
2 turos. plus in oratione tali dignitatis quam fidei erat; Tiberi-
oque etiam in rebus quas non occuleret, seu natura siue
adsuetudine, suspensa semper et obscura uerba: tunc uero
nitenti ut sensus suos penitus abderet, in incertum et ambi-
3 guum magis implicabantur. at patres, quibus unus metus
si intellegere uiderentur, in questus lacrimas uota effundi;
ad deos, ad effigiem Augusti, ad genua ipsius manus tendere,
4 cum proferri libellum recitarique iussit. opes publicae con-
tinebantur, quantum ciuium sociorumque in armis, quot
classes, regna, prouinciae, tributa aut uectigalia, et necessitates ac largitiones. quae cuncta sua manu perscripserat

Augustus addideratque consilium coercendi intra terminos imperii, incertum metu an per inuidiam.

12. Inter quae senatu ad infimas obtestationes procumbente, dixit forte Tiberius se ut non toti rei publicae parem, ita quaecumque pars sibi mandaretur eius tutelam suscepturum. 2 tum Asinius Gallus 'interrogo' inquit, 'Caesar, quam partem rei publicae mandari tibi uelis.' perculsus inprouisa interrogatione paulum reticuit: dein collecto animo respondit nequaquam decorum pudori suo legere aliquid aut euitare 3 ex eo cui in uniuersum excusari mallet. rursum Gallus (etenim uultu offensionem coniectauerat) non idcirco interrogatum ait, ut diuideret quae separari nequirent sed ut sua confessione argueretur unum esse rei publicae corpus atque unius animo regendum. addidit laudem de Augusto Tiberiumque ipsum uictoriarum suarum quaeque in toga per tot 4 annos egregie fecisset admonuit. nec ideo iram eius leniuit, pridem inuisus, tamquam ducta in matrimonium Vipsania M. Agrippae filia, quae quondam Tiberii uxor fuerat, plus quam ciuilia agitaret Pollionisque Asinii patris ferociam retineret.

13. Post quae L. Arruntius haud multum discrepans a Galli oratione perinde offendit, quamquam Tiberio nulla uetus in Arruntium ira: sed diuitem, promptum, artibus 2 egregiis et pari fama publice, suspectabat. quippe Augustus supremis sermonibus cum tractaret quinam adipisci principem locum suffecturi abnuerent aut inpares uellent uel idem possent cuperentque, M.[1] Lepidum dixerat capacem sed aspernantem, Gallum Asinium auidum et minorem, L. 3 Arruntium non indignum et si casus daretur ausurum. de prioribus consentitur, pro Arruntio quidam Cn. Pisonem tradidere; omnesque praeter Lepidum uariis mox criminibus 4 struente Tiberio circumuenti sunt. etiam Q. Haterius et

[1] M'. O.T.

Mamercus Scaurus suspicacem animum perstrinxere, Haterius cum dixisset 'quo usque patieris, Caesar, non adesse caput rei publicae?' Scaurus quia dixerat spem esse ex eo non inritas fore senatus preces quod relationi consulum iure tribuniciae potestatis non intercessisset. in Haterium statim inuectus est; Scaurum, cui inplacabilius irascebatur, silentio
5 tramisit. fessusque clamore omnium, expostulatione singulorum flexit paulatim, non ut fateretur suscipi a se imperium,
6 sed ut negare et rogari desineret. constat Haterium, cum deprecandi causa Palatium introisset ambulantisque Tiberii genua aduolueretur, prope a militibus interfectum quia Tiberius casu an manibus eius inpeditus prociderat. neque tamen periculo talis uiri mitigatus est, donec Haterius Augustam oraret eiusque curatissimis precibus protegeretur.

14. Multa patrum et in Augustam adulatio. alii parentem, alii matrem patriae appellandam, plerique ut nomini Caesa-
2 ris adscriberetur 'Iuliae filius' censebant. ille moderandos feminarum honores dictitans eademque se temperantia usurum in iis quae sibi tribuerentur, ceterum anxius inuidia et muliebre fastigium in deminutionem sui accipiens ne lictorem quidem ei decerni passus est aramque adoptionis et
3 alia huiusce modi prohibuit. at Germanico Caesari proconsulare imperium petiuit, missique legati qui deferrent, simul maestitiam eius ob excessum Augusti solarentur. quo minus idem pro Druso postularetur, ea causa quod designatus
4 consul Drusus praesensque erat. candidatos praeturae duodecim nominauit, numerum ab Augusto traditum; et hortante senatu ut augeret, iure iurando obstrinxit se non excessurum.

15. Tum primum e campo comitia ad patres translata sunt: nam ad eam diem, etsi potissima arbitrio principis, quaedam tamen studiis tribuum fiebant. neque populus ademptum ius questus est nisi inani rumore, et senatus

largitionibus ac precibus sordidis exsolutus libens tenuit,
moderante Tiberio ne plures quam quattuor candidatos
2 commendaret sine repulsa et ambitu designandos. inter quae
tribuni plebei petiuere ut proprio sumptu ederent ludos
qui de nomine Augusti fastis additi Augustales uocarentur.
sed decreta pecunia ex aerario, utque per circum triumphali
3 ueste uterentur: curru uehi haud permissum. mox celebratio
annua ad praetorem translata cui inter ciuis et peregrinos
iurisdictio euenisset.

16. Hic rerum urbanarum status erat, cum Pannonicas
legiones seditio incessit, nullis nouis causis nisi quod mutatus
princeps licentiam turbarum et ex ciuili bello spem praemio-
2 rum ostendebat. castris aestiuis tres simul legiones habebantur, praesidente Iunio Blaeso, qui fine Augusti et initiis
Tiberii auditis ob iustitium aut gaudium intermiserat solita
munia. eo principio lasciuire miles, discordare, pessimi
cuiusque sermonibus praebere auris, denique luxum et otium
3 cupere, disciplinam et laborem aspernari. erat in castris
Percennius quidam, dux olim theatralium operarum, dein
gregarius miles, procax lingua et miscere coetus histrionali
studio doctus. is imperitos animos et quaenam post Augustum
militiae condicio ambigentis inpellere paulatim nocturnis
conloquiis aut flexo in uesperam die et dilapsis melioribus
deterrimum quemque congregare.

17. Postremo promptis iam et aliis seditionis ministris
uelut contionabundus interrogabat cur paucis centurionibus
paucioribus tribunis in modum seruorum oboedirent.
quando ausuros exposcere remedia, nisi nouum et nutantem
2 adhuc principem precibus uel armis adirent? satis per tot
annos ignauia peccatum, quod tricena aut quadragena
stipendia senes et plerique truncato ex uulneribus corpore
3 tolerent. ne dimissis quidem finem esse militiae, sed apud
uexillum tendentis alio uocabulo eosdem labores perferre.

ac si quis tot casus uita superauerit, trahi adhuc diuersas
in terras ubi per nomen agrorum uligines paludum uel
4 inculta montium accipiant. enimuero militiam ipsam grauem,
infructuosam: denis in diem assibus animam et corpus
aestimari: hinc uestem arma tentoria, hinc saeuitiam centurionum et uacationes munerum redimi. at hercule uerbera
et uulnera, duram hiemem, exercitas aestates, bellum atrox
5 aut sterilem pacem sempiterna. nec aliud leuamentum quam
si certis sub legibus militia iniretur, ut singulos denarios
mererent, sextus decumus stipendii annus finem adferret,
ne ultra sub uexillis tenerentur, sed isdem in castris praemium
6 pecunia solueretur. an praetorias cohortis, quae binos
denarios acceperint, quae post sedecim annos penatibus suis
reddantur, plus periculorum suscipere? non obtrectari a se
urbanas excubias: sibi tamen apud horridas gentis e contuberniis hostem aspici.

18. Adstrepebat uulgus, diuersis incitamentis, hi uerberum
notas, illi canitiem, plurimi detrita tegmina et nudum corpus
2 exprobrantes. postremo eo furoris uenere ut tres legiones
miscere in unam agitauerint. depulsi aemulatione, quia suae
quisque legioni eum honorem quaerebant, alio uertunt atque
una tres aquilas et signa cohortium locant; simul congerunt
caespites, exstruunt tribunal, quo magis conspicua sedes
3 foret. properantibus Blaesus aduenit, increpabatque ac
retinebat singulos, clamitans 'mea potius caede imbuite
manus: leuiore flagitio legatum interficietis quam ab imperatore desciscitis. aut incolumis fidem legionum retinebo aut
iugulatus paenitentiam adcelerabo.'

19. Aggerebatur[1] nihilo minus caespes iamque pectori
usque adcreuerat, cum tandem peruicacia uicti inceptum
2 omisere. Blaesus multa dicendi arte non per seditionem et
turbas desideria militum ad Caesarem ferenda ait, neque

---

[1] aggerauatur O.T.

ueteres ab imperatoribus priscis neque ipsos a diuo Augusto
tam noua petiuisse; et parum in tempore incipientis principis
3 curas onerari. si tamen tenderent in pace temptare quae ne
ciuilium quidem bellorum uictores expostulauerint, cur
contra morem obsequii, contra fas disciplinae uim meditentur? decernerent legatos seque coram mandata darent.
4 adclamauere ut filius Blaesi tribunus legatione ea fungeretur
peteretque militibus missionem ab sedecim annis: cetera
5 mandaturos ubi prima prouenissent. profecto iuuene modicum otium: sed superbire miles quod filius legati orator
publicae causae satis ostenderet necessitate expressa quae per
modestiam non obtinuissent.

20. Interea manipuli ante coeptam seditionem Nauportum missi ob itinera et pontes et alios usus, postquam
turbatum in castris accepere, uexilla conuellunt direptisque
proximis uicis ipsoque Nauporto, quod municipii instar
erat, retinentis centuriones inrisu et contumeliis, postremo
uerberibus insectantur, praecipua in Aufidienum Rufum
praefectum castrorum ira, quem dereptum uehiculo sarcinis
grauant aguntque primo in agmine per ludibrium rogitantes
an tam immensa onera, tam longa itinera libenter ferret.
2 quippe Rufus diu manipularis, dein centurio, mox castris
praefectus, antiquam duramque militiam reuocabat, intentus ¹ operis ac laboris et eo inmitior quia tolerauerat.

21. Horum aduentu redintegratur seditio et uagi circumiecta populabantur. Blaesus paucos, maxime praeda onustos,
ad terrorem ceterorum adfici uerberibus, claudi carcere
iubet; nam etiam tum legato a centurionibus et optimo
2 quoque manipularium parebatur. illi obniti trahentibus,
prensare circumstantium genua, ciere modo nomina singulorum, modo centuriam quisque cuius manipularis erat, cohor-
tem, legionem, eadem omnibus inminere clamitantes. simul

---

¹ uetus O.T.

probra in legatum cumulant, caelum ac deos obtestantur, nihil reliqui faciunt quo minus inuidiam misericordiam
3 metum et iras permouerent. adcurritur ab uniuersis, et carcere effracto soluunt uincula desertoresque ac rerum capitalium damnatos sibi iam miscent.

22. Flagrantior inde uis, plures seditioni duces. et Vibulenus quidam gregarius miles, ante tribunal Blaesi adleuatus circumstantium umeris, apud turbatos et quid pararet intentos 'uos quidem' inquit 'his innocentibus et miserrimis lucem et spiritum reddidistis: sed quis fratri meo uitam, quis fratrem mihi reddit? quem missum ad uos a Germanico exercitu de communibus commodis nocte proxima iugulauit per gladiatores suos, quos in exitium militum habet atque
2 armat. responde, Blaese, ubi cadauer abieceris: ne hostes quidem sepultura inuident. cum osculis, cum lacrimis dolorem meum impleuero, me quoque trucidari iube, dum interfectos nullum ob scelus sed quia utilitati legionum consulebamus hi sepeliant.'

23. Incendebat haec fletu et pectus atque os manibus uerberans. mox disiectis quorum per umeros sustinebatur, praeceps et singulorum pedibus aduolutus tantum consternationis inuidiaeque conciuit, ut pars militum gladiatores, qui e seruitio Blaesi erant, pars ceteram eiusdem familiam
2 uincirent, alii ad quaerendum corpus effunderentur. ac ni propere neque corpus ullum reperiri, et seruos adhibitis cruciatibus abnuere caedem, neque illi fuisse umquam fratrem pernotuisset, haud multum ab exitio legati aberant.
3 tribunos tamen ac praefectum castrorum extrusere, sarcinae fugientium direptae, et centurio Lucilius interficitur cui militaribus facetiis uocabulum 'cedo alteram' indiderant, quia fracta uite in tergo militis alteram clara uoce ac rursus
4 aliam poscebat. ceteros latebrae texere, uno retento Clemente Iulio qui perferendis militum mandatis habebatur idoneus

5 ob promptum ingenium. quin ipsae inter se legiones octaua
et quinta decuma ferrum parabant, dum centurionem
cognomento Sirpicum illa morti deposcit, quintadecumani
tuentur, ni miles nonanus preces et aduersum asperantis
minas interiecisset.

asperantis

24. Haec audita quamquam abstrusum et tristissima quaeque maxime occultantem Tiberium perpulere, ut Drusum
filium cum primoribus ciuitatis duabusque praetoriis cohortibus mitteret, nullis satis certis mandatis, ex re consulturum.
2 et cohortes delecto milite supra solitum firmatae. additur
magna pars praetoriani equitis et robora Germanorum, qui
tum custodes imperatori aderant; simul praetorii praefectus
Aelius Seianus, collega Straboni patri suo datus, magna
apud Tiberium auctoritate, rector iuueni et ceteris pericu-
3 lorum praemiorumque ostentator. Druso propinquanti
quasi per officium obuiae fuere legiones, non laetae, ut
adsolet, neque insignibus fulgentes, sed inluuie deformi et
uultu, quamquam maestitiam imitarentur contumaciae
propiores.

25. Postquam uallum introiit, portas stationibus firmant,
globos armatorum certis castrorum locis opperiri iubent:
ceteri tribunal ingenti agmine circumueniunt. stabat Drusus
2 silentium manu poscens. illi quoties oculos ad multitudinem
rettulerant, uocibus truculentis strepere, rursum uiso Caesare
trepidare; murmur incertum, atrox clamor et repente
quies; diuersis animorum motibus pauebant terrebantque.
3 tandem interrupto tumultu litteras patris recitat, in quis
perscriptum erat, praecipuam ipsi fortissimarum legionum
curam, quibuscum plurima bella tolerauisset; ubi primum
a luctu requiesset animus, acturum apud patres de postulatis
eorum; misisse interim filium ut sine cunctatione concederet
quae statim tribui possent; cetera senatui seruanda quem
neque gratiae neque seueritatis expertem haberi par esset.

26. Responsum est a contione mandata Clementi centurioni quae perferret. is orditur de missione a sedecim annis, de praemiis finitae militiae, ut denarius diurnum stipendium foret, ne ueterani sub uexillo haberentur. ad ea Drusus cum arbitrium senatus et patris obtenderet, clamore turba-2 tur. cur uenisset neque augendis militum stipendiis neque adleuandis laboribus, denique nulla bene faciendi licentia? at hercule uerbera et necem cunctis permitti. Tiberium olim nomine Augusti desideria legionum frustrari solitum: easdem artis Drusum rettulisse. numquamne ad se nisi filios 3 familiarum uenturos? nouum id plane quod imperator sola militis commoda ad senatum reiciat. eundem ergo senatum consulendum quotiens supplicia aut proelia indicantur: an praemia sub dominis, poenas sine arbitro esse?

27. Postremo deserunt tribunal, ut quis praetorianorum militum amicorumue Caesaris occurreret, manus intentantes, causam discordiae et initium armorum, maxime infensi Cn. Lentulo, quod is ante alios aetate et gloria belli firmare Drusum credebatur et illa militiae flagitia primus aspernari. 2 nec multo post digredientem eum[1] Caesare ac prouisu periculi hiberna castra repetentem circumsistunt, rogitantes quo pergeret, ad imperatorem an ad patres, ut illic quoque commodis legionum aduersaretur; simul ingruunt, saxa iaciunt. iamque lapidis ictu cruentus et exitii certus adcursu multitudinis quae cum Druso aduenerat protectus est.

28. Noctem minacem et in scelus erupturam fors leniuit: nam luna claro repente caelo uisa languescere. id miles rationis ignarus omen praesentium accepit, suis laboribus defectionem sideris adsimulans, prosperque cessura quae [2] 2 pergerent si fulgor et claritudo deae redderetur. igitur aeris sono, tubarum cornuumque concentu strepere; prout splendidior obscuriorue laetari aut maerere; et postquam

[1] cum *O.T.*   [2] qua *O.T.*

ortae nubes offecere uisui creditumque conditam tenebris,
ut sunt mobiles ad superstitionem perculsae semel mentes,
sibi aeternum laborem portendi, sua facinora auersari deos
3 lamentantur. utendum inclinatione ea Caesar et quae casus
obtulerat in sapientiam uertenda ratus circumiri tentoria
iubet; accitur centurio Clemens et si *qui* [1] alii bonis artibus
4 grati in uulgus. hi uigiliis, stationibus, custodiis portarum
se inserunt, spem offerunt, metum intendunt. 'quo usque
filium imperatoris obsidebimus? quis certaminum finis?
Percennione et Vibuleno sacramentum dicturi sumus? Percennius et Vibulenus stipendia militibus, agros emeritis
largientur? denique pro Neronibus et Drusis imperium
5 populi Romani capessent? quin potius, ut nouissimi in
culpam, ita primi ad paenitentiam sumus? tarda sunt quae
in commune expostulantur: priuatam gratiam statim mereare,
6 statim recipias.' commotis per haec mentibus et inter se
suspectis, tironem a ueterano, legionem a legione dissociant.
tum redire paulatim amor obsequii: omittunt portas, signa
unum in locum principio seditionis congregata suas in sedes
referunt.

29. Drusus orto die et uocata contione, quamquam rudis
dicendi, nobilitate ingenita incusat priora, probat praesentia;
negat se terrore et minis uinci: flexos ad modestiam si uideat,
si supplices audiat, scripturum patri ut placatus legionum
2 preces exciperet. orantibus rursum idem Blaesus et L.
Aponius, eques Romanus e cohorte Drusi, Iustusque Cato-
3 nius, primi ordinis centurio, ad Tiberium mittuntur. certa-
tum inde sententiis, cum alii opperiendos legatos atque
interim comitate permulcendum militem censerent, alii
fortioribus remediis agendum: nihil in uulgo modicum;
terrere ni paueant, ubi pertimuerint inpune contemni:
dum superstitio urgeat, adiciendos ex duce metus sublatis

---

[1] et si alii *O.T.*

4 seditionis auctoribus. promptum ad asperiora ingenium Druso
erat: uocatos Vibulenum et Percennium interfici iubet.
tradunt plerique intra tabernaculum ducis obrutos, alii
corpora extra uallum abiecta ostentui.

30. Tum ut quisque praecipuus turbator conquisiti, et
pars, extra castra palantes, a centurionibus aut praetoriarum
cohortium militibus caesi: quosdam ipsi manipuli documen-
2 tum fidei tradidere. auxerat militum curas praematura
hiems imbribus continuis adeoque saeuis, ut non egredi
tentoria, congregari inter se, uix tutari signa possent, quae
3 turbine atque unda raptabantur. durabat et formido caelestis
irae, nec frustra aduersus impios hebescere sidera, ruere
tempestates: non aliud malorum leuamentum, quam si
linquerent castra infausta temerataque et soluti piaculo
4 suis quisque hibernis redderentur. primum octaua, dein
quinta decuma legio rediere: nonanus opperiendas Tiberii
epistulas clamitauerat, mox desolatus aliorum discessione
5 imminentem necessitatem sponte praeuenit. et Drusus non
exspectato legatorum regressu, quia praesentia satis consederant, in urbem rediit.

31. Isdem ferme diebus isdem causis Germanicae legiones
turbatae, quanto plures tanto uiolentius, et magna spe fore
ut Germanicus Caesar imperium alterius pati nequiret
2 daretque se legionibus ui sua cuncta tracturis. duo apud
ripam Rheni exercitus erant: cui nomen superiori sub C.
Silio legato, inferiorem A. Caecina curabat. regimen summae
rei penes Germanicum agendo Galliarum censui tum inten-
3 tum. sed quibus Silius moderabatur, mente ambigua fortunam
seditionis alienae speculabantur: inferioris exercitus miles in
rabiem prolapsus est, orto ab unetuicesimanis quintanisque
initio, et tractis prima quoque ac uicesima legionibus: nam
isdem aestiuis in finibus Vbiorum habebantur per otium
4 aut leuia munia. igitur audito fine Augusti uernacula multi-

tudo, nuper acto in urbe dilectu, lasciuiae sueta, laborum
intolerans, implere ceterorum rudes animos: uenisse tempus
quo ueterani maturam missionem, iuuenes largiora stipendia,
cuncti modum miseriarum exposcerent saeuitiamque centu-
5 rionum ulciscerentur. non unus haec, ut Pannonicas inter
legiones Percennius, nec apud trepidas militum auris, alios
ualidiores exercitus respicientium, sed multa seditionis ora
uocesque: sua in manu sitam rem Romanam, suis uictoriis
augeri rem publicam, in suum cognomentum adscisci imperatores.

32. Nec legatus obuiam ibat: quippe plurium uaecordia
constantiam exemerat. repente lymphati destrictis gladiis
in centuriones inuadunt: ea uetustissima militaribus odiis
materies et saeuiendi principium. prostratos uerberibus
mulcant, sexagenis [1] singulos, ut numerum centurionum
adaequarent: tum conuulsos laniatosque et partim exanimos
2 ante uallum aut in amnem Rhenum proiciunt. Septimius
cum perfugisset ad tribunal pedibusque Caecinae aduolueretur, eo usque flagitatus est donec ad exitium dederetur.
Cassius Chaerea, mox caede Gai Caesaris memoriam apud
posteros adeptus, tum adulescens et animi ferox, inter obstan-
3 tis et armatos ferro uiam patefecit. non tribunus ultra, non
castrorum praefectus ius obtinuit: uigilias, stationes, et
si qua alia praesens usus indixerat, ipsi partiebantur. id
militaris animos altius coniectantibus praecipuum indicium
magni atque inplacabilis motus, quod neque disiecti nec
paucorum instinctu, set pariter ardescerent, pariter silerent,
tanta aequalitate et constantia ut regi crederes.

33. Interea Germanico per Gallias, ut diximus, census
accipienti excessisse Augustum adfertur. neptem eius Agrippinam in matrimonio pluresque ex ea liberos habebat, ipse
Druso fratre Tiberii genitus, Augustae nepos, set anxius

---

[1] sexageni O.T.

occultis in se patrui auiaeque odiis quorum causae acriores
2 quia iniquae. quippe Drusi magna apud populum Romanum
memoria, credebaturque, si rerum potitus foret, libertatem
redditurus; unde in Germanicum fauor et spes eadem. nam
iuueni ciuile ingenium, mira comitas et diuersa ab Tiberii
3 sermone uultu, adrogantibus et obscuris. accedebant mulie-
bres offensiones nouercalibus Liuiae in Agrippinam stimulis,
atque ipsa Agrippina paulo commotior, nisi quod castitate
et mariti amore quamuis indomitum animum in bonum
uertebat.

34. Sed Germanicus quanto summae spei propior, tanto
impensius pro Tiberio niti. seque et [1] proximos et Belgarum
ciuitates in uerba eius adigit. dehinc audito legionum tumultu
raptim profectus obuias extra castra habuit, deiectis in
2 terram oculis uelut paenitentia. postquam uallum iniit
dissoni questus audiri coepere. et quidam prensa manu
eius per speciem exosculandi inseruerunt digitos ut uacua
dentibus ora contingeret; alii curuata senio membra osten-
3 debant. adsistentem contionem, quia permixta uidebatur,
discedere in manipulos iubet: sic melius audituros responsum;
uexilla praeferri ut id saltem discerneret cohortis: tarde
4 obtemperauere. tunc a ueneratione Augusti orsus flexit ad
uictorias triumphosque Tiberii, praecipuis laudibus celebrans
quae apud Germanias illis cum legionibus pulcherrima
fecisset. Italiae inde consensum, Galliarum fidem extollit;
nil usquam turbidum aut discors. silentio haec uel murmure
modico audita sunt.

35. Vt seditionem attigit, ubi modestia militaris, ubi
ueteris disciplinae decus, quonam tribunos, quo centuriones
exegissent, rogitans, nudant uniuersi corpora, cicatrices ex
uulneribus, uerberum notas exprobrant; mox indiscretis
uocibus pretia uacationum, angustias stipendii, duritiam

[1] Sequanos O.T.

operum ac propriis nominibus incusant uallum, fossas,
pabuli materiae lignorum adgestus, et si qua alia ex neces-

2 sitate aut aduersus otium castrorum quaeruntur. atrocissi-
mus ueteranorum clamor oriebatur, qui tricena aut supra
stipendia numerantes, mederetur fessis, neu mortem in isdem
laboribus, sed finem tam exercitae militiae neque inopem

3 requiem orabant. fuere etiam qui legatam a diuo Augusto
pecuniam reposcerent, faustis in Germanicum ominibus; et

4 si uellet imperium promptos ostentauere. tum uero, quasi
scelere contaminaretur, praeceps tribunali desiluit. opposue-
runt abeunti arma, minitantes, ni regrederetur; at ille mori-
turum potius quam fidem exueret clamitans, ferrum a latere
diripuit elatumque deferebat in pectus, ni proximi prensam

5 dextram ui attinuissent. extrema et conglobata inter se pars
contionis ac, uix credibile dictu, quidam singuli propius
incedentes feriret hortabantur; et miles nomine Calusidius
strictum obtulit gladium, addito acutiorem esse. saeuum id
malique moris etiam furentibus uisum, ac spatium fuit quo
Caesar ab amicis in tabernaculum raperetur.

36. Consultatum ibi de remedio; etenim nuntiabatur
parari legatos qui superiorem exercitum ad causam eandem
traherent; destinatum excidio Vbiorum oppidum, imbutasque

2 praeda manus in direptionem Galliarum erupturas. augebat
metum gnarus Romanae seditionis et, si omitteretur ripa,
inuasurus hostis: at si auxilia et socii aduersum abscedentis
legiones armarentur, ciuile bellum suscipi. periculosa seueritas, flagitiosa largitio: seu nihil militi siue omnia concedentur

3 in ancipiti res publica. igitur uolutatis inter se rationibus
placitum ut epistulae nomine principis scriberentur: missionem dari uicena stipendia meritis, exauctorari qui sena
dena fecissent ac retineri sub uexillo ceterorum inmunes
nisi propulsandi hostis, legata quae petiuerant exsolui
duplicarique.

37. Sensit miles in tempus conficta statimque flagitauit. missio per tribunos maturatur, largitio differebatur in hiberna cuiusque. non abscessere quintani unetuicesimanique donec isdem in aestiuis contracta ex uiatico amicorum ipsiusque
2 Caesaris pecunia persolueretur. primam ac uicesimam legiones Caecina legatus in ciuitatem Vbiorum reduxit turpi agmine cum fisci de imperatore rapti inter signa interque aquilas
3 ueherentur. Germanicus superiorem ad exercitum profectus secundam et tertiam decumam et sextam decumam legiones nihil cunctatas sacramento adigit. quartadecumani paulum dubitauerant: pecunia et missio quamuis non flagitantibus oblata est.

38. At in Chaucis coeptauere seditionem praesidium agitantes uexillarii discordium legionum et praesenti duorum militum supplicio paulum repressi sunt. iusserat id M'. Ennius castrorum praefectus, bono magis exemplo quam
2 concesso iure. deinde intumescente motu profugus repertusque, postquam intutae latebrae, praesidium ab audacia mutuatur: non praefectum ab iis, sed Germanicum ducem, sed Tiberium imperatorem uiolari. simul exterritis qui obstiterant, raptum uexillum ad ripam uertit, et si quis agmine decessisset, pro desertore fore clamitans, reduxit in hiberna turbidos et nihil ausos.

39. Interea legati ab senatu regressum iam apud aram Vbiorum Germanicum adeunt. duae ibi legiones, prima atque uicesima, ueteranique nuper missi sub uexillo hiemabant.
2 pauidos et conscientia uaecordes intrat metus uenisse patrum iussu qui inrita facerent quae per seditionem expresserant.
3 utque mos uulgo quamuis falsis reum subdere, Munatium Plancum consulatu functum, principem legationis, auctorem senatus consulti incusant; et nocte concubia uexillum in domo Germanici situm flagitare occipiunt, concursuque ad ianuam facto moliuntur foris, extractum cubili Caesarem

4 tradere uexillum intento mortis metu subigunt. mox uagi
per uias obuios habuere legatos, audita consternatione ad
Germanicum tendentis. ingerunt contumelias, caedem parant,
Planco maxime, quem dignitas fuga impediuerat; neque
aliud periclitanti subsidium quam castra primae legionis.
illic signa et aquilam amplexus religione sese tutabatur, ac
ni aquilifer Calpurnius uim extremam arcuisset, rarum etiam
inter hostis, legatus populi Romani Romanis in castris san-
5 guine suo altaria deum commaculauisset. luce demum,
postquam dux et miles et facta noscebantur, ingressus castra
Germanicus perduci ad se Plancum imperat recepitque in
6 tribunal. tum fatalem increpans rabiem, neque militum sed
deum ira resurgere, cur uenerint legati aperit; ius legationis
atque ipsius Planci grauem et immeritum casum, simul
quantum dedecoris adierit legio, facunde miseratur, attoni-
taque magis quam quieta contione legatos praesidio
auxiliarium equitum dimittit.

40. Eo in metu arguere Germanicum omnes quod non ad
superiorem exercitum pergeret, ubi obsequia et contra rebellis
auxilium: satis superque missione et pecunia et mollibus
2 consultis peccatum. uel si uilis ipsi salus, cur filium paruulum,
cur grauidam coniugem inter furentis et omnis humani
iuris uiolatores haberet? illos saltem auo et rei publicae red-
3 deret. diu cunctatus aspernantem uxorem, cum se diuo
Augusto ortam neque degenerem ad pericula testaretur,
postremo uterum eius et communem filium multo cum fletu
4 complexus, ut abiret perpulit. incedebat muliebre et misera-
bile agmen, profuga ducis uxor, paruulum sinu filium gerens,
lamentantes circum amicorum coniuges quae simul trahebantur nec minus tristes qui manebant.

41. Non florentis Caesaris neque suis in castris, sed uelut
in urbe uicta facies gemitusque ac planctus etiam militum
auris oraque aduertere: progrediuntur contuberniis. quis

ille flebilis sonus? quod tam triste? feminas inlustris, non centurionem ad tutelam, non militem, nihil imperatoriae uxoris aut comitatus soliti: pergere ad Treuiros et [1] externae

2 fidei. pudor inde et miseratio et patris Agrippae, Augusti aui memoria, socer Drusus, ipsa insigni fecunditate, praeclara pudicitia; iam infans in castris genitus, in contubernio legionum eductus, quem militari uocabulo Caligulam appellabant, quia plerumque ad concilianda uulgi studia eo

3 tegmine pedum induebatur. sed nihil aeque flexit quam inuidia in Treuiros: orant obsistunt, rediret maneret, pars Agrippinae occursantes, plurimi ad Germanicum regressi. isque ut erat recens dolore et ira apud circumfusos ita coepit.

42. 'Non mihi uxor aut filius patre et re publica cariores sunt, sed illum quidem sua maiestas, imperium Romanum ceteri exercitus defendent. coniugem et liberos meos quos pro gloria uestra libens ad exitium offerrem, nunc procul a furentibus summoueo, ut quidquid istud sceleris imminet, meo tantum sanguine pietur, neue occisus Augusti pronepos,

2 interfecta Tiberii nurus nocentiores uos faciant. quid enim per hos dies inausum intemeratumue uobis? quod nomen huic coetui dabo? militesne appellem, qui filium imperatoris uestri uallo et armis circumsedistis? an ciuis, quibus tam proiecta senatus auctoritas? hostium quoque ius et sacra

3 legationis et fas gentium rupistis. diuus Iulius seditionem exercitus uerbo uno compescuit, Quirites uocando qui sacramentum eius detrectabant: diuus Augustus uultu et aspectu Actiacas legiones exterruit: nos ut nondum eosdem, ita ex illis ortos, si Hispaniae Syriaeue miles aspernaretur, tamen mirum et indignum erat. primane et uicesima legiones, illa signis a Tiberio acceptis, tu tot proeliorum socia, tot

4 praemiis aucta, egregiam duci uestro gratiam refertis? hunc ego nuntium patri laeta omnia aliis e prouinciis audient

[1] [et] O.T.

feram? ipsius tirones, ipsius ueteranos non missione, non
pecunia satiatos: hic tantum interfici centuriones, eici tribunos, includi legatos, infecta sanguine castra, flumina, meque
precariam animam inter infensos trahere.

43. 'Cur enim primo contionis die ferrum illud, quod
pectori meo infigere parabam, detraxistis, o inprouidi amici?
melius et amantius ille qui gladium offerebat. cecidissem
certe nondum tot flagitiorum exercitui [1] meo conscius;
legissetis ducem, qui meam quidem mortem inpunitam
2 sineret, Vari tamen et trium legionum ulcisceretur. neque
enim di sinant ut Belgarum quamquam offerentium decus
istud et claritudo sit subuenisse Romano nomini, compressisse
3 Germaniae populos. tua, diue Auguste, caelo recepta mens,
tua, pater Druse, imago, tui memoria isdem istis cum militibus, quos iam pudor et gloria intrat, eluant hanc maculam
4 irasque ciuilis in exitium hostibus uertant. uos quoque,
quorum alia nunc ora, alia pectora contueor, si legatos
senatui, obsequium imperatori, si mihi coniugem et filium
redditis, discedite a contactu ac diuidite turbidos: id stabile
ad paenitentiam, id fidei uinculum erit.'

44. Supplices ad haec et uera exprobrari fatentes orabant
puniret noxios, ignosceret lapsis et duceret in hostem:
reuocaretur coniunx, rediret legionum alumnus neue obses
Gallis traderetur. reditum Agrippinae excusauit ob inmi-
nentem partum et hiemem: uenturum filium: cetera ipsi
2 exsequerentur. discurrunt mutati et seditiosissimum quemque
uinctos trahunt ad legatum legionis primae C. Caetronium,
qui iudicium et poenas de singulis in hunc modum exercuit.
stabant pro contione legiones destrictis gladiis: reus in
suggestu per tribunum ostendebatur: si nocentem adclama-
3 uerant, praeceps datus trucidabatur. et gaudebat caedibus
miles tamquam semet absolueret; nec Caesar arcebat, quando

[1] exercitu *O.T.*

nullo ipsius iussu penes eosdem sacuitia facti et inuidia
4 erat. secuti exemplum ueterani haud multo post in Raetiam
mittuntur, specie defendendae prouinciae ob imminentis
Suebos ceterum ut auellerentur castris trucibus adhuc non
5 minus asperitate remedii quam sceleris memoria. centurionatum inde egit. citatus ab imperatore nomen, ordinem,
patriam, numerum stipendiorum, quae strenue in proeliis
fecisset, et cui erant, dona militaria edebat. si tribuni, si legio
industriam innocentiamque adprobauerant, retinebat ordinem: ubi auaritiam aut crudelitatem consensu obiectauissent,
soluebatur militia.

45. Sic compositis praesentibus haud minor moles supererat ob ferociam quintae et unetuicesimae legionum, sexa-
gesimum apud lapidem (loco Vetera nomen est) hibernantium.
2 nam primi seditionem coeptauerant: atrocissimum quodque
facinus horum manibus patratum; nec poena commilitonum
exterriti nec paenitentia conuersi iras retinebant. igitur
Caesar arma classem socios demittere Rheno parat, si imperium detrectetur, bello certaturus.

46. At Romae nondum cognito qui fuisset exitus in Illyrico, et legionum Germanicarum motu audito, trepida
ciuitas incusare Tiberium quod, dum patres et plebem, inualida et inermia, cunctatione ficta ludificetur, dissideat interim
miles neque duorum adulescentium nondum adulta auctori-
2 tate comprimi queat. ire ipsum et opponere maiestatem impe-
ratoriam debuisse cessuris ubi principem longa experientia
eundemque seueritatis et munificentiae summum uidissent.
3 an Augustum fessa aetate totiens in Germanias commeare
potuisse: Tiberium uigentem annis sedere in senatu, uerba
patrum cauillantem? satis prospectum urbanae seruituti:
militaribus animis adhibenda fomenta ut ferre pacem uelint.

47. Immotum aduersus eos sermones fixumque Tiberio
fuit non omittere caput rerum neque se remque publicam in

casum dare. multa quippe et diuersa angebant: ualidior per
Germaniam exercitus, propior apud Pannoniam; ille Galliarum opibus subnixus, hic Italiae inminens: quos igitur ante-
2 ferret? ac ne postpositi contumelia incenderentur. at per
filios pariter adiri maiestate salua, cui maior e longinquo
reuerentia. simul adulescentibus excusatum quaedam ad
patrem reicere, resistentisque Germanico aut Druso posse a
se mitigari uel infringi: quod aliud subsidium si imperatorem
3 spreuissent? ceterum ut iam iamque iturus legit comites,
conquisiuit impedimenta, adornauit nauis: mox hiemem aut
negotia uarie causatus primo prudentis, dein uulgum,
diutissime prouincias fefellit.

48. At Germanicus, quamquam contracto exercitu et
parata in defectores ultione, dandum adhuc spatium ratus, si
recenti exemplo sibi ipsi consulerent, praemittit litteras ad
Caecinam, uenire se ualida manu ac, ni supplicium in malos
2 praesumant, usurum promisca caede. eas Caecina aquiliferis
signiferisque et quod maxime castrorum sincerum erat
occulte recitat, utque cunctos infamiae, se ipsos morti eximant
hortatur: nam in pace causas et merita spectari, ubi bellum
3 ingruat innocentis ac noxios iuxta cadere. illi temptatis quos
idoneos rebantur, postquam maiorem legionum partem in
officio uident, de sententia legati statuunt tempus, quo
foedissimum quemque et seditioni promptum ferro inuadant.
tunc signo inter se dato inrumpunt contubernia, trucidant
ignaros, nullo nisi consciis noscente quod caedis initium, quis
finis.

49. Diuersa omnium, quae umquam accidere, ciuilium
armorum facies. non proelio, non aduersis e castris, sed isdem
e cubilibus, quos simul uescentis dies, simul quietos nox
habuerat, discedunt in partis, ingerunt tela. clamor uulnera
sanguis palam, causa in occulto; cetera fors regit. et quidam
bonorum caesi, postquam intellecto in quos saeuiretur

2 pessimi quoque arma rapuerant. neque legatus aut tribunus
moderator adfuit: permissa uulgo licentia atque ultio et
satietas. mox ingressus castra Germanicus, non medicinam
illud plurimis cum lacrimis sed cladem appellans, cremari
corpora iubet.

3   Truces etiam tum animos cupido inuolat eundi in hostem,
piaculum furoris; nec aliter posse placari commilitonum
manis quam si pectoribus impiis honesta uulnera accepissent.

4 sequitur ardorem militum Caesar iunctoque ponte tramittit
duodecim milia e legionibus, sex et uiginti socias cohortis,
octo equitum alas, quarum ea seditione intemerata modestia
fuit.

   50. Laeti neque procul Germani agitabant, dum iustitio
ob amissum Augustum, post discordiis attinemur. at Romanus
agmine propero siluam Caesiam limitemque a Tiberio
coeptum scindit, castra in limite locat, frontem ac tergum

2 uallo, latera concaedibus munitus. inde saltus obscuros
permeat consultatque ex duobus itineribus breue et solitum
sequatur an inpeditius et intemptatum eoque hostibus in-

3 cautum. delecta longiore uia cetera adcelerantur: etenim
attulerant exploratores festam eam Germanis noctem ac
sollemnibus epulis ludicram. Caecina cum expeditis cohortibus praeire et obstantia siluarum amoliri iubetur: legiones

4 modico interuallo sequuntur. iuuit nox sideribus inlustris,
uentumque ad uicos Marsorum et circumdatae stationes
stratis etiam tum per cubilia propterque mensas, nullo metu,
non antepositis uigiliis: adeo cuncta incuria disiecta erant
neque belli timor, ac ne pax quidem nisi languida et soluta
inter temulentos.

   51. Caesar auidas legiones quo latior populatio foret
quattuor in cuneos dispertit; quinquaginta milium spatium
ferro flammisque peruastat. non sexus, non aetas miserationem attulit: profana simul et sacra et celeberrimum illis

gentibus templum quod Tanfanae uocabant solo aequantur.
sine uulnere milites, qui semisomnos, inermos aut palantis
2 ceciderant. exciuit ea caedes Bructeros, Tubantes, Vsipetes,
saltusque, per quos exercitui regressus, insedere. quod gnarum
duci incessitque itineri et proelio. pars equitum et auxiliariae
cohortes ducebant, mox prima legio, et mediis impedimentis
sinistrum latus unetuicesimani, dextrum quintani clausere,
3 uicesima legio terga firmauit, post ceteri sociorum. sed
hostes, donec agmen per saltus porrigeretur, immoti, dein
latera et frontem modice adsultantes, tota ui nouissimos
incurrere. turbabanturque densis Germanorum cateruis leues
cohortes, cum Caesar aduectus ad uicesimanos uoce magna
hoc illud tempus obliterandae seditionis clamitabat: pergerent,
4 properarent culpam in decus uertere. exarsere animis unoque
impetu perruptum hostem redigunt in aperta caeduntque:
simul primi agminis copiae euasere siluas castraque com-
muniuere. quietum inde iter, fidensque recentibus ac priorum
oblitus miles in hibernis locatur.

52. Nuntiata ea Tiberium laetitia curaque adfecere: gaudebat oppressam seditionem, sed quod largiendis pecuniis et
missione festinata fauorem militum quaesiuisset, bellica
2 quoque Germanici gloria angebatur. rettulit tamen ad senatum de rebus gestis multaque de uirtute eius memorauit,
magis in speciem uerbis adornata quam ut penitus sentire
3 crederetur. paucioribus Drusum et finem Illyrici motus
laudauit, sed intentior et fida oratione. cunctaque quae
Germanicus indulserat seruauit etiam apud Pannonicos
exercitus.

53. Eodem anno Iulia supremum diem obiit, ob impudi-
citiam olim a patre Augusto Pandateria insula, mox oppido
Reginorum, qui Siculum fretum accolunt, clausa. fuerat in
matrimonio Tiberii florentibus Gaio et Lucio Caesaribus
spreueratque ut inparem; nec alia tam intima Tiberio causa

2 cur Rhodum abscederet. imperium adeptus extorrem, infamem et post interfectum Postumum Agrippam omnis spei
egenam inopia ac tabe longa peremit, obscuram fore necem
3 longinquitate exilii ratus. par causa saeuitiae in Sempronium
Gracchum, qui familia nobili, sollers ingenio et praue facun-
dus, eandem Iuliam in matrimonio Marci Agrippae temer-
auerat. nec is libidini finis: traditam Tiberio peruicax adulter
contumacia et odiis in maritum accendebat; litteraeque
quas Iulia patri Augusto cum insectatione Tiberii scripsit
4 a Graccho compositae credebantur. igitur amotus Cercinam,
Africi maris insulam, quattuordecim annis exilium tolerauit.
5 tunc milites ad caedem missi inuenere in prominenti litoris
nihil laetum opperientem. quorum aduentu breue tempus
petiuit ut suprema mandata uxori Alliariae per litteras daret,
ceruicemque percussoribus obtulit; constantia mortis haud
6 indignus Sempronio nomine uita degenerauerat. quidam
non Roma eos milites, sed ab L. Asprenate pro consule
Africae missos tradidere auctore Tiberio, qui famam caedis
posse in Asprenatem uerti frustra sperauerat.

54. Idem annus nouas caerimonias accepit addito sodalium
Augustalium sacerdotio, ut quondam Titus Tatius retinendis
Sabinorum sacris sodalis Titios instituerat. sorte ducti e
primoribus ciuitatis unus et uiginti: Tiberius Drususque
2 et Claudius et Germanicus adiciuntur. ludos Augustalis tunc
primum coeptos turbauit discordia ex certamine histrionum.
indulserat ei ludicro Augustus, dum Maecenati obtemperat
effuso in amorem Bathylli; neque ipse abhorrebat talibus
studiis, et ciuile rebatur misceri uoluptatibus uulgi. alia
Tiberio morum uia: sed populum per tot annos molliter
habitum nondum audebat ad duriora uertere.

55. Druso Caesare C. Norbano consulibus decernitur
Germanico triumphus manente bello; quod quamquam in
aestatem summa ope parabat, initio ueris et repentino in

Chattos excursu praecepit. nam spes incesserat dissidere hostem in Arminium ac Segestem, insignem utrumque 2 perfidia in nos aut fide. Arminius turbator Germaniae, Segestes parari rebellionem saepe alias et supremo convivio, post quod in arma itum, aperuit suasitque Varo ut se et Arminium et ceteros proceres uinciret: nihil ausuram plebem principibus amotis; atque ipsi tempus fore quo crimina et 3 innoxios discerneret. sed Varus fato et ui Armini cecidit: Segestes quamquam consensu gentis in bellum tractus discors manebat, auctis priuatim odiis, quod Arminius filiam eius alii pactam rapuerat: gener inuisus inimici soceri; quaeque apud concordes uincula caritatis, incitamenta irarum apud infensos erant.

56. Igitur Germanicus quattuor legiones, quinque auxiliarium milia et tumultuarias cateruas Germanorum cis Rhenum colentium Caecinae tradit; totidem legiones, duplicem sociorum numerum ipse ducit, positoque castello super uestigia paterni praesidii in monte Tauno expeditum exercitum in Chattos rapit, L. Apronio ad munitiones uiarum et fluminum 2 relicto. nam (rarum illi caelo) siccitate et amnibus modicis inoffensum iter properauerat, imbresque et fluminum auctus 3 regredienti metuebatur.[1] sed Chattis adeo inprouisus aduenit, ut quod imbecillum aetate ac sexu statim captum aut trucidatum sit. iuuentus flumen Adranam nando tramiserat, Romanosque pontem coeptantis arcebant. dein tormentis sagittisque pulsi, temptatis frustra condicionibus pacis, cum quidam ad Germanicum perfugissent, reliqui omissis pagis 4 uicisque in siluas disperguntur. Caesar incenso Mattio (id genti caput) aperta populatus uertit ad Rhenum, non auso hoste terga abeuntium lacessere, quod illi moris, quotiens 5 astu magis quam per formidinem cessit. fuerat animus Cheruscis iuuare Chattos, sed exterruit Caecina huc illuc

---

[1] metuebantur O.T.

ferens arma; et Marsos congredi ausos prospero proelio cohibuit.

57. Neque multo post legati a Segeste uenerunt auxilium orantes aduersus uim popularium a quis circumsedebatur, ualidiore apud eos Arminio quoniam bellum suadebat: nam barbaris, quanto quis audacia promptus, tanto magis fidus 2 rebusque motis potior habetur. addiderat Segestes legatis filium, nomine Segimundum: sed iuuenis conscientia cunctabatur. quippe anno quo Germaniae desciuere sacerdos apud aram Vbiorum creatus ruperat uittas, profugus ad rebellis. adductus tamen in spem clementiae Romanae pertulit patris mandata benigneque exceptus cum praesidio Gallicam in 3 ripam missus est. Germanico pretium fuit conuertere agmen, pugnatumque in obsidentis, et ereptus Segestes magna cum 4 propinquorum et clientium manu. inerant feminae nobiles, inter quas uxor Arminii eademque filia Segestis, mariti magis quam parentis animo, neque euicta ¹ in lacrimas neque uoce supplex; compressis intra sinum manibus grauidum uterum 5 intuens. ferebantur et spolia Varianae cladis, plerisque eorum qui tum in deditionem ueniebant praedae data: simul Segestes ipse, ingens uisu et memoria bonae societatis inpauidus.

58. Verba eius in hunc modum fuere: 'non hic mihi primus erga populum Romanum fidei et constantiae dies. ex quo a diuo Augusto ciuitate donatus sum, amicos inimicosque ex uestris utilitatibus delegi, neque odio patriae (quippe proditores etiam iis quos anteponunt inuisi sunt), uerum quia Romanis Germanisque idem conducere et pacem quam 2 bellum probabam. ergo raptorem filiae meae, uiolatorem foederis uestri, Arminium apud Varum, qui tum exercitui praesidebat, reum feci. dilatus segnitia ducis, quia parum praesidii in legibus erat, ut me et Arminium et conscios uinciret flagitaui: testis illa nox, mihi utinam potius nouissima!

¹ uicta O.T.

3 quae secuta sunt defleri magis quam defendi possunt: ceterum et inieci catenas Arminio et a factione eius iniectas perpessus sum. atque ubi primum tui copia, uetera nouis et quieta turbidis antehabeo, neque ob praemium, sed ut me perfidia exsoluam, simul genti Germanorum idoneus conciliator, si

4 paenitentiam quam perniciem maluerit. pro iuuenta et errore filii ueniam precor: filiam necessitate huc adductam fateor. tuum erit consultare utrum praeualeat quod ex Arminio

5 concepit an quod ex me genita est.' Caesar clementi responso liberis propinquisque eius incolumitatem, ipsi sedem uetere in prouincia pollicetur. exercitum reduxit nomenque im-

6 peratoris auctore Tiberio accepit. Arminii uxor uirilis sexus stirpem edidit: educatus Rauennae puer quo mox ludibrio conflictatus sit in tempore memorabo.

59. Fama dediti benigneque excepti Segestis uulgata, ut quibusque bellum inuitis aut cupientibus erat, spe uel dolore accipitur. Arminium super insitam uiolentiam rapta uxor, subiectus seruitio uxoris uterus uaecordem agebant, uolita-batque per Cheruscos, arma in Segestem, arma in Caesarem

2 poscens. neque probris temperabat: egregium patrem, magnum imperatorem, fortem exercitum, quorum tot manus

3 unam mulierculam auexerint. sibi tres legiones, totidem lega-tos procubuisse; non enim se proditione neque aduersus femi-nas grauidas, sed palam aduersus armatos bellum tractare. cerni adhuc Germanorum in lucis signa Romana, quae dis patriis

4 suspenderit. coleret Segestes uictam ripam, redderet filio sacerdotium hominum: Germanos numquam satis excusa-turos quod inter Albim et Rhenum uirgas et securis et togam

5 uiderint. aliis gentibus ignorantia imperi Romani inexperta esse supplicia, nescia tributa: quae quoniam exuerint in-ritusque discesserit ille inter numina dicatus Augustus, ille delectus Tiberius, ne inperitum adulescentulum, ne seditiosum

6 exercitum pauescerent. si patriam parentes antiqua mallent

quam dominos et colonias nouas, Arminium potius gloriae
ac libertatis quam Segestem flagitiosae seruitutis ducem
sequerentur.

60. Conciti per haec non modo Cherusci, sed conterminae
gentes, tractusque in partis Inguiomerus Arminii patruus,
uetere apud Romanos auctoritate; unde maior Caesari metus.
2 et ne bellum mole una ingrueret Caecinam cum quadraginta
cohortibus Romanis distrahendo hosti per Bructeros ad
flumen Amisiam mittit, equitem Pedo praefectus finibus
Frisiorum ducit. ipse inpositas nauibus quattuor legiones per
lacus uexit; simulque pedes eques classis apud praedictum
amnem conuenere. Chauci cum auxilia pollicerentur, in
3 commilitium adsciti sunt. Bructeros sua urentis expedita
cum manu L. Stertinius missu Germanici fudit; interque
caedem et praedam repperit undeuicesimae legionis aquilam
cum Varo amissam. ductum inde agmen ad ultimos Bruc-
terorum, quantumque Amisiam et Lupiam amnis inter
uastatum, haud procul Teutoburgiensi saltu in quo reliquiae
Vari legionumque insepultae dicebantur.

61. Igitur cupido Caesarem inuadit soluendi suprema
militibus ducique, permoto ad miserationem omni qui aderat
exercitu ob propinquos, amicos, denique ob casus bellorum
et sortem hominum. praemisso Caecina ut occulta saltuum
scrutaretur pontesque et aggeres umido paludum et fallacibus
campis inponeret, incedunt maestos locos uisuque ac memoria
2 deformis. prima Vari castra lato ambitu et dimensis principiis
trium legionum manus ostentabant; dein semiruto uallo,
humili fossa accisae iam reliquiae consedisse intellegebantur:
medio campi albentia ossa, ut fugerant, ut restiterant, disiecta
3 uel aggerata. adiacebant fragmina telorum equorumque
artus, simul truncis arborum antefixa ora. lucis propinquis
barbarae arae, apud quas tribunos ac primorum ordinum
4 centuriones mactauerant. et cladis eius superstites, pugnam

aut uincula elapsi, referebant hic cecidisse legatos, illic raptas
aquilas; primum ubi uulnus Varo adactum, ubi infelici
dextera et suo ictu mortem inuenerit; quo tribunali contiona-
tus Arminius, quot patibula captiuis, quae scrobes, utque
signis et aquilis per superbiam inluserit.

62. Igitur Romanus qui aderat exercitus sextum post cladis
annum trium legionum ossa, nullo noscente alienas reliquias
an suorum humo tegeret, omnis ut coniunctos, ut consan-
guineos, aucta in hostem ira, maesti simul et infensi conde-
bant. primum extruendo tumulo caespitem Caesar posuit,
gratissimo munere in defunctos et praesentibus doloris socius.
2 quod Tiberio haud probatum, seu cuncta Germanici in
deterius trahenti, siue exercitum imagine caesorum insepulto-
rumque tardatum ad proelia et formidolosiorem hostium
credebat; neque imperatorem auguratu et uetustissimis caeri-
moniis praeditum adtrectare feralia debuisse.

63. Sed Germanicus cedentem in auia Arminium secutus,
ubi primum copia fuit, euehi equites campumque quem
hostis insederat eripi iubet. Arminius colligi suos et propin-
quare siluis monitos uertit repente : mox signum prorumpendi
2 dedit iis quos per saltus occultauerat. tunc noua acie turbatus
eques, missaeque subsidiariae cohortes et fugientium agmine
impulsae auxerant consternationem; trudebanturque in
paludem gnaram uincentibus, iniquam nesciis, ni Caesar
productas legiones instruxisset: inde hostibus terror, fiducia
3 militi; et manibus aequis abscessum. mox reducto ad Amisiam
exercitu legiones classe, ut aduexerat, reportat; pars equitum
litore Oceani petere Rhenum iussa; Caecina, qui suum
militem ducebat, monitus, quamquam notis itineribus
regrederetur, pontes longos quam maturrime superare.
4 angustus is trames uastas inter paludes et quondam a L.
Domitio aggeratus, cetera limosa, tenacia graui caeno aut
riuis incerta erant; circum siluae paulatim adcliues, quas tum

Arminius inpleuit, compendiis uiarum et cito agmine onu-
5 stum sarcinis armisque militem cum anteuenisset. Caecinae
dubitanti quonam modo ruptos uetustate pontes reponeret
simulque propulsaret hostem, castra metari in loco placuit,
ut opus et alii proelium inciperent.

64. Barbari perfringere stationes seque inferre munitoribus
nisi lacessunt, circumgrediuntur, occursant: miscetur operan-
2 tium bellantiumque clamor. et cuncta pariter Romanis
aduersa, locus uligine profunda, idem ad gradum instabilis,
procedentibus lubricus, corpora grauia loricis; neque librare
pila inter undas poterant. contra Cheruscis sueta apud paludes
proelia, procera membra, hastae ingentes ad uulnera facienda
3 quamuis procul. nox demum inclinantis iam legiones aduersae pugnae exemit. Germani ob prospera indefessi, ne tum
quidem sumpta quiete, quantum aquarum circum surgentibus
iugis oritur uertere in subiecta, mersaque humo et obruto
4 quod effectum operis duplicatus militi labor. quadragesimum
id stipendium Caecina parendi aut imperitandi habebat,
secundarum ambiguarumque rerum sciens eoque interritus.
igitur futura uoluens non aliud repperit quam ut hostem
siluis coerceret, donec saucii quantumque grauioris agminis
anteirent; nam medio montium et paludum porrigebatur
5 planities, quae tenuem aciem pateretur. deliguntur legiones
quinta dextro lateri, unetuicesima in laeuum, primani
ducendum ad agmen, uicesimanus aduersum secuturos.

65. Nox per diuersa inquies, cum barbari festis epulis,
laeto cantu aut truci sonore subiecta uallium ac resultantis
saltus complerent, apud Romanos inualidi ignes, interruptae
uoces, atque ipsi passim adiacerent uallo, oberrarent tentoriis,
2 insomnes magis quam peruigiles. ducemque terruit dira quies:
nam Quintilium Varum sanguine oblitum et paludibus
emersum cernere et audire uisus est uelut uocantem, non
3 tamen obsecutus et manum intendentis reppulisse. coepta

luce missae in latera legiones, metu an contumacia, locum
4 deseruere, capto propere campo umentia ultra. neque tamen
Arminius quamquam libero incursu statim prorupit: sed ut
haesere caeno fossisque impedimenta, turbati circum milites,
incertus signorum ordo, utque tali in tempore sibi quisque
properus et lentae aduersum imperia aures, inrumpere Germanos iubet, clamitans 'en Varus eodemque iterum fato
uinctae legiones!' simul haec et cum delectis scindit agmen
5 equisque maxime uulnera ingerit. illi sanguine suo et lubrico
paludum lapsantes excussis rectoribus disicere obuios, pro-
terere iacentis. plurimus circa aquilas labor, quae neque ferri
aduersum ingruentia tela neque figi limosa humo poterant.
6 Caecina dum sustentat aciem, suffosso equo delapsus circumueniebatur, ni prima legio sese opposuisset. iuuit hostium
auiditas, omissa caede praedam sectantium, enisaeque legiones
7 uesperascente die in aperta et solida. neque is miseriarum
finis. struendum uallum, petendus agger, amissa magna ex
parte per quae egeritur humus aut exciditur caespes; non
tentoria manipulis, non fomenta sauciis; infectos caeno aut
cruore cibos diuidentes funestas tenebras et tot hominum
milibus unum iam reliquum diem lamentabantur.

66. Forte equus abruptis uinculis uagus et clamore territus
quosdam occurrentium obturbauit. tanta inde consternatio
inrupisse Germanos credentium ut cuncti ruerent ad portas,
quarum decumana maxime petebatur, auersa hosti et fugien-
2 tibus tutior. Caecina comperto uanam esse formidinem,
cum tamen neque auctoritate neque precibus, ne manu
quidem obsistere aut retinere militem quiret, proiectus in
limine portae miseratione demum, quia per corpus legati
eundum erat, clausit uiam: simul tribuni et centuriones
falsum pauorem esse docuerunt.

67. Tunc contractos in principia iussosque dicta cum
silentio accipere temporis ac necessitatis monet. unam in

armis salutem, sed ea consilio temperanda manendumque intra uallum, donec expugnandi hostis spe propius succederent;
mox undique erumpendum: illa eruptione ad Rhenum
2 perueniri. quod si fugerent, pluris siluas, profundas magis
paludes, saeuitiam hostium superesse; at uictoribus decus
gloriam. quae domi cara, quae in castris honesta, memorat;
3 reticuit de aduersis. equos dehinc, orsus a suis, legatorum
tribunorumque nulla ambitione fortissimo cuique bellatori
tradit, ut hi, mox pedes in hostem inuaderent.

68. Haud minus inquies Germanus spe, cupidine et diuersis
ducum sententiis agebat, Arminio sinerent egredi egressosque
rursum per umida et inpedita circumuenirent suadente,
atrociora Inguiomero et laeta barbaris, ut uallum armis
ambirent: promptam expugnationem, plures captiuos, in-
2 corruptam praedam fore. igitur orta die proruunt fossas,
iniciunt cratis, summa ualli prensant, raro super milite et
3 quasi ob metum defixo. postquam haesere munimentis, datur
cohortibus signum cornuaque ac tubae concinuere. exim
clamore et impetu tergis Germanorum circumfunduntur,
exprobrantes non hic siluas nec paludes, sed aequis locis
4 aequos deos. hosti facile excidium et paucos ac semermos
cogitanti sonus tubarum, fulgor armorum, quanto inopina
tanto maiora offunduntur, caděbantque, ut rebus secundis
5 auidi, ita aduersis incauti. Arminius integer, Inguiomerus post
graue uulnus pugnam deseruere: uulgus trucidatum est, donec
ira et dies permansit. nocte demum reuersae legiones,
quamuis plus uulnerum, eadem ciborum egestas fatigaret,
uim sanitatem copias, cuncta in uictoria habuere.

69. Peruaserat interim circumuenti exercitus fama et infesto
Germanorum agmine Gallias peti, ac ni Agrippina inpositum
Rheno pontem solui prohibuisset, erant qui id flagitium
formidine auderent. sed femina ingens animi munia ducis
per eos dies induit, militibusque, ut quis inops aut saucius,

2 uestem et fomenta dilargita est. tradit C. Plinius, Germani-
corum bellorum scriptor, stetisse apud principium ponti
3 laudes et grates reuersis legionibus habentem. id Tiberii
animum altius penetrauit: non enim simplicis eas curas, nec
4 aduersus externos *studia* militum quaeri. nihil relictum
imperatoribus, ubi femina manipulos interuisat, signa adeat,
largitionem temptet, tamquam parum ambitiose filium
ducis gregali habitu circumferat Caesaremque Caligulam
appellari uelit. potiorem iam apud exercitus Agrippinam
quam legatos, quam duces; conpressam a muliere seditionem,
5 cui nomen principis obsistere non quiuerit. accendebat haec
onerabatque Seianus, peritia morum Tiberii odia in longum
iaciens, quae reconderet auctaque promeret.

70. At Germanicus legionum, quas nauibus uexerat,
secundam et quartam decimam itinere terrestri P. Vitellio
ducendas tradit, quo leuior classis uadoso mari innaret uel
2 reciproco sideret. Vitellius primum iter sicca humo aut
modice adlabente aestu quietum habuit: mox inpulsu aqui-
lonis, simul sidere aequinoctii, quo maxime tumescit Oceanus,
rapi agique agmen. et opplebantur terrae: eadem freto litori
campis facies, neque discerni poterant incerta ab solidis,
3 breuia a profundis. sternuntur fluctibus, hauriuntur gurgiti-
bus; iumenta, sarcinae, corpora exanima interfluunt, occursant. permiscentur inter se manipuli, modo pectore, modo
ore tenus extantes, aliquando subtracto solo disiecti aut obruti.
non uox et mutui hortatus iuuabant aduersante unda; nihil
strenuus ab ignauo, sapiens ab inprudenti, consilia a casu
4 differre: cuncta pari uiolentia inuoluebantur. tandem Vitellius in editiora enisus eodem agmen subduxit. pernoctauere
sine utensilibus, sine igni, magna pars nudo aut mulcato
corpore, haud minus miserabiles quam quos hostis circumsidet: quippe illic etiam honestae mortis usus, his inglorium
5 exitium. lux reddidit terram, penetratumque ad amnem

[Visurgin], quo Caesar classe contenderat. inpositae dein legiones, uagante fama submersas; nec fides salutis, antequam Caesarem exercitumque reducem uidere.

71. Iam Stertinius, ad accipiendum in deditionem Segimerum fratrem Segestis praemissus, ipsum et filium eius in ciuitatem Vbiorum perduxerat. data utrique uenia, facile Segimero, cunctantius filio, quia Quintilii Vari corpus in-
2 lusisse dicebatur. ceterum ad supplenda exercitus damna certauere Galliae Hispaniae Italia, quod cuique promptum, arma equos aurum offerentes. quorum laudato studio Germanicus, armis modo et equis ad bellum sumptis, propria
3 pecunia militem iuuit. utque cladis memoriam etiam comitate leniret, circumire saucios, facta singulorum extollere; uulnera intuens alium spe, alium gloria, cunctos adloquio et cura sibique et proelio firmabat.

72. Decreta eo anno triumphalia insignia A. Caecinae, L. Apronio, C. Silio ob res cum Germanico gestas. nomen patris patriae Tiberius, a populo saepius ingestum, repudiauit; neque in acta sua iurari quamquam censente senatu permisit, cuncta mortalium incerta, quantoque plus adeptus foret,
2 tanto se magis in lubrico dictitans.•non tamen ideo faciebat fidem ciuilis animi; nam legem maiestatis reduxerat, cui nomen apud ueteres idem, sed alia in iudicium ueniebant, si quis proditione exercitum aut plebem seditionibus, denique male gesta re publica maiestatem populi Romani minuisset:
3 facta arguebantur, dicta inpune erant. primus Augustus cognitionem de famosis libellis specie legis eius tractauit, commotus Cassii Seueri libidine, qua uiros feminasque inlustris procacibus scriptis diffamauerat; mox Tiberius, consultante Pompeio Macro praetore an iudicia maiestatis
4 redderentur, exercendas leges esse respondit. hunc quoque asperauere carmina incertis auctoribus uulgata in saeuitiam superbiamque eius et discordem cum matre animum.

73. Haud pigebit referre in Falanio et Rubrio, modicis equitibus Romanis, praetemptata crimina, ut quibus initiis, quanta Tiberii arte grauissimum exitium inrepserit, dein repressum sit, postremo arserit cunctaque corripuerit, no-
2 scatur. Falanio obiciebat accusator, quod inter cultores Augusti, qui per omnis domos in modum collegiorum habebantur, Cassium quendam mimum corpore infamem adsciuisset, quodque uenditis hortis statuam Augusti simul mancipasset. Rubrio crimini dabatur uiolatum periurio
3 numen Augusti. quae ubi Tiberio notuere, scripsit consulibus non ideo decretum patri suo caelum, ut in perniciem ciuium is honor uerteretur. Cassium histrionem solitum inter alios eiusdem artis interesse ludis, quos mater sua in memoriam Augusti sacrasset; nec contra religiones fieri quod effigies eius, ut alia numinum simulacra, uenditionibus hortorum et
4 domuum accedant. ius iurandum perinde aestimandum quam si Iouem fefellisset: deorum iniurias dis curae.

74. Nec multo post Granium Marcellum praetorem Bithyniae quaestor ipsius Caepio Crispinus maiestatis postu-lauit, subscribente Romanio [1] Hispone: qui formam uitae iniit, quam postea celebrem miseriae temporum et audaciae
2 hominum fecerunt. nam egens, ignotus, inquies, dum occultis libellis saeuitiae principis adrepit, mox clarissimo cuique periculum facessit, potentiam apud unum, odium apud omnis adeptus dedit exemplum, quod secuti ex pauperibus diuites, ex contemptis metuendi perniciem aliis ac postremum sibi
3 inuenere. sed Marcellum insimulabat sinistros de Tiberio sermones habuisse, ineuitabile crimen, cum ex moribus principis foedissima quaeque deligeret accusator obiectaret-que reo. nam quia uera erant, etiam dicta credebantur. addidit Hispo statuam Marcelli altius quam Caesarum sitam, et alia in statua amputato capite Augusti effigiem Tiberii

[1] Romano O.T.

4 inditam. ad quod exarsit adeo, ut rupta taciturnitate proclamaret se quoque in ea causa laturum sententiam palam et
5 iuratum, quo ceteris eadem necessitas fieret. manebant
etiam tum uestigia morientis libertatis. igitur Cn. Piso 'quo'
inquit 'loco censebis, Caesar? si primus, habebo quod sequar:
9 si post omnis, uereor ne inprudens dissentiam.' permotus
his, quantoque incautius efferuerat, paenitentia patiens tulit
absolui reum criminibus maiestatis: de pecuniis repetundis
ad reciperatores itum est.

75. Nec patrum cognitionibus satiatus iudiciis adsidebat
in cornu tribunalis, ne praetorem curuli depelleret; multaque
eo coram aduersus ambitum et potentium preces constituta.
2 set dum ueritati consulitur, libertas corrumpebatur. inter
quae Pius Aurelius senator questus mole publicae uiae
ductuque aquarum labefactas aedis suas, auxilium patrum
inuocabat. resistentibus aerarii praetoribus subuenit Caesar
pretiumque aedium Aurelio tribuit, erogandae per honesta
pecuniae cupiens, quam uirtutem diu retinuit, cum ceteras
3 exueret. Propertio Celeri praetorio, ueniam ordinis ob
paupertatem petenti, decies sestertium largitus est, satis
4 conperto paternas ei angustias esse. temptantis eadem alios
probare causam senatui iussit, cupidine seueritatis in iis
etiam quae rite faceret acerbus. unde ceteri silentium et
paupertatem confessioni et beneficio praeposuere.

76. Eodem anno continuis imbribus auctus Tiberis plana
urbis stagnauerat; relabentem secuta est aedificiorum et
hominum strages. igitur censuit Asinius Gallus ut libri
Sibyllini adirentur. renuit Tiberius, perinde diuina humanaque obtegens; sed remedium coercendi fluminis Ateio Capi
2 toni et L. Arruntio mandatum. Achaiam ac Macedoniam
onera deprecantis leuari in praesens proconsulari imperio
3 tradique Caesari placuit. edendis gladiatoribus, quos Germanici fratris ac suo nomine obtulerat, Drusus praesedit, quam-

quam uili sanguine nimis gaudens; quod *in* uulgus formi-
4 dolosum et pater arguisse dicebatur. cur abstinuerit spectaculo
ipse, uarie trahebant; alii taedio coetus, quidam tristitia
ingenii et metu conparationis, quia Augustus comiter interfuisset. non crediderim ad ostentandam saeuitiam mouendas-
que populi offensiones concessam filio materiem, quamquam
id quoque dictum est.

77. At theatri licentia, proximo priore anno coepta,
grauius tum erupit, occisis non modo e plebe set militibus
et centurione, uulnerato tribuno praetoriae cohortis, dum
probra in magistratus et dissensionem uulgi prohibent.
2 actum de ea seditione apud patres dicebanturque sententiae,
3 ut praetoribus ius uirgarum in histriones esset. intercessit
Haterius Agrippa tribunus plebei increpitusque est Asinii
Galli oratione, silente Tiberio, qui ea simulacra libertatis
senatui praebebat. ualuit tamen intercessio, quia diuus
Augustus immunis uerberum histriones quondam respon-
4 derat, neque fas Tiberio infringere dicta eius. de modo lucaris
et aduersus lasciuiam fautorum multa decernuntur; ex quis
maxime insignia, ne domos pantomimorum senator introir-
et, ne egredientis in publicum equites Romani cingerent
aut alibi quam in theatro spectarentur, et spectantium
immodestiam exilio multandi potestas praetoribus fieret.

78. Templum ut in colonia Tarraconensi strueretur
Augusto petentibus Hispanis permissum, datumque in omnis
2 prouincias exemplum. centesimam rerum uenalium post
bella ciuilia institutam deprecante populo edixit Tiberius
militare aerarium eo subsidio niti; simul imparem oneri rem
publicam, nisi uicesimo militiae anno ueterani dimitterentur.
ita proximae seditionis male consulta, quibus sedecim
stipendiorum finem expresserant, abolita in posterum.

79. Actum deinde in senatu ab Arruntio et Ateio an ob
moderandas Tiberis exundationes uerterentur flumina et

lacus, per quos augescit; auditaeque municipiorum et coloniarum legationes, orantibus Florentinis ne Clanis solito alueo demotus in amnem Arnum transferretur idque ipsis 2 perniciem adferret. congruentia his Interamnates disseruere: pessum ituros fecundissimos Italiae campos, si amnis Nar 3 (id enim parabatur) in riuos diductus superstagnauisset. nec Reatini silebant, Velinum lacum, qua in Narem effunditur, obstrui recusantes, quippe in adiacentia erupturum; optume rebus mortalium consuluisse naturam, quae sua ora flumini-bus, suos cursus utque originem, ita finis dederit; spectandas etiam religiones sociorum, qui sacra et lucos et aras patriis amnibus dicauerint: quin ipsum Tiberim nolle prorsus 4 accolis fluuiis orbatum minore gloria fluere. seu preces coloniarum seu difficultas operum siue superstitio ualuit, ut in sententiam Pisonis concederetur, qui nil mutandum censuerat.

80. Prorogatur Poppaeo Sabino prouincia Moesia, additis Achaia ac Macedonia. id quoque morum Tiberii fuit, con-tinuare imperia ac plerosque ad finem uitae in isdem exer-2 citibus aut iurisdictionibus habere. causae uariae traduntur: alii taedio nouae curae semel placita pro aeternis seruauisse, quidam inuidia, ne plures fruerentur; sunt qui existiment, ut callidum eius ingenium, ita anxium iudicium; neque enim eminentis uirtutes sectabatur, et rursum uitia oderat: ex optimis periculum sibi, a pessimis dedecus publicum metue-3 bat. qua haesitatione postremo eo prouectus est ut mandauerit quibusdam prouincias, quos egredi urbe non erat passurus.

81. De comitiis consularibus, quae tum primum illo principe ac deinceps fuere, uix quicquam firmare ausim: adeo diuersa non modo apud auctores, sed in ipsius oratio-2 nibus reperiuntur. modo subtractis candidatorum nominibus originem cuiusque et uitam et stipendia descripsit ut qui forent intellegeretur; aliquando ea quoque significatione subtracta candidatos hortatus ne ambitu comitia turbarent, suam ad id curam pollicitus est. plerumque eos tantum apud se professos disseruit, quorum nomina consulibus edidisset; posse et alios profiteri, si gratiae aut meritis confiderent: speciosa uerbis, re inania aut subdola, quantoque maiore libertatis imagine tegebantur, tanto eruptura ad infensius seruitium.

NOTES

I. § I. urbem . . . habuere, an hexameter line—not rhythmically a great line, but gaining emphasis from its position. The use of complete lines of verse in prose writing is deprecated by the stylists (e.g. Cic. *De Or.* III, 182), but they do occur occasionally in the works of Livy and Tacitus (cf. *Germ.* 39, 2, *auguriis patrum et prisca formidine sacram*). Most of them are probably accidental, but it is difficult to believe that this one is: rather is Tacitus starting his great historical work on a deliberately heroic note. There is in the sentence a double link with his predecessors, because Livy began his history with two thirds of an hexameter (*Praef.* 1) and Sallust in describing the early history of Rome (*Cat.* 6) uses words which Tacitus obviously echoes here (*urbem Romam . . . habuere initio Troiani*).

a principio. Tacitus' rapid survey of the History of Rome is not merely a synopsis of necessary facts with the serialist's 'Now Read On' implied at the relevant spot. It implies a conception of historical development, of the place of the Principate in Roman History as a whole; and the subjects chosen for mention provide the constitutional background to the establishment of the Principate and set the atmosphere in which its history will be treated.

reges. The detailed history of the Kings of Rome (traditionally six in number) remains obscure, but it is certain that the city was originally ruled by kings, that some of them were of Etruscan origin and that they were finally expelled at (probably) the end of the sixth century B.C.

libertatem, here = 'political freedom', especially freedom from monarchical rule; to Cicero the prerogative of the Roman people (*Phil.* VI, 7, 19), to Tacitus, who saw in the Principate a new monarchy, a term synonymous with the vanished Republic. Cf. 33, 2.

consulatum. The creation of the office (of two chief magistrates, annually elected, in whom the power of the state was vested) does date from the founding of the Republic (probably *c.* 510 B.C.). But they were, until some time in the early fourth century, known as 'praetors' (Livy, III, 55, 12).

L. Brutus, L. Iunius Brutus, a legendary hero of Rome. It is probable that he existed and was largely responsible for the founding of the Republic: but most of the exploits associated with his name are purely legendary, being folk tales of a type which tend to cluster round one known and famous name.

dictaturae. *ad tempus* 'for the occasion' shows that dacitus is referring to the original office of dictator and not to its later development under, e.g. Sulla. The appointment was temporary, for not more than six months, and gave the holder supreme power to deal with some particular crisis. No appointments are recorded after the end of the third century B.C.

decemuiralis potestas. It is difficult to separate fact from legend in the traditional account of the *decemuiri*, but it is generally agreed that in 451 B.C. a board of ten patricians was appointed to prepare a code of law, and that a second board (450–449) completed their work. The code (the Twelve Tables) was published in 449. Whether in fact the *decemuiri* attempted to retain their office beyond its legal limits, as tradition related (Livy, III, 37 sq.) is uncertain. If the story is true, Tacitus' statement may be taken either as a reference to their *legal* tenure of office (*potestas*), or as a convenient round number: if they succeeded in prolonging their rule, it was only for a few months.

tribunorum militum. The traditional explanation of the institution of *tribuni militum consulari potestate* (Livy, IV, 6, 8) is this. In 445 B.C. the struggle between patricians and plebeians in Rome reached an impasse: the plebeians demanded the right to be consuls, the patricians refused, and the tribunes of the people used their veto to prevent any business being done in the Senate. The problem was temporarily resolved by the election of Consular Tribunes instead of consuls, the office being open to plebeians and patricians alike.

That this explanation is unsatisfactory has been demonstrated by Professor F. E. Adcock in *J.R.S.* 1957, pp. 9 sq. He concludes that political reasons may have caused the election of the first set of Tribunes, but that during the next eighty years administrative and military reasons were also relevant. Political manoeuvres probably also ended the Tribunate: in 367 B.C. the consulship was finally opened to the *plebs*, and no more Consular Tribunes were appointed.

Although the Tribunate existed for about eighty years, it was never more than a temporary expedient and made little impression on Rome's constitutional history. Tacitus is therefore justified in describing the term of office as *non diu*.

non Cinnae, non Sullae. Anaphora (the repetition of a word at the beginning of successive phrases or clauses, its presence making a conjunction unnecessary) is used by Tacitus to produce various stylistic effects. Here the repeated *non* keeps firmly before the reader the impression that none of these systems lasted for long. In 51, 1, *non sexus, non aetas* is rather pathetic: while 7, 5, *miles in forum, miles in curiam comitabatur* emphasizes the armed guard precisely as

> Cannon to right of them
> Cannon to left of them . . .

emphasizes the artillery.

L. Cornelius Cinna contrived to hold the consulship continuously from 87–84 B.C., thus assuming a virtual dictatorship over the city. He was the champion of the popular party and the enemy of Sulla, and was killed in a fracas at Brundisium, while on his way to Greece to meet Sulla's army. It is unlikely that he could have preserved his power for much longer: Sulla had the better army and was the greater man.

Sulla's march on Rome in 88 B.C. was the first open use of military power for political purposes. But his dictatorship proper dates from 82 B.C., on his return from the East. It was quite legally conferred upon him, but the fact that it was unlimited in period of tenure and scope of activities, and extorted by the presence of an army under his control, made it a dictatorship of a kind very different from the earlier ones— a fact which Tacitus recognizes by his use of the word *dominatio*. Sulla resigned his dictatorship in 79 and died in the following year.

Pompei Crassique potentia. In 60 B.C. was formed what is conveniently termed the First Triumvirate, a political alliance for mutual benefit between Julius Caesar and Pompey, with the wealthy Crassus as the third man. Crassus was a competent general, but a man without a policy, and his influence on the coalition would have been negligible even if he had not died in 53. Pompey was a greater man, but his abilities too were military and his political moves were unrealistic and shortsighted. He gradually found himself in opposition to Caesar, and was finally defeated by him at Pharsalus in 48. From this year dates the military dictatorship of Caesar, which provided both a precedent and a warning for Augustus.

Note the double meaning conveyed by *potentia*. It indicates not only an alliance of influence as opposed to the military alliance (*arma*) of the Second Triumvirate: but also a power that did not depend on constitutional forms, but was unofficial. Contrast the *potestas* (officially granted) of the *decemuiri*.

Lepidi atque Antonii arma. The alliance between Octavian, Lepidus and Antony was concluded in 43 B.C., appropriately enough in the presence of their legions. They then marched on Rome and ensured their legal status by having a law passed which created them *tresuiri reipublicae constituendae* for a term of five years. Their power was later extended for another five years, to 33 B.C. But this Triumvirate, like the First, broke up, and the deposition of Lepidus in 36 and the defeat of Antony at Actium in 31 left Octavian master of the Roman world.

cessere. With *in* and the acc. *cedere* means 'fall to', 'pass to'. Cf. Livy, I, 52, 2, *res omnis Albana in Romanum cesserit imperium*. Tacitus alone seems to use the construction with a personal object, cf. *Ag.* 5, *gloria in ducem cessit*.

cuncta ... fessa. Rome and Italy had, by 28 B.C., been suffering from civil disturbances for the greater part of a century. They had become discouraged and almost hopeless of any settled existence, and the psychological effect of the firm, stable government of Augustus can hardly be exaggerated.

nomine principis. Warned by Caesar's fate, and guided by his own temperament, Augustus refused to be called 'dictator' or 'king' and was known simply as *princeps*, 'the leading citizen'. The term was a Republican one (cf. Cic. *De Dom.* 25, 66, *Cn. Pompeium, quem omnium iudicio longe principem esse ciuitatis uidebat*) and free from monarchical associations. It defined his *auctoritas*, influence or standing in the state, rather than his *imperium*, the official power which he possessed; but the power was there, and the significance of *nomine* should not be missed (cf. 9, 5). On Augustus' *imperium* see note on 2, 1 (*consulem ... contentum*) and cf. *J.R.S.* 1946, pp. 157 sq. and *C.R.* 1953, p. 10.

§ 2. claris scriptoribus. See Introd. IV, 3 (iv). The writers dealing with the Republican period would include Sallust and Livy. Tacitus' feeling that the interesting subject matter of history vanished with the Republic is partly responsible for the deliberate elaboration of his style.

temporibus ... dicendis, 'there was no lack of gifted men to describe the times of Augustus'. The dative does not follow *desum* but is dat. of purpose (Introd. IV, 3 (v)).

ingenia. From meaning the quality of genius, *ingenium* is extended to mean 'a man of genius'. It is found occasionally in Cicero (*Brut.* 147, e.g.), but is most common in the Silver Latin writers and in the plural. Cf. *Hist.* I, 1, *magna ingenia*. The reference here is to writers such as Livy, Velleius Paterculus and Aufidius Bassus, who included part or whole of Augustus' reign in their work.

gliscente. *gliscere* 'to grow', 'to increase' is an old and poetic word, so much used by Tacitus as to be almost a hallmark of his style. It implies a secret or gradual growth in power or force, and is therefore used of things as diverse as wind (*uento gliscente*, Sall. *Hist.* III, 31), war (*ne glisceret ... bellum*, Livy, XXIX, 2, 2) and personal influence (*gliscere singulos*, *Ann.*, II, 33). Tacitus extends it to mean increase in numbers (*multitudo ... gliscebat, Ann.* III, 25; *gliscentibus negotiis, Ann.* XI, 22). But its predominant use is with qualities, mainly undesirable, e.g. *saeuitia* (*Ann.* VI, 19), *inuidia* (*Ann.* XV, 64), *adulatio;* but occasionally *gloria* (*Ann.* XV, 23), *gaudium* (Lucr. V, 1061), &c.

donec ... deterrerentur. See Introd. IV, 5 (ii).

Tiberii ... Neronis. Tacitus is defining his period and explaining his reasons for choosing it. With the loss of *Ann.* VII–X has been lost his account of the reign of Gaius and much of that of Claudius. Note that *et* joins the two major divisions of Julian and Claudian Emperors, while *-que* and *ac* subdivide the respective sections. See Nipperdey *ad loc.*

metum . . . odiis. Fear produces over-laudatory histories during the lifetime of the Emperor, hatred unnecessarily harsh accounts after his death (cf. e.g. the venomous attack on Claudius in Seneca's *Apocolocyntosis*). Neither is sound history. On Tacitus' own merits as an historian and his claim to write *sine ira et studio*, see Introd. II.

This sentence is typically Tacitean, the two phrases *florentibus . . . falsae* and *postquam . . . sunt* presenting a balanced meaning and a careful avoidance of balance in structure: the first shows a temporal abl. abs., a causal *ob* with acc., and an adj. agreeing with the subject; while the second is composed of a temporal clause, an abl. of attendant circumstances, and the main verb. 'As for Tiberius and Gaius, Claudius and Nero, the histories composed in their lifetimes were falsified through fear, while those written after their deaths were produced in the light of recent bitter hatred.'

postquam occiderant. The pluperfect after *postquam* is not common. It indicates that the action of the temporal clause has been completed before the action of the main clause began. *postquam occiderunt* would simply imply temporal precedence—first they died, then the histories were written: the pluperfect implies a temporal relationship—their being dead was necessary before histories of this kind could be written. Cf. Cic. *Verr.* IV, 24, 54, *posteaquam multitudinem collegerat emblematum, instituit officinam*, where he had to have his works of art before he could open his shop. Cf. 49, 1, *postquam . . . rapuerant.*

§ 3. **pauca . . . et extrema**, 'to say a little about Augustus, especially about the end of his reign'. For the use of *et* to introduce the stronger adjective, cf. Cic. *Acad.* II, 127, *haec nostra ut exigua et minima contemnimus.*

causas, 'motives' or 'incentives'.

2. § 1. For an analysis of the sentence-structure, see Introd. III. 'With Brutus and Cassius dead there was now no national army: Pompeius had been crushed in Sicily: and with Lepidus cast off and Antony dead even the Julian party had no leader left but Caesar. He relinquished the title of "triumvir", styling himself consul and stating that he was content to protect the people by virtue of his tribunician power. He first enticed the support of the army by gifts, of the populace by a good corn supply, and of the whole nation by the sweet prospect of peace, then gradually increased his power, taking to himself the functions of Senate, magistrates and laws—without any opposition, because the fieriest spirits had fallen in battle or the proscription, and the rest of the nobility, their wealth or political importance increased in proportion to their readiness to serve, were the gainers from the new régime, and preferred present safety to the old Republic and its dangers.'

postquam. *erant* is understood with *arma*, *est* with *oppressus*, and *erat* with *reliquus*. Tacitus omits the verb 'to be' much more freely than do other Latin writers. For similar exx. in subordinate clauses, cf. 7, 6, *in cuius manu*, 38, 2, *postquam intutae latebrae*; 58, 3, *ubi primum tui copia*; 69, 1, *ut quis*; and see note on 7, 1.

Bruto et Cassio caesis. They committed suicide at Philippi (42 B.C.).

publica arma. Brutus and Cassius had in April 43 been granted *maius imperium* by the Senate; their armies had therefore some official standing, which those of Antony and Octavian had not.

Pompeius. Sextus Pompeius, younger son of Pompey the Great, was appointed commander of the fleet by the Senate in 44 B.C. He was proscribed, but escaped, was later reconciled to Antony and Octavian, but for several years continued to cause Octavian considerable trouble. He was finally crushed (*oppressus*—cf. Cic. *Font.* 12, 26, *ab hoc ipso bello superati et oppressi*) in the naval battle of Naulochus in 36.

exuto, 'Lepidus having been discarded', like a garment. This seems better than 'having been stripped of power'—in which usage of *exuere* the abl. is usually expressed. The point is discussed by Walker, *Annals of Tacitus*, p. 63, n. 2. Cf. 4, 1, *exuta aequalitate* and *Ann*. XIV, 52, *exueret magistrum*. Lepidus never counted for much in the Triumvirate, and in 36 B.C. was forced into private life and virtual exile.

Antonio. After his defeat at Actium he fled to Egypt, but failed to hold it, and committed suicide before Octavian reached Alexandria.

ne . . . quidem. The Republican leaders were dead: and even the Caesarian party could now offer only Octavian ('Caesar' by adoption). It sounds derogatory and is probably intentionally so.

posito triumuiri nomine. The Triumvirate's (second) legal term of office ended with 33 B.C. Antony continued to style himself *triumuir* (his denarii of 32 B.C. bear the titles ANT. AUG. IIIVIR R.P.C.—see Matt., *Pl.* XX, 17–19), and to use triumviral powers (Dio, L, 7); Octavian, as far as we know, dropped the title, and perhaps the powers also (though Tacitus obviously does not think so.) See T. Rice Holmes, *The Architect of the Roman Empire*, I, pp. 231 sq. For the gen. *triumuiri* see Introd. IV, 2 (iv).

consulem . . . contentum. Octavian (Augustus) was consul continuously from 31–23 B.C., holding his *imperium maius* in Rome by virtue of that office. When he resigned it in 23, he was granted *proconsulare imperium maius*, and the loss of various privileges attached to the office of chief magistrate was made good by the use of *tribunicia potestas* (i.e. by the use of a tribune's powers, without the limitations and inconveniences of the office itself; see *Ann*. III, 56). Augustus numbers his *trib. pot.* from 23, but whether it was first granted in that year (Dio, LIII, 32, 5; cf. Last in *R.I.L.* 1951, pp. 93 sq.) or granted in 30 (Dio, LI, 19, 6) and not used until 23 (*C.A.H.* X, pp. 121 and 139 sq.) is still debated. Dr Last reasonably suggests that it is improbable that a power so important should not be mentioned among Augustus' titles until

23 if he had in fact possessed it since 30; and points out that Dio in LI, 19, 6 merely records the *offer* of *trib. pot.* among other honours, some at least of which Augustus refused (LI, 20, 4). He may therefore have been offered the power in 30, but have accepted it only in 23 when he needed it. This chapter does little to resolve the difficulty, for it is (as Haverfield saw, *J.R.S.* 1912, pp. 195 sq.; cf. Syme in *J.R.S.* 1946, p. 157) not a chronological description of Augustus' constitutional position, but an impressionistic account of his rise to power. The general context shows that, as do such points as the placing of *interfecto Antonio* before *posito triumuiri nomine*, and the implication that the consulship and *trib. pot.* were equally important at the same time: there is no period of which this is true. Tacitus is producing a pictorial interpretation of a set of facts and is not at the moment concerned with detailed chronology.

ad tuendam plebem. This was the original function of the tribunate.

donis. Augustus lists his benefactions in the *R.G.*:

(*a*) His general policy of granting veterans land or money, *R.G.* 3, 3 and 16, 1–2.

(*b*) A special grant of 1,000 sesterces to each of about 120,000 veterans settled in colonies, *R.G.* 15, 3.

(*c*) His establishment of the military chest in A.D. 6 by a gift of 170 m. sesterces from his own patrimony, *R.G.* 17, 2. See 78, 2 n.

annona. Rome's food-supply presented a perpetual problem; most of the corn had to be imported, so that it was expensive and its transport uncertain because of bad weather, pirates or war. The problem of its price was met by allowing a regular dole of cheap or free corn to the urban population: to ensure its transport various emergency measures were taken from time to time. In 23 B.C., to meet a scarcity, Augustus made twelve special grants of corn at his own expense (*R.G.* 15, 1) and in the following year agreed to undertake the *cura annonae* as his own responsibility, and reorganized it so speedily that famine was averted (*R.G.* 5, 2). Later, a special *praefectus annonae* was appointed, a man of equestrian rank, responsible to Augustus. Egypt, the source of most of Rome's corn, remained directly under the control of the Princeps.

insurgere . . . trahere. hist. infins. (Introd. IV, 6 (ii)).

munia . . . in se trahere. The phrase is repeated in *Ann.* XI, 5. Augustus claims (*R.G.* 34, 3), *potestatis autem nihilo amplius habui quam ceteri, qui mihi quoque in magistratu conlegae fuerunt.* But in fact his *imperium* was *maius*, he had no 'colleagues' of any significance (after 23 rarely any colleagues at all), and he held an unprecedented concentration of powers, many of them divorced from their offices and so less restricted. Tacitus' statement is therefore much nearer the truth than Augustus' own, though the process was not so blatant as his words suggest.

From the Senate Augustus took over, e.g. the supreme command over all armies (Dio, LIII, 12, 3), the right to make peace and war

(Strabo, XVII, 840) and the right to receive foreign embassies (*R.G.* 31–3). Of magistrates' powers he exercised *trib. pot.* and *proc. imp.*, and assumed consular and censorial powers (*R.G.* 8, 3–4) when he required them. He promoted legislation (the *leges Iuliae* of 18 B.C., e.g. see Dio, LIII, 21) by virtue of his *trib. pot.*, exercised a general appellate jurisdiction (Dig. *passim;* Dio, LI, 19, 7) and had his own private court (Suet. *Aug.* 32–3).

acies, Philippi and Actium.

proscriptione. At the end of November 43 B.C., the Second Triumvirate published a list of persons who were declared outlaws, with rewards offered for their execution. Panic and slaughter followed, wiping out many of the old aristocracy who had supported Pompey and the Senate (Dio, XLVII, 3–13).

nobilium. For the gen. see Introd. IV, 2 (iii).

quanto. For the omission of the balancing *tanto* see 57, 1 n.

quis. The indefinite pronoun is used not only 'after *si, nisi, ne* and *num*' but also in certain interrogative and relative expressions. Cf. 27, 1, *ut quis occurreret;* 57, 1, *quanto quis audacia promptus;* 69, 1, *ut quis inops.*

seruitio, dat. of purpose (Introd. IV, 3 (v)).

tuta . . . periculosa. A neat chiasmus (the figure takes its name from the Greek letter X—'chi'; instead of the adjectives being balanced

in parallel they are crossed in the form of a 'chi'). The accusative

with *malo* is poetical, cf. Livy II, 39, 8 *plebes omnia quam bellum malebat* and 58, 3.

§ 2. prouinciae sq. The Republic was not successful in its government of provinces. Governors were ex-magistrates of Rome, often elected on purely political grounds and with no experience of provincial government, frequently gaining their provinces by lot and having no permanent officials or standing army to assist them: the taxes were collected by the *publicani* and much of the money collected never reached Rome; a dishonest Governor could be prosecuted at Rome in the *quaestio de repetundis,* but was quite likely to be acquitted through political influence or bribery. Not that all Governors were corrupt or all provincials exploited all the time: but the welfare of the provincials depended too much on the character of the individual Governor.

Augustus adopted the theory of the Republican system, ensured that it really worked and hedged it about with safeguards. The peaceful provinces he left to the government of ex-magistrates appointed by lot: the rest were governed by *legati,* selected by Augustus and holding office as long as was necessary: every province had an imperial pro-curator responsible for its finances, so that the money in fact went to the treasury: and it was much more difficult for a dishonest Governor to oppress his provincials, and much easier for them to prosecute him if he did. Augustus applied his mind to the organization of the provinces and created a workable system from the haphazard arrangements of the Republic: and the provincials naturally appreciated it.

certamina potentium. Rivals like Marius and Sulla, or Caesar and Pompey, often fought in the provinces their battles for political ascendancy at Rome.

3. § 1. ceterum, not adversative, but marking a transition to a new point in the narrative. Lit. 'for the rest'; tr. 'Meanwhile Augustus . . .' Cf. 71, 2.

subsidia, acc. in apposition to the phrase: see Introd. IV, 1 (iv). Augustus was anxious to form a dynasty, but his desire to secure the succession was also based on sound political sense. If there was no obvious successor, there might be attempts to overthrow his rule and there would certainly be trouble after his death—as there was in A.D. 69, after the death of Nero.

dominationi. For the dat. see Introd. IV, 3 (v); for the emotional significance of the word see Introd. III.

Marcellum. For the family relationships mentioned in this chapter, see the genealogical table, page 49. Marcellus was the son by her first husband of the Octavia who later married Mark Antony. He died in 23 B.C., aged 19, after holding the aedileship for that year and celebrating it with magnificent games. That so young a man should hold the offices of pontiff and aedile marked him out for special attention. Virgil in a famous passage (*Aen.* VI, 860 sq.) praises and laments him.

admodum, 'to the limit' and so 'very'. It is especially common with adjs. denoting age, cf. Cic. *Phil.* V, 48, *admodum adulescentes consules facti*; 'a mere boy'.

M. Agrippam. This is the official form of his name—the inscription on the Pantheon, e.g. reads M. AGRIPPA L. F. COS. TERTIUM FECIT. He was M. Vipsanius Agrippa, but dropped the gentile name *quasi argumentum paternae humilitatis* (Sen. *Contr.* II, 4, 13). A soldier and a loyal supporter of Augustus, he was associated with him in the grants of *proconsulare imperium* and *tribunicia potestas*. He was an ener-getic and capable man, and served Augustus well. See *C.A.H.* X, especially chs. 3 and 5.

ignobilem loco, a variation on the classical *humili loco natus*, where the abl. is local: here the adj. is transferred to the person, and the abl. is one of respect. (See 16, 3 n.)

uictoriae socium. Agrippa's manoeuvres with the fleet did much to win the victory of Actium.

geminatis, two *consecutive* consulships. Agrippa was consul three times, in 37, 28 and 27 B.C. It was rare for anyone to hold the consulship for two successive years, and under the Principate only the Emperor or members of his immediate family did so.

generum. In 21 Agrippa married, at Augustus' request, Julia—daughter of Augustus and widow of Marcellus.

Tiberium . . . Drusum. Livia's sons by her former marriage. (Introd. V.)

imperatoriis nominibus. Inscriptions (e.g. *E. and J.* 39 and 79) confirm that Tiberius and Drusus had the title *imperator*, though there is some doubt about the date of conferment. No. 39, which is datable to 7 B.C. mentions Tiberius as *cos. iterum, imp. iterum* and that, with other evidence (Suet. *Tib.* 9; id. *Claud.* 1) makes it likely that the title was first conferred in 9 B.C.

integra etiam tum. His grandson Lucius lived until A.D. 2, Gaius until 4.

§ 2. induxerat. He adopted them in 17 B.C.

praetexta. The *toga praetexta*, a toga with a purple border, was worn by boys until they came of age (about 15), and then formally dedicated to the Lares. Thereafter the boy was *pubes* and wore the *toga uirilis*. The ceremony was not only a domestic one but marked the entry of the young man into public life. Augustus used it as a convenient opportunity to acquire honours for his possible successor. Tacitus exaggerates with *necdum,* for the honours were associated with the ceremony: the exaggeration emphasizes the extreme youth of the boys who were being so honoured.

principes iuuentutis. The six squadrons of *equites equo publico* who paraded before the Emperor each year (*trauectio equitum*) consisted of members of the Equestrian order under 35 years of age, and young men of Senatorial rank who had not yet held office. This body in 5 B.C. elected Gaius, and in 2 B.C. Lucius, as *princeps iuuentutis* (*R.G.* 14). They were thus recognized as the leaders of Roman youth, and carried a title reminiscent of Augustus' own. Coins of 2 B.C. onwards show the youths, with the title C. L. CAESARES AUGUSTI F. COS. DESIG. PRINC. IVVENT.; see *R.I.C.* I, Pl. III, 47.

destinari consules. In 5 B.C. Gaius was designated consul, to hold office five years later, and in 2 B.C. Lucius was accorded a similar honour (*R.G.* 14).

specie recusantis. According to Dio, LV, 9, 2, the people had wished to elect Gaius consul in 6 B.C.: this Augustus refused, but Tacitus may be right in his insinuation that he was merely preparing the way for the conferment of exceptional honours on Gaius and Lucius.

§ 3. uita concessit. Tacitus uses a great variety of expressions to describe death, whether natural death, suicide or murder. In this chapter note *defuncto Marcello* (§ 1), *uita concessit, mors . . . abstulit, extincto* (§ 3); c. 6 shows a similar range of expressions, mainly for murder or execution—*morte adficere, supremum diem expleuisset* (§ 1), *in . . . necem durauit, mortem . . . inlatam, caedem festinauisse* (§ 2). Cf. also *quaesita morte* (5, 2), *cecidissem* (43, 1), *supplicium praesumant* (48, 1), *supremum diem obiit* (53, 1), *mortem inuenerit* (61, 4), *honestae mortis usus, inglorium exitium* (70, 4). Agrippa died in 12 B.C.

This sentence shows in miniature Tacitus' 'affective' use of language (see Introd. II). His facts are correctly stated, but by using archaic and poetic words (*remeantem, cuncta, uergere*), unusual constructions (*mors fato propera, illuc*), a rhetorical commonplace (*nouerca*, the 'cruel stepmother') and an insinuating alternative (*uel . . . Liuiae dolus*—see Introd. II) he produces, by association, an atmosphere of romance, pathos and mystery to surround the facts and affect our interpretation of them. It is extremely improbable that Livia (the 'stepmother' of Gaius and Lucius since Augustus had adopted them) had anything to do with their deaths.

Armenia, 'from Armenia'; see Introd. IV, 4 (i).

fato propera, 'a death quick in the natural course of fate', i.e. 'an early but natural death'. Tacitus frequently uses *fatum* of natural as opposed to violent death. Cf. *Ann.* VI, 10, *L. Piso, rarum in tanta claritudine, fato obiit.*

Druso. He died in Germany in 9 B.C.

illuc, 'on him'. Cf. *Hist.* II, 24, *ne omne belli decus illuc concederet;* and *illic* in 70, 4. The personal application of this adverb is rare, although *unde=a quo* is common.

filius. Tiberius was adopted by Augustus in A.D. 4, and had his *trib. pot.* (which he had already held from 6–1 B.C.: Dio, LV, 9, 4) renewed for ten years; it was not until A.D. 13 that he was given a co-regency with Augustus (Vell. II, 121). For his campaigns with the various armies, between A.D. 4 and 14, see Introd. V. Here, as in the description of Octavian's rise to power (2, 1), Tacitus is giving an impressionistic account, not a chronological sequence.

omnis, all those that counted at this time.

palam. The adverb is used adjectivally, as commonly in Greek—οἱ νῦν ἄνθρωποι = 'men of today'. The usage is found early in Latin (Plaut. *Pers.* 385, *non tu nunc hominum mores uides?*) but classical prose prefers it either enclosed in a phrase (Livy, I, 17, *multarum circa ciuitatium*) as the Greek definite article and noun enclose it, or so arranged that syntactically it may be taken with the verb (Cic. *N.D.* II, 166, *deorum saepe praesentiae declarant*). Poetical usage is freer (Virg. *Aen.* I, 198, *neque enim ignari sumus ante malorum*) as is Tacitus'. Here the use is made easier by the fact that *hortatu* is derived from a verb. Cf. *Ann.* XV, 7, *nulla palam causa; Ann.* I, 13, 1, *pari fama publice.*

§ 4. Postumum. Born after Agrippa's death, he was now the only surviving son of Julia and Agrippa: according to the sources (cf. Suet. *Aug. 65*), he was a youth of depraved character. Augustus adopted him along with Tiberius in A.D. 4, but later had him disinherited and exiled. Cf. 6, 1–2.

Planasiam, a small island lying between Elba and Corsica.

proiecerit. A consecutive clause depending on a secondary verb may use either the imperfect or the perfect subj. Broadly speaking, the imperfect indicates a result which is quoted to emphasize the main action, of which it is considered a part, while the perfect stresses the result as an actual happening in past time, incidental to the main action but not its inevitable result. *ira ita commotus est ut loqui non posset* describes the degree of his anger: *non potuerit* would emphasize his inability to speak. The sequence of tenses used in other subordinate clauses sometimes caused the imperfect to be used where the perfect might be expected: but the perfect remained none the less in fairly common use. For a similar ex. after the pluperfect, cf. *Ann*. II, 81, *seditionem adeo commouerat, ut signifer signum transtulerit.*

bonarum artium. *ars* in this sense is the motive behind behaviour, or the means by which we act: and so means something like 'character'. Cf. Sall. *Cat*. 11, 2 *huic quia bonae artes desunt, dolis atque fallaciis contendit.* Tacitus uses the phrase, and its opposite (*malae artes*) quite frequently. Cf. 9, 3; 28, 3. The gen. here is partitive, and is common with adjs. of fullness and emptiness.

stolide ferocem, 'stupidly arrogant as regards the strength of his body'. The adverb limits the meaning of the adj. Cf. Livy, VII, 10, 5, *Gallum stolide laetum*. Postumus was therefore 'admittedly devoid of every good quality, with the brute confidence of purely physical strength, but not yet detected in any open offence'.

flagitii, 'legal' gen. (Introd. IV, 2 (ii)).

§ 5. at hercule, strongly adversative—Postumus he drove into exile, but *Germanicus* he honoured.

Germanicum. He was adopted by Tiberius in A.D. 4 (Suet. *Tib*. 15) but his command on the Rhine dated only from A.D. 13 (Suet. *Cal*. 8; Vell. II, 123). Tacitus continues to disregard exact chronology: see note on *filius* § 3.

octo ... legionibus. Inscriptions confirm Tacitus' allocation of these:

V Alaudae and XXI at Vetera (Xanten)	
I Germanica and XX Valeria at Oppidum Vbiorum (Cologne)	} Lower Germany, cf. 31, 3.
XIV Gemina and XVI at Moguntiacum (Mainz)	
II Augusta at Argentoratum (Strasbourg)	} Upper Germany, cf. 37, 3.
XIII Gemina at Vindonissa (Windisch)	

adsciri. This is a rare word, meaning to 'receive', 'admit' (cf. the much commoner *adscisco*); it is borrowed by Tacitus from Virgil.

quamquam esset. The original (and usual) construction of *quamquam* is with the indicative, but the analogy of the subjunctive used with *quamuis* inevitably produced a similar usage with *quamquam*. It is rare in Ciceronian prose, commoner in Virgil and Livy, and used by Tacitus more frequently than the indicative. Cf. 24, 3, *quamquam maestitiam imitarentur*.

filius. Drusus, son of Tiberius and Vipsania, was born about 13 B.C.

pluribus munimentis. Augustus had been so unfortunate in his previous attempts to secure the succession that he was determined this time to have several lines of defence.

§ 6. ea tempestate, i.e. after A.D. 9 not, as might be imagined from this passage, in A.D. 4. *tempestas*='time' is archaic and poetical.

abolendae . . . infamiae. This may be either dat. of purpose (Introd. IV, 3 (v)) or gen. (Introd. IV, 2 (v)): probably the latter.

ob amissum . . . exercitum. See 8, 6 n.

Quintilio Varo. See Introd. VI.

cupidine. Cicero uses *cupiditas* for 'desire', and *Cupido* only as a personification. But the latter is common in the sense of 'desire' in all the historians, especially Livy and Tacitus.

proferendi imperii. On the reasons for the various invasions of Germany, see Introd. VI.

§ 7. uocabula, 'the magistrates' *titles* remained the same'; a typically Tacitean shaft, and one not without justification. The great public offices of the Republic were still there, but much of the reality of their power had vanished.

iuniores. Technically, these are the men under 45. Actium was fought in 31 B.C. and the reference here is to the last years of Augustus' reign, A.D. 13–14.

senes. The First Triumvirate had been formed in 60 B.C. and from that date, through the Civil War, Caesar's Dictatorship and the Second Triumvirate, the power of the Republican constitution had been virtually in abeyance.

inter. See 12, 1 n.

quotus quisque. This phrase literally asks 'each man was how many-th?' Used, as it invariably is, in a rhetorical question, it means, 'How many are there? Very few!' and therefore 'How few there are!'

rem publicam. In this and similar contexts it means 'the Republic'.

uidisset. This use of the subjunctive in relative clauses it is convenient to describe as 'generic', though the term is much abused. The antecedent is indefinite or negative (*nemo est qui*), and the subjunctive characterises the person described by the antecedent, while the indicative would merely identify or paraphrase it (i.e. *ille erat qui diceret* means 'he was the kind of man to say' while *ille erat qui dixit* means 'he was the speaker'). It is not possible to make a definite statement of fact (which is implied by an indicative verb) about such a general or negative antecedent: hence the subjunctive, which is almost certainly potential in origin, though other factors may have contributed to its development. Note the significant difference of mood in the relative clauses in Hor. *Ep.* II, 2, 182, *sunt qui non habeant, est qui non curat habere*; and cf. Cic. *Tusc.* II, 4, 11, *quotus enim quisque . . . inuenitur, qui sit moratus.* In *Ann.* I, cf. 11, 2, *occuleret*; 75, 4, *faceret.*

4. § 1. igitur. The word is, in classical prose, normally placed second in the phrase. Cicero rarely puts it first, but its placing there becomes increasingly common in Sallust and Livy, while in Tacitus, apart from seven examples (one of them *quos igitur?* 47, 1) it is invariable.

et. *neque* would separate and distinguish the adjs., *et* joins them closely as part of a single idea, with *nihil* standing, as it were, outside the bracket. Cf. 29, 1, *negat se (terrore et minis) uinci*; 70, 3, *non (uox et mutui hortatus) iuuabant.*

moris, 'conduct' or 'behaviour'. Tacitus considers that the loss of political freedom has had a bad effect on the moral fibre of the Romans. The 'good old way' is no more.

aequalitate, 'political equality', as in *Ann.* III, 26; the juxtaposition of *iussa principis* adds emphasis to both phrases. For *exuta* see 2, 1 n.

aspectare. The verb is rare in this sense of 'look to', being so used perhaps only here: *specto* is common in this sense (Livy, V, 16, 8, *Romani, desperata ope humana, fata et deos spectabant*). *aspectare* is a poetical word (cf. Virg. *Aen.* I, 420) and unusual, and is therefore employed by Tacitus to draw attention to a point he considers to be important. It is, too, a frequentative verb, and Tacitus likes to use the frequentative instead of the simple form of a verb; it is more emphatic in itself, and gains in effect from being unusually employed. Cf. *sustentauit* at the end of § 1; *suspectabat* 13, 1.

aetate, abl. of respect (16, 3 n.): *aetas* means here 'the prime of life' and the phrase is an extension of such usages as *ualidus mente* Horace) and *ualidus corpore* (*Hist.* I, 57). 'In the vigour of life.'

§ 2. postquam. For its use with the imperf. indic. see 39, 5 n.

prouecta senectus. The more usual phrases are *uir prouectus aetate* and *uir prouecta aetate* (cf. *Ann.* VI, 11). Here *prouecta senectus* is personified as the subject of *fatigabatur.* For a similar personification, cf. *Hist.* I, 16, *ut nec mea senectus conferre plus possit.*

aegro et corpore. *et*=*etiam.* 'When he was advanced in years and, in addition, worn out by illness.'

aderat . . . nouae. This is typically Tacitean arrangement: it was *because* the end was near that hopes of revolution were raised, but

Tacitus simply states the two facts and leaves the juxtaposition to make its own effect.

in cassum, 'vainly', 'foolishly'; the acc. and abl. neut. sing. of certain adjs. are used with prepositions to form adverbial phrases expressing respectively aim or manner and attendant circumstances. Cf. *in incertum et ambiguum* (11, 2), *in deterius* (62, 2), *in occulto* (49, 1). These phrases are commonest in the poets and post-Augustan writers, and the Greek use of εἰς and ἐν clearly influenced the Latin formations. Cf. too *in speciem* (52, 2). Note that Tacitus hates the Empire, but sees quite clearly that the only alternative to an Emperor is another Emperor.

disserere. Cicero confines his use of the acc. after *dissero* to neuter pronouns (*haec disseruissem*, Brut. 201): Tacitus, like the other historians, extends it to neuter adjs. or participles (*congruentia*, 79, 2) and nouns (*eius negotii initium disseram*, Ann. II, 27).

bellum. For the acc. after *pauescere* see Introd. IV, 1 (ii).

multo. The abl. of measure of difference, common with comparatives (*multo maior*, &c.), is used with the superlative mainly by the poets and historians. A few examples occur in Cicero, cf. *Cat.* IV, 17, *multo' uero maxima pars eorum.*

rumoribus. On Tacitus' use of rumour see Introd. II.

differebant. *differre* means 'to spread abroad', 'to publish', and in particular (of personal objects) 'to publish evil reports of', i.e. 'to defame'. Cf. Plaut. *Pseud.* 359, *te differam dictis meis* and Prop. I, iv, 22, *te circum omnes alias . . . puellas differet.*

§ 3. **rerum experientia.** Tiberius' training too was inadequate; see Introd. V. For *experientia*='experience', cf. 46, 2, *principem longa experientia.* The classical meaning is 'trial' or 'effort'.

Tiberium Neronem. For the use of the name Nero see note on **5,** 4.

annis . . . bello . . . superbia. It is typical of Tacitus that the three abls. are different usages—respect, instrumental and quality respectively. The appearance of balance is illusory.

Claudiae familiae. Since the days of Appius Claudius the *decemuir,* the *gens Claudia* had given to Rome a series of administrators and soldiers, many of them able men: in this family ability Tiberius shared. If the Claudii were proud, it was not entirely without justification.

premantur. *Repraesentatio;* Introd. IV, 5 (iv).

§ 4. **et.** If this were, as Nipperdey and Furneaux suggest, the first half of *et . . . et* or *et . . . neque,* the latter half being lost in the stronger *ne . . . quidem,* surely *congestos iuueni* too would require an *et?* It is probably intensive, =*uel,* like Suet. *Galba* 3, *temporum suorum et eloquentissimus.*

regnatrice. *regnatrix* seems to have been invented by Tacitus and is used only here. He has a special fondness for verbal substantives and adjs. in -*tor* and -*trix,* and makes full use of the 'professional' meaning which they often carry. Here he boldly classes as a professional 'ruling family' the house of Augustus, who so carefully concealed any connexion with kingly power. Cf. *machinator*, 10, 2; *ostentator*, 24, 2; *turbator*, 30, 1 and 55, 2; *moderator*, 49, 2; *conciliator*, 58, 3.

congestos . . . triumphos, an exaggeration. Tiberius held the consulship twice in Augustus' lifetime, in 13 and 7 B.C., at the ages of 29 and 35: and the triumphs which he celebrated for Germany and Illyria were well earned.

Rhodi specie secessus. For Tiberius' retirement to Rhodes see Introd. V.

exulem. This is the reading of M, and should be retained. It has been objected that Tiberius cannot have been pretending both to withdraw and be an exile; but (i) *personam agere* is a metaphor from the stage, means 'to take the part of', 'to behave as' and need not involve any idea of pretence. Cf. *Hist.* IV, 2, *filium principis agebat* (Domitian *was* the Emperor's son) and Val. Max. V, 8, 1, *exuit patrem, ut consulem ageret* (L. Brutus was both a father and a consul, but the consul was for the moment uppermost). (ii) The whole point of the accusation is that Tiberius pretended voluntary withdrawal but in fact behaved like an exile: that is what *exulem egerit* means and there is therefore no need to change the text. 'On the pretext of voluntary withdrawal, he took the exile's part.' See Brink in *J.R.S.* 1951, p. 38.

aliquid quam. This is the reading of M, and not without difficulty. *aliquid* is certainly used in contexts where the contrast with other words produces a sense resembling 'something other' (Cic. *Verr.* V, 72, *cum mercaturas facerent aut aliquam ob causam nauigarent*), but it is nowhere in itself=*aliud quid* and is not followed by *quam* or any other comparative adverb. But the *quam* here can be explained (see Eriksson, p. 91) as following a suppressed *potius* (58, 1 n.); and *aliquid* following a negative and meaning 'anything' is in an emphatic context like this quite reasonable. 'Not even in those years (in Rhodes) were his thoughts of anything but resentment. . . .'

iram sq. For the 'resentment', 'hypocrisy' and 'excesses' of Tiberius, see Introd. V.

§ 5. **muliebri inpotentia.** Basically, *impotens* means 'lacking control' and can therefore be 'weak' or 'unbridled', according to which control we visualize as lacking. The noun *impotentia* almost invariably means 'lack of self-control' and so 'fury', 'violence'. 'There was his mother too, an imperious woman'; or 'with a woman's violence'. For the abl. see Introd. IV, 4 (ii d).

seruiendum. The emphasis on this word, and its close connexion with *feminae* shows Tacitus' sympathy with those who thus complained.

duobus . . . adulescentibus, i.e. Drusus, Tiberius' own son, now about 27 years old: and Germanicus, his adopted son.

interim, while Tiberius lived.

quandoque, 'at some time', i.e. 'one day', cf. *Ann.* VI, 20, *et tu, Galba, quandoque degustabis imperium.* With joint heirs, there was a possibility of civil war on the death of Tiberius.

5. § 1. agitantibus. *eis,* the subject of the abl. abs., is understood from the general sense of the preceding chapter. Cf. 29, 2, *orantibus*; 50, 4, *stratis.* This usage is common in Livy and Tacitus, but rare in classical Latin, occurring only when the subject can be directly derived from the previous sentence, cf. Caes. *B.G.* IV, 12, *at hostes nostros perturbauerunt: rursus resistentibus* (sc. *nostris*) . . .

grauescere, for the classical *ingrauescere.* The use of the simple verb in the sense of one of its compounds is a characteristic of Tacitean style. It is poetical in origin (cf. Lucr. IV, 1069, *aerumna grauescit*) and must have been especially congenial to Tacitus' liking for compression in style. Cf. 7, 3, *posuit* for *proposuit*; 14, 3, *solarentur* for *consolarentur*; 42, 1, *pietur* for *expietur*; 56, 4, *uertit* for *reuertit*; 70, 1, *uexerat* for *aduexerat*; 79, 1, *uerterentur* for *auerterentur*; 81, 1, *firmare* for *affirmare.*

suspectabant. For the story of the poisoned figs see Dio, LVI, 30. Neither this nor the story of Augustus' visit to Planasia (related by Dio as fact) is at all likely to be true. Both the details and the conception of the stories have been effectively disposed of by M. P. Charlesworth in *A.J.P.* 1923, pp. 145 sq.

quippe. From being an interjected question (*quid-pe* 'precisely why?') *quippe* developed into an explanatory conjunction 'for', 'inasmuch as'. It is not so used by Cicero, who prefers to employ it as an adverb emphasizing a causal *cum* or causal *qui* clause, but is common in the historians. Cf. Sall. *Cat.* 11, 7, *ii milites nihil reliqui uictis fecere. quippe secundae res sapientium animos fatigant.* Cf. 13, 2; 20, 2; 58, 1; 70, 4.

consciis . . . comite. Several people knew of the visit, but only Fabius had gone with him.

Fabio Maximo. Paullus Fabius Maximus, consul in 11 B.C., was later proconsul of Asia and *legatus Augusti* in Northern Spain. He was a friend of Ovid's, and several of the *Ep. ex Pont.* are addressed to him.

§ 2. quod . . . aperuisse. When the rel. pron. is purely formal, i.e. serving only to link main clauses and representing *et* with a demonstrative, it is found, in *Oratio Obliqua,* with an acc. and inf. This sentence therefore represents *et hoc Maximum . . . aperuisse.* Cf. Cic. *Fin.* III, 19, 64 (*philosophi*) *censent unum quemque nostrum mundi esse partem, ex quo illud natura consequi ut . . .* 'and that the natural consequence of this is . . .'. Cf. the similar use of the inf. with *ut—ita,* 12, 1 n.

Marciae. She was a cousin of Augustus', being the daughter of Atia Minor, sister of Augustus' mother Atia Maior. See Ovid, *Fasti* VI, 803–10.

gnarum. This passive use (=*notus*) is found first and almost exclusively in Tacitus. Cf. 51, 2; 63, 2; and the similar uses of *incautum*, 50, 2; *nescia*, 59, 5.

extincto Maximo . . . eius. The frequently quoted rule of the grammar books that the abl. abs. is not used if its subject appears elsewhere in the sentence in another case, is only relatively true. The rule is often disregarded—but always with the purpose of emphasizing the contents of the participial phrase. Here the detaching of *extincto* from *eius* makes it much more important. Cf. Caes. B.G. VI, 4, 4, (*Caesar*) *obsidibus imperatis hos Haeduis custodiendos tradit; Ann.* XVI,14, *hausto ueneno, tarditatem eius perosus . . . mortem adproperauit.* Cic. *Att.* X, 4, 6, *me libente eripies mihi hunc errorem.*

dubium an. For the innuendo see Introd. II. This phrase, like *incertum an*, develops from its use to introduce an indirect question a purely adverbial meaning ('doubtfully', 'perhaps') which has no effect on the construction; cf. *Ann.* XI, 18, *quae nimia et incertum an falso iacta.* The development begins in classical prose (cf. Cic. *De Sen.* 74; *Off.* III, 105) but is commoner in Livy and Tacitus.

§ 3. accitur. The historic present tense is used by most Roman writers to give a vivid picture of the action which is being related. Modern English accepts the present as a narrative tense only in colloquial (and some poetic) contexts, and it should therefore be avoided in translations of the historians.

neque satis conpertum. Velleius (II, 123) and Suetonius (*Aug.* 98) state that Augustus was still alive. Whether he was or not, the machinations here attributed to Livia are almost certainly pure invention—though not necessarily by Tacitus. See Charlesworth *loc. cit.*

spirantem. The omission of *utrum* is not unknown in classical Latin (Cic. *Part. Orat.* 65, *disputandum est aliud an idem sit*), but it is particularly common in Tacitus.

apud, 'in'—a meaning very common in the post-Augustan historians. Cf. *Ann.* VI, 11, *apud Romam.*

§ 4. namque. Cicero and Caesar use this only at the beginning of a phrase: its placing in second or third position begins with the poets and from there passes into post-Augustan prose. It is commonly so used by Livy.

rerum potiri. *potior* is found with the acc. (an archaic usage, found once in Tacitus—*Ann.* XI, 10, *potitusque regiam*), with the abl. (the normal classical usage) and with the gen., which is partitive in origin and is reasonably common all through the classical period: the gen. is invariable in this phrase.

Neronem. Of the nine references to Tiberius as Tiberius Nero or Nero, seven are unexceptionable because they refer to him before his adoption by Augustus (when he legally ceased to be a Nero). But in

4, 3 and 5, 4 the reference is to A.D. 14 and the use of the name must be deliberate and malicious—whether on the part of Tacitus, branding Tiberius as by birth no member of the house of Augustus, or on the part of his source, reflecting contemporary gossip and backbiting, cannot be certainly decided. (See Fabia in *W. K. Ph.* 1909, pp. 334–5; Martin in *C.Q.* 1955, p. 123, n. 1.)

fama tulit. For *fama fert* followed by an acc. and inf. clause, cf. Cic. *Rep.* II, 13, 25; Virg. *Aen.* VI, 502–3.

This account of the death of Augustus resembles the story of the death of Claudius in *Ann.* XII. See Introd. II, p. 8, n. 1.

6. § 1. primum facinus. Tacitus specializes in setting the emotional tone of a section of narrative by its opening sentence. With this chapter he turns from his synopsis of earlier history and starts on the reign of Tiberius, making no concealment of the kind of reign he considers it to be. Cf. *Ann.* XIII, 1, *prima nouo principatu mors.*

caedes. It has been suggested (*T.A.P.A.* 1947, p. 131) that the 'murder' of Postumus is part of the anti-Tiberian legend, and that in fact he died a natural death. It seems a remarkable and convenient coincidence if he did.

centurio. Suet. *Tib.* 22 states that the tribune *custos appositus* did the deed himself.

simulabat. The orders may well have come from Augustus, but Tacitus obviously feels that any villainy is likely to be Tiberius'.

praescripsisset. The subj. is virtual oblique: 'by which (so he said) Augustus had previously directed . . .'

custodiae. Probably not dat. of purpose ('set over him as a guard') but 'officer in charge of the guard'. Cf. *Ann.* II, 68, *Remmius . . . priori custodiae regis adpositus.*

quandoque. Here a relative adv.='at what time soever'. In this sense it usually has (as here) a future reference; cf. Cic. *Rep.* VI, 24, *quandoque sol iterum defecerit expletum annum habeto.* For the indefinite meaning see 4, 5.

§ 2. sine dubio. This grants a point—'admittedly'. Cf. 10, 4.

exilium. The word had become a general term for every kind of voluntary and involuntary banishment. Had Augustus simply banished Agrippa on his own authority, the sentence would have been revoked by his own death: he used the senatorial decree to ensure perpetual exile (Suet. *Aug.* 65).

in . . . necem durauit. This sense of *duro* 'to be hard, callous' is post-classical. For its use with *in* or *ad* and the acc. of goal, cf. *Ann.* XIV, 1 *credente nullo usque ad caedem eius duratura filii odia.* 'But he had never been callous enough to kill any of his family.'

credibile erat, 'men did not find it easy to believe that . . .'. It is not in fact difficult to credit, if Augustus thought Tiberius the more suitable successor.

nouercalibus. Augustus had adopted Postumus in A.D. 4. For the rhetorical use of *nouerca* see 3, 3 n. and cf. 10, 5; 33, 3.

festinauisse. The transitive use of this verb is, before the Silver Age, mainly poetical; cf. Virg. *Aen.* IV, 575, *festinare fugam*. See 52, 1.

§ 3. **mos militiae,** *factum est quod imperasti* was the formula in which a soldier reported 'operation completed'. Cf. Suet. *Tib.* 22 (which bears a close verbal resemblance to this passage) and id. *Claud.* 29.

neque . . . et. These conjunctions are used with two balancing statements when the first is negative, the second affirmative. Cf. 15, 1; 54, 2; 80, 2.

Sallustius Crispus. Tacitus, recording his death (A.D. 20) in *Ann.* III, 30, gives a brief sketch of his career. He was the great-nephew and adopted son of Sallust the historian, and was an adviser of Augustus and Tiberius, but preferred, like Maecenas, to exercise his influence privately and not through high office. As with Maecenas, his influence apparently waned in the later years of his life.

particeps secretorum, cf. *Ann.* III, 30, *praecipuus cui secreta imperatorum initerentur.* He was one of the *amici principis*, the men of experience and ability who had the entrée to the house of the Princeps. From this body Augustus and his successors drew a *consilium* of counsellors whenever they required one, and their immediate retinue (*cohors amicorum, comites*) for court or travel. It had no constitutional standing, but was to some extent formal in character—the *amici* were divided into *prima* and *secunda admissio* (to the morning reception) and used *ex prima admissione* and *amicus* as formal titles on inscriptions (*E. and J.* 230a and *I.L.S.* 5864). Their influence on imperial policy must at times have been great. See Crook, *Consilium Principis*, ch. III. Crispus belonged to the *prima admissio* (Sen. *Clem.* I, 10, 1), i.e. to the politically more important group.

subderetur. As often, the compound with *sub* suggests underhand dealing; cf. *surripio.* The meaning of 'substitute' is normal, but 'substitute falsely' is a special sense, found in Terence and developed by the historians. Cf. 39, 3, *reum subdere; Ann.* XIV, 40, *subdidit testamentum.*

iuxta periculoso, 'lying or telling the truth being equally dangerous'. The clauses stand as the subject of the abl. abs. Note the omission of the first *seu. promeret* is the protasis of an ideal condition (the apodosis being represented by the abl. abs.), becoming imperf. subj. because it is virtual oblique after *metuens.* 'For (he reflected) it would be equally dangerous whether he were to speak truth or falsehood.'

eam condicionem, 'it is the essential condition of autocracy that accounts do not balance unless submitted to (the autocrat) alone'. If

the ruler wishes to have supreme power, he must also have the ultimate
authority. The metaphors are taken from commercial life. For the
characteristic closing epigram see Introd. III.

7. § 1. ruere in seruitium. On Tacitus' attitude to the servility
of the Senate see Introd. II.

quis. See 2, 1 n. Under certain Emperors it was the distinguished
men who were in greatest danger.

uultuque composito, abl. of quality, giving variety of construction
after the participles.

ne. Tacitus omits subj. verbs only when the construction makes it
clear that it is a subj. which has to be supplied. The following categories
are found in *Ann.* I; (*a*) when another subj. follows in a connected
construction, e.g. 9, 1, two clauses with *quod*; 65, 1, with *cum*. (*b*) When
the conjunction (as here) or construction used makes a subj. verb inevitable, e.g. the indirect questions in 11, 1 and 4; 16, 3; 48, 3; 61, 4,
subord. clauses in indirect speech as in 9, 3; 40, 1 and 2; 47, 2, or
following *utinam* in 58, 2.

tristiores, 'over-gloomy'; the meanings 'rather' and 'too' are basic
to the comparative form, and persist although 'more' has become the
general meaning. Cf. Cic. *Sest.* 59, *suspicio durior* 'especially searching'.

§ 2. Sex. Pompeius. Both he and Appuleius were, according to
Dio, LVI, 29, related to Augustus. There was a connexion by marriage
between the *gens Pompeia* and Scribonia, first wife of Augustus (*Ann.*
II, 27): and the Appuleia mentioned in *Ann.* II, 50 as a great-niece of
Augustus is probably the sister of Sex. Appuleius. This relationship
may account for their holding the consulship for a whole year, by
this time an unusual practice.

in uerba . . . iurauere. This is not the specific oath *in acta principis*
(for which see 72, 1) but a general expression of loyalty from the whole
state and (eventually, see 34, 1) provinces. It did not of itself make
Tiberius Princeps, but it helped to show that he was the obvious
successor. The phrase means 'they swore to a formula concerning T.',
i.e. 'allegiance to T'. Cf. Livy, XXVIII, 29, *in uerba P. Scipionis iurarunt*.

Seius Strabo. A native of Vulsinii in Etruria (*Ann.* IV, 1), he was
father of Sejanus, for whom see 24, 2.

C. Turranius. He was still holding the office (for which see 2, 1)
in A.D. 48 (*Ann.* XI, 31). These two prefectures were the great Equestrian offices in Rome.

praetoriarum . . . praefectus. The Praetorian Guard was a development of the *cohors praetoria*, the bodyguard of Republican
generals. Augustus formed a permanent body of nine cohorts, and
these were stationed in various parts of Rome and Italy. Their duties
were to preserve law and order in Italy and to attend the Emperor and
his family (cf. 24, 1); their period of service was shorter and their pay

much higher than that of the legionary soldiers, and they did not see much active service. Somewhat naturally, the legions looked on them with envy. See 17, 6. Normally they had two prefects, but Sejanus, e.g. held office alone and it was he who gave the Guard its political importance by uniting all nine cohorts in one camp, just outside Rome. From then on the Praetorians played a considerable part in the making of Emperors.

senatus . . . populus. The Equites are presumably not mentioned specifically because they had not as a separate body the constitutional importance of the Senate or people, nor the military importance of the army.

§ 3. **consules.** With one Princeps dead and another not yet elected, the consuls were the magistrates on whom formal authority naturally devolved.

tamquam, here used with an abl. abs. As participial phrases came to be used more and more in the sense of certain subordinate clauses (temporal, conditional, concessive, causal), they began to have attached to them, to put the meaning beyond dispute, the relevant conjunction. This usage is found in the classical period (Cic. *Verr.* V, 64, *iste quasi praeda sibi aduecta . . . ducit*) and is greatly extended by the Silver Latin writers. It was probably encouraged by the parallel Greek construction of ὡς, ἅτε, &c. with the participle. Cf. § 5, *tamquam adepto principatu. quamquam* is similarly used in 24, 1; 48, 1; 55, 3; 65, 4; 72, 1; 76, 3; *quippe* in 79, 3; and *ut* (where the Greek influence is very clear) in 47, 3.

ambiguus imperandi. On the gen. see Introd. IV, 2 (i). Note the different constructions joined by *et*. Tiberius cannot have been at all uncertain of obtaining the Principate, though he may well have been genuinely disinclined to take it on. Hypocrisy is a possible explanation of his behaviour, but natural diffidence (cf. 80, 2, *anxium iudicium*) and a desire to act correctly are much more probable ones.

tribuniciae potestatis. See on 2, 1. He issued the edict as *Ti. Caesar trib. pot. xvi*, thus carefully emphasizing the legality of the power by which he did so.

posuit, for *proposuit*. See 5, 1 n.

sub Augusto. The use of *sub* with a proper name to indicate 'in the reign of', 'under the rule of', first becomes common in Livy.

§ 4. **parentis.** The word has more religious significance than *pater*. 'He would arrange about the honours to be paid to his father, but in the meantime was staying with the body.' He was escorting it on its journey from Nola to Rome.

idque unum, i.e. the summoning of the Senate.

§ 5. **signum,** the password or countersign for the guard. It is difficult to see who else had a better right to give it, Tiberius having been admitted as *collega imperii* in the previous year (Suet. *Tib.* 21); this would also justify the *excubiae*, &c. of the next sentence. Even if his *prouincia* did not yet extend to Italy (see *J.R.S.* 1951, p. 112), certain machinery clearly had to be kept in motion, and Tiberius was clearly the man to do it.

cetera, lictors, e.g. and *fasces* bound with laurel; the indefinite phrase makes them sound more in number and importance than they actually were.

miles. For the anaphora see on 1, 1. They must have escorted him only *to* the Senate House, because it is not until A.D. 33 (*Ann.* VI, 15) that we find Tiberius asking for a military escort to be permitted inside the House.

tamquam. See § 3.

adepto. Some deponents are occasionally used passively, especially in the perfect participle; cf. the common *meditatus* 'studied', 'considered' and Sall. *Cat.* 7, *adepta libertate.*

cum . . . loqueretur, 'whenever he spoke in the Senate'. For the subj. see Introd. IV, 5 (i).

§ 6. causa praecipua. Germanicus himself showed no signs of wishing to be *princeps.*

tot legiones, the eight legions on the Rhine (3, 5). These with the *auxilia* would give Germanicus an army of something under 100,000 men.

§ 7. dabat . . . famae, 'he conceded to public opinion that he should . . .' i.e. 'in deference to public opinion he wished . . .'. The phrase is used by Cicero (*quantum famae dandum sit, Tusc.* I, 109), Horace (*das aliquid famae, Sat.* II, 2, 94) and Seneca (*multa famae dare, Clem.* I, 15, 5); Tacitus alone substitutes an *ut* clause for the direct object.

uxorium . . . senili. Tacitus here uses adjs. in place of the commoner defining gen.: he also reverses the process—cf. *uirgines Vestae,* 8, 1 and *in campo Martis,* 8, 5. Both devices draw attention to the phrase because of its unusual form.

inductam, 'assumed' as a cloak (Luc. II, 387, *membra super induxisse togam*), or 'spread over' as a covering (Plaut. *Most.* 827, *si sunt (postes) inducti pice*).

nam uerba, 'every word, every look he would twist to some criminal significance, and store up in his memory'.

8. § 1. passus. The addition of *est* is unnecessary. Sörbom, pp. 151–6 has shown by examples that Tacitus and others do sometimes use a transitive deponent verb without the auxiliary. Cf. *Hist.* IV, 2, *locutus*; Livy, XXXIV, 17, 6, *passi* (as here, the only verb of the sentence); id. XLIV, 27, 8, *passus* (where, as here, an acc. and inf. clause depends on it).

supremis, 'last rites', 'funeral', cf. 61, 1. It is a general term for death and all the circumstances connected with it.

uirgines Vestae. The Romans used temples as safe-deposits, storing there important documents and money. The temple of Vesta was considered particularly sacred and so particularly safe. For the gen. replacing the more usual adj. see 7, 7 n.

Tiberium et Liuiam. Two thirds of the estate went to Tiberius, one third to Livia (Suet. *Aug.* 101).

in familiam Iuliam. She is accordingly after A.D. 14 called Augusta or Julia Augusta and, as Augustus' will adopted her, *diui Augusti filia.* Cf. *R.I.C.* I, Pl. VI, 104 SPQR IULIAE AUGUST. and *E. and J.* 126, *Iuliae Augustae, diui Augusti.*

nomen Augustum. See 9, 5 n.

in spem secundam, heirs in default; these were Drusus, son of Tiberius, and Germanicus, nephew of Tiberius; and the three sons of Germanicus. According to Suet. *Aug.* 101, one third was to go to Drusus and the rest to Germanicus and his sons.

plerosque inuisos. This seems a gratuitous slight on Augustus. Suetonius simply says *propinquos amicosque complures.*

iactantia, 'but (he had named them) from ostentation and a desire for glory in the eyes of posterity'. The clause is loosely attached, cut to the bones of the essential meaning, with that meaning expressed by the juxtaposition of nouns. *ad posteros* is almost equal to an adj., 'posthumous'. Livy uses it (II, 10, 11; IX, 29, 6) but Tacitus' use is bolder; cf. *Ann.* VI, 46, *in posteros ambitio.* Classical Latin prose did not make very free use of prepositional phrases directly attached to nouns: but the poets used them freely and it is from them that the Silver Age borrows the usage.

§ 2. **ciuilem,** 'of an ordinary citizen' and therefore not beyond the bounds of propriety.

populo et plebi. This must be a variation on the old formula *populo plebique,* and a reference to a legacy to the *plebs Romana.* There is no suggestion that it is a gift to the treasury, and against it are the facts that (*a*) the context deals with legacies to individuals and classes, not official benefactions, (*b*) *populo* in *Ann.* VI, 17 certainly means 'the State' but it stands in a constitutional context and is not a parallel, (*c*) Augustus was obviously accustomed to giving largess (*R.G.* 15) and would never have omitted the *plebs* from such a distribution. If the number of the *plebs* receiving largess is taken as about 200,000 (*R.G.* 15, referring to 2 B.C.), from 43,500,000 sesterces they would each receive about 200 sesterces—a slightly smaller sum than Augustus had previously distributed; but (i) he estimated his estate as smaller than it actually was (Suet. *Aug.* 101), (ii) Dio, LVII, 14, 2 states that Tiberius gave them 260 sesterces, but he may have increased it himself; cf.

Suet. *Tib.* 48 where a similar increase is recorded, (iii) he did give different sums at different times (Suet. *Aug.* 41 mentions 400, 300, 250).

quadringenties tricies. The sum is 43,500,000—435 times 100,000 sesterces. Large sums of sesterces are expressed by *centena milia sestertium* (gen. plural) multiplied by the necessary adverb, e.g. *decies centena milia sest.* = 1,000,000; *centena milia* is frequently omitted and *sestertium* then declined as a neuter singular, so that for 1,000,000 is found *decies sestertium(-ii)*—see 75, 3. Occasionally, as here in Tacitus, *sestertium* also is omitted: it was the regular unit of monetary measurement, and the presence of the adverb is sufficient to indicate that '100,000 sesterces' is to be supplied. Cf. Mart. V, 37, 24.

nummum. This is the original form of the gen. plural, which has been preserved in conservative contexts (mainly religious and legal, cf. *deum*), and in poetry.

urbanis quingenos. The phrase is missing from M but supplied from Suetonius and Dio. These cohorts, founded by Augustus, acted as the police force of Rome.

aut cohortibus ciuium R. These were composed of volunteers, often Italians, coming probably from areas from which the legions were no longer recruited. They seem to have been classed with legionary troops, though not part of a legion. We know from inscriptions of 32 or 33 such cohorts. 'To those who were members of a legion or citizen cohort he gave . . .'. Similar uses of *aut* = 'or in turn' are found in 9, 5; 16, 2; 30, 1; 55, 1; 64, 4.

§ 3. **quis**, a by-form of *quibus*, much used by Tacitus. Cf. 25, 3; 57, 1.

qui. Either the addition of *qui* or the omission of *uisi* is necessary in order to construe the sentence, and this is the easier change. 'The proposals which seemed most notable were those of Asinius Gallus and L. Arruntius, Gallus suggesting that . . .'

porta triumphali. By this gate a victorious general's triumphal procession entered Rome; its exact position is not certain, but it gave access to the Campus Martius. For the abl. see Introd. IV, 4, (iia).

Gallus Asinius. Asinius Gallus was the son of Asinius Pollio, the great literary patron of the Augustan age. He was consul in 8 B.C. and two year laters proconsul of Asia. Augustus judged him to be ambitious but not outstanding (13, 2) and Tiberius disliked him (12, 4). He was arrested in 30 (Dio, LVIII, 3) and died of starvation three years later (*Ann.* VI, 23).

Note the reversal of nomen and cognomen. It is found occasionally in Cicero (*Mil.* 8, Ahala Seruilius) where it seems to be connected with the omission of the praenomen. In Tacitus such reversal is frequet and quite arbitrary, probably being used simply to produce variety of style. Cf. Messala Valerius § 4.

tituli, *de ambitu, de maiestate, de maritandis ordinibus,* &c.—the titles of the Leges Iuliae.

L. Arruntius, cf. 76, 1; 79, 1. He was consul in A.D. 6 and a famous pleader. He incurred the enmity of Sejanus and later of Macro, was accused on a trumped-up charge in A.D. 37, and rather than fight a hopeless battle committed suicide (*Ann.* VI, 48).

§ 4. **Messala Valerius.** Son of Messala Corvinus and inheritor of his rhetorical gifts (*Ann.* III, 34), he was consul in 3 B.C. and legate of Illyricum during the rebellion of A.D. 6, gaining the *ornamenta triumphalia* for his work in Pannonia at that time (Vell. II, 112). Judging by the references in the *Annals* (cf. III, 18), he was over-anxious to be obsequious.

sacramentum. See 7, 2 n.

sponte. Its use without *sua* (*mea, tua,* &c.) is poetical. Cf. Virg. *Aen.* IV, 361.

ea sola species, 'that (show of independence) was the only form of flattery left': a bitter remark but, as far as Messala was concerned, perhaps not without justification.

§ 5. **remisit,** 'excused them'. Cf. Livy, V, 12, 13, *tribuni . . . de tributo remiserunt.* This apparent moderation showed arrogance (Tacitus thinks) because it implied that Tiberius claimed the right to demand or excuse the duty. According to Suet. *Aug.* 100 the Senators, though excused, did in fact bear Augustus' body to the Campus Martius.

funus diui Iulii. The bier was removed from the pyre prepared in the Campus, and carried to the Forum, where benches, robes, arms and jewels were thrown on to it as it was burned there. See Suet. *Iul.* 84.

Martis. For the gen. see 7, 7 n.

sede destinata. This was a site near the Mausoleum, a circular tomb for the Imperial family, begun by Augustus in 28 B.C. (Suet. *Aug.* 100). It stood on the Campus Martius near the Tiber, and part of it is still preserved.

§ 6. **seruitii . . . libertatis,** gen. of quality; *crudus* is 'raw', 'immature'.

occisus . . . Caesar, 'the murder of Caesar'. This use of noun and participle in the sense of an abstract verbal noun begins with prepositional phrases (*ab urbe condita, ante solem occasum*—in *Ann.* I, cf. 3, 6, *ob amissum . . . exercitum:* 20, 1, *ante coeptam seditionem;* 50, 1, *ob amissum Augustum;* 53, 2, *post interfectum Postumum*) but soon extends to the useful nominative, cf. Caes. *B.C.* I, 26, 2, *ea res saepe temptata . . . tardabat.* It is the action or state denoted by the participle which is important in these phrases, more important than the person or thing which is, sometimes quite illogically, the grammatical subject. Cf. 16, 1, *mutatus princeps;* 36, 2, *gnarus et inuasurus hostis;* 42, 1, *occisus* *pronepos, interfecta nurus*; 52, 1, *nuntiata ea*; 59, 1, *rapta uxor, subiectus uterus*. See also Introd. IV, 7 (iv).

senem. Augustus was 76 when he died, and had been princeps for 41 years.

longa potentia, abl. of attendant circumstances. (Introd. IV, 4 (iic)).

foret. *forem* is an archaic subjunctive form which is very rarely used by the strictly classical writers, but which the historians made peculiarly their own. Sallust, Livy and Tacitus all use it as the equivalent of *essem*. In *Ann.* I–XII it occurs at least twice as often as *essem*.

9. § 1. multus . . . sermo. The presentation of cc. 9 and 10 is important. See Introd. II.

uana. Certain coincidences, which some people thought significant, Tacitus dismisses as meaningless.

dies. On 19th August 43 B.C. he was elected to his first consulship. Supply *esset*—see 7, 1 n.

Octauius, a necessary addition, because Julius Caesar was also his 'father' by adoption.

finiuisset, subj. of virtual oblique, giving the reason they put forward for their amazement.

§ 2. numerus. He held the consulship 13 times, Marius 7 times and Corvus 6. Corvus was a hero of the fourth-century B.C. See Livy, VII–X.

septem et triginta annos, consecutively from 23 B.C. See on 2, 1.

nomen inperatoris. Not the praenomen (Imperator Caesar), but the salutation formerly granted on the field to a successful general. As the Princeps was Commander-in-Chief and the armies fought under his auspices, successes by his legates brought salutations to him. Both uses of *imperator* are found in Augustus' titles, e.g. *E. and J.* 82, *imp. Caesar diui f. Augustus pontifex maxim. cos. XIII, imp. XX, tribunic. potest. XXXVII P.P.* For the gen. see Introd. IV, 2 (iv).

alia honorum, partitive gen. See Introd. IV, 2 (iii).

multiplicata aut noua, e.g. he celebrated three triumphs and two ovations, and fifty-five *supplicationes* were offered for his successes (*R.G.* 4); the name Augustus was a unique honour, as was the complimentary mission which met him in Campania on his return from the East in 19 B.C. (*qui honos ad hoc tempus nemini praeter me est decretus, R.G.* 12).

§ 3. hi. The verb of saying is understood from the immediate context.

parentem, Julius Caesar, his adoptive father. Cf. *patris*, § 4.

in qua. For the omission of the subj. see 7, 1 n.

per bonas artis. See 3, 4 n. Here it means rather 'by honourable methods'.

§ 4. dum. Octavian used Antony and Lepidus as long as it was convenient to himself, and then shed them. The point for the defence

is that, while avenging Caesar, he was forced to countenance deeds
he would otherwise have abhorred, in order to get the help he needed.

ut, a necessary addition to the text: *quam* appears with the subj.
after *potius, prius,* &c. (35, 4), but there the subj. clause stands in its own
right: whereas after a comparative adj. + noun, an explanatory *ut*
clause is required to balance the noun. See Brink in *J.R.S.* 1951, p. 45,
n. 71.

§ 5. **non regno.** See note on *principis* 1, 1.

mari Oceano. The adjectival use of nouns in apposition is commonest in the poets (*aduena exercitus*, Virg. *Aen.* VII, 38), but not
unknown in prose writers. Cf. Cic. *Phil.* XI, 39, *tirones milites.* Personal
names are also used in this way, cf. 8, 1, *nomen Augustum.*

amnibus longinquis, esp. the Rhine, the Danube and the Euph-
rates. This is a somewhat optimistic definition of the boundaries of the
Empire, but even if these were not entirely the ocean and the great
rivers, they were far enough away to give Rome a sense of security.

conexa. Augustus' was the first real attempt at centralization.

magnifico ornatu, abl. of quality (Introd. IV, 4 (*iid*)) used as the
predicate of the sentence. Augustus boasted (Suet. *Aug.* 28) that he had
found a city of brick and left one of marble. His buildings, which
included the Temple of Palatine Apollo and the Theatre of Marcellus,
are listed, with restorations and other public works, in *R.G.* 19 sq.
He not only built, he planned, so that whole areas of fine new buildings
stood as a memorial to him.

10. § 1. **dicebatur,** 'it was said that . . .'. This passive of *dico, trado,*
&c. is regularly personal in the present tenses (*Aristaeus inuentor olei
fuisse dicitur*) and impersonal in the perfect stem (*traditum est Homerum
caecum fuisse*). But the impersonal construction is also regular when
(*a*) there is an auxiliary verb (*dici potest*), (*b*) there is an adverb or dative
attached to the verb (*contra dicitur; nuntiatur Afranio magnos commeatus
ad flumen constitisse*), (*c*) the verb is essentially impersonal in meaning,
e.g. *adfertur* 'news was brought' (cf. 33, 1 and Livy, IV, 55, 1). There
are a few exx. even in classical prose of impersonal *dicitur* without
these qualifications, and they become increasingly common in the
later writers.

obtentui, dat. of purpose. See Introd. IV, 3 (v).

ceterum, 'but in fact'; for this meaning, cf. 14, 2 and 44, 4. It is a
strengthening and particularizing of the ordinary adversative meaning
which, used in contrast to a word meaning 'pretence', can itself indicate
'but in reality'. Cf. Sall. *Jug.* 76, *simulabat . . . ceterum.*

ueteranos. In 44 B.C. Octavian raised (without authorization, hence
priuato) the veterans settled in Casilinum and Calatia, by a gift of
500 denarii to each (Cic. *Att.* XVI, 8). *adulescens* adds further disapproval
—'a mere youth'.

legiones. The IVth legion and the legio Martia deserted Antony (consul of 44) in November of that year. Cic. (*Phil*. III, 6–7) argues that the *legio Martia* judged Antony to be no longer consul. Tacitus implies an unconstitutional act on the part of Octavian.

Pompeianarum . . . partium, 'and that his support for the Senatorial party was feigned'. The gen. is objective. Antony's refusal to have anything to do with the young Octavian drove him to associate with the Senatorial party, to whom also Antony was an enemy. Octavian was willing to use any means to establish his position. That *Pompeianae* here means 'Senatorial', i.e. the party which had been Pompey the Great's, and not that of Sextus Pompeius, is made clear by a specific reference to his treatment of Sextus in § 3.

§ 2. fascis. He was granted the status of senator with the rank of pro-praetor, on the motion of Cicero on 1st January, 43 (Cic. *Phil*. V, 46), and shared with the consuls a military command against Antony (Suet. *Aug*. 10; *R.G.* 1). Note the innuendo of *inuaserit* to describe a perfectly legal action.

Hirtio et Pansa, consuls of 43 B.C. Pansa, on his way to join his colleague at Mutina, was attacked by Antony and suffered a serious wound from which he afterwards died; Hirtius was killed in the victory at Mutina. The suggestions of foul play are entirely without foundation. See Introd. II.

sui. See 12, 3 n.

machinator. See 4, 4 n.

abstulerat. The indicative shows that this is an aside by Tacitus and not part of the main statement. The verb is singular because Caesar is not only the nearer but the more important subject. Cf. 56, 2 n.

occupauisse, again an exaggeration. Octavian refused to surrender Pansa's legions, the others refused to be surrendered.

senatu, probably dat.: the form is well attested (*Ann*. III, 47, *senatu scripsit*) and it was in fact *from* the Senate that Octavian extorted the consulship (Suet. *Aug*. 26). It is therefore likely that *senatu* is dat. of disadvantage, and not abl. abs.

contra rem publicam. Antony was necessary to Octavian's plans and therefore, having established his right to treat with him on equal terms, he joined forces with him.

proscriptionem. See 2, 1 n.

diuisiones agrorum. After the formation of the Triumvirate in 43 B.C., its members allotted land to their veterans: in this allocation Virgil lost his patrimony.

ipsis . . . qui fecere, 'not even by their perpetrators'. When a relative clause is a pure paraphrase of a noun, it frequently retains its ndic. verb even in *Oratio Obliqua*. Cf. Cic. *Arch*. 9, 20, *putabat ea, quae* *gesserat, posse celebrari* 'his exploits'; c. 28, 3, *quae casus obtulerat*; 36, 3, *quae petiuerant*; 39, 2, *quae . . . expresserant*; 58, 4, *quod . . . concepit, quod . . . est*; 39, 2, *quae . . . expresserant. ipsis* is dat. of the agent, see Introd. IV, 3 (iv).

§ 3. **Brutorum,** Marcus, who committed suicide after his defeat at Philippi, and Decimus, killed in Gaul in 43.

quamquam. This limits the concession made by *sane.* 'Granted that the deaths of Cassius and the Bruti had been an offering to an hereditary quarrel (though private enmities ought to be sacrificed to the public good).'

sed . . . sed. The anaphora (1, 1 n.) emphasizes that no excuse is possible here.

Pompeium. Sextus Pompeius had been granted certain concessions by the treaty of Misenum in 39, but in the following year Octavian accused him of violating the treaty and attacked him.

Lepidum. See 2, 1 n.

Tarentino . . . foedere. The treaties of Brundisium (40 B.C.) and Tarentum (37 B.C.) marked uneasy and temporary reconciliations between Octavian and Antony. They are here out of chronological order because of the connexion with the marriage of Octavia, which was provided for by the treaty of Brundisium: and because it is a common rhetorical device so to reverse normal order.

§ 4. **cladis.** M. Lollius suffered defeat at the hands of raiding Germans in (probably) 17 B.C. It seems likely that the 'disaster' was magnified by Velleius (see *J.R.S.* 1933, p. 17) and was in fact no more than a temporary setback. For Varus see Introd. VI.

Varrones. The plurals are generalizing—'men like Varro'; also, the executions sound more impressive in the plural. Varro Murena, brother-in-law of Maecenas, was involved in a conspiracy against Augustus in 23 B.C. and executed; Egnatius Rufus was executed for leading a similar conspiracy in 19 B.C., and Iullus Antonius, son of M. Antony and Fulvia, was forced to commit suicide in 2 B.C. because of his adultery with Julia, daughter of Augustus.

§ 5. **abstinebatur.** Tacitus suddenly inserts a passage of narrative to relieve the monotony of extensive *Oratio Obliqua.* With *nihil* the indirect quotation is resumed.

abducta. A verb such as *memorabatur* is understood from the general sense of gossip in the context. Tiberius Nero's willingness to divorce Livia makes it difficult to justify *abducta.*

que tedii et. The text is corrupt beyond certain restoration. The best suggestions seem to be *C. Matii et* (Matius was a friend of Augustus' (Plin. *H.N.* XII, 13) and is mentioned with Pollio in *Ann.* XII, 60) or *Q. Vitellii et* (mentioned as *prodigus* in *Ann.* II, 48 where M has *que* for Q.).

Vedii Pollionis. He was an *eques* whose one piece of public service appears to have been the organization of taxation in Asia, after Actium. He was noted for his wealth and cruelty (Dio, LIV, 23), especially for his practice of throwing live slaves to his lampreys.

grauis . . . nouerca. She was disastrous as a mother because she contrived to make her son Tiberius Princeps (which Tacitus considers ruinous to the state), and as a stepmother because, according to the charges mentioned in c. 3, she was responsible for the death of Augustus' natural heirs.

§ 6. **templis et effigie,** instrumental abls. *effigie numinum* means 'with statues like those of the gods', in divine guise and with divine attributes.

coli uellet. The paying of divine honours to a living Emperor or his *Genius* was not 'deification' in the strict sense (that had to be awarded after the Emperor's death). For Augustus it was politically necessary to succeed to the attributes of the Hellenistic monarchs, and his worship in the East meant little more than an expression of gratitude and a recognition of the great position of the Emperor. It was also a convenient expression of loyalty. In Italy his *Genius* was honoured, as the *genius* of the head of a family was honoured in private worship: he was recognized as head of the family of the state. In the Western provinces the imperial cult was deliberately instituted as a political measure, in the hope that the peoples who met in assembly to honour Rome and Augustus would gradually become more Romanized and tractable. There was thus great variety of Emperor-worship, the different forms depending on local political necessity.

Tacitus' statement here is misleading. Only in the East were there temples to the living Augustus, elsewhere the worship was at altars (cf. *ara Vbiorum*, 39, 1); he did not have a *flamen* until he was dead and *diuus*: and he encouraged the imperial cult, not from any desire for personal divinity, but from a recognition of its political importance.

§ 7. **ne . . . quidem,** 'he had not even adopted Tiberius from any personal affection or regard for the interests of the state'.

comparatione deterrima. The phrase is compressed from *comparatione cum deterrimo homine*, 'comparison with one so inferior'.

paucis ante annis, probably in A.D. 4, when Tiberius was granted the power for the second time. See 3, 3 n.

quamquam. See 7, 3 n.

honora, a poetic word. Cf. Val. Fl. 4, 342.

habitu, 'deportment, style of dress and habits'. Suet. *Tib.* 68 describes his mannerisms, and Augustus' attempt to excuse them as *naturae uitia, non animi.*

excusando. See Introd. IV, 4 (ii e).

exprobraret, a final relative clause, indicating the intention of Augustus to criticize.

§ 8. **templum.** This was begun shortly afterwards by Tiberius and Livia (Dio, LVI, 46, 3), and dedicated by Gaius (Dio, LIX, 7, 1).

caelestes religiones, a variation on the usual *caelestes honores*. Augustus was now *diuus* and worshipped as such.

11. § 1. **modestia,** 'diffidence'. Cf. *Ann*. III, 56. See Introd. V.

diui, the normal reference to a dead and deified Emperor. Sometimes it is merely formal, with no more emotional meaning than 'the late Emperor'; here it has deeper significance—'the Great Augustus'. 'Divine' is misleading, because the divinity conferred was more formal than the English adj. implies.

tantae molis. The phrase echoes one of Virgil's. See Introd. III.

in partem curarum, 'to share his responsibilities'. *curae* is similarly used of affairs of state in *Hist*. II, 67, *numquam ita ad curas intento Vitellio* and *Hist*. IV, 2, *Domitianus nondum ad curas intentus*.

experiendo, 'from experience'. Only the past participle is at all common in this meaning in the classical period. See note on *experientia*, 4, 3.

quam arduum. *esset* is understood. See 7, 1 n.

non. The verb is jussive but the negative is *non* because it belongs not to the verb but to *unum*. Cf. Cic. *Cael*. 42, *non omnia uoluptatibus denegentur*.

§ 2. **Tiberio.** For the dat. see Introd. IV, 3 (ii).

occuleret. For the subj. see 3, 7 n.

suspensa, 'hesitant'. Cf. Suetonius' description of the scene (*Tib*. 24) *ambiguis responsis et callida cunctatione suspendens*. For a more literal use of the participle, cf. *suspenso gradu* 'on tiptoe'.

in incertum. See 4, 2 n.

§ 3. **si ... uiderentur,** 'whose only fear was to seem to understand'. The *si* clause is here an explanatory noun clause. Cf. Cic. *Fam*. VII, 10, 4, *unum mihi esse solacium, si sciam* ('my only consolation is, to know'). In Tacitus, cf. *Ann*. I, 49, 3, *nec aliter posse placari ... quam si ... honesta uulnera accepissent; Ann*. XVI, 5, *grauior inerat metus, si spectaculo defuissent*. The subj. is virtual oblique, representing the fear in their minds.

cum ... iussit, 'inverse' *cum*, containing the main statement of the sentence and so having an indicative verb. Cf. 16, 1, *cum ... incessit*; 19, 1, *cum ... omisere*; 51, 3, *cum ... clamitabat*.

libellum. Suet. *Aug*. 101 records that three documents were deposited by Augustus along with his will, (*a*) one containing directions for his funeral, (*b*) the Res Gestae, (*c*) the list here referred to—a summary of the military and financial resources and expenditure of the Empire. Tiberius wished it to be read to emphasize the greatness of the Empire and the consequent burden of rule for one man.

§ 4. **opes publicae** sq. Note how Tacitus avoids a monotonous catalogue by variety of arrangement—*quantum* with a partitive gen.

is followed by the adjectival *quot*, the asyndeton *classes, regna, prouinciae* is followed by a phrase subdivided by *aut* and that in turn by a phrase connected by *et* and itself divided by *ac*.

regna, the client kingdoms, such as Cappadocia and Commagene, whose rulers acknowledged Rome's suzerainty.

tributa . . . uectigalia. *tributum* was money paid in direct taxation by the provincials, on land and property. *uectigalia* were indirect taxes—dues on goods using harbours and certain frontiers, death duties, taxes on auction sales, &c.; Italians as well as provincials paid these. The difference between *tributum* and *uectigal* is the difference between Income Tax and e.g. Entertainment Tax.

necessitates . . . largitiones, 'essential expenditure' (upkeep of the army and public services, e.g.) and 'gifts' (the largess expected of the Emperor from time to time).

incertum. This is not the adverbial usage noted in 5, 2 but an ellipse of *incertum* (*est utrum*) . . . *an*. On the suggested motives see Introd. II.

12. § 1. inter quae. *inter* is used in a temporal sense='during'. Cf. 3, 7, *inter bella ciuium* and Cic. *Q. fr.* III, 1, 19, *haec inter cenam Tironi dictaui*. The historians extend the usage to produce *inter haec* (Livy, I, 29, 1) and *inter quae* as equivalents of the adverb *interea*, 'meanwhile'. Cf. 15, 2; 75, 2. Similarly they use *post quae*=*postea*: cf. 13, 1.

obtestationes, 'supplications', 'entreaties'; a rare sense of the word, but cf. Livy, XXVII, 50, *matronae . . . in preces obtestationesque uersae*.

procumbente, 'with the Senate sinking to the most abject entreaties'. Suet. *Tib.* 24 says that they actually fell at his feet (*procumbentem sibi ad genua*), but the verb is here metaphorical. Its use is, however, significant.

forte, 'casually', 'incidentally', without realizing the possible consequences of his remark.

ut . . . ita. These adverbs, which properly mark a comparison, are also used to indicate a contrast ('though . . . yet', 'granted . . . but'). Cf. 42, 3. The *ut* clause is by strict grammar subordinate, but the subordination is purely formal and the clauses are, logically, parallel main statements, both becoming acc. and inf. in *Or. Ob.* (See note on *quod . . . aperuisse*, 5, 2). Cf. Cic. *Cluent.* 138, *ex quo intellegi potuit, ut mare uentorum ui agitari, sic populum Romanum hominum seditiosorum uocibus concitari*.

§ 2. Asinius Gallus. See 8, 3 n. Taking this question in conjunction with Augustus' opinion of Gallus (13, 2), we may perhaps assume it to have had malicious intent.

respondit. Dio, LVII, 2, 6 gives as his answer 'How can the same man both divide and choose?'

cui. The dat. is rare with *excuso*: it is an extension of that used with *adimere*, &c. (Introd. IV, 3 (i)). For *in uniuersum* ('altogether') see 4, 2 n.

§ 3. **etenim** sq., 'for he had guessed from Tiberius' expression that he was offended'.

sua. *suus* is often used thus to indicate an emphatic 'his *own*' even though it does not strictly refer to the subject of the clause or sentence. Cf. Caes. *B.G.* I, 28, 3, *Heluetios . . . in fines suos reuerti iussit*: in *Ann.* I, 10, 2, *sui milites Hirtium et . . . Caesar abstulerat*; 41, 1, *non florentis Caesaris neque suis in castris (erat) facies*; 79, 3, *quae sua ora fluminibus . . . dederit*.

laudem de Augusto. The construction with *de* is explained by the fact that *laus*='an expression of praise', a meaning commoner in the plural (*funebres laudes*, e.g.='funeral oration'). Nouns of statement or speech are followed by *de*, cf. Cic. *Vat.* 1, 3, *nullum sermonem de Sestio accusando fuisse*.

quaeque in toga, 'in civil life', the toga being a cumbersome garment, suitable only for peaceful pursuits. Cf. the common *togatus*= civilian.

§ 4. **nec ideo,** 'but in spite of that he did not appease his anger'. For a similar use, cf. Cic. *Balb.* 35, *neque ideo est Gaditanorum causa deterior*.

tamquam . . . agitaret. See Introd. IV, 5 (iii).

Vipsania. See Introd. V.

ferociam. Pollio's literary judgments were famous for their severity—in most of the criticisms quoted by Quintilian &c., he appears as the subject of *reprehendit*. For a general estimate of him, see Sen. *Contr.* IV, *praef.* 3.

13. § 1. **post quae.** See 12, 1 n.

L. Arruntius. See 8, 3 n.

haud multum discrepans, an abbreviated statement: 'with a speech little different from that of Gallus, gave equal offence'.

Tiberio. For the dat. of possession see Introd. IV, 3 (ii).

Arruntium. Nipperdey points out Tacitus' habit of repeating a proper name when a pronoun appears to him too unemphatic. This happens especially when, as here, one of a pair is being singled out. Cf. 14, 3, *quo minus idem pro Druso postularetur, . . . quod designatus consul Drusus praesensque erat*. Tr. 'though Tiberius harboured no long-standing grievance against *him*'.

artibus egregiis, pari fama. For the abls. see Introd. IV, 4 (ii *d*). 'He mistrusted him as being wealthy, active, a man of considerable accomplishments and with a comparable reputation among the people.'

publice. For the adv. used with a noun see 3, 3 n.

§ 2. **quippe.** See 5, 1 n.

adipisci. This depends alike on *abnuerent*, *uellent* and *possent cuperentque*. Augustus divided possible aspirants into three classes, (*a*) those with capacity but no desire to rule. (*b*) those with the desire but no capacity, (c) those with both capacity and desire: obviously the last was the most dangerous category.

aut ... uel. *uel* is sometimes used = *aut*, i.e. to present incompatible alternatives. It rarely has this meaning in classical Latin, except in the poets. Tacitus uses it several times (cf. *Ann.* XIV, 35, *uincendum illa acie uel cadendum esse*), but only here do *aut* and *uel* appear together with complete identity of meaning.

M. Lepidum. Professor Syme (*J.R.S.* 1955, pp. 22–33) has shown beyond reasonable doubt that here, and in all other passages except *Ann.* III, 22 and 32, the Lepidus referred to must be Marcus (M.) and not Manius (M'.). The Manius Lepidus of the period (consul A.D. 11), grandson of the Triumvir, seems to have been a comparative nonentity, while Marcus Lepidus (consul A.D. 6) had marriage connexions with the Imperial family, distinguished himself in the Illyrian campaign, was awarded the *ornamenta triumphalia*, and is described by Velleius (II, 114–15) as *uir nomini ac fortunae Caesarum proximus*. He is clearly the better candidate for the description *capacem (imperii)*.

casus, 'opportunity'. This meaning is not common, but cf. *Ann.* IV, 50, *ne ... casum insidiantibus aperirent* and Sall. *Jug.* 56, 4, *fortunam illis praeclari facinoris casum dare.*

§ 3. consentitur. For Tacitus' use of historical sources see Introd. II.

Cn. Pisonem. He figures largely in *Ann.* II and III. Appointed legate of Syria in A.D. 17, he quarrelled with Germanicus and was suspected of poisoning him. He returned to Rome and stood his trial before the Senate; though the charge of poisoning was obviously absurd, that of insubordination was not, and Piso committed suicide to avoid condemnation (A.D. 20, *Ann.* III, 9 sq.).

omnes sq. There is exaggeration here. *omnes* cannot have been more than two; Tiberius did not trump up a charge against Piso; Gallus was not arrested until 30 and died in prison in 33; and Arruntius was Macro's victim, not Tiberius' (*Ann.* VI, 48). The vague statement gives an impression of Tiberius' agency, which is not borne out by the facts.

§ 4. Q. Haterius. Already an old man (he died in A.D. 26 aged nearly 90), he was an orator noted for his impetuous delivery. Tacitus' notice of his death (*Ann.* IV, 61) discusses his rhetorical powers.

Mamercus Scaurus. Again his obituary (*Ann.* VI, 29) gives us some information. He was of noble family and a distinguished orator, but of low character. He was twice accused of treason, in 32 (*Ann.* VI, 9) and 34 (ibid. 29), and in 34 committed suicide before the verdict was pronounced.

perstrinxere. *perstringere* = 'to graze', 'chafe', 'grate upon'. Cf. Hor. *Od.* II, 1, 17, *iam nunc minaci murmure cornuum perstringis aures* and **Tac.** *Dial.* 27, *si quid forte aures uestras perstringat.*

quo usque, 'how long'? lit. 'to what point?' Cf. Cic. *Cat.* I, 1, *quo usque tandem abutere, Catilina, patientia nostra?*

ex eo, explained by the *quod* clause: 'from the fact that . . .'.

relationi. The consuls' motion is nowhere quoted by Tacitus, but it is obvious that some proposal to elect Tiberius as Augustus' successor must have been before the house.

intercessisset. The power of veto belonged peculiarly to the tribune. On *trib. pot.* see 2, 1 n.

tramisit. This verb is common in Silver Latin for the classical *praetermitto,* 'pass over', 'disregard'.

§ 5. flexit. *flecto* is used intransitively mainly by the poets and post-Augustan writers, both literally and metaphorically. Cf. *Hist.* II, 70, *inde Vitellius Cremonam flexit* 'turned his course to': *Ann.* IV, 37, *arguebatur in ambitionem flexisse* 'turned his attention to'; *Ann.* I, 34, *flexit ad uictorias triumphosque* 'turned to the topic of'.

suscipi, i.e. he did not say *suscipio imperium*: the tense is the present of agreement, not the future of promise. Tacitus implies that the decision went by default, but surely some definite acceptance must have been made. Suet. *Tib.* 24 supports this: *recepit imperium,* he says, and quotes a condition of acceptance made by Tiberius.

rogari desineret. See 34, 2 n.

§ 6. deprecandi causa, 'to apologize'.

genua. *aduolui* is usually followed by a dat. (cf. 23, 1, *pedibus aduolutus:* 32, 2, *cum . . . pedibus Caecinae aduolueretur*), but on four occasions Tacitus uses the acc. See Introd. IV, 1 (i), and cf. *Ann.* XV, 71, *genua ipsius aduolui.*

an. From its proper use in disjunctive clauses, *an* came to be used as a disjunctive particle between nouns, showing no essential difference in meaning or construction from *aut* or *uel.* Cicero uses it in this way in his letters and later philosophical and rhetorical works (*Att.* VII, 1, 9, *quibusdam litteris ex Epiro an Athenis datis*), and it is also found in Livy and Sallust. Tacitus makes frequent use of it, cf. 65, 3, *metu an contumacia.*

donec . . . oraret, purely temporal. For the subj. see Introd. IV, 5 (ii).

curatissimis, 'over which care is taken' and so here 'urgent': *accuratus* is the common classical word, but cf. Plin. *Ep.* IX, 13, 10, *secreto curatoque sermone.*

14. § 1. parentem . . . matrem. Holders of the title *pater patriae* (72, 1 n.) seem to be referred to equally as *parens patriae* (cf. *I.L.S.* 71 and 72). It is probably here suggested simply as the form in which, without adaptation, a traditional title could be conferred on a woman.

appellandam . . . ut. These are equally possible constructions with *censeo,* and are here used together to introduce variety into the construction.

Iuliae filius, i.e. that his official title, instead of the usual *Ti. Caesar Aug. f.* should be *Ti. Caesar Aug. f. Iuliae f.*, which was unprecedented in Roman nomenclature.

§ 2. **feminarum,** objective gen.—'honours paid to women'.

dictitans. Tacitus does use the frequentative in the sense of the simple verb (see 4, 1 n.), but here *dictito* has its proper meaning 'saying repeatedly', i.e. on each occasion when honours were offered to Livia.

eadem . . . temperantia. Tiberius refused all unusual honours, even some that Augustus had held, e.g. *Imperator* as praenomen and *pater patriae*.

ceterum. See 10, 1 n.

inuidia, abl. of cause. Cf. Livy, IX, 46, 9, *anxios inuidia*.

in deminutionem. *in* with the acc. here expresses the end of the action; 'regarding high rank in a woman as tending to diminish his own'.

lictorem. Tiberius himself, as Emperor, was attended by twelve lictors.

aram. As well as its proper meaning of 'sacrificial altar' *ara* can mean a tombstone or monument erected *honoris causa*. Cf. Cic. *Phil.* XIV, 34 and Suet. *Nero 50*. The *ara* here suggested would have commemorated Livia's adoption by Augustus, as *arae* commemorated the delivery of Agrippina (Suet. *Gaius 8*).

§ 3. **proconsulare imperium.** This is clearly not simply a renewal of his command, made necessary by the death of Augustus (as Furneaux says), but the association in the general power which indicates a possible successor: the reference to Drusus shows that.

solarentur, for *consolarentur*. See 5, 1 n.

quo minus. *quominus* and *quin* are found after *causa* when *causa* expresses a reason for prevention. Cf. Sall. *Cat.* 51, 41, *hanc ego causam, quo minus nouum consilium capiamus, magnam puto*. Here *ea causa* is nom. and *fuit* is understood; 'the fact that D. was consul designate and in Rome was the reason that prevented the same request being made for him'. Tr. 'But the same request was not made for Drusus, because he was consul designate and in Rome'. For the repetition of the name Drusus, see 13, 1 n.

quod sq. He was to hold *imperium* as consul: and *proconsulare imperium* (other than *maius*) could not be exercised in the city.

praesens erat. The periphrastic conjugation, found in early and colloquial Latin (Plaut. *Poen.* 1038, *ut tu sis sciens*) is used by the classical writers only in special circumstances, usually where the participle is still strongly adjectival. Cf. Cic. *Off.* I, 4, 11, *quod adest quodque praesens est* and see Introd. IV, 7 (i). *praesens* is all but an adj., and the periphrasis is here convenient for it allows *erat* to be used as a common verb.

§ 4. **nominauit,** examined their qualifications and formally approved their candidature (by issuing a list of the names approved, hence the verb). This had been, in Republican times, the duty of the consul as presiding magistrate, and the Princeps seems to have continued to do it even when not holding office as consul. It remained possible for the presiding consul to 'nominate' other suitable candidates. From the complete list of nominations the elections were made. See also note on *commendaret*, 15, 1.

numerum. Tacitus has either misunderstood his source or compressed it into obscurity. What Tiberius refused to raise must have been the number, not of nominations, but of praetorships. The normal number of praetors elected was twelve (Dio, LVI, 25, 4) and it is difficult to see what benefit or honour would have come to Tiberius from nominating more. Admittedly about A.D. 33, more than twelve praetors were occasionally and for special reasons elected (Dio, LVIII, 20, 5): but Tiberius may perhaps be allowed to change his mind in 20 years and adapt his oath to the needs of the moment. See Marsh, pp. 296 sq.; *J.R.S.* 1955, p. 19.

obstrinxit. Tacitus again uses this verb intransitively (= *affirmo*) in *Ann.* IV, 31, *ut iure iurando obstringeret e re publica id esse.*

15. § 1. **tum primum** sq. When Augustus 'restored the Republic' in 27 B.C., he also restored the ancient system of election of magistrates, by the *comitia centuriata* and *comitia tributa* (Suet. *Aug.* 40, 2). These continued to make the formal election, but Tiberius in A.D. 14 gave to the Senate effective control of the elections by allowing it to select names to form a list of nominations exactly corresponding to the number of offices to be filled, and to send this list to the centuries and tribes purely for ratification. Tacitus is here talking of elections to the Praetorship, which happened to be the first to occur after the accession of Tiberius, but there is no reason to suppose that the Senate's privilege was limited to these. There is no record of legislation about this transfer simply because it *was* a privilege and the formal method of election remained unchanged. See 81, 1 on the consular elections.

e campo. The Assemblies met in the Campus Martius, and the word is sometimes used for the Assemblies themselves. Cf. Cic. *De Or.* III, 42, 167 (on Metonymy), *ex quo genere haec sunt . . . campum (appellare) pro comitiis.*

arbitrio principis. The view that the elections for the higher offices were 'arranged' by Augustus has been challenged by Professor A. H. M. Jones (*J.R.S.* 1955, pp. 9 sq.). Obviously the Emperor's wishes must to some extent have influenced the elections but he seldom if ever 'commended' (see below) candidates for the consulship, and only a small number of those for other offices; elections were frequently and sometimes bitterly contested and bribery was common—which does not suggest successful 'arrangement'.

tribuum. Tribunes, quaestors and aediles (the minor officials) were elected by the *comitia tributa.*

neque ... questus est. This was partly because the formal act of election was still theirs, and partly because they were satisfied as long as they had peace and relative plenty.

rumore. Its meaning of 'common talk' is classical. Cf. Livy, XXVII, 20, *Marcellus etiam aduerso rumore esse.* Tr. 'idle talk'.

largitionibus ac precibus. Canvassing the centuries and tribes was an expensive and tiresome necessity, and most senators would be concerned in it, either as candidates themselves (for offices above the quaestorship) or as patrons and supporters of other candidates. They could now settle the list themselves by debate, agreement or lot (see Dio, LVIII, 20, 3).

moderante Tiberio. This is typical of Tacitus' habit of adding a major statement in an abl. abs. phrase. It is not logically subordinate to the main verb. The present participle indicates a continuing state, 'Tiberius guaranteed to confine himself to . . .' The *ne* clause is similar to that found with verbs of preventing and hindering.

commendaret. This is the first recorded mention of a practice which had become a right by Vespasian's time. Augustus had continued the practice of Republican consulars and canvassed for his friends at election times. After A.D. 8 he ceased to do it in person, and instead published a list of those candidates he supported. These men (a small proportion of the whole) appear to have been automatically elected. Certainly by A.D. 14 the custom that they be returned *sine repulsa et ambitu* had been established. Tiberius is to limit his *commendatio* to four out of the twelve praetorships. We know from Velleius (II, 124, 4) that he and his brother were two of the four 'commended' on this occasion.

§ 2. proprio sumptu. This may have shown a desire to honour Augustus and serve the state, but popularity could be won by lavish games, and support gained for the next election.

de nomine, 'named after', a poetical construction. Cf. Virg. *Aen.* I, 277, *Romulus . . . Romanos suo de nomine dicet.*

Augustales. These were an adaptation and enlargement of an existing festival. 12th October, the day of Augustus' return from the East in 19 B.C., had been declared a public holiday (Dio, LIV, 10, 3; *R.G.* 11; *Fast. Amit.* 12th Oct.) and was known as the Augustalia: it had become a more formal festival by 11 B.C., when it was 'celebrated by decree' (Dio, LIV, 34, 2); now from A.D. 14 on it became a regular annual festival, the Ludi Augustales, was put in the Calendar and celebrated with several days of games, beginning on 5th October. See *E. and J.* under 5th October and 12th October, and cf. 54, 2.

uocarentur. This represents the future indic. (or present subj.) of their request: 'to be added to the Calendar as Ludi Augustales'.

utque, dependent on *decretum*, understood from *decreta*.

per circum, i.e. the Circus Maximus, where the games were held.

triumphali ueste. The presiding magistrate of the games wore triumphal dress and normally drove in a triumphal chariot. This latter the tribunes were not permitted to do, probably because they were not curule officials. For *uehi . . . permissum* see 72, 1 n.

§ 3. **annua.** The adj. is not otiose. The games had just been *fastis additi,* and their new annual character is emphasised.

praetorem. This praetorship dates from the time when Rome began to acquire provinces, the last quarter of the third century B.C. The praetor, who later and more conveniently became known as the *praetor peregrinus,* dealt first with lawsuits between foreigners, and afterwards also with those between citizens and foreigners.

euenisset, i.e. *sorte euenisset.* The praetors were elected by vote to the praetorship, but the allocation of the various duties they performed was determined by lot. The subj. is indefinite; see Introd. IV, 5 (i).

16. § 1. **Pannonicas.** Pannonia was the imperial province lying between the Danube and the Austrian Alps, occupying roughly the area of modern Hungary. It had originally been joined to Illyricum, but after the great Illyrian/Pannonian revolt of A.D. 6 it was made a separate province with its own governor.

incessit. The historians commonly use *incedere* with the simple acc. when the subject is abstract. Cf. Livy, I, 17, 4, *timor deinde patres incessit:* so here with *seditio.* Tacitus extends the use to the personal and literal meaning of the verb ('to proceed to'), cf. 61, 1, *incedunt maestos locos.* See Introd. IV, 1 (i). For the indic. after *cum* see 11, 3 n.

mutatus princeps, 'the change of Emperor'. See 8, 6 n.

licentiam turbarum, 'offered the prospect of rioting at will and the hope of profit from civil war'. For the gen. see Introd. IV, 2 (i).

§ 2. **tres simul legiones.** VIII Augusta, XV Apollinaris (23, 5) and IX Hispana (30, 4); their titles are known from inscriptions. It was at this time quite common for two or three legions to share a camp: Domitian (Suet. *Dom.* 7) was the first to see the dangers of this policy and decree one legion to one camp.

Iunio Blaeso, uncle of Sejanus. He was afterwards proconsul of Africa (*Ann.* III, 35), and for his service there was awarded triumphal insignia (III, 72) and later the title of Imperator (III, 74)—the last instance of this award to someone not of the Imperial family.

iustitium, lit. 'a stopping of law' and therefore of public business: then, as that happened especially for a period of mourning, 'public mourning'. Mourning here would be for Augustus, rejoicing for the accession of the new Emperor.

§ 3. **dux . . . theatralium operarum.** The following phrase *miscere . . . doctus* makes it clear that he was the leader of a claque, hired to applaud one actor and barrack his rivals. The factions supporting different actors were almost as bitterly divided as those supporting different racing colours in the Circus, and Suet. (*Tib.* 37) records a quarrel in the theatre that ended in bloodshed and the consequent banishment of the leaders of the claques concerned. *operae* from meaning 'day's work' comes to mean 'day labourers' and then especially those hired as a gang of trouble-makers: this sense is classical, cf. Cic. *Sest.* 38, *erat autem mihi contentio . . . cum operis conductis et ad diripiendam urbem concitatis.*

lingua, abl. of respect, which gives the point of view from which a statement (commonly an adj.) is true. Cf. 3, 1, *ignobilem loco*; 4, 1, *aetate ualidus*; 57, 4, *uoce supplex*; 73, 2, *corpore infamem.*

histrionali. Tacitus seems to have coined this word. It is found only here and in *Dial.* 26 and 29. It means 'connected with actors' and takes its precise colour from its context on each occasion. Here and in *Dial.* 29 it means 'support *for* actors', in *Dial.* 26 'rhythms used *by* actors'.

quaenam . . . condicio. Supply *esset*; see 7, 1 n. Lit. 'he worked on minds ignorant and doubtful about what would be the condition of service after Augustus', i.e. 'on men who were ignorant, and worried about their terms of service now that Augustus was dead'.

nocturnis conloquiis sq. The two major conditions, darkness and the absence of the more stable elements, are joined by *et*: the first is then subdivided by *aut* into complete darkness and twilight.

flexo . . . die. The phrase is an extension of the common *se flectere* used of journeying. Such extension to expressions of time is not common; Amm. XXXI, 15, 15 repeats Tacitus' phrase, and Sil. XIII, 414 has *a medio cum se nox humida cursu flexerit.*

dilapsis, 'dispersed', to their tents.

17. § 1. promptis . . . ministris, 'at last, when others too were ready to help in mutiny'.

contionabundus. Apart from this ex., the adj. (formed from *contionari*) is found only in Livy. *uelut* indicates that it was not a formal meeting, but a crowd gathered round an impromptu speaker; 'a kind of harangue' or 'something like a public speech'. Cf. Livy's use of *prope contionabundus* (XXI, 53, 6).

paucis . . . paucioribus. A legion had sixty centurions, each commanding about eighty men, and six tribunes, for whom see 19, 4 n.

quando ausuros. Rhetorical questions in *Oratio Obliqua* retain their interrogative word, but are otherwise expressed by the acc. and inf., because they are in fact statements cast in the form of a question to give greater emphasis. *quando auderent* would expect an answer ('tomorrow', 'in a week's time'), whereas Percennius is simply saying 'we shall never dare it, if not now.' Cf. § 6; 46, 3.

nutantem, 'faltering'—simply because *nouum*; 'not yet firmly established'. The general uncertainty caused by the death of an established Princeps and the appointment of a new and untried one, presented a good opportunity for pressing claims.

§ 2. **per tot annos** sq. In 13 B.C. (Dio, LIV, 25, 6) the legionaries' term of service was fixed at sixteen years, after which they would serve for four years as veterans in a special brigade, with certain privileges and exemptions, and receive a sum of money on discharge. In A.D. 6 (Dio, LV, 23, 1) this was altered to twenty years' service, with 12,000 sesterces discharge money after several years as veterans. But there was not enough money in the military treasury to pay these gratuities regularly, and the men were kept on, technically as veterans but not always with their recognized privileges (see § 3) for periods far beyond that officially recognized. This rebellion produced a temporary return to the original conditions (36, 3), but in the following year (78, 2) Tiberius had to request that the term of service be again twenty years. Discharge seems to have continued to be haphazard until Vespasian's time.

senes, deliberately placed beside *tricena . . . stipendia* to give cause and effect. 'They endured 30 or 40 years' service, which turned them into old men, many with their bodies mutilated by wounds.'

truncato . . . corpore, abl. of quality.   See Introd. IV, 4 (ii *d*).

§ 3. **dimissis,** i.e. those who had completed their term of service in the legion proper (*sub aquila*) and were now veterans with a special standard (*sub uexillo*). They were nominally exempt from various routine duties and to be called upon only in case of an enemy attack (36, 3).

uexillum. Here=the special standard of the veteran brigade (cf. 36, 3; 39, 1). The word is used for all kinds of standard, from those of the legions (*Ann.* V, 4) or maniples (34, 3) to that of any special detachment from a legion (38, 1 and 2) or of cavalry or auxiliaries (*Hist.* III, 17; *Ag.* 35).

tendentis, i.e. *tentoria tendentis* 'stretching their tents' and therefore 'encamping', 'quartered'. Cf. *Hist.* I, 55, *isdem hibernis tendentes.*

alio uocabulo, *uexillarii* or *missicii,* instead of *legionarii.*

uita superauerit, 'outstripped by life' and so 'survived'.

adhuc, 'still', i.e. 'even then'—for the commoner *etiamnunc.* This meaning is mainly poetical and post-Augustan.

diuersas, 'remote', a secondary meaning of the word. Cf. Ov. *Ep. Sapph.* 11, *arua celebras diuersa Aetnae.*

per nomen, instead of the modal abl. *nomine.* This type of variation is common in the historians, cf. Caes. *B.C.* III, 24, *per causam exercendorum remigum.* The use of *nomen* as 'pretext', 'guise', is classical, cf. Cic. *Leg. Agr.* II, 15, *legis agrariae simulatione atque nomine.*

paludum . . . montium. For the gens. see Introd. IV, 2 (iv) and IV, 2 (iii). The complaint about allocations of land is probably not purely rhetorical. There was not enough money to pay the promised 12,000 sesterces on discharge, and some of it may well have been paid in land: also, colonies of veterans (e.g. Colchester, Cologne) were still being established in the time of Claudius.

§ 4. **denis . . . assibus.** In the third century B.C. when the *denarius* was worth ten *asses*, the legionaries received just over three *asses* per day (Polyb. VI, 39); with the depreciation of the coinage during the Second Punic War, the *denarius* became worth sixteen *asses*, but the soldiers received a corresponding rise in pay, i.e. they had 5⅓ of the new *asses* instead of 3⅓ of the old (Plin. *H.N.* XXXIII, 45). Julius Caesar doubled their pay (Suet. *Jul.* 26) to the nearest round number, and they were therefore at this time receiving 10 *asses* per day. From this certain deductions were made; a papyrus account of Domitian's time (see Parker, p. 217) shows regular deductions for food, bedding and boots, with varying amounts for clothing. It appears therefore that Percennius is complaining not about the regular and calculable charges on the legionary's pay, but about the expenses which would fall at irregular intervals and sometimes unexpectedly and heavily. That explains why food is not mentioned.

saeuitiam. To the centurion belonged the prerogative of flogging soldiers, and no doubt unscrupulous officers used the threat of punishment to produce money to 'buy them off'.

uacationes. There were unpleasant duties to be done in camp, and bribery of the centurion in charge would ensure that they were allocated to others. *Hist.* I, 46 gives an account of the abuses of this practice.

redimi. The verb has three distinct meanings for *uestem*, *saeuitiam* and *uacationes*. For the first it supplies the sense of the simple verb *emi* 'to make a material purchase'; for the second it = 'to buy off', cf. Cic. *Mil.* 87, *se a iudicibus palam redemerat*; for the third 'to acquire something not material', cf. *pacem, gratiam, amicitiam redimere*. This figure is known as Zeugma ('a joining'): the word used in zeugma has its proper meaning with part of the sentence (here *saeuitiam* and *uacationes*) and from it must be understood the connected and appropriate meaning for the other part. Cf. *Ann.* II, 29, *manus ac supplices uoces ad Tiberium tendens; Ann.* I, 49, 1; 58, 1. The figure is quite classical.

aestates. It was, naturally, during the summer that the army did most of its training.

§ 5. **iniretur.** The sudden series of imperfect subjs. is not merely a return to regular sequence after a section of *repraesentatio* (Introd. IV, 5 (iv)); these verbs represent present *subjunctives* of the direct speech, and to retain them in that tense would be confusing. So Tacitus, who in the early part of the chapter has been retaining the vivid *tense*, now changes that tense to indicate a change of *mood* in the original. See *C.R.* 1951, p. 145.

singulos denarios. 16 *asses* instead of 10 per day. They demand (*a*) more pay, (*b*) a return to the original Augustan limit of 16 years' service, (*c*) the abolition of the extra service as veterans, (*d*) the payment of their gratuity in cash (*pecunia* is emphatic).

§ 6. **an.** So used, it frequently marks an indignant or ironical question. 'Do you really imagine that . . .' For the praetorians, see 7, 2n.

acceperint. This represents the perf. indic. of the direct, which refers to the most recent increase; 'who have got their two *denarii*.'

suscipere, rhet. question. See § 1 n.

sibi, dat. of the agent. See Introd. IV, 3 (iv). The whole of this clause, with its increasing emphasis, gives the lie to his statement that he is 'not disparaging guard-duty in the capital'.

18. § 1. **adstrepebat,** 'noisily applauded'. The word is rare both before (Sen. *Hipp.* 1026: Calp. Sic. IV, 2) and after Tacitus. He uses it several times, both intransitively, as here, and transitively—cf. *Hist.* IV, 49, *ut eadem adstreperent.*

diuersis incitamentis. Different men made a noise and displayed their different signs of ill treatment at the appropriate parts of Percennius' speech, *uerberum notas* being induced by *saeuitiam centurionum* and *uerbera* § 4, *canities* by *senes* § 2 and *detrita tegmina* by *uestem* § 4. 'As the different points struck home.'

et nudum corpus, set alongside *detrita tegmina* but logically subordinate to it; 'clothing so worn that their bodies showed through'.

exprobrantes, used with the acc. of the thing objected to; 'indignantly pointing to . . .' The verb most commonly means 'reproach' but cf. 35, 1 and Livy, II, 27, 2, *milites exprobrabant . . . cicatrices.*

§ 2. **eo furoris,** 'to such a pitch of madness'. The gen. is partitive.

miscere. For the infin. see Introd. IV, 6 (i) and cf. Nepos, *Hamil.* 1, 4, *ut mente agitaret bellum renouare.* The idea was 'mad', because such a legion would be an impossible fighting unit, and also because the legionary *aquila* (see below) had a kind of sanctity as a symbol of identity and could not be lightly discarded.

eum honorem, i.e. the honour of having its *aquila* accepted as that of the new legion, and therefore of giving its name to it.

aquilas . . . signa. Marius first gave each legion its own particular standard, an eagle of silver or gold set on top of a pole. The *signa* are the standards of the maniples within each cohort, and usually consisted of a spear-head on a pole, bearing various decorations. These were used mainly as a rallying point in battle for the smaller units, but the *aquila* was the *numen legionis* (*Ann.* II, 17) and regarded with religious veneration.

foret. Note that the historic present (5, 3 n.) is an historic tense, and that its dependent subjs. may therefore follow historic sequence.

§ 3. **properantibus.** This may be an abl. abs. with *eis* understood (5, 1 n.) or possibly dat. after *aduenit.*

increpabat. The change of tense is significant—'began to chide', describing a process and not an isolated action like his arrival.

leuiore flagitio, lit. 'with a lighter crime will you kill an officer', —a compressed way of saying 'it will be less of a crime to kill an officer than to revolt from the Emperor, as you are now doing'.

aut iugulatus, again a compression, this time rather of thought than of language. He will either live and keep his men loyal, or die in the attempt: if death is necessary, he hopes that the loss of their own general will help to show them the enormity of their crime and so eventually restore them to loyalty.

19. § 1. aggerebatur. There is no need to alter this, the reading of M, which in fact gives better sense. *adcreuerat* deals adequately with the growth of the structure, and there is no need to have *aggerare* too. While Blaesus was speaking, turf 'was still being brought up and the structure was breast-high when . . .' See *L.E.C.* 1940, p. 388; *B.P.E.C.* 1941, pp. 97 sq.

pectori usque, 'quite breast high'. For the dat. expressing motion towards a goal see Introd. IV, 3 (vi).

peruicacia, 'by his (Blaesus') persistent firmness'.

cum . . . omisere, 'inverse' *cum*. See 11, 3 n.

§ 2. desideria. In such contexts it almost = 'petition'. Cf. 26, 2.

parum in tempore, οὐκ ἐν καιρῷ, 'not at the right time', 'inopportunely'. For this use of *in tempore* (which is at least as early as Terence), cf. 58, 6. Tacitus makes great use of *parum* (lit. 'too little') as a strong negative.

incipientis, with *principis*, = 'at the beginning of his reign'. Cf. Plin. *Paneg.* 57, *et incipientes principes et desinentes.* For *onerare* in the sense of 'aggravate', cf. *Ann.* XVI, 30, *cuius onerasse pericula uidebatur*; this meaning is first found in Livy.

§ 3. tenderent . . . expostulauerint . . . meditentur. This represents *tenditis . . . expostulauerunt . . . meditamini* of the direct speech. Tacitus has chosen to use regular sequence for the first verb, and *repraesentatio* (Introd. IV, 5 (iv)) for the other two. For the subj. verb in an indirect rhetorical question, see 40, 2 n.

temptare. *tendere* with the infin. in the meaning of 'aim at' occurs mainly in the poets and post-Augustan writers. See Introd. IV, 6 (i).

fas disciplinae, 'the just demands of discipline'—a stronger phrase than *morem obsequii,* 'the habit of obedience'.

legatos. For *decernere* with the acc. = 'officially appoint', cf. Cic. *Phil.* V, 4, *senatus decernit legatos ad Antonium*.

coram. For its position see 60, 3 n.

§ 4. tribunus. The six *tribuni militum* of each legion formed the administrative staff of the legionary commander. They dealt with such things as leave, discharge and discipline within the camp. Under the

Principate they were normally young men who hoped to follow a senatorial or equestrian career, for which this service was a necessary qualification.

ab sedecim annis, 'after sixteen years'. For this use of *ab*, cf. Cic. *Att.* I, 5, 4, *ut primum a tuo digressu Romam ueni*. The prepositional phrase qualifies the noun, cf. 26, 1 and see 8, 1 n.

§ 5. **filius . . . orator . . . ostenderet,** 'because (the fact that) the commander's son (had been chosen) as the pleader of the common cause . . . showed . . .' In principle, the construction is the same as that of *occisus Caesar* (8, 6 n.), the fact of the appointment and not the person being the logical subject. *ostenderet* is subj. because the construction is virtual oblique; 'because (they felt that) . . .'

necessitate expressa, 'they had extorted by force what they would not have obtained by correct behaviour'.

obtinuissent. Cicero regularly, in an indirect construction such as this, represents the apodosis of a condition of the type *quae per modestiam* (= *si modestia usi essemus*) *non obtinuissemus* by the periphrasis *obtenturi fuerint*, so contriving to preserve both the original potential meaning of the verb and its present subordination to another verb. But later writers tended to avoid this precise linguistic convention, and to use instead the simple pluperfect. *obtinuissent*, therefore, may well represent an original *obtinuissemus*. But it could also be the indirect form of an original *obtinueramus*, the vivid construction whereby the apodosis is regarded as so certain, if the protasis stands, that it is expressed as completed fact in the indicative. Cf. Cic. *Fam.* XII, 10, 3, *praeclare uiceramus, nisi . . . Lepidus recepisset Antonium*; Sen. *Contr.* X, 1 (30), 1 *perieramus, si magistratus esset*; and 36, 2 n.

20. § 1. **Nauportum,** in modern Yugoslavia, about 40 miles behind Trieste and 10 miles S.W. of Ljubljana.

ob itinera, 'to make roads'—a duty which served the double purpose of making communications easier and of occupying the troops.

uexilla conuelliunt. Other exx. of *signa conuellere* (e.g. Cic. *Div.* I, 77; Livy, III, 7, 3) make it clear that the phrase means to take up the standards from the ground, where they were fixed while the army was stationary, and use them to lead the march. *uexilla* here = the standards of a special detachment: see 17, 3 n.

municipii. The word has here no technical political significance, but simply means 'town'. Cf. *Hist.* I, 67, *in modum municipii extructus locus*, and see 79, 1 n.

praecipua . . . ira, abl. abs. expressing accompanying circumstances.

Aufidienum Rufum. He is otherwise unknown.

praefectum castrorum. This officer was responsible for the organization and running of the camp, and commanded soldiers in the field only in the absence of the *legatus*. Rufus had been sent out in command of this special detachment.

uehiculo, abl. case. It is not always possible, in constructions with *deripere*, to distinguish dat. from abl. by form alone: but if the emphasis lies on the *person* deprived of something, the case may be safely assumed to be dat. (of disadvantage; cf. *Ann.* II, 45, *tela Romanis derepta*); while if a person or thing is dragged *from* something, the case is probably abl. of separation (cf. Hor. *Epod.* V, 46, *lunamque caelo deripit*.) This assumption is supported by the occasional use of prepositions with the abl., cf. Plaut. *Men.* 870, *me de curru deripit*.

an. The indignant *an* (17, 6 n.) of the direct question is retained in the indirect form.

§ 2. **quippe.** See 5, 1 n.

castris. For the dat. cf. *praefectus urbi*.

reuocabat. The imperfect implies 'wished to revive', 'was for reviving'. Cf. 2, 2, *abnuebant* 'were not for objecting'.

intentus. The manuscript reads *intus*. In spite of the ingenious suggestion (*C.R.* 1954, p. 209) that *intus* is a preposition meaning 'inside the range of' and therefore 'safe from', it seems an unlikely reading; the meaning of *intus* is unparalleled in Latin and would be an imitation of a Greek construction, itself very rare. *uetus* is possible Latin (meaning, with a gen. of reference, 'experienced in', cf. *Ann.* VI, 12, *caerimoniarum uetus*) and reasonable sense: but not the best possible sense. The emphasis of the sentence lies rather on his present severity as an officer, and *intentus* ('strict' cf. *Ann.* XI, 18, *intentumque et magnis delictis inexorabilem scias*) is probably the best reading (see Brink in *J.R.S.* 1951, pp. 39–40). For the gen. see Introd. IV, 2 (i).

21. § 1. **circumiecta,** 'surrounding district'. Cf. Plin. *H.N.* XXIII, 37, *hoc distat orbis medius et mitior plaga circumiectis*.

populabantur, 'began to plunder'.

carcere, the guard-room of the camp. Cf. Juv. VI, 561, *si longe castrorum in carcere mansit*. The abl. is instrumental—'enclosed by the prison' lit.

etiam tum. Later, the rage of the soldiers prevented their being of much use. Cf. 23.

§ 2. **illi,** the *pauci* of § 1.

quisque cuius. This, the traditional order, is correct; *quisque* belongs to *ciere* and should not be included in the relative clause.

manipularis. The maniple was by now purely an administrative unit (= two centuries); *manipularis* has here no technical meaning, but simply = 'ordinary soldier'; 'the century to which he belonged'.

cumulant. For a similar construction, cf. *Ann.* XIV, 53, *tantum honorum in me cumulasti*. Tacitus alone seems to use *in* and the acc. with *cumulare*.

nihil reliqui faciunt, 'they left nothing undone'. Such negative expressions are constantly, in classical Latin, followed by *quominus* (Cic. *Att.* II, 4, 5, *nihil desideramus quominus*; id. *Inv.* II, 130, *neque ullam facultatem defuisse quominus*). There seems therefore no need to class this (as Furneaux and Nipperdey do) as an ex. of *quominus* used for *quin*.

et iras. For the use of *et* see 25, 2 n. and for the plural *iras* = 'expressions of rage' see 74, 1 n.

permouerent. *permoueo* with the acc. of the passion excited is a post-Augustan usage. Cf. Quint. XII, 10, 36, *permouendi omnes affectus erunt.*

§ 3. **rerum capitalium.** For the gen. see Introd. IV, 2 (ii).

iam, not here a temporal adv., but one adding emphasis—'and actually added to their numbers', 'and went so far as to add'. Cf. Cic. *Fam.* I, 1, 2, *Pompeium et hortari et orare et iam liberius accusare.*

22. § 1. **seditioni,** dat. of purpose. See Introd. IV, 3 (v).

quid pararet intentos, 'intent upon what he would contrive' lit.; the phrase is a natural extension of such expressions as *intenti ludo* (Virg. *Aen.* VII, 380) and *aduersus insidias intentae* (*Ann.* XIV, 3). 'Eagerly waiting to see what he would do.'

lucem et spiritum, 'light and life'.

missum . . . a Germanico exercitu. It is unlikely that news of the German revolt could yet have reached Pannonia. As the brother was invented (23, 2), presumably the errand was also.

iugulauit. Blaesus, the subject, is understood from the context.

gladiatores. He probably kept them, as did other provincial officials (see *Ann.* XIII, 31), to provide shows and so win popularity for himself. But as they were his slaves he could use them for any purpose he thought fit.

§ 2. **sepultura,** abl. This construction of *inuideo* with the dat. of the person and abl. of the thing first occurs in Livy (II, 40, 11, *non inuiderunt laude sua mulieribus uiri Romani*) and was current usage by Quintilian's time (IX, iii, 1, *paene iam quidquid loquimur figura est, ut hac re inuidere, non ut ueteres et Cicero praecipue, hanc rem*). Cf. *Germ.* 33, *ne spectaculo quidem proelii inuidere.*

dum, 'provided that', with the subj. 'Only, let them bury us . . .'

23. § 1. **incendebat,** 'he inflamed these words' lit., i.e. made them more inflammatory, increased their effect. Cf. 69, 5, *accendebat haec.*

pedibus, dat. indicating the goal of motion. See Introd. IV, 3 (vi) and cf. 13, 6 n.

e seruitio, 'of the number of Blaesus' slaves', i.e. 'numbered among Blaesus' slaves'.

familiam. The word is used particularly of the slaves of a household. 'Family' in the narrower sense is *domus*.

§ 2. **pernotuisset.** *pernotescere* ('to become known') is post-Augustan and usually, as here, constructed impersonally with the acc. and inf.

Cf. *Ann.* XIII, 25, *ubi Caesarem esse . . . pernotuit*. The apparently 'mixed' condition is produced because the real apodosis is suppressed, and replaced by a kindred *fact*. 'They were not far from murdering the general (and would have murdered him) had it not become known . . .' The construction is very common with the imperfect. Cf. § 5, *quin . . . ferrum parabant . . . ni miles . . . interiecisset*; 35, 4, *deferebat . . . ni . . . attinuissent*; 63, 2, *trudebantur . . . ni . . . instruxisset*; 65, 6, *circumueniebatur, ni . . . opposuisset*; 69, 1, *ni . . . prohibuisset, erant qui . . .*; Cic. *Leg.* I, 52, *labebar longius, nisi me retinuissem*. Usually the apodosis comes first but, cf. Cic. *Verr.* V, 129, *si per L. Metellum licitum esset, matres . . . ueniebant.*

§ 3. **uocabulum,** here 'nickname', cf. 41, 2, *militari uocabulo Caligulam appellabant*. His nickname was 'Another please', *cedo* being an old imperative form (the particle *ce* + an old imperative of *do*) meaning 'give'. Cf. Plaut. *Most.* 308, *cedo aquam manibus.*

uite. The *uitis*, vine-rod, was the mark of the centurion's office, and his instrument of punishment.

poscebat, 'he would (i.e. was accustomed to) demand'. The imperfect of its very nature frequently represents habitual action. Cf. Ter. *And.* 83, *obseruabam* 'I would watch', *rogitabam* 'I would ask'.

§ 4. **Clemente Iulio.** He is known only from these chapters of *Ann.* I.

perferendis . . . mandatis, dat. of purpose. See Introd. IV, 3 (v).

§ 5. **quin.** Originally *qui-ne* 'how not?', *quin* comes to be used as an introductory particle meaning 'indeed', 'in fact'. 'The Eighth and Fifteenth legions were actually preparing to fight.' Cf. 79, 3.

dum. Not here purely temporal, but causal also—'with one demanding the death of S.' The usage is classical, cf. Cic. *Div.* II, 37, *dum haruspicinam ueram esse uultis, physiologiam totam peruertitis* 'in your desire for divination to be true . . .'

cognomento Sirpicum. Sirpicus is his real name, not a nickname. It is paralleled in *C.I.L.* VIII, 6167; and the phrase is in accordance with Tacitus' normal use of *cognomentum* for a genuine name, cf. *Ann.* II, 9, *cognomento Flauus*. See Syme in *J.R.S.* 1949, p. 15.

morti, dat. of purpose. See Introd. IV, 3 (v).

24. § 1. **haec audita,** 'news of this'. See 8, 6 n.

quamquam. For its use with a participle see 7, 3 n.

abstrusum. The metaphorical use of *abstrusus* is common in classical Latin with such words as *disputatio* (Cic. *Acad.* II, 30) and *dolor* (id. *Dom.* 25), but Tacitus alone, and only here, seems to use it of a person. It means 'reserved' and emphasizes the almost violently secretive attitude which Tacitus conceives to be Tiberius'.

tristissima quaeque. In classical Latin *quisque* with the superlative is normally singular in the masculine and feminine, but the neuter plural (as here) is quite common. Cf. Cic. *Acad.* I, 13, *recentissima quaeque.*

nullis . . . mandatis, abl. abs. 'He was given no definite instructions, but was to act as circumstances required.' Note the future participle expressing purpose (Introd. IV, 7 (ii)).

delecto, picked men from the remaining Praetorian Cohorts.

§ 2. **praetoriani equitis.** Cavalry belonging to the Praetorian Guard is again mentioned in *Ann.* XII, 56, *praetoriarum cohortium manipuli turmaeque.*

robora, 'flower', 'strength of', and therefore 'the best of'. The usage is classical.

Germanorum, mainly Batavians, who from Augustus to Galba formed a private bodyguard for the Imperial family. Augustus disbanded them after the Varian disaster (Suet. *Aug.* 49) but they had by this time obviously been reconstituted. Tacitus mentions Nero's *Germani* in *Ann.* XIII, 18 and XV, 58.

tum. They were no longer so by Tacitus' own time.

Aelius Seianus. This is the first mention in the Annals of Tiberius' famous minister, who later gained such ascendancy that he even aimed at the Principate—an attempt which caused his downfall. Tacitus describes his early life and character in *Ann.* IV, 1, where he calls his ascendancy the result of *deum ira in rem Romanam.* He was a clever and unscrupulous man, whose strength of character probably appealed to Tiberius' diffidence.

collega. Normally the Praetorian Guard had two prefects, but when Strabo (shortly after this) became Prefect of Egypt, Sejanus was left in sole charge, and his use of the Guard greatly increased his power. See note on 7, 2.

magna . . . auctoritate. For the abl. of quality see Introd. IV, 4 (ii *d*).

iuueni, poss. dat. See Introd. IV, 3 (ii). Sentences like *est Marco amicus* gave an opportunity to take the dat. with the noun instead of with the verb, and the poets and later writers use such descriptions as *Philocomasio amator* (Plaut.) and *Othoni comes* (Tac.). Some of the exx. express (as here) not only poss. but purpose—a natural development in the light of the very similar dat. of purpose (Introd. IV, 3 (v*d*)).

ceteris, the Praetorians who were to accompany him.

periculorum . . . ostentator. For nouns in *-tor* see 4, 4 n. Sejanus' job was to keep the soldiers in order, as (4, 4) it was the job of the *domus Augusta* to rule. He was to show them what they had to lose by disobedience (*periculorum*) and what they would gain by obedience (*praemiorum*).

§ 3. **per officium,** 'as a mark of respect'.

laetae, i.e. showing their happiness—'with demonstrations of welcome'.

insignibus. The *insignia* are the decorations, corresponding to our medals, which were awarded to individual soldiers and worn on dress parades. The arrival of the Emperor's son would normally have been the occasion for such a parade, but the legions made no effort to make it so.

inluuie . . . uultu. The first is abl. of quality (Introd. IV, 4 (ii *d*), the second abl. of respect (16, 3) with *propiores*.

quamquam. For its use with the subj. see 3, 5 n.

25. § 1. portas . . . firmant. There is no reason to suppose, as Furneaux does, that the main body of Drusus' retinue did not enter the camp and that these precautions were to prevent their doing so. They were more probably intended to prevent Drusus from leaving before he had granted their demands, and the Praetorians from unexpectedly seizing key positions.

certis . . . locis. *locus* is one of the few words which even in classical Latin are found in the local abl. without *in*. Almost invariably, when it is so used, it has an attributive adj. Cf. 68, 3 *aequis locis*.

§ 2. illi quoties sq. The sound of the words and the short abrupt phrases help to convey the wavering of their emotions.

et repente quies. When the last unit of a series in asyndeton (i.e. without formal connexion) sums up the series or (as here) adds a new and slightly different idea, it is regularly joined to the series by *et*. Cf. 21, 2, *inuidiam misericordiam metum et iras*; *Hist.* IV, 1, *ubique lamenta, conclamationes et fortuna captae urbis*. See *C.R.* 1897, p. 327.

§ 3. plurima bella tolerauisset. He had commanded in Pannonia from 12–9 B.C. and again during the Illyrian revolt of A.D. 6–9.

acturum . . . de, 'he would bring their demands before the Senate'.

seueritatis, not 'punishment', because 26, 3 shows that that was a matter never referred to the Senate. Tiberius' plea is that the Senate should have a share in the indulgence or refusal of the soldiers' present demands. Cf. the similar contrast between *seueritas* and *largitio* in 36, 2.

26. § 1. de missione sq. These are the remedies demanded for the grievances listed in c. 17.

obtenderet, 'put forward as an excuse'. Cf. *obtentui* 10, 1 'as an excuse' and *Ann.* XII, 45, *quia multitudinem hostium Pollio, iussa patris Radamistus obtendebant*. The meaning is post-Augustan, and is found also in Pliny and Quintilian. 'When he pleaded that the decision must be the Senate's and his father's . . .'

§ 2. cur uenisset. For the subj. verb in an indirect rhetorical question, see 40, 2 n.

augendis . . . stipendiis, dat. of purpose. See Introd. IV, 3 (v).

nulla . . . licentia, abl. of attendant circumstances (Introd. IV, 4 (ii *c*)). 'In fact, with no power at all to help them.'

at hercule. See 3, 5 n.

cunctis. In actual fact, only the provincial governor had capital jurisdiction. But the soldiers' point is that no ratification had to be sought from Rome for punishments but only, apparently, for reforms.

rettulisse, 'had revived the same tricks'.

filios familiarum, a technical legal term for 'minors.' The soldiers complain that all members of the Imperial family who visit them act as if they were still under parental jurisdiction and incapable of independent action. Contrast *patres familiarum, qui sunt suae potestatis* (Dig. 1, 6, 4).

§ 3. **nouum id plane,** ironical. 'It was certainly very strange that it was only army *reforms* which the Emperor referred to the Senate.'

supplicia. The word is used especially of the death penalty.

an. See 17, 6 n.; 20, 1.

sub dominis. The word *dominus* is deliberate and invidious, and both Augustus and Tiberius deprecated its use. Cf. Dio, LVII, 8, 2.

sine arbitro, 'without a controller' lit., i.e. 'without appeal'.

27. § 1. **ut . . . occurreret.** The subj. is frequentative—see Introd. IV, 5 (i). For *quis* = 'anyone' see 2, 1 n.; the classical phrase is *ut quisque.* Cf. Cic. *Verr.* V, 143.

manus intentantes, 'making threatening gestures'. Cf. *Ann.* III, 36, *cum uoces, cum manus intentarent.*

causam . . . initium, acc. in apposition to the phrase. See Introd. IV, 1 (iv).

Cn. Lentulo. The evidence (examined by Groag in *P.I.R.*² C 1379) seems to suggest that it was not the consul of 18 B.C. (as Nipperdey and Furneaux state) but Cn. Cornelius Cn. f. Lentulus the augur, consul in 14 B.C., who campaigned against the Dacians and acquired great wealth; and that it is that Lentulus who is here meant. Cf. *Ann.* III, 59 and IV, 44.

ante alios, 'before others' and therefore 'especially'. The phrase is mainly poetical and post-Augustan, and is common with superlatives and emphatic adjs. or descriptive phrases. Cf. Virg. *Aen.* VII, 55, *ante alios pulcherrimus omnes Turnus*; *Hist.* IV, 55.

illa . . . aspernari, 'and to be particularly disgusted at the outrageous conduct of the soldiers'.

§ 2. **digredientem eum Caesare.** This has been very generally changed into *digredientem cum Caesare.* But the sense is then wrong; Drusus did not leave the camp (see 28, 3 and 29, 1); it seems unlikely that such an attack would have been made on Lentulus in his presence; his escort was obviously elsewhere (*adcursu multitudinis* sq.), which makes it likely that he was too. The only way to preserve the sense and read *cum* is to translate 'parting *with* Caesar'. But although *cum* is so used with, e.g. *discedere* (Livy, II, 40, 14), it is unparalleled with *digredi*; and the tense of the participle is wrong because Caesar, as we have seen, was almost certainly not there. Further, it is desirable to have *eum*. Tacitus does not make great use of *is*, but he does use it with participles where a person has to be distinguished or emphasized (cf. *Ann.* II, 42, 2) and both are necessary here. The difficulty of this reading lies in the omission of *a* with *Caesare*. *digredi* occurs with a simple abl. of separation (Suet. *Nero* 43), but none of the exx. is a person—*digredi a* is the normal construction there. If, however, an *a* originally stood before *Caesare*, it is difficult to see why it was ever lost.

It seems better, on balance, to accept the simple abl. as a Tacitean extension or eccentricity, than to read *cum*, which is doubtful idiom and doubtful sense. For a discussion of the passage see *L.E.C.* 1940, p. 390; *Maia* 1950, p. 261.

prouisu. The word is used only by Tacitus and only in the abl. sing.; once (here) meaning 'foreseeing', once (*Hist.* III, 22) a literal 'looking forward', and four times (*Ann.* XII, 6 and 12; *Ann.* XV, 8; *Hist.* II, 5) in the sense of 'precaution', 'provision'.

hiberna castra, presumably some short distance away. They had obviously already halted there (*repetentem*) on their way to the present legionary camp.

exitii, simple objective gen. after *certus*; 'sure that his end was near'.

multitudinis. There is no reason to assume, as Furneaux does, that they were outside the camp.

28. § 1. minacem ... leniuit. Note the personification of *nox* and *fors*. 'The night threatened to end in an outbreak of crime: but this was averted by a stroke of fortune.'

claro repente. This is Lipsius' emendation of *clamore pena* M, and the best of the suggested readings. *repente* belongs to *uisa*, but the interwoven order is not unparalleled in Tacitus (cf. 10, 1, *simulatam Pompeianarum gratiam partium*; 40, 4, *paruulum sinu filium gerens*; 67, 1, *expugnandi hostis spe succederent*; *Ann.* XIV, 2, *tradit ardore retinendae Agrippinam potentiae*), and the juxtaposition of *claro* and *repente* adds emphasis to the phenomenon. See *J.R.S.* 1951, p. 43.

languescere. The eclipse is usually dated to 26th September, but Mr D. H. Sadler, O.B.E., Superintendent of H.M. Nautical Almanac Office at Herstmonceux, tells me that in terms of Universal Time it occurred at about 5 a.m. on 27th September, A.D. 14.

rationis ignarus. The cause of eclipses had long since been discovered and was known to educated men of Cicero's day (cf. *Div.* II, 6, 17). But popular superstition remained.

suis laboribus, 'likening the failure of the moon to (the failure of) their own efforts'. This shortened form of comparison is fairly common in Latin, both in prose and verse. Cf. Caes. *B.G.* VI, 22, *cum suas quisque opes cum potentissimis aequari uideat.*

sideris. *sidus*, while chiefly used of stars and planets, is also found for the sun and the moon. Cf. Plin. *H.N.* II, 57, *utrumque sidus* 'both sun and moon'.

prospereque. The acc. and inf. clause depends on the verb of saying or thinking implicit in *adsimulans.* Cf. 30, 3, *nec frustra* sq.; 49, 3, *nec aliter* sq.

quae pergerent. This is the reading of M, and preferable to any of the emendations. The required sense is clearly 'and considering that success would attend their efforts if her bright splendour were restored to the moon-goddess'; this requires *quae* not *qua.* The difficulty lies in the transitive use of *pergo; peragerent* is an obvious emendation (the *a* has actually been inserted in M, but by a later hand), but it is so obvious as to be suspect. *iter pergo* is found (*Ann.* III, 66), and verbs of similar meaning are found with *id* as an internal acc. (*id perseuerare,* Livy, XXII, 38, 13); that being so, it seems better to retain the manuscript reading and explain it as a Tacitean extension of a known usage. See *J.R.S.* 1951, p. 42.

claritudo. Tacitus prefers this form of the word to the classical *claritas.*

§ 2. **aeris sono.** The noise was intended to discourage the magic power which they believed to be drawing the moon's light away. Cf. Livy, XXVI, 5, *cum aeris crepitu, qualis in defectu lunae silenti nocte cieri solet, edidit clamorem.*

prout splendidior obscuriorue. The progress of an eclipse is steady, not fluctuating, so this can only mean 'as the light *seemed* brighter or dimmer'. The eclipse moves slowly, and at times the soldiers would imagine that their magic was having effect.

offecere uisui, lit. 'obstructed their sight'. Cf. *Bell. Afr.* 52, *prospectui offecisset.* 'Hid it from view.'

§ 3. **quae . . . obtulerat,** 'the gift of fortune'. For the indicative see 10, 2 n. on *fecere.*

et si qui alii, 'and any others who . . .' There seems to be no other ex. in Tacitus (or elsewhere) of *alius* so used without *quis,* and many exx. of the standard usage with *quis* (cf. 32, 3; 35, 1; *Ann.* VI, 43; XII, 38). That being so, it seems better to insert *qui* here.

bonis artibus. See 3, 4 n.

in uulgus. The dat. is more usual after *gratus* = 'pleasing'.

§ 4. **uigiliis, stationibus, custodiis.** Strictly, *uigiliae* are the night-guard, *stationes* guards in general. But the distinction is not always made, and probably all that Tacitus means here is that they approached the men on guard-duty, patrols, pickets and sentries alike.

Neronibus et Drusis, two of the surnames of the *gens Claudia* (4, 3 n.).

§ 5. **mereare . . . recipias.** The subj. is potential, indefinite second person. Cf. the common *dicas, credas,* etc.

§ 6. **inter se suspectis,** 'rendered mutually suspicious'.

tironem. Obviously *tiro* is not here strictly technical (= 'new recruit'), but used generally of the younger soldiers.

signa, cf. 18, 2.

29. § 1. dicendi, gen. of reference. See Introd. IV, 2 (i).

nobilitate ingenita, 'natural dignity'.

negat . . . et. See 4, 1 n.

§ 2. orantibus, *eis* is understood. See 5, 1 n.

idem. Blaesus had previously gone on a similar mission (19, 4). 'Blaesus was again despatched to Tiberius, and with him . . .'

L. Aponius. He may be the man mentioned in *C.I.L.* XII, 4230 as tribune of the VIIth and XXIInd legions, and a *praefectus castrorum*.

cohorte, his retinue, i.e. his personal friends and companions, not his official staff. This use of the word dates from C I B.C. Cf. Cic. *Q. Fr.* I, 1, 12; Hor. *Ep.* I, iii, 6.

Iustus Catonius. He became Prefect of Praetorians under Claudius, and was put to death by Messalina in A.D. 43 (Dio, LX, 18, 3; Sen. *Apocol.* 13).

primi ordinis centurio. The *primi ordines* were probably the six centurions of the First Cohort and the leading centurion of each of the other nine cohorts. See Parker, pp. 281–2.

§ 3. terrere . . . contemni, a chiasmus. See 2, 1 n. The present infins. describe a permanent characteristic—'they inspired fear (they argued) unless themselves made afraid, but once intimidated they could safely be ignored.'

ex duce. This phrase, giving the source of the fear inspired, belongs to *metus.* Cf. *Ann.* II, 72, *metum ex Tiberio.*

§ 4. ingenium. All the sources depict Drusus unfavourably, as harsh and quarrelsome and even cruel. He may well have been a difficult young man, but Tacitus' account of him in the Annals shows him also to have had sense and ability.

Druso, possessive dat. See Introd. IV, 3 (ii).

tradunt plerique . . . alii. See Introd. II.

ostentui, 'for display'—dat. of purpose (Introd. IV, 3 (v)).

30. § 1. ut quisque sq., lit. 'as each (was) a particular trouble-maker, they were sought out', i.e. 'search was made for all the chief trouble-makers'. *ut quisque* subdivides the subject into units and so adds importance to the individuals concerned. Cf. Ovid, *Met.* II, 210, *corripitur flammis ut quaeque altissima tellus.* For *turbator* see 4, 4 n.

pars . . . palantes . . . caesi. See 44, 2 n.

documentum, acc. in apposition to the phrase. See Introd. IV, 1 (iv).

§ 2. egredi tentoria. The transitive use of *egredior*, both literal and metaphorical, belongs to the historians and post-Augustan prose. Cf. Livy, I, 29, 6, *egressis urbem Albanis*; id. II, 61, 4, *modum . . . egressum (propugnatorem).* See Introd. IV, 1 (i).

tutari signa. It would be a bad omen if they fell.

§ 3. **nec frustra.** See 28, 1 n. For the phrase in the meaning 'it was not for nothing that', cf. *Ann.* XI, 7.

hebescere, lit. 'to grow blunt'. For a very similar usage, cf. Sil. XII, 653, *fulgor hebescere caeli . . . coepit.*

piaculo. *piaculum* is originally an expiatory offering, and then the sin for which such an offering was necessary.

§ 4. **epistulas,** presumably only one letter. This use of the plural is probably induced by *litterae*, which does mean '*a letter*'. Cf. 36, 3.

nonanus. *miles* is understood.

desolatus, 'left alone', 'abandoned'. Cf. *Ann.* XVI, 30, *uiduata desolataque.* Its use of persons is post-Augustan.

aliorum. *alii* in the sense of *ceteri*, occasionally found in classical Latin, is fairly common in Livy and later writers. Cf. Livy, I, 7, 3, *sacra diis aliis Albano ritu, Graeco Herculi facit.*

§ 5. **quia . . . consederant,** lit. 'as the present state of affairs had settled', i.e. 'as things were quiet for the moment'.

31. § 1. **tracturis,** 'who would carry all before them (with their power)'. For the future participle see Introd. IV, 7 (ii).

§ 2. **duo . . . exercitus.** The Germanies, Upper and Lower, were military districts rather than provinces proper. Their governors were appointed not to the province but to the army (as late as A.D. 74 Cornelius Clemens is referred to as *leg. eius pro pr. exercitus Germanici superioris, I.L.S.* 5957), because the districts primarily served the military organization of the North and were not being developed as provinces. Not until C 2 A.D. do references to *prouincia Germania inferior/superior* become common (cf. *I.L.S.* 1052, 1057, 1065). For the distribution of the German legions see 3, 5 n.

superiori. It is possible to say either *nomen est mihi Marcus*, or *nomen est mihi Marco*, attracting the name to the case of the pronoun. Most classical writers use both constructions, Cicero preferring the nom. and Livy the dat. Tacitus too prefers the nom. and generally uses the dat. only when the appellation is an adj. (as here). Cf. *Ann.* II, 8, *cui Drusianae nomen.* The gen. of definition is also, but much more rarely, used with *nomen*; see Introd. IV, 2 (iv). 'The one called "Upper" was under the legate C. Silius, the Lower A. Caecina had in his charge.'

C. Silio. He held this command for seven years (*Ann.* IV, 18) and was in A.D. 15 awarded the triumphal insignia for his share in Germanicus' campaign (72, 1). Accused of treason in A.D. 24, he committed suicide. He was the father of the Silius concerned in Messalina's scandalous doings (see *Ann.* XI).

Caecina. Aulus Caecina Severus had a command in Moesia and Pannonia during the great rebellion of A.D. 6. He too was awarded *triumphalia* in A.D. 15 (72, 1).

summae rei. Germanicus had *imperium maius* (3, 5).

agendo . . . censui, dat. of purpose (Introd. IV, 3 (v)). Julius Caesar had assessed the tax to be paid by Gaul at 40,000,000 sesterces (Suet. *Jul.* 25). The purpose of the census was to distribute this burden equitably. The first census of Gaul was taken in 27 B.C. (Dio, LIII, 22, 5), revised by Drusus *c.* 12 B.C. (*I.L.S.* 212; Livy, *Epit.* CXXXVI–VII) and now again by Germanicus.

§ 3. **Vbiorum.** The Ubii were a Germanic tribe friendly to Rome. Originally settled on the east bank of the Rhine, in 38 B.C. they were, at their own request, transferred by Agrippa to the west bank. Their capital (*oppidum Vbiorum*, 36, 1) was later the site chosen for Claudius' *Colonia Agrippinensis*, the modern Cologne.

§ 4. **uernacula multitudo,** the ἀστικὸς ὄχλος of Dio, LVII, 5, 4 —non-citizens enrolled by Augustus to fill the gaps left in the army by the destruction of Varus' three legions in A.D. 9 (Suet. *Aug.* 25). These were not, as Mommsen held and Furneaux accepted, formed into new legions XXI and XXII: papyri show that XXII existed at least as early as 8 B.C. They were simply fresh drafts to the already existing legions. See Parker, pp. 88–9.

nuper, five years before—not long enough to make real legionaries of them.

implere, 'filled the silly minds of the rest (with the idea that) the time had come'.

missionem. The complaints are the same as those of the Pannonian legions (17).

§ 5. **non unus haec.** A verb of saying is understood.

apud . . . auris, 'nor was it said to timid soldiers'.

sua in manu sitam, 'in their power lay the fate of Rome'. Cf. Sall. *Jug.* 31, 5, *in uostra manu situm est, Quirites* (quoted by Fletcher, *C.R.* 1945, p. 45).

cognomentum, the surname Germanicus, borne by Drusus and his descendants in recognition of his conquests in Germany (Suet. *Claud.* 1).

imperatores, not 'Emperors', but those with the title *imperator* (3, 1). Drusus Germanicus had held the title, and it is probable that Germanicus also had already been given it for the first time.

32. § 1. **legatus,** Caecina. His behaviour is contrasted by implication with that of Blaesus in Pannonia.

plurium uaecordia, 'mob-madness'. Note that *uaecordia* is almost personified. Cf. *nox* and *fors* in 28, 1 and the very similar construction in *Ann.* XI, 32, *quamquam res aduersae consilium eximerent.*

ea. They were 'the immemorial object of the army's resentment', but according to the usual Latin idiom the demonstrative pronoun in such a sentence is attracted to the number and gender of the predicate. Cf.

Virg. *Aen.* VI, 129, *hoc opus, hic labor est.* For similar resentment against centurions see 17.

sexagenis. The abl., referring to the lashes, makes better sense: soldiers suffering from *uaecordia* would hardly take time solemnly to divide themselves into companies of sixty to deal with each centurion, but might easily see sixty as a grimly appropriate number of lashes when deciding on their punishment. There were sixty centurions in each legion.

§ 2. **Septimius.** He is otherwise unknown.

pedibus. See 23, 1 n.

donec . . . dederetur. See Introd. IV, 5 (ii).

Cassius Chaerea. The story of his assassination of Gaius is told by Suet. (*Gaius* 56–58). He was opposed to the choice of Claudius as Gaius' successor (Jos. *Ant. Jud.* XIX, 258) and was executed by him (ibid. 269).

animi. For the gen. see Introd. IV, 2 (i).

§ 3. **si qua alia,** 'and anything else which the needs of the moment required'.

coniectantibus, lit. 'to those guessing the soldiers' feelings more deeply', i.e. 'to students of military psychology'. For the dat. see Introd. IV, 3 (iii).

ardescerent . . . silerent, subj., because the clauses are virtual oblique.

ut . . . crederes, 'that you would have believed', 'that they might almost have been under orders'. The subj. is past potential, cf. the common *scires, putares,* etc.; for its use with *ut,* cf. Livy, XLI, 13, 8, *taciti, ut iratos esse scires, secuti sunt currum.*

33. § 1. **ut diximus,** in 31, 2.

adfertur, 'news was brought'. Cf. 10, 1 n.

eius, i.e. of Augustus. For the relationships see table on p. 49

plures, for the commoner *complures* 'several'. Cf. *Ann.* XIII, 39, *plura simul in loca ibatur.*

set. Germanicus was married to a descendant of Augustus, and by their children the succession was secured: he was himself related by blood to Tiberius and Augusta: *and yet* he was hated by them.

§ 2. **libertatem.** See on 1, 1.

redditurus. *fuisse* is understood. 'They believed that if he had come into power, he would have restored the Republic.'

spes eadem, lit. 'the same hope', i.e. the hope that he would do the same.

ciuile. See 8, 2 n.; here perhaps 'unassuming'.

adrogantibus et obscuris, plural, because each adj. belongs to both nouns. Cf. 70, 1 *secundam et quartam decimam . . . ducendas tradit.* The principles governing the use of singular or plural adjs. when the adj. belongs to more than one noun, are similar to those governing the use of a verb with more than one subject. See 68, 5 n.; 70, 5 n.

§ 3. nouercalibus . . . stimulis. Livia was in fact the stepmother of Julia, Agrippina's mother: but she is represented as carrying the bitterness on to the next generation.

nisi quod. She had the qualities of her defects; an excitable temperament can cause trouble, but can in other circumstances be used to advantage.

34. § 1. seque et proximos. This is the reading of M, perfectly good Latin, and much better sense than the emendation *Sequanos*. There is no real doubt that *seque*[7] of the manuscript is *seque et* (the sign occurs again at *Ann*. III, 44); the use of *-que . . . et* and *-que . . . et . . . et* with balancing words is quite common in Tacitus, and the *-que* is nearly always joined to *se* or *sibi* (cf. 4, 1, *seque et domum et pacem*; *Hist*. IV, 34, *seque et proximos*); there was every reason why Germanicus should himself take the oath to the new Princeps, but none whatever for singling out the Sequani. 'He administered to himself and his circle and the Belgic communities the oath of loyalty to Tiberius.'

in uerba eius. See 7, 2 n.

§ 2. audiri coepere. The rule that *coepi* (and to a lesser extent *desino*) become passive in form before a passive infin., is frequently disregarded by the poets and later writers. Tacitus himself never in such phrases uses the passive form of either verb. Cf. 13, 5, *ut . . . rogari desineret*; *Hist*. III, 34, *occidi coepere*.

§ 3. sic, 'like this', i.e. 'as they were'.

uexilla, here the standards of the maniples (see 17, 3 n. and 18, 2 n.). The cohort as such seems to have had no standard: probably that of its first maniple was used (see Parker, p. 42).

praeferri. *iubet* is understood from the beginning of the sentence.

ut . . . discerneret. The men would range themselves roughly behind their own standard.

§ 4. flexit. See 13, 5 n.

quae apud Germanias. See Introd. VI.

illis cum legionibus. I and XX are particularly mentioned in 42, 3.

consensum. Germanicus is deliberately exaggerating the lack of trouble elsewhere, in order to impress upon the legions that they stand alone. Note that he also implies that they are opposed to Tiberius' election, which is not in fact the cause of the trouble.

35. § 1. ubi . . . ubi . . . quonam . . . quo. The indignant effect of Germanicus' rhetoric is cleverly suggested by the rapid questions. For the omission of the subj. verb see 7, 1 n.

modestia. See 11, 1 n. Here it means 'proper behaviour', 'behaviour proper to soldiers', as in 49, 4.

quonam. *nam*, like γάρ, is used to give vivacity and vigour to a query. It can be used to introduce the question (Plaut. *Epid*. 132, *perdidisti omnem operam./Nam qui perdidi?*) or, as here, be attached as a suffix to the interrogatory word. Cf. Cic. *N.D.* I, 24, *in qua non uideo, ubinam uita beata possit insistere.*

exprobrant. See 18, 1 n. Note that many of the grievances are the same as those put forward in 17 sq., but that variety in treatment avoids an impression of idle repetition.

indiscretis, 'with indistinguishable shouts' lit., i.e. 'there was a confused roar of bitter complaint about . . .'

uacationum. See 17, 4 n.

propriis nominibus, 'by their particular names', i.e. 'specifically'.

materiae lignorum, wood, for construction and destruction.

aduersus otium, 'to prevent idleness in the camp'.

quaeruntur. The indic. shows that this is a general comment by Tacitus, and not part of the soldiers' complaint.

§ 2. **mederetur . . . orabant.** There is something wrong with the sentence, but the fault would appear to be Tacitus' and not that of his manuscript. He has started to say *mederetur . . . neu mortem (se obire pateretur)* but has branched off before reaching the second verb, to introduce a positive contrast to 'not death' (*non mortem, sed finem . . . daret*) and then finished the sentence by putting this contrasting phrase in the acc. after *orabant*—in itself a perfectly possible construction. The result is not a balance of two equally possible constructions, but a confusion of them. It is just possible that the confusion is deliberate, to indicate the incoherently shouted demands of the soldiers. 'He should help the weary before death claimed them at the same drudgery: an end of such harassing service, they begged, and retirement without destitution.'

§ 3. **faustis . . . ominibus.** They indicated their support, if he should wish to try for the throne.

promptos. This seems the best emendation of *promtas* M. The brevity and compression of the statement is very Tacitean, and the omission of *se* (which causes no difficulty of translation) can be paralleled. See *Ann.* IV, 59 *extimulatur ut erectum et fidentem animi ostenderet.*

§ 4. **tribunali.** The normal prose construction of *desilio* is *de, ex, ab* with the abl.: but the poets made much freer use of the simple abl. and it is found occasionally in prose from Livy onward. Its use is especially easy after a compound like *desilio*, where the case can depend on the preposition compounded with the verb. Cf. *Ann.* XV, 28, *equo desiluit.*

minitantes, ni . . ., 'threatening (violence) if he did not return'.

potius quam . . . exueret. *quam,* as a co-ordinating conjunction, originally and naturally produced two co-ordinate clauses in the same mood, e.g. (*a*) *perdam operam potius quam carebo filia* (Plaut.); (*b*) *dem potius aurum quam illum corrumpi sinam* (Plaut.); (*c*) *affirmaui quiduis me* *potius perpessurum quam ex Italia me exiturum* (Cic.). But by its very nature, a statement with *potius quam* was more frequently associated with some kind of subj.—potential, voluntative, jussive—and this came to be accepted as the regular construction after *quam* when one alternative was being deliberately rejected, so that (*a*) becomes *perdam* . . . *quam caream* or (in past time) *perdidi* . . . *quam carerem.* The simple comparison of two actions naturally remains indic. (i.e. *abiit potius quam eos iuuit* means 'his action was departure rather than assistance', 'he went away instead of helping', while *abiit potius quam iuuaret* means 'he went away rather than help them').

In indirect speech, in the classical period, the normal construction is still two infins. (*c*) above. But the common use of the subj. in the *quam* clause was making it look more and more like a subordinate clause, and from Livy on it is regularly so treated and kept in the subj. Cf. *Ann.* XIII, 42, *omnia potius toleraturum quam . . . submitteret.* It will be seen from this explanation that the subj. is a natural development in the *quam* clause and requires no *ut* 'understood' to explain it. Livy sometimes *inserts* an *ut*, but it is grammatically quite unnecessary.

deferebat . . . ni . . . attinuissent. For the condition see 23, 2 n.

§ 5. uix credibile dictu. It was safe enough for the mob at the back to suggest that he use his sword, but highly dangerous for individuals to thrust themselves forward with the suggestion. Obviously they were marked, because the name of Calusidius is known. *dictu* is the Second Supine, in origin either the dat. or abl. case of a verbal noun. If it is dat. (forms in -*u* do exist, see 10, 2 n.), it expresses purpose (*facile factu* 'easy for doing'); if abl., it is one of respect ('easy in respect of the doing'). It is used to complete the sense of certain adjs. describing moral characteristics, or probability. Cf. *mirabile dictu.*

feriret. The omission of *ut* brings this nearer to a direct quotation and makes it more vivid. Not 'they encouraged him to strike' but 'let him strike, they urged'.

addito, impersonal abl. abs. See Introd. IV, 4 (iv); 'adding that it was sharper'.

mali moris. For the gen. see 56, 4 n.

spatium . . . quo, 'there was time for Caesar to be hurried to his tent'. The subj. is generic.

36. § 1. superiorem. See 31, 2 n.

Vbiorum oppidum. See 31, 3 n.

manus, not 'troops', as Furneaux says, but 'hands'. The metaphor lies more in *erupturas* than in *imbutas*—'hands once dipped in loot would soon be stretching out to plunder the Gallic provinces too'. Cf. ps.-Quint. *Decl. Mai.* II, 9, *ad quod erumpant manus* and see Fletcher in *C.Q.* 1943, p. 90.

Galliarum, plural, because Gaul consisted of four provinces.

§ 2. **gnarus,** 'the fact that the enemy knew' . . . See 8, 6 n. 'Their apprehension was increased by the enemy's knowledge of the Roman rebellion and by the certainty of invasion if they neglected the Rhine bank.' For an interesting dispute about the meaning of *omittere*, see *J.R.S.* 1937-39, esp. 1939, p. 5 sq.

inuasurus. For the future part. see Introd. IV, 7 (iv). This particular ex. is complicated, because it also supplies the apodosis to *si omitteretur* (Introd. IV, 7 (ii)), and acts as a vivid apodosis to the more remote protasis (see note on *suscipi* below). *omitteretur* is imperf. subj. because the sentence is virtually oblique—'the certainty that, if the bank were to be neglected, the enemy would invade'.

auxilia et socii, the auxiliary forces of the army and the local tribesmen.

suscipi. The original condition was *si . . . armentur . . . suscipitur,* the indic. implying the inevitability of the result if the protasis were carried out (cf. 19, 5 n.). Cf. Ovid, *Trist.* IV, iii, 78, *si ualeant homines, ars tua, Phoebe, iacet.* 'On the other hand, if they armed the allies . . . that was civil war.'

periculosa. With this we return abruptly to narrative. Tacitus clearly intends the change to be vivid and dramatic, and it therefore seems likely that the manuscript reading *concedentur* is correct: it is the future counterpart of the historic present to be supplied with *seueritas,* &c. The emendation *concederentur* loses both the dramatic quality and the necessary future meaning.

§ 3. **uolutatis inter se,** 'when all the arguments had been weighed and compared'.

epistulae. See 30, 4 n.

missionem . . . exauctorari. The context makes it clear that *missio* here means absolute, and *exauctorari* conditional, discharge. On the conditions of service see 17, 2 n.

sub uexillo. See 17, 3 n.

ceterorum inmunes, exempt from all duties except that of beating off the enemy. The pres. infins. make the letter sound almost like a legal document—'that discharge be hereby granted', &c.

petiuerant. For the indic. see 10, 2 n. on *abstulerat.*

37. § 1. in tempus conficta, 'improvized for the occasion', 'emergency measures'.

in hiberna, (postponed) 'until they reached winter quarters'. This is an extension of the normal *in posterum diem, in aduentum tuum,* &c.

isdem in aestiuis, 'on the spot', 'there and then'.

contracta, 'scraped together'. The order of *amicorum ipsiusque Caesaris* emphasizes the oddity of this measure—not only his friends, but Germanicus himself had to contribute money to make up the necessary sum.

persolueretur. This is the normal classical use of the temporal subj.—they refused to leave until the money should be paid. For the Silver Latin use see Introd. IV, 5 (ii).

§ 2. turpi agmine, 'in a disgraceful column' lit. 'It was a disgraceful march, for . . .'

inter signa. Each soldier had a savings account *ad signa*, consisting of half of any donative paid, together with any savings of his own (Veg. II, 20; cf. Suet. *Dom.* 7). This was therefore the natural place for the money to be: what Tacitus is objecting to is the semi-sacrilege involved in the association of the standards with money extorted from Germanicus.

There is some difficulty here in the I and XX legions' possession oı the money which apparently only the V and XXI had demanded on the spot. But once the demand had been made, it would surely have been very difficult to pay two legions immediately, and defer payment to the others. The V and XXI caused the change of plan, but I and XX must then have shared in the payment.

38. § 1. in Chaucis, in the territory of the Chauci, who occupied that part of N. Germany now bounded by Emden and Hamburg.

coeptauere. *coepto* is used perhaps more often by Tacitus than by any other writer, and it is very commonly (though not exclusively) used of rebellion and conspiracy. Cf. 45, 2; *Ann.* II, 81 (both *seditionem*).

praesidium agitantes, 'on garrison duty'.

uexillarii, 'units'—not necessarily of veterans, but merely men detailed for special duty. See 17, 3 n.

praesenti, 'immediate'. A classical meaning of the word. Cf. Cic. *Div.* II, 122, *praesens poena sit.*

M'. Ennius, a very probable emendation for *Mennius* M. A M'. Ennius is mentioned by Dio, LV, 33, 2.

exemplo . . . iure, abls. of attendant circumstances (Introd. IV, 4 (ii *c*)). It appears from Dio, LIII, 13, 6 that even for Augustus' *legati* the right to execute soldiers was a concession. It was certainly not possessed by *praefecti castrorum.*

§ 2. postquam. For the omission of the verb of the subordinate clause see 2, 1 n.

mutuatur, 'he borrowed protection from boldness' lit.—'he found safety in boldness'. Cf. Livy, XXX, 12, 19, *ab amore mutuatur consilium.*

qui obstiterant, 'whosoever resisted', i.e. 'all resistance'. For the constructions used in indefinite clauses see Introd. IV, 5 (i).

ad ripam, 'towards the Rhine' (where their winter camp was).

decessisset. This represents the future perfect indic. of his original statement.

turbidos et nihil ausos, 'rebellious but under control'. *et* = 'and yet' is relatively common at all periods of Latin, when the context

makes the meaning clear. Cf. *Hist.* II, 20, *speciosis et irritis nominibus.*
et nihil shows the collocation of conjunction and negative which is
usual when it is desirable to define and emphasize the negative. Cf. Cic.
De Or. I, 32, *sermo facetus ac nulla in re rudis.*

39. § 1. legati ab senatu. On prepositional phrases attached to
nouns see 8, 1 n. The envoys were those sent by Tiberius (14, 3) but
the guilty conscience of the legionaries connected them with the
rebellion.

regressum, from the Upper army (37, 3).

apud aram. An altar to Rome and Augustus was established in the
Ubian capital some time after 9 B.C. It was, like the more famous one
at Lugdunum, intended to be a cult centre for a whole province: the
province did not materialize, but the altar remained.

sub uexillo, with *missi.* The reference is to those granted conditional
discharge (*exauctorari qui sena dena fecissent ac retineri sub uexillo,* 36, 3).

§ 2. conscientia, 'guilty conscience'. Latin, like English (e.g. 'an
attack of conscience') uses the word without qualification when the
context makes the meaning clear. Cf. 57, 2.

metus uenisse. When expressions of fearing indicate not a fear that
something will happen, but an apprehensive belief that it has happened,
they are often treated like verbs of perception and constructed with an
acc. and infin. This construction is rare in Cicero, but fairly common in
Livy, the poets and the post-Augustan writers. Cf. Livy, XXIII, 14, 8,
senatum metus cepit resisti multitudini non posse.

expresserant. For the indic. see 10, 2 n. on *fecere.*

§ 3. quamuis falsis. *criminibus* is understood. The presence of *reum*
is sufficient to recall the standard phrase. The abl. is one of attendant
circumstances. For *reum subdere* see 6, 3 n.

Munatium Plancum, L. Munatius Plancus, the consul of A.D. 13
and (probably) son of the famous Plancus of the Civil Wars.

senatus consulti, the decree they imagined the delegation had
come to enforce.

uexillum. This can here hardly be anything but their own (veteran)
standard, already mentioned in § 1. It would not be necessary to explain
Germanicus' personal standard as *in domo G. situm,* and it is difficult
to see what the soldiers could want with it. But their own standard was
the symbol of their conditional release, and with it in their possession they
would feel they had some guarantee that they would not be returned
to ordinary service. The veterans are naturally the soldiers most concerned here, because they have most to lose if the terms (36, 3) are
revoked. Why the standard was kept *in domo G.* is not clear: it may
have been only for safe keeping.

moliuntur foris, 'worked at the doors', i.e. 'broke down the doors'
Cf. *Ann.* II, 82, *moliuntur templorum foris.*

tradere. For the infin. after *subigere* see Introd. IV, 6 (i).

intento . . . metu, a confused but vivid phrase: they threatened death, which caused him to fear. 'Under threat of death.'

§ 4. **dignitas.** He was an ex-consul, and leader of the delegation.

signa et aquilam. The shrine of the standards was the nearest available approach to a temple and sanctuary.

tutabatur, 'tried to protect'. See 18, 3 n.

uim extremam, 'warded off the extreme violence', i.e. 'saved him from the last outrage'.

rarum. The parenthesis, as often, comments on the following clause. Cf. 35, 5: 56, 2. The sentence as it stands is rather illogical, because it is compressed. Its force is 'a Roman envoy would have been killed in sanctuary (a thing rare enough even at an enemy's hands) and it would have happened *in a Roman camp*'.

§ 5. **noscebantur.** *postquam* with the imperf. indic. describes an action which continues right up to the time of the main verb, and is not simply an isolated incident in the past. There is often an underlying causal sense, with *postquam* meaning 'now that' rather than 'after'. This causal meaning of *postquam* is found at all periods of Latin and with all tenses, but when used with the imperfect it is especially characteristic of Livy and Tacitus. Cf. 4, 2, *postquam . . . fatigabatur.* 'Now that general, soldiers and the events (of the night) were being recognized for what they were . . .'

perduci. *impero* is sometimes so used (with a passive infin.) even in classical prose. Cf. Cic. *Verr.* V, 69, *eodem ceteros piratas condi imperarat.*

§ 6. **neque.** The sense of 'saying' is understood from *increpans,* and on that this clause depends.

miseratur, 'bewailed' not 'pitied'.

40. §·1. **eo in metu,** 'in this alarming situation'.

pergeret, 'because (they said) he was not proceeding'. The subj. is virtual oblique. The *ubi* clause is also clearly part of their statement, and therefore the omitted verb would be subj. (7, 1 n.). With *satis* the Latin slips into straightforward Or. Ob.

§ 2. **si.** A subj. verb is again omitted. See 7, 1 n.

filium, the later Emperor Gaius.

haberet. When a rhetorical question represents not a statement (17, 1 n.) but a command, it quite logically has a subj. verb in Or. Ob. Here the original *cur habes?* meant *noli habere*; in Or. Ob. the interrogative word is retained, and the verb becomes the subj. of indirect command. Cf. 19, 3, *cur . . . meditentur?*; 26, 2, *cur uenisset?*

auo. Tiberius had adopted Germanicus (3, 5), and is therefore reckoned as Gaius' grandfather.

§ 3. **ortam.** See table on p. 49.

ad pericula. *ad* with the acc. frequently conveys the meaning of respect or reference, especially with adjs. Cf. Cic. *Font.* 43, *uirum ad labores belli impigrum, ad pericula fortem.* 'In face of danger.'

§ 4. **incedebat.** This sentence is a series of verbal pictures, held together with the minimum of syntax, and producing its effect from the careful placing of words and phrases. It is best translated by a series of short sentences.

profuga, put first to give it emphasis, and next to *ducis* for additional effect.

qui manebant, i.e. Germanicus and the other husbands.

41. § 1. non florentis Caesaris, 'the appearance (of things in general was) not of a successful Caesar nor (of one) in his own camp, but as (of one) in a captured city', i.e. 'the scene did not suggest a successful Caesar in his own camp, but rather a captured city'. For *suis* see 12, 3 n.

gemitusque ac planctus. *-que* joins the clause to *non . . . facies, ac* joins the two halves of the subject of the clause.

etiam militum. They, presumably, had not until now known of the decision to send away the women and children.

contuberniis. For the abl. see Introd. IV, 4 (i).

quis ille. This is the beginning of the Or. Ob., so the verb to be supplied is subj. (7, 1 n.). The sudden indignant questions are dramatic; Or. Ob. is used in preference to direct quotation, because it better expresses mass feeling, and allows Tacitus to reserve his rhetorical guns for Germanicus' speech immediately following.

quod tam triste. To justify the adj. *quod, triste* must be taken as a substantive. This is not entirely satisfactory, but neither are the suggested emendations. The run of the phrase is against *quid* (a predicative adj., not a pronoun is required); more likely is the provision of a noun like *agmen* or *iter*, but it is difficult to see why that was ever lost.

feminas sq. The staccato phrases give the impression of puzzled and rather indignant spectators tossing comments to and fro.

ad tutelam. *ad* here expresses purpose, like Greek ἐπί. Cf. the common *ad praesidium.*

imperatoriae uxoris, partitive gen. 'Nothing to mark the general's wife, no sign of the usual escort.'

et externae fidei. Löfstedt (*Synt.* I, p. 190, n. 2) seems to be right in taking *externae fidei* as a dat. of goal (Introd. IV, 3 (vi)), and the *et* as necessary to join the two expressions of goal. The Latin is bold, but not impossible, especially for Tacitus, who often joins two possible constructions of the same verb (see 14, 1 n. and cf. *Ann.* XIV, 38, *aduersa prauitati ipsius, prospera ad fortunam referebat*). And the sense is the sense required—'they were going to the Treviri and the protection of foreigners'. For a very similar use of *fides,* cf. Curtius, VI, 7, 9, *quod caput suum permisisset fidei adhuc inexpertae.*

§ 2. socer Drusus. Instead of further narrative ('they remembered that . . .'), we now have a vivid list of the points as they occurred to the soldiers. 'There was Drusus her father-in-law, her own virtue, her infant son . . .'

pudicitia, abl. of quality, balancing *fecunditate.*

in castris genitus. He was, in fact, as Suet. *Gaius* 8 shows, born at Antium. But he spent the early years of his life in military camps, and there was a popular legend that he had been born there. Whether Tacitus is here accepting the legend, or merely indicating the soldiers as accepting it, is uncertain.

uocabulo. See 23, 3 n.

Caligulam, 'Little Boots', from the *caliga* or military boot. Cf. Suet. *Gaius* 9, *manipulario habitu.* The boot was not worn by officers, hence *uulgi.*

§ 3. **quam,** for the classical *ac.* This extended use of *quam* becomes increasingly frequent after Livy. Cf. 73, 4, *perinde . . . quam.*

orant . . . maneret. The arrangement of the verbs without connexion gives a vivid picture of the confusion. 'They begged, they blocked the way: she must stop, she must return.'

occursantes, 'running to meet', i.e. 'to intercept her'.

recens dolore, 'fresh from grief and anger' ('his grief and anger still fresh'). The normal construction is *recens a* and the abl. (Virg. *Aen.* VI, 450, *recens a uulnere Dido*) but Tacitus dispenses with the preposition. Cf. *Ann.* IV, 52, *is recens praetura.*

42. § 1. **uxor . . . filius . . . sunt.** See 68, 5 n.

liberos meos, 'my family', i.e. Gaius and the child soon to be born.

quidquid istud sceleris. *sceleris* is partitive gen. after *quidquid,* and *istud* qualifies the whole phrase. 'Whatever criminal action of yours is impending.'

pietur, for *expietur* (5, 1 n.). The meaning is rather 'be appeased by' than 'be atoned for', cf. Livy, IX, 1, 3, *expiatum est, quidquid . . . irarum in nos caelestium fuit.* Complications arise from the facts that (*a*) Germanicus is picturing himself as a kind of blood-sacrifice, and so *piare* has something of the sense of 'atonement', and (*b*) the 'appeasement' is not, as it usually was, an act of propitiation, but the putting into effect of a criminal impulse—'satisfaction' only in a limited sense. Cf. Prop. III, xix, 18, *quo tempore matris|iram natorum caede piauit amor.*

occisus . . . pronepos. See 8, 6 n.

faciant. This is Ritter's correction of *faciat* M. For the reasons which make a plural verb desirable here, see 68, 5 n.

§ 2. **inausum intemeratumue.** Both are poetical words, borrowed from Virgil. *uobis* is dative of the agent, cf. *quibus* below and Introd. IV, 3 (iv).

quod nomen. Editors have noted the similarity of this section to the opening of Scipio's speech in Livy, XXVIII, 27. But this does not make the speech necessarily Tacitus' own invention. Addresses by generals to their troops tend to be of limited range, and although the style is Tacitus' own and the rhetoric highly developed for dramatic purposes, it is unsafe to assume that such speeches have no foundation at all in fact. See *Rhein. Mus.* 1956, p. 304.

uallo et armis. This refers to the events of cc. 34–5.

proiecta, 'cast aside', 'rejected'. The *legatio* came from the Senate.

hostium . . . gentium. The three expressions form a climax. By their behaviour they have 'failed to recognize the rights granted even to enemies, the sanctity of ambassadors and international law'.

§ 3. **diuus Iulius.** According to Suet. *Jul.* 70, this happened in 47 B.C., just before Caesar went to Africa.

diuus Augustus. The reference appears to be to the complaints made by the veterans at Brundisium shortly after Actium, though according to other accounts (Suet. *Aug.* 17; Dio, LI, 3–4) Augustus rather appeased the soldiers than cowed them. But Suet. *Aug.* 24 says, *disciplinam seuerissime rexit* and records the dismissal of a legion; whether this refers to the period immediately after Actium or not, there was obviously a tradition of firmness connected with Augustus' handling of the legions.

nos, 'I'. Lit. 'people like myself'—a more modest expression than the singular pronoun.

ut . . . ita. See 12, 1 n. He was *ortus* only by adoption.

erat, 'would be'. With words expressing a standard (*par, rectum, dignum, longum,* &c., and gerundives) Latin uses the indic., not the subj. So *longum est* = 'it would be tedious', *longum erat* = 'it would have been tedious'. The absoluteness of the standard is thus emphasized, and not the condition in which it happens temporarily to be involved: to the Romans a thing *was* right or wrong, and it is stated in that form, any necessary conditions being drawn from the context. Note that here *erat* means 'would be', not (as in *longum erat* and 66, 2, *eundum erat*) 'would have been'. The imperf. subj. is normally used in conditions unfulfilled in present time, and by analogy we commonly find the corresponding tense of the indic. in phrases such as this. Cf. Cic. *Fin.* IV, 2, *illud erat aptius.*

'I am not yet what they were: but I am descended from them, and if it were the legions of Spain and Syria who were rejecting me, that would be surprising and disgraceful enough.' The offenders were, in fact, his own familiar German legions.

illa signis . . . acceptis. This cannot, in the context, refer to anything but the First Legion. It has been plausibly suggested that this is the legion whose degradation is recorded by Dio, LIV, 11, 5. In which case it would have been, until 19 B.C., Legio I Augusta and thereafter simply Legio I; it was probably reconstituted by Tiberius shortly after 19. See Syme in *J.R.S.* 1933, p. 15.

tu . . . socia. Legio XX had fought in Pannonia during the great rebellion of A.D. 6 (Vell. II, 112).

duci, i.e. Tiberius, who has just been shown to have particular claims on the loyalties of both legions.

§ 4. tirones . . . ueteranos, the I and XX legions respectively.

legatos. Almost certainly = the commanding officers of the legions, and not the envoys from the Senate. Germanicus has already (§ 2) dealt with their treatment of the delegation, and is now attacking their military misdemeanours. *intercludi* is not an adequate description of their attack on the envoys (39), but a reasonable account of the obvious helplessness of the *legati legionum* (32, 1).

precariam animam . . . trahere, 'drawing precarious breath' lit. Cf. Pliny, *H.N.* XI, 6, *nec uideo cur magis possint non trahere animam talia et uiuere quam spirare sine uisceribus* and see *C.Q.* 1943, p. 90. A *precarium* is something which depends on favour and not on right, and Germanicus is therefore representing himself as at the mercy of the legions.

43. § 1. enim. The connexion of thought is 'I am living on sufferance and it would be better not to live at all: why then . . .?' There is also a suggestion of the rhetorical and emphatic use of *enim* which is found in the common *quid enim?*

parabam. See 35, 4.

melius et amantius. *agebat* or *fecit* is understood. Tacitus is often very bold in his omission of verbs, when the context makes the meaning clear. Cf. *Ann.* XIV, 8, *anxia Agrippina quod nemo a filio.* The style in English is that of the diarist, cf. Pepys 'By water to my office and there all the morning and so home to dinner'.

offerebat. See 35, 5.

exercitui, 'involved with my army in so many crimes' lit. Germanicus pictures himself as tainted by the crimes of the soldiers under his command. For the double construction (dat. of the person and gen. of the crime) with *conscius,* cf. Ter. *Phorm.* 156, *audacis facinoris mihi consciu's. exercitu* in the Oxford Text appears to be a misprint.

sineret . . . ulcisceretur, 'such as would allow . . . but would avenge'. The subj. is akin to that used in generic relative clauses (3, 7 n.), but is here not only descriptive but potential. Cf. *pateretur,* 64, 4.

§ 2. neque . . . sinant, 'and may Heaven forbid'. *neque* and not *neue* is the regular negative conjunction with the *independent* jussive subj., except when another negative clause precedes, i.e. *mulier . . . ne adsit neue uideat* (Cato, *R.R.* 83) but *hanc sequamur neque discamus* (Cic. *De Or.* III, 44). It is common when, as here, it introduces a new sentence. *sino ut* is rare, but cf. Livy, XXXIV, 24, 2, *ne Iuppiter sirit ut.*

quamquam. See 7, 3 n.

subuenisse . . . compressisse. The infins. explain the demonstrative phrase—'that glory, namely, to have helped', i.e. 'the glory of having helped'. Cf. Cic. *Tusc.* III, 30, *haec est illa diuina sapientia, nihil admirari.*

§ 3. **imago,** 'vision', 'thought'. The word is not technical, of an ancestral image, but used as Cicero uses it in *De Amic.* 102, *qui sibi non illius memoriam atque imaginem proponendam putet.*

gloria, 'pride' or 'ambition'.

hanc maculam, the stain of rebellion.

§ 4. **alia . . . pectora,** 'a change of expression, a change of heart'.

si . . . redditis, 'if you are ready to restore'. The tense refers to their present intentions rather than their future actions. *reddere* has a slightly different meaning with each phrase—they will give the Senate's envoys their proper status, render renewed obedience to Tiberius, and by their behaviour make it possible for Germanicus' wife and child to return. *imperator* here clearly refers to Tiberius.

diuidite, 'single out', 'separate out'. The meaning is unusual, but helped by the context.

stabile ad, 'firm for repentance', i.e. 'a guarantee of your repentance'. For the construction, cf. Cic. *De Or.* I, 129, *nihil est tam ad diuturnitatem memoriae stabile.*

44. § 1. **neue.** Contrast *neque* in 43, 2. The subj. here is dependent, and with that *neue* is common, even after an affirmative. Cf. Caes. *B.G.* V, 58, *praecipit unum omnes peterent Indutiomarum neu quis uulneret.*

reditum . . . excusauit. *excusare* in the meaning of apologetic refusal is not common, and most of the exx. are Silver Latin or later.

exsequerentur, indirect jussive. 'The rest they must do themselves.'

§ 2. **uinctos.** This belongs to *seditiosissimum quemque* by *constructio ad sensum.* The plural is often so used with collective singulars. Cf. 30, 1 *pars . . . caesi;* 56, 3 *iuuentus . . . arcebant;* 67, 1 *hostis . . . succederent.*

exercuit. *exercere,* used with *iudicium,* is a technical legal term: its use with *poenas* is an extension of this, which is found occasionally in the poets (Virg. *Aen.* VI, 543; Stat. *Theb.* III, 5—with *supplicium*) and several times in the later jurists.

pro contione. The evidence for *contio* in the meaning of 'speaker's platform' is dubious and therefore this is best taken as 'in the manner of an assembly', i.e. 'in assembly', in reasonably ordered array.

adclamauerant, the normal classical construction of indefinite frequency.

§ 4. **Raetiam,** an Alpine province, covering parts of Switzerland, Bavaria and Austria. The Suebi are probably the Marcomanni, followers of Maroboduus.

ceterum, 'but in reality'. See 10, 1 n.

castris, probably abl. depending on the preposition compounded with the verb.

§ 5. centurionatum. The word is rare, but the phrase will stand if *agere* is taken in the general sense of 'manage', 'handle' as in Suet. *Dom.* 12, *Iudaicus fiscus acerbissime actus est.* 'Next he dealt with the (office of) centurions.'

ordinem. Some centurions ranked above others. See on *primi ordines,* 29, 2.

et cui erant, 'and (if he had any) . . .' The parenthesis is Tacitus' and therefore the verb is indic.

dona militaria. See the note (24, 3) on *insignia.*

adprobauerant . . . obiectauissent. The change to the subj. of indefinite frequency (Introd. IV, 5 (i)) probably indicates no more than Tacitus' usual desire for variety of expression.

45. § 1. Vetera, castra Vetera, near Xanten, at the junction of the Rhine and the Lippe, sixty Roman miles (*c.* 56 English miles) north of Cologne (*oppidum Vbiorum*), where the events described in the last few chapters took place.

hibernantium. Their departure from the summer camp is implied in 37, 1.

§ 2. primi. They had started the rebellion (31, 3) and committed its worst excesses (32) and were correspondingly difficult to suppress.

commilitonum. This belongs both to *poena* and to *paenitentia.* They were neither frightened into submission by the punishment of the other legions, nor softened by their change of heart.

arma, 'an armed force'. The fleet is probably part of the regular Rhine fleet used by Drusus, Tiberius and Germanicus. Cf. *Ann.* II, 7–8

certaturus, 'determined to decide the issue by force, should his authority be flouted'. For the use of the future participle see Introd. IV, 7 (iic). The subj. *detrectetur* is virtual oblique.

46. § 1. at Romae. Tacitus indicates a change of scene and subject by using a strong adversative, and putting the operative word (*Romae*) in a conspicuous position.

cognito, impersonal abl. abs. See Introd. IV, 4 (iv).

Illyrico. Although Pannonia as a province had been separated from Illyricum (16, 1 n.), Illyricum is still used to describe the geographical area of which Pannonia was a part.

inualida et inermia, 'things weak and unarmed'; the neuter adjs. are used as substantives and represent the class to which *patres* and *plebs* belong. Cf. *Hist.* V, 5, *parentes liberos fratres uilia habere*; Virg. *Aen.* IV, 569, *uarium et mutabile semper femina.*

cunctatione ficta, 'assumed hesitation' (about accepting the Principate; cf. 11–13).

ludificetur, dissideat . . . queat. The subjs. are virtual oblique, representing the city's complaint.

adulescentium. Germanicus was 29, Drusus about 27 years old.

§ 2. **cessuris,** 'to those sure to yield when they had seen', i.e. 'who would have given way when they saw . . .' For the fut. part. see Introd. IV, 7 (ii *c*).

longa experientia, 'their experienced Emperor'. For the abl. of quality see Introd. IV, 4 (ii *d*); for *experientia* 4, 3 n.

seueritatis et munificentiae summum, 'supreme as regards punishment and reward'—'with sovereign powers of punishment and reward'. The gen. is one of reference (Introd. IV, 2 (i)). *seueritas* is here probably stronger than the mere refusal of requests, as in 25, 3 and 36, 2.

§ 3. **Augustum.** Augustus spent the years 16–13 B.C. in Gaul, when he was 47–50 years of age. (It is very doubtful that Dio, LV, 6 really implies another visit in 8 B.C.) Tiberius was at the moment 56 years old. This is therefore a rhetorical flourish, but whether Tacitus' or his source's seems impossible to decide.

annis. The instrumental abl. is the normal classical construction with *uigeo.* Cf. Cic. *De Or.* II, 355, *qui memoria uigent.* For the acc. and inf. in rhetorical questions in Or. Ob. see 17, 1 n.

prospectum, 'slavery in Rome had been sufficiently provided for'.

47. § 1. **immotum . . . fixumque,** a Virgilian echo. See Introd. III. 'In spite of such talk Tiberius remained determined not to leave the capital.' *non omittere* is the subject of *fuit, Tiberio* dat. of the person interested.

ualidior sq. Tiberius' dilemma is presented to us dramatically. For the inference of motive see Introd. II.

quos. The use of *quis* for *uter,* though rare, is classical. Cf. Cic. *Att.* XVI, 14, 1, *ut quem* (i.e. Antony or Octavian) *uelis nescias.* On the position of *igitur* see 4, 1 n.

§ 2. **ac.** The *ne* clause depends on the sense of fear in *angebant,* as the question depends on its meaning of tortured doubt. *ac* is required to join the two.

cui . . . reuerentia. On the omission of the subj. verb see 7, 1 n.

excusatum, 'excusable'. This usage of *excusatus,* both personal and impersonal, is found occasionally in the post-Augustan writers. Cf. Sen. *Contr.* VII, 1, 20, *excusatius est in malum colorem incidere quam transire.*

quod aliud. *esset* is understood. See 7, 1 n.

§ 3. **iam iamque.** A strengthened form of *iam,* meaning 'at any moment'. Cf. Cic. *Att.* XII, 5 *c, cum Romae essem et te iam iamque uisurum me putarem.*

ut . . . iturus. See 7, 3 n. ⌐

uulgum. This form of the acc. of *uulgus* (n.) is also found in Virgil and Livy.

48. § 1. at Germanicus. See note on *at Romae*, 46, 1.

quamquam. On its use with the abl. abs. see 7, 3 n.

si . . . consulerent, 'in the hope that they might profit by what had just happened (to the other legions—44) and look to their own safety'. This use of *si* and the subj. is very common after verbs of waiting and trying (cf. Cic. *Att.* XVI, 2, 4, *exspectabamque, si quid de eo ad me scriberes*); it also found where (as here), there is a general sense of effort or expectation in the main clause. The connexion of *dandum . . . spatium* with waiting is fairly close; there are much looser examples. Cf. Cic. *Att.* XI, 9, 2, *solui (fasciculum), si quid ad me esset litterarum*—'I opened the packet, in the hope that there might be a letter for me.'

Caecinam. Last heard of (37, 2) taking I and XX back to Cologne, he is now apparently in Vetera with V and XXI. All four legions were under his command (31, 2).

in malos, a variation on the usual phrase *supplicium sumere de aliquo*.

§ 2. aquiliferis signiferisque, the legionary and manipular standard-bearers respectively, who ranked next after the centurions: there being at the moment no centurions left (32), these were their obvious deputies.

quod . . . sincerum erat, 'and all the most reliable element in camp'.

infamiae. The dat. with *eximere* is more commonly used of persons (dat. of person concerned), but in the post-Augustan writers, and especially in Tacitus, it is also used of things. Cf. Livy, VIII, 35, 5, *non noxae eximitur Q. Fabius*: *Ann.* I, 64, 3, *nox . . . legiones aduersae pugnae exemit*.

§ 3. postquam . . . uident. The historic present is, quite naturally, used with *postquam* by writers of all periods. Cf. Cic. *Verr.* II, 92, *quem posteaquam uidet non adesse*.

in officio, 'in their duty', i.e. 'loyal'. Cf. *Ann.* III, 42, *pauci equitum corrupti, plures in officio mansere*.

seditioni promptum, dat. of purpose. See Introd. IV, 3 (v).

quod . . . quis. The statutory distinction between *quis* and *qui*, the interrogative pronoun and adj., is that *quis* demands information about identity, *qui* about character and condition: thus *quis philosophus* requires the answer (say) Plato, while *qui philosophus* could be answered by *Stoicus*. But this distinction is not always observed, and here there is probably no motive behind the change from adj. to pronoun, except desire for variety. On the omission of the verbs of the indirect questions, see 7, 1 n.

49. § 1. omnium . . . armorum. Furneaux may be right in suggesting that the gen. is 'Greek' and dependent on *diuersa*; but *facies* (cf. 41,

1) seems to need the gen. to complete its meaning. 'Quite different (from this) was the appearance of any other civil war.'

proelio . . . e castris. The verb for these phrases is supplied by a kind of Zeugma (17, 4 n.) from *discedunt*. 'Not in battle (did they meet), nor from opposing camps (did they start), but from the same tents they separated into parties . . .'

dies . . . nox. Note the personification. Perhaps 'men from the same tents, which had seen them eating together by day and sleeping together at night'.

cetera. *cetera* is rather difficult, but Andresen's *cuncta* is even more difficult, besides being untrue. There was some method in the action, though not all could see it. The uproar was obvious, the reason for it obscure: everything else (the ultimate outcome, as becomes clear from the next sentence) was unpredictable.

intellecto, impersonal abl. abs. See Introd. IV, 4 (iv).

rapuerant. On the tense see 1, 2 n.

§ 2. **moderator.** See 4, 4 n. ?

licentia atque ultio et satietas. English would subordinate some of these nouns ('a free hand to exact vengeance to their complete satisfaction'). Tacitus gives them additional force by giving them equal grammatical weight in the sentence.

illud. This use of the neuter demonstrative pronoun with a feminine predicate is contrary to the normal rule of attraction (32, 1 n.). Similar exceptions are found in Cicero, but they can there be explained either as pronouns attached to a relative which cannot be attracted (*Phil.* I, 26, *quod ita erit gestum, id lex erit*), or, in philosophical contexts, as referring briefly to the point under discussion (*Fin.* IV, 12, *Zeno id dixit esse ignem*). This use, without such justifications, is found in the poets and later prose writers. Cf. Livy, II, 38, 5, *si hoc profectio et non fuga est.*

The unusual placing of *plurimis cum lacrimis* puts more emphasis on *cladem*, by separating it from the rest of its phrase.

§ 3. **cupido inuolat,** a vivid personification and metaphor. 'They were still savage, and were seized with the desire to march against the enemy.' For the acc. after *inuolo* see Introd. IV, 1 (i).

piaculum, acc. in apposition to the phrase. See Introd. IV, 1 (iv).

posse. The Or. Ob. represents their feelings. 'In no other way (they felt) . . .'

si . . . accepissent. For the *si* clause see 11, 3 n.

§ 4. **e legionibus,** from all four legions of Lower Germany, as appears from 51, 2.

quarum, the auxiliary *cohortes* and *alae*, who had taken no part in the legionary rebellion.

modestia, 'discipline', as in 35, 1.

50. § 1. agitabant. *agito* is used intransitively in the sense of 'act' or 'behave', describing a temporary or permanent condition of individuals or peoples; it is especially common in Sallust and Tacitus. Cf. *Ann.* IV, 46, *ferocius agitabant. agere* is also, and more commonly, used in this way. Cf. 68, 1, *inquies Germanus . . . agebat*: Sall. *Jug.* 55, *ciuitas laeta agere.*

iustitio. See 16, 2 n.

attinemur. This use of the first person plural in the meaning 'we Romans' and therefore 'the Romans', is fairly common in the historians. Cf. *nos* 55, 1.

Romanus. This appears to mean here both 'the Romans' and 'the Roman general'. It starts as a collective singular in contrast to *Germani*, but as the statement proceeds, the subject becomes more and more the man directing the army's movements and not the army itself.

siluam Caesiam. The exact site of this forest is uncertain, but it probably lay not far east of the Rhine, between the rivers Lippe and Ruhr. It seems fairly clear, from the next few chapters and from *Ann.* II, 25 and Strabo VII, 290, that the country of the Marsi lay between the upper waters of these rivers, and the army obviously crossed the forest before reaching the Marsian villages. The reference to Tiberius supports this placing, because in the campaigns obviously meant here, he did not penetrate far beyond the Rhine (Vell. II, 120). Gomoll (*Rhein. Mus.* 1938, p. 177) discusses the various suggested sites.

limitem. *limes* is a technical military term, not at this time having the specialized later meaning of 'fortified boundary line' but simply meaning a military road made to penetrate enemy territory. Velleius (II, 120), speaking of Tiberius' campaigns of A.D. 10–11, says *ultro Rhenum cum exercitu transgreditur. penetrat interius, aperit limites*, and this is pretty certainly one of these *limites*. That being so, there seems to be no difficulty about taking *coeptum* in its obvious sense of 'begun'. Tiberius did not in fact carry his invasion to any definite conclusion.

frontem . . . tergum . . . latera, accs. of respect. See Introd. IV, 1 (v).

§ 2. incautum, 'unguarded'. This passive meaning of the adj. (cf. *gnarum,* 5, 2 n.) is rare, especially in prose, but cf. Sall. *Hist.* fr. inc. 46D, *repente incautos agros inuasit.*

§ 3. cetera. Once the choice of route was made, everything else (i.e. the advance) was rapid.

ludicram. *ludicer* means 'sportive', and is used (by the post-Augustan writers) especially of theatrical and similar performances. Cf. *Ann.* XIV, 14, *ludicrum in modum.* The festival was being celebrated with due ceremony, with statutory (*sollemnibus*) banquet and show, not with informal junketings. The Germans, according to Tacitus, had only one kind of public show, a form of war-dance performed by the young men: it is described in *Germ.* 24.

siluarum, 'to clear a way through the woods'. For the gen. see Introd. IV, 2 (iii).

§ 4. **nox,** again almost personified.

Marsorum. For the probable location of the Marsi see the note on *silua Caesia* § 1. The name perhaps indicates a small confederacy of tribes, who appear to have gained historical importance only twice— in the defeat of Varus (*Ann.* II, 25) and in the present campaign.

stratis. This is probably not dat. after *circumdatae*, but abl. abs. Not the drunkards but the villages needed to be surrounded by pickets. *stratis* is then the first of a series of abls. abs. describing the situation: its subject is easily supplied (5, 1 n.) from *Marsorum*.

antepositis. *anteponere* is rare in the literal meaning. Cf. *Ann.* XII, 56, *antepositis propugnaculis*.

ne pax quidem. Tacitus means that they are not in the condition of positive peace, but in the negative state of drunken stupor. It was peace only in so far as the careless relaxation of drunkenness can be so called.

51. § 1. **auidas,** 'eager' (for battle). The context gives the shade of meaning required. Cf. 68, 4, *rebus secundis auidi*.

cuneos. *cuneus* ('wedge'), originally applied to a battle formation, is used by the later Latin writers to mean something like a 'flying column'. Cf. *Ann.* XVI, 27, *dispersique per fora ac basilicas cunei militares*.

non . . . non. For the anaphora see 1, 1 n.

templum. The Germans, as appears from *Germ.* 9 and other sources, made no temples for their gods: this should therefore be taken to mean 'sacred place' or 'sanctuary', the original meaning of *templum*. Cf. *Germ.* 40, *sacerdos . . . deam templo reddat* and Anderson's note *ad loc*. The site was probably a sacred grove with an altar in the middle.

sine uulnere, 'unwounded'. Even in classical Latin, phrases with *sine* had become almost stereotyped as equivalents of adjs. Cf. Cic. *Cael.* 78, *hominem sine re, sine fide, sine spe*.

§ 2. **Bructeros** &c. These tribes occupied (roughly) the territory between the Lippe and the present German-Dutch frontier.

gnarum. See 5, 2 n.

itineri et proelio, dat. of purpose (Introd. IV, 3 (v)). Cf. *Ann.* XIII, 40, *uiae pariter et pugnae composuerat exercitum*. Slight difficulty is caused by Tacitus' brief use of *incessit* instead of, e.g. *incessum instituit*; but the construction is unmistakable and there is no need to supply *paratus*. See Löfstedt, I, p. 190 n. 2.

auxiliariae cohortes. It is fairly obvious that only some of the auxiliary infantry is here meant. The normal order of march (see Parker, pp. 252-4) put auxiliary cavalry and infantry in the van, and auxiliary infantry and cavalry in the rear, and *ceteri sociorum* implies that order here. Nipperdey supposed the loss of a numeral, but loose writing is a more likely explanation. For the gen. *sociorum* see Introd. IV, 2 (iii).

§ 3. **porrigeretur.** The subj. is here normal classical usage, cf. 37, 1 n The Romans could not march through the forest in the square formation mentioned above: their line would of necessity become longer and thinner.

adsultantes. The verb is Silver Latin and used normally with the dat. But cf. Stat. *Theb.* XI, 244, *portarumque moras . . . assultat.* For the acc. here and with *incurrere* see Introd. IV, 1 (i).

turbabanturque. Note the tense—they were in process of being disorganized when Caesar rode up.

leues. The *auxilia* were the light infantry of the Roman army.

cum, 'inverse' *cum* (11, 3 n.).

hoc illud, 'this was that opportunity', i.e. the one which they had desired (49, 3).

§ 4. **siluas.** For the acc. see Introd. IV, 1 (i). Cf. *Ann.* V, 10, *angustiasque Isthmi euadit.*

recentibus, 'recent events' (cf. *praesentia* and *futura*). The case is probably dat.

52. § 1. **festinata.** For the transitive use of this verb see 6, 2 n.

quaesiuisset, 'because Germanicus had (he felt) courted the army's good will'. The subj. is virtual oblique, representing the thought of Tiberius. The subject is supplied from *Germanici* below, and the clause represents the first reason for Tiberius' displeasure, as *bellica gloria* (abl. of cause) represents the second. For a similar change of construction, cf. *Ann.* IV, 38, *alii modestiam, multi quia diffideret . . . interpretabantur.* Note how the mixture of pleasure and anxiety is expressed by *gaudebat* and *angebatur* bracketing the sentence.

§ 2. **rettulit,** 'reported'.

magis in speciem, 'in language too ostentatiously elaborate for him to be credited with real sincerity'. *in speciem* 'to make a show' is an adverbial phrase like *in cassum,* 4, 2. See note *ad loc.* The *ut* clause is consecutive. Cf. the corresponding Greek construction ἢ ὥστε with infin.

§ 3. **paucioribus.** The absolute use of *pauca* = 'a few words' is well established in Latin. Cf. Virg. *Aen.* IV, 116, *paucis docebo.*

intentior, 'with more enthusiasm'.

fida, 'trustworthy', i.e. 'sincere'. The use of *fidus* of things is mainly poetical and post-Augustan. Cf. *Ann.* XV, 28, *consilium fidum.*

etiam. It was obviously politic to make the same concessions to both armies. But Tacitus contrives to make it sound like an attempt by Tiberius to give to Drusus some of the credit that belonged to Germanicus.

53. § 1. **Iulia.** The only child of Augustus, Julia was the daughter of Scribonia, and was born in 39 B.C. on the day on which Augustus divorced her mother (Dio, XLVIII, 34, 3). At the age of 14 she was married to Marcellus (3, 1), and after his death she became (21 B.C.) the wife of Agrippa, by whom she had five children, including Gaius, Lucius and Agrippa Postumus (c. 3); finally in 11 B.C. she married Tiberius. All these marriages were arranged by Augustus in an attempt to secure the succession. In 2 B.C. her immorality became too flagrant to be ignored, and Augustus banished her under the *Lex Iulia de adulteriis*. She lived in exile until her death in A.D. 14.

Pandateria, Ventotene, in the Gulf of Gaeta, north of Naples. The abl. is local (Introd. IV, 4 (iii *a*)).

mox, in fact after five years (Suet. *Aug.* 65).

qui . . . accolunt. Perhaps this is intended, as Nipperdey suggests, to distinguish the town from Regium Lepidi in the north, near Mutina: or perhaps it merely emphasizes the geographical position to indicate the change from island to mainland, which was an alleviation of the exile.

matrimonio. On Tiberius' marriage to Julia, and his retirement to Rhodes see Introd. V.

inparem, 'her social inferior'. Cf. *Hist.* II, 50, *maternum genus impar*.

intima, 'inmost', i.e. 'fundamental'.

Tiberio. For the dat. see Introd. IV, 3 (ii).

§ 2. extorrem sq. All the sources agree about Julia's infamy, but Tacitus is here claiming pity for her, as a victim of Tiberius.

omnis spei egenam. Postumus (her own son) was the only rival to Tiberius who would have been likely to do anything for her. *egenus* is a poetical word, found both with gen. and abl. as *egeo* is. Cf. *Ann.* XV, 3, *egena aquarum regio*.

inopia ac tabe longa. The two things are interdependent; by leaving her destitute (for the stopping of her allowance see Suet. *Tib.* 50), he allowed her to waste away.

obscuram, 'would not be noticed'.

longinquitate, 'duration'. Cf. Cic. *Phil.* X, 16, *ex longinquitate grauissimi morbi.*

§ 3. Sempronium Gracchum. He is usually identified with Ti. Sempronius Gracchus, the *triumuir monetalis* (official of the Mint) who certainly held office under Augustus. There is little definite evidence for his career.

praue. He misused his eloquence.

contumacia et odiis. These are the feelings he inspired in her against Tiberius, not the means he used to inflame her.

§ 4. Cercinam, one of the Kerkenna islands, in the Gulf of Gabes, off the coast of Tunisia.

quattuordecim annis. For the abl. expressing extent of time see Introd. IV, 4 (iii *b*). The years of his exile here given are one less than those of Julia's: he may therefore have been the tribune mentioned by

Dio (LV, 10, 15) who could not be tried until the year of his office was over.

§ 5. **litoris,** part. gen. See Introd. IV, 2 (iii).

uita, modal abl.—'by his life'.

§ 6. **L. Asprenate.** L. Nonius Asprenas, consul in A.D. 6, was a nephew of Varus and served under him in Germany (Vell. II, 120). He was proconsul of Africa in A.D. 14/15, and a milestone is extant (*E. and J.* 290) recording the making of a road under his rule. He died before A.D. 30.

quidam . . . tradidere. On Tacitus' sources see Introd. II.

sperauerat. The indic. of narrative makes this sound like a statement of fact, which it hardly is. To Tacitus this is the true explanation, and to be stated bluntly as such. Cf. *sectabatur*, 80, 2 and see Introd. II.

54. § 1. **addito . . . sacerdotio.** On 17th September, A.D. 14, Augustus was formally deified and accepted as one of the gods of Rome. A special priest was appointed for his worship, and a priestly college (the *sodales Augustales*) established to act in all matters connected with his cult. This college was modelled on one of the oldest Roman religious bodies (see next note) and was an extra honour for the deified Emperor.

ut quondam, 'on the analogy of the *Titii sodales*, long ago instituted by T. Tatius'. The religious brotherhood of the Titii Sodales is well attested (Augustus himself was a member of it, *R.G.* 7), but its origins and functions are quite uncertain. Tacitus here and in *Hist.* II, 95 connects it (though with different explanations) with Tatius, a Sabine who may have been an early king of Rome. But the name may also be connected with augury or phallic rites. It seems clear that even the Romans could only conjecture about its meaning, and that alternative explanations were current. Tacitus is using the story that seems relevan here.

retinendis . . . sacris, dat. of purpose. Introd. IV, 3 (v).

sorte. Election by lot was not practised in Rome as it was in Athens. No ordinary elections to magistracies were made by lot, though subsidiary allocations might be (division of duties among praetors, e.g.). But the system was used quite frequently, though not exclusively, for the appointment of members of priestly colleges. Cf. Suet. *Aug.* 31.

Drususque. The different conjunction here may indicate the closer connexion of Tiberius with his son than any of the others.

Claudius, brother of Germanicus, later Emperor.

adiciuntur, i.e. added as supernumerary members, over and above the regular 21. Cf. Suet. *Claud.* 6.

§ 2. **primum coeptos,** i.e. they were now first celebrated as an annual official festival. Cf. 15, 2 n.

ex certamine histrionum. The mention of Bathyllus and our knowledge of Imperial theatrical performances make it clear that the *pantomimi* are meant—dancers who by mime and gesture represented mythological and tragic themes. These performers were tremendously popular and each had his own faction of supporters (*fautores histrionum, Ann.* XIII, 25); temperament, professional jealousy and faction-loyalty constantly caused trouble at performances, and on several occasions actors were banished from Italy in an attempt to stop such rioting. Cf. *Ann.* IV, 14 and XIII, 25.

Augustus. Suet. *Aug.* 45 makes it plain that Augustus enjoyed the performances, but did not tolerate the lawlessness, of the actors.

Bathylli. Bathyllus of Alexandria was, with Pylades, the inventor of the pantomimic art, and one of its most famous exponents. He was a favourite of Maecenas, and may have been one of his freedmen.

neque . . . et. See 6, 3 n.

talibus studiis. Probably abl. *abhorreo* is normally followed by *a*, but there are a few examples of the simple abl. (e.g. Curt. VI, 7, 11, *animum tanto facinore procul abhorrentem*). The use of the dat. seems to be confined to the secondary meaning of 'inconsistent with', and therefore here and in *Ann.* XIV, 21 and *Hist.* IV, 55 the case may be assumed to be abl.

ciuile, cf. 8, 2 and 33, 2; 'democratic' seems right here. Suet. *Aug.* 45 gives the same two reasons for Augustus' attendance at the performances—*seu uitandi rumoris causa . . . seu studio spectandi.*

nondum. He did in A.D. 23 (*Ann.* IV, 14) introduce a motion expelling the actors from Italy.

55. § 1. With this chapter Tacitus begins his account of A.D. 15.

triumphus. Under the Principate a full-scale triumph could be celebrated only by the Princeps (as C.-in-C. all forces) or his immediate family. Other generals were granted an *ouatio* (minor triumph) or, more commonly, the triumphal insignia only (cf. 72, 1). The fact that a full triumph was voted to Germanicus at this time, when he was doing little of real value for Rome, is a mark both of his popularity and of Tiberius' forbearance. He did not return to celebrate the triumph until May, A.D. 17.

manente bello. Normally triumphs were granted only after the successful conclusion of a campaign.

et. The conjunction may be grammatically unnecessary, but its effect on the emphasis is considerable. By separating the time from the manner of anticipation, Tacitus emphasizes both, giving the effect of '*at* the beginning of spring and *by* a sudden raid'.

Chattos. The Chatti, a powerful German tribe and a persistent enemy of Rome, inhabited the country about the waters of the Upper Weser, the modern district of Hesse.

dissidere, 'hope that the enemy was divided into A. and S.', i.e. 'between (the parties of) A. and S.' The acc. and inf. depends on *spes* as it would on *spero.* Cf. Cic. *Tusc.* I, 97, *magna me spes tenet bene mihi euenire.*

Arminium, one of Rome's most bitter enemies. Leader of the Cherusci (56, 5), he was a Roman citizen, had the rank of *eques* and had served in the Roman army (Vell. II, 118); hence the charge of *perfidia.* It was he who was responsible for the defeat of Varus (Introd. VI), and he continued to harass the Romans until he was treacherously killed in A.D. 17 at the age of 37 (*Ann.* II, 88).

Segestem, father-in-law of Arminius and his bitter enemy.

perfidia . . . aut fide. *perfidia* refers only to Arminius, *fide* only to Segestes, by the literary figure called by Professor Brink (*C.R.* 1944, p. 43) 'Double Zeugma'. Cf. 69, 1, *ut quis inops aut saucius, uestem et fomenta dilargita est.* For *nos* see 50, 1 n.

§ 2. turbator. See 4, 4 n.

conuiuio. According to Dio, LVI, 19, 2, Arminius often dined with Varus.

principibus. On the *principes* or prominent nobles of the German tribes see *Germ.* (ed. Anderson), Introd., pp. lii sq.

crimina et innoxios, the guilty and the innocent'. Instead of using either a pair of abstract nouns or a pair of personal ones, Tacitus has used one of each. Cf. *Ann.* XI, 26, *insontibus . . . flagitiis manifestis.* Virg. *Ecl.* I, 62, *aut Ararim Parthus bibet aut Germania Tigrim.*

§ 3. fato. Velleius (II, 118), speaking of Varus' refusal to heed the warnings of Segestes, says *ita se res habet, plerumque cui fortunam mutaturus est deus, consilia corrumpat.*

quamquam . . . tractus. See 7. 3 n.

gener . . . soceri, 'he was the hated son-in-law of a hostile father-in-law' lit., i.e. son-in-law and father-in-law hated one another.

56. § 1. igitur. The connexion of this sentence is not with the end of c. 55 but with the end of its first sentence (*praecepit*). The rest of c. 55 is logically an explanatory parenthesis within the main narrative.

tumultuarias, 'raised in a hurry', i.e. 'for the occasion'.

cis, on the left bank. The tribes would include the Ubii (31, 3).

totidem, the legions of the Upper army.

in monte Tauno. The Taunus mountains are the range of high ground lying between Frankfurt-on-Main and Coblenz. Drusus' fort is probably the one mentioned by Dio, LIV, 33, 4 as built 'among the Chatti', but its exact site remains uncertain.

rapit. *rapio* is so used by Virgil (e.g. *Aen.* VII, 725) to indicate rapid movement.

L. Apronio. Apronius was consul suffectus in A.D. 8. He had already served with distinction in Dalmatia (Vell. II, 116), and for this campaign with Germanicus was awarded triumphal insignia (72, 1). He was procurator of Africa from A.D. 18–21 (*Ann.* III, 21) and for some years after 28 was legate of Lower Germany (*Ann.* IV, 73).

§ 2. **rarum.** For the parenthesis see 39, 4 n.

inoffensum, 'without incident' perhaps.

properauerat. The transitive use of *properare* ('to hurry on') is mainly poetical.

metuebatur. This, the reading of M, is best retained. *auctus* is almost certainly singular (*auctus aquarum* seems to be invariably singular, and it was the fact of a possible rise in the water-level that was worrying, not individual increases). That being so, there is no necessity to emend, because the singular verb is often found in similar sentences especially when, as here, the singular subject is the more important and closer to the verb. Cf. *abstulerat* 10, 2 and n.; *Ann.* XII, 12, *illustres Parthi rexque Arabum . . . aduenerat.*

§ 3. **aetate ac sexu,** abl. of respect. See 16, 3 n. The phrase includes women, children and the aged. *iuuentus* means the men of military age.

Adranam, the Eder, which joins the Weser at Kassel.

arcebant, 'were for preventing' (20, 2 n.), i.e. 'tried to prevent'. The verb is plural to match the sense, not the form, of *iuuentus*. The variation with the singular *tramiserat* is typical of Tacitus.

pagis. The German *pagi* were clan territories, districts held by subdivisions of the tribes.

§ 4. **Mattio,** probably to be identified with the Altenburg by Metze-Niedenstein.

uertit, for *reuertit.* See 5, 1 n.

moris, 'as was his custom'. *mos est* is the commoner classical construction, but some exx. of the gen. are found, and it becomes commoner in the Silver Latin writers. The gen. is basically one of sphere ('it is within the sphere of his custom') and if a narrower definition is required, may be considered either as a part. gen. or gen. of characteristic. Cf. 80, 1.

astu, cf. *Germ.* 6, *cedere loco consilii quam formidinis arbitrantur.* 'Tactical withdrawal' did not seem to the Romans a virtue.

§ 5. **Cheruscis.** The Cherusci lived north of the Chatti, around the middle Weser and the Harz mountains. They had led the rebellion of A.D. 9, and were still very powerful, but after the death of Arminius they were torn by internal feuds and gradually lost importance.

iuuare. *animus est* with the infin. is a poetic construction. Cf. Virg. *Aen.* IV, 638–9, *sacra Ioui Stygio perficere est animus,* and see Introd. IV, 6 (i).

57. § 1. circumsedebatur. The indic. here and in *suadebat* shows that the passage is narrative and not part of Segestes' request.

barbaris. For the dat. see Introd. IV, 3 (iv).

quis. See 2, 1 n.

audacia. This is abl. of respect ('ready *in* daring'). Contrast 2, 1, *seruitio promptior*, which is dat. of purpose ('ready *for* slavery').

promptus. The regular construction of comparative sentences is *quanto . . . tanto* (or *quo . . . eo*), with a comparative in each clause— *uia quanto tutior, tanto fere longior*, Livy, IX, 2, 6. But from the time of Livy on, and especially in Tacitus, such sentences are also found with a positive in one or other of the clauses. The effect of this disjointed construction is to emphasize the clause containing the positive, making it more of an independent statement which does not rely for its full meaning on its relationship with another clause. So the meaning here is 'it is the bold man who is preferred'. Cf. 68, 4, *quanto inopina, tanto maiora offunduntur*.

When the positive appears in the demonstrative clause, as in 2, 1, *quanto quis seruitio promptior, opibus et honoribus extollerentur* and 74, 6, *quantoque incautius efferuerat paenitentia patiens tulit*, Tacitus almost invariably further emphasizes the independence of that clause by omitting the *tanto* or *eo* which would be its formal connexion with the relative clause.

§ 2. **conscientia.** See 39, 2 n.

anno. A.D. 9.

Germaniae. Like *Galliae*, this plural is used of Roman-conquered territory, both of the districts of Upper and Lower Germany and of districts which at the time under discussion were under Roman rule. It means 'the administrative districts of Germany', rather than the whole country, which is *Germania*. Cf. *Ag.* 15, *sic Germanias excussisse iugum*.

aram. See 39, 1 n.

Gallicam. In fact the districts of Upper and Lower Germany lay on the left bank of the Rhine, but it was still called the bank 'towards Gaul'.

§ 3. **pretium.** The classical phrase is *operae pretium est*, but Livy uses *operae est* (IX, 23, 12, e.g.) and Tacitus *pretium est*. Once the phrase is established usage, it can be abbreviated without loss of meaning. Cf. *Ann.* II, 35, *ni pretium foret noscere*.

clientium. The household and retinue of a German *princeps* are described in *Germ.* 13–14.

§ 4. **animo,** abl. of quality. Introd. IV, 4 (ii *d*).

euicta. This seems preferable to *uicta* M. In the sense of 'overcome with emotion' *euictus* is not only commoner in Latin generally, but in keeping with Tacitus' own practice. Cf. *Hist.* II, 64, *in gaudium euicta*; *Ann.* XI, 37, *ad miserationem euicta*.

uoce, abl. of respect. See 16, 3 n. Note the structure of the sentence from *filia Segestis*; the woman is described in five phrases loosely attached to the sentence—an abl. of quality, a participle and a descriptive adjectival phrase which are given an illusory balance by the use of *neque . . . neque*; then an abl. abs. and a present participle. Some of the phrases describe character, others appearance or situation. It is very odd Latin structure, but a very effective description.

§ 5. **praedae,** predicative dat. (Introd. IV, 3 (v)). 'Which had been given (distributed) as loot to many of those who were now surrendering.'

uisu, abl. of respect. See 16, 3 n. *memoria* is abl. of cause.

58. § 1. **ciuitate.** He may have been granted citizenship for services rendered with the auxiliary forces of the Roman army.

amicos inimicosque, cf. the Greek phrase for making an alliance— τοὺς αὐτοὺς ἐχθροὺς καὶ φίλους νομίζειν, 'to consider the same people enemies and friends' (as the other partner does).

neque . . . uerum. Cf. *neque . . . sed*, § 3. Tacitus uses this collocation several times. It produces a balanced construction, being reminiscent of the more usual *neque . . . et*, but has the merit of novelty. In almost every example Tacitus contrives variation of construction within the balancing phrases. Cf. *Hist*. V, 20, *nec omnia patrandi fiducia, sed multa ausis aliqua in parte fortunam fore.*

quippe. See 5, 1 n.

idem conducere. The acc. and inf. depend on a verb of thinking or judging supplied by zeugma (17, 4 n.) from *probabam.*

pacem quam bellum. For the omission of *potius*, cf. *Ann*. XIV, 61, *libens quam coactus*. It is not peculiar to Tacitus, but is very common in his works.

§ 2. **nox,** the night of the *conuiuium* (55, 2).

utinam. On the omission of the subj. see 7, 1 n. The elliptical use of *utinam* is not confined to Tacitus. Cf. Cic. *De Or*. II, 361, *habetis sermonem bene longum hominis, utinam non impudentis!*

§ 3. **quae secuta sunt.** He was forced into war with the Romans (55, 3).

tui copia, 'access to you'. *copia* is commonly used with the gen. of the gerundive (*copia tui uidendi*), but there are also, from Plautus onward, exx. of this simple personal gen. Cf. Plaut. *Mil*. 1229, *ut eius mihi sit copia*; Ovid, *Met*. III, 391, 'ante' ait 'emoriar quam sit tibi copia nostri'. For the omission of the verb in this clause see 2, 1 n.

uetera, the old system of Roman rule.

antehabeo. This word seems to be an invention of Tacitus. It is used again in *Ann*. IV, 11 and nowhere else.

neque . . . sed. See § 1.

perfidia, 'clear myself of the charge of treachery'.

conciliator. For nouns in *-tor* see 4, 4 n. *conciliator* stands in apposition to the subject: the real apodosis of the condition is suppressed. He *is* (in fact and now) a suitable agent (and could be so used) should the Germans require one. Their change of heart must precede his services, hence the future perfect tense. For the acc. after *malo* see 2, 1 n.

§ 4. **iuuenta et errore**, 'youthful folly'. For the hendiadys see 75, 1 n.

quod . . . concepit. The two *quod* clauses retain their indic. verbs within the indirect question because they are mere circumlocutions for the subject of *praeualeat*. See 10, 2 n.

§ 5. **liberis . . . incolumitatem.** But, according to Strabo, VII, 291, not only Segestes' daughter and her child, but also Segimundus were displayed in Germanicus' triumph in A.D. 17.

uetere in prouincia, in the districts on the left bank of the Rhine as 59, 4, *coleret Segestes uictam ripam* shows. Cf. *Ann*. III, 74 where *ueteris prouinciae* refers to the part of Africa first conquered, the original province.

imperatoris, probably the second conferment of this title. See 31, 5. For the gen. see Introd. IV, 2 (iv).

auctore Tiberio, i.e. Tiberius had brought the motion before the Senate.

§ 6. **in tempore**, 'at the proper time' (in his annalistic survey). For the phrase see 19, 2 n.

memorabo. If Tacitus did relate the insult, he did it in the lost books of the *Annals* and nothing further is known of it. *Ann*. II, 10 and 46 show that the child (Thumelicus by name, according to Strabo, VII, 292) spent some time in captivity. *Ann*. XI, 16, being hypothetical, leaves it uncertain whether he did in fact reach manhood.

59. § 1. quibusque. Strictly speaking, *quisque* should not be used in the plural, but as the meaning of 'each' so easily becomes 'all', so the form of *quisque* sometimes conforms to general sense and not strict grammatical requirement. The plural is found occasionally even in Cicero (*Amic*. 34, *in optimis quibusque*) and is fairly common in the poets and post-Augustan writers.

inuitis aut cupientibus, 'according as men did or did not wish for war'. The native Latin construction would be *ut bellum ingratum aut optatum erat*, but this is an imitation of a Greek construction, whereby participles expressing pleasure or displeasure are used in agreement with the dat. of the person (Thuc. II, 3, τῷ πλήθει οὐ βουλομένῳ ἦν 'it was not the wish of the majority'). The construction first appears in Latin with Sallust; there is one example in Livy, and a few in Tacitus and later writers. Cf. *Ag*. 18, *quibus bellum uolentibus erat*. See also Introd. IV, 3 (iii).

spe uel dolore. The modal abl. (expressing manner) is in classical Latin normally used either with *cum* (*cum labore*) or with an adj. (*magno labore*). Certain conventional, almost adverbial, uses of the simple abl. do appear (*iure, iniuria, consilio, ui*, &c.), and Tacitus' bolder usage is based on these. Cf. 68, 3, *clamore et impetu*.

super, 'over and above'. Cf. Livy XLII, 25, 8, *alii super alios legati.*

rapta uxor, subiectus . . . uterus. See 8, 6 n. For the plur. verb *agebant* see 68, 5 n.

uolitabat. The frequentative verb and the imperfect tense help to give an impression of constant movement.

§ 2. **mulierculam,** 'one poor, helpless woman'. Latin, like Scots, uses the diminutive to express not only size but emotion. 'The bonnie wee boatie' expresses approval and admiration, as Catullus' *turgiduli ocelli* expresses affectionate sympathy, and *adulescentulum* in § 5 contempt. The usage belongs to the spoken rather than to the literary language: it is common in Plautus and the letters of Cicero, and is a mark of the passionate poet Catullus, but is rare in the deliberate stylists.

§ 3. **sibi.** For the dat. see Introd. IV, 3 (i).

tres legiones, XVII, XVIII, XIX. The last is proved by 60, 3; a stone from Vetera (*E. and J.* 45) commemorates a centurion of Leg. XVIII who *cecidit bello Variano*; and XVII is the only other legion of which there is no record after A.D. 9, and may safely be assumed to be the third lost then.

totidem legatos, 'and their commanders with them'. In this context the *legati* can only be the *legati legionum*, and do not include Varus, the *legatus Augusti*.

§ 4. **hominum.** This, though presenting difficulty, is probably the correct reading. *sacerdotium* needs some defining word, the more contemptuous the better. Segimundus (57, 2) had been a priest concerned with the worship of Augustus, to the Germans a mere man. The gen. is objective, loosely used to indicate general reference (see Introd. IV, 2, (i)) and the word is contemptuous and emphatic, both from its position and from the contrast with *dis patriis*.

Germanos, 'real Germans'—unlike Segestes.

excusaturos, 'never quite wipe out the shame of having seen . . .'

uirgas sq. These are the symbols of Roman civil (here provincial) rule. The lictors' *fasces* and the garb peculiar to a Roman citizen mark Roman officialdom.

§ 5. **inexperta . . . nescia.** Both adjs. are passive in meaning—'untried' and 'unknown'. See note on *gnarus* 5, 2. Arminius' point is that they know just how bad Roman rule can be; and that, having defeated more experienced generals, they must not now give way to the young Germanicus.

inritus, 'frustrated'; the application of the adj. to persons is confined to the poets and post-Augustan writers. Cf. Virg. *Aen.* V, 442, *uariis adsultibus inritus urget; Ann.* XIV, 7, *ne inriti dissuaderent.*

dicatus, 'proclaimed among the gods', i.e. 'proclaimed a god'. This use of the verb is rare, but cf. Plin. *Pan.* 11, *dicauit caelo Tiberius Augustum.*

delectus, 'chosen' (to be *princeps*).

adulescentulum. For the diminutive see § 2. In fact Arminius and Germanicus were much of an age, but Arminius is contemptuous of Germanicus' more sheltered life. For the acc. see Introd. IV, 1 (ii).

§ 6. **colonias.** The reference is not to Roman colonies but to settlements of German tribes in new sites, under the supervision of Rome. The Ubii (31, 3) had already made such a move, and Arminius has scornfully suggested the same course to Segestes (§ 4).

gloriae. The gens. are loosely attached to define *ducem*—'a leader concerned with glory . . .'; 'who will lead you to glory and freedom'. See Introd. IV, 2 (i).

60. § 1. **non modo . . . sed.** The omission of *etiam* is not merely for the sake of brevity, but to make the contrast more stark and so emphasize the second statement. It was to be expected that Arminius would inflame the Cherusci: that he should bring in other tribes too was more serious. Cf. Cic. *Verr.* II, 58, *non modo eques Romanus, sed quiuis liber*; and 77, 1; 81, 1.

Inguiomerus. He also fought with Arminius against Germanicus in the campaign of A.D. 16 (*Ann.* II, 17, 21), but in 17, when fighting began between Arminius and Maroboduus, he deserted to Maroboduus (*Ann.* II, 45) 'because he scorned to serve under his young nephew'.

uetere . . . auctoritate, abl. of quality. Introd. IV, 4 (ii *d*).

§ 2. **ne . . . ingrueret,** 'lest the war might fall upon them with one mass', i.e. 'to prevent a single concentrated attack'.

quadraginta cohortibus, i.e. four legions. See 56, 1.

distrahendo hosti, dat. of purpose. Introd. IV, 3 (v).

Amisiam, the Ems.

Pedo. Almost certainly = Albinovanus Pedo, the poet-friend of Ovid (*Pont.* IV, x). The elder Seneca (*Suas.* I, 15) quotes a fragment of his poem 'On Germanicus' Voyage'. Germanicus' father also made such a voyage (Suet. *Claud.* 1), but his title of Germanicus was posthumously conferred and he is never mentioned by that title alone. It may therefore be safely assumed that the poem deals with Germanicus' expedition of A.D. 16 (*Ann.* II, 8, 23–4), and it seems likely that its author was the officer here named.

finibus, 'by way of the territory of the Friesians'. For the abl. see Introd. IV, 4 (ii *a*).

Frisiorum. They occupied the land round what is now the Ijsselmeer (formerly Zuider Zee), from Utrecht to Groningen, including the district still called Friesland. They revolted from Rome in A.D. 28 (*Ann.* IV, 72) and in 68 joined the rising of Civilis (*Hist.* IV).

per lacus, cf. *Germ.* 34. These lakes are now merged in the Ijsselmeer.

praedictum. This must mean 'aforementioned'. Tacitus normally uses *praedico* to mean 'appoint', 'fix', but that would be ambiguous here: the river is certainly the Ems, and it has just been mentioned. The meaning 'say beforehand' is well attested, cf. Velleius' common use of *ut praediximus* and Livy, X, 14, 7, *ad praedictas hostium latebras*.

§ 3. **L. Stertinius.** Judging by the references to him in *Ann.* I–II, he was a skilled and trusted leader of flying columns.

undeuicesimae legionis. See 59, 3 n.

aquilam. *Ann.* II, 25, records the recovery of another of the lost standards, and a coin of the period shows Germanicus standing with an eagle in his left hand, and the legend SIGNIS RECEPT. DEVICTIS GERM. (*R.I.C.* I, Pl. VIII, 124).

agmen. Here = the whole army, not simply Stertinius' column.

inter. The placing of the preposition after its noun (anastrophe of the preposition) is much commoner in poetry than in prose. Cicero employs the device only after a relative pronoun (*quibus de scriptum est*), but the historians and later prose writers adopt the poetical usage more freely. Cf. 19, 3, *seque coram*; 65, 3, *umentia ultra*; 75, 1, *eo coram*. Caes. *B.C.* III, 6, 3, *saxa inter et alia loca periculosa* shows the preposition placed between two co-ordinate nouns, while Virg. *Aen.* I, 218, *spemque metumque inter* has (as here) both nouns preceding the preposition. Cf. too *Ann.* XV, 61, *Poppaea et Tigellino coram*.

Teutoburgiensi saltu. The exact site remains uncertain.

61. § 1. Caesarem inuadit. See Introd. IV, 1 (i) and cf. Sall. *Jug.* 89, *eius potiundi Marium maxuma cupido inuaserat*.

suprema. See 8, 1 n.

omni, 'the whole army'. *omnis* properly means 'every', but it occasionally carries the kindred meaning of 'whole' which properly belongs to *totus*. Cf. Caes. *B.G.* I, 1, *Gallia est omnis diuisa in partes tres*.

saltuum . . . paludum. For the gens. see Introd. IV, 2 (iii).

incedunt. Introd. IV, 1 (i).

locos. These are individual points mentioned in turn. For places considered as a unit ('region', 'district') the neuter plural *loca* is normally used.

uisuque ac memoria. They presented a horrible sight and had horrible associations. *-que . . . ac* for 'both . . . and' is not common, but cf. *Hist.* III, 63, *seque ac liberos suos*, and see note on *-que . . . et*, 34, 1.

§ 2. **prima Vari castra.** The various accounts of the disaster (Vell. II, 119; Dio, LVI, 21; Flor. IV, 12) are difficult to correlate and none of them is clear. The latest attempt to explain the sequence of events comes from W. John, *Die Örtlichkeit der Varusschlacht*, based largely on Tacitus' account. He plausibly suggests that the *prima castra* is not Varus' summer camp from which he had been enticed by reports of trouble, but the ordinary marching camp pitched after his first day's march and the initial attack. The following day they marched on, but were

more seriously attacked, and the remnant (*reliquiae*) of the army fell
back to the marching camp, where they attempted to defend part of it
by the rampart (*semiruto uallo*) seen by Germanicus. The final rout took
place *medio campi*, not in the open country, but in the courtyard of the
camp, for which *campus* is a technical term (cf. Amm. XXVII, 6, 5).
This picture is convincing: there is certainly no suggestion in Tacitus
that the various *loci* were any distance apart, and his facts probably
come from Pliny (Elder), who himself knew the district.

lato ambitu et dimensis principiis. The abls. may express either
quality (Introd. IV, 4 (ii *d*)) or means. The wide extent and the fact
that headquarters were marked out do not necessarily indicate a
permanent camp, but merely the Roman instinct for doing things
decently and in due order, even when under attack. A camp is
established by Caecina under very similar circumstances (65, 7), and
we find references to the regular gates (66, 1) and to the *principia*
(67, 1).

manus ostentabant, 'showed the handiwork'—'was obviously the
work of (all) three legions (the whole army)'. The whole passage is
reminiscent of a fragment of Sallust (*Hist.* II, D21), *semiruta moenia,
domus intectae . . . manus Punicas ostentabant.* See *C.R.* 1945, p. 45.

semiruto uallo, humili fossa, local abls. (Introd. IV, 4 (iii *a*)) but
they are also the reason for the inference, and their position makes
that clear. The adj. *semirutus* was probably suggested to Tacitus by the
passage of Sallust quoted above.

medio campi. *medio* is local abl. (see above): for the gen. see Introd.
IV, 2 (iii).

ut fugerant sq., 'scattered where (lit. 'as') men had fled, heaped up
where they had made a stand'.

§ 3. **ora,** probably the skulls of those men offered in sacrifice.

lucis, 'in the groves'. Local abl.

barbarae, not merely 'non-Roman' but 'barbarous', whereon human
sacrifice was offered.

primorum ordinum. See 29, 2 n.

§ 4. **elapsi.** For the acc. after this verb see Introd. IV, i (i). Cf. *Ann.*
IV, 64 and *Hist.* III, 59. According to Dio, LVI, 22, some did manage
to escape capture, and others were later ransomed by their families.

ubi. For the omission of the subj. verbs, here and in the following
sentence, see 7, 1 n.

infelici. It had not been conspicuously successful at its proper task
of winning Roman victories.

scrobes. As they obviously did not bury the slain (*ossa* § 2), and as
they displayed the sacrificial victims (*ora* § 3), these must have been
used for burying yet others alive. That such practices were possible is
clear from *Germ.* 12.

ut, 'how'. The clause is an indirect question.

62. § 1. qui aderat. The repetition of the phrase from 61, 1 is surely deliberate. It gives something of the solemnity of poetry or ritual, where repetition is regular, and contrasts vividly the vanished army with its living and present successor.

sextum post cladis annum, 'after the sixth year of the disaster', i.e. 'six years after the disaster'. This method of expressing length of time before or after a definite occasion, by means of *ante* or *post* and the acc., with a dependent gen., is rare before the Silver Age. Cf. Vell. I, 10, *ante paucos triumphi dies.*

extruendo tumulo, dat. of purpose. Introd. IV, 3 (v).

munere, 'by way of a tribute'. The abl. is instrumental. Cf. Cat. CI, 8, *tradita sunt tristi munere ad inferias.*

in defunctos. Fletcher (*C.Q.* 1943, p. 90) is surely right in taking this as dependent on *munere.* It is similar in construction to *in Augustam adulatio* (14, 1), and the variation of construction is between *munere in defunctos* and *praesentibus socius.*

§ 2. Tiberio, dat. of agent. Introd. IV, 3 (iv).

in deterius trahenti, 'interpreting unfavourably'. *traho* 'to draw' easily becomes 'to ascribe', with *in* or *ad* and the acc. Cf. 76, 4; Sall. *Jug.* 92, *omnia . . . in uirtutem trahebantur.* The construction of the verb makes easier the adverbial use of *in deterius,* for which see 4, 2 n.

siue . . . credebat. The change of construction is not only for variety, but indicates the more probable explanation. But the insinuation that Tiberius hates Germanicus has been neatly made: see Introd. II. *siue = siue quod,* as often.

formidolosiorem, 'more fearful of the enemy'. This meaning of the adj. is rare (cf. Ter. *Eun.* 757, *egon formidulosus?*) and this appears to be the only example (until Late Latin) of its use with the gen.; the gen. is one of reference (Introd. IV, 2 (i)) its use here being an extension of the gen. with the commoner *trepidus, timidus,* &c. For the more usual active meaning of *formidolosus* ('inspiring fear') see 76, 3.

auguratu. The Romans learned their augury (the science of telling the possible outcome of events from signs, especially the activities of birds) from the Etruscans, and therefore the ritual was very old indeed. 'Invested with the ancient ritual (office) of augur.'

feralia. Many, perhaps all, of the priests of Rome suffered formal pollution if they handled dead bodies or objects closely connected with them. Cf. Dio, LVI, 31, 3.

63. § 1. eripi, 'to be rushed'.

colligi . . . monitos. *moneo* is occasionally found with an infin., even in classical prose (Cic. *Verr.* II, 1, 63, *ut eum suae libidines facere monebant*). But it is much commoner in the poets and later prose writers. Cf. § 3, and see Introd. IV ,6 (i).

§ 2. **impulsae**, 'broken into' and therefore 'forced back'. Cf. Vell. II, 70, *impulsis hostibus castra Caesaris cepit.*

trudebantur . . . ni . . . instruxisset. See 23, 2 n.

gnaram, 5, 2 n. Note the neat 'balance-with-variation' in *gnaram uincentibus, iniquam nesciis.*

manibus aequis, cf. *aequo Marte;* 'indecisive'.

§ 3. **legiones . . . reportat.** Objections have been made to these words on the grounds that (*a*) *legiones* implies all eight legions and only four can here be meant, for Caecina took his own four by a different route; (*b*) from 70, 1 it appears that in fact only two returned by sea. The objection cannot be sustained because (i) in a sentence which carefully echoes the three-fold division mentioned in 60, 2 and with a verb whose subject is obviously Germanicus, there is no difficulty in understanding *legiones* to be 'his' legions, i.e. four; (ii) this is merely a general indication that the three-fold division was maintained for the return journey. Details are then given about Caecina's journey, and with 70 we begin the detailed account of Germanicus'. There is no contradiction, only expansion. All four legions did in fact *complete* the journey by water. See note on 70, 5.

litore. Introd. IV, 4 (ii *a*).

quamquam. For its use with the subj. see 3, 5 n.; in this example the subj. may equally well be virtual oblique within *monitus . . . superare.*

pontes longos. It is clear from the following sentence that this was a regular causeway, though fallen into disrepair.

§ 4. **L. Domitio.** L. Domitius Ahenobarbus, who married Antonia *maior,* daughter of M. Antony and Octavia, was the grandfather of the Emperor Nero. His great expedition across the Elbe is related by Dio (LV, 10*a*, 2–3) and Tacitus (*Ann.* IV, 44). See Introd. VI.

§ 5. **in loco,** 'on the spot'.

ut opus et alii. The omission of the first *alii* indicates that *opus . . . inciperent* is the main point of the sentence, and *et alii proelium inciperent* an afterthought, involving a smaller number of people. Cf. Livy, III, 37, 8, *uirgis caedi, alii securi subici.* There are several examples of this construction in Tacitus (e.g. *Ann.* XII, 41; XV, 54), all showing *alii* joined by *et;* this is parallel with the corresponding Greek construction of οἱ δέ without the preceding οἱ μέν. Cf. Andoc. *Myst.* 38, ἑστάναι δὲ κύκλῳ ἀνὰ πέντε καὶ δέκα ἄνδρας τοὺς δὲ ἀνὰ εἴκοσιν.

64. § 1. **perfringere . . . nisi.** *nitor* with the infin. is rare in classical prose, but cf. Caes. *B.G.* VI, 37, *perrumpere nituntur.* See Introd. IV, 6 (i).

§ 2. **uligine profunda,** abl. of quality. Introd. IV, 4 (ii *d*).

ad gradum, 'for making a stand'. This meaning of *gradus* is common in the historians and poets; cf. Livy, VII, 8, 3, *primum gradu mouerunt hostem, deinde pepulerunt.*

inter undas, 'standing in the water'.

sueta. The participle is more commonly used of people and in the meaning of 'accustomed'. For this meaning of 'customary', cf. *Ann.* XIV, 49, *sueta firmitudine animi.*

procera. The height of the Germans is constantly mentioned as an outstanding characteristic. Cf. *Germ.* 4; *Hist.* IV, 1.

§ 3. **inclinantis.** Tacitus and Livy use both the active and the passive of this verb intransitively. Cf. *Hist.* III, 83, *quotiens pars altera inclinasset* and *Germ.* 8, *acies inclinatas iam.*

pugnae. For the dat. see 48, 2 n.

subiecta, 'the lower ground'.

quod effectum operis, 'what of work had been done', i.e. 'the work which had been done'. The gen. is partitive, and the clause stands as the subject of the abl. abs.

§ 4. **quadragesimum . . . stipendium,** cf. Caecina's speech in *Ann.* III, 33, *quamquam ipse quadraginta stipendia expleuisset.*

rerum sciens. When the pres. part. is used adjectivally (Introd. IV, 7 (i)) with the gen. of reference (Introd. IV, 2 (i)), it denotes a permanent characteristic and not an isolated action. Cf. 75, 2 *erogandae . . . pecuniae cupiens.*

uoluens, 'thinking over'; the original phrase is *secum* or *animo uoluere.*

quantum . . . agminis, 'as much of heavy column as (there was)', i.e. 'all the heavy part of his army'; the gen. is partitive. See § 3.

medio. See Introd. IV, 4 (iii *a*). For the gens. see Introd. IV, 2 (iii *a*).

pateretur, 'such as would admit a thin battle-line'. For the subj. see 43, 1 n.

§ 5. **legiones.** Note the typical variation both in the adjs. describing the legions, and in the phrases describing the duties to which they were assigned. *quinta* and *unetuicesima* agree straightforwardly with *legiones*: *primani* = 'the men of the 1st', and *uicesimanus* = 'the soldiery (*miles*) of the XXth.

65. § 1. This whole chapter is written in a very fine style, with elaborate pictorial effects obtained by deliberately unco-ordinated structure, and with strong poetic colouring (*inquies, resultantis, insomnes, inuigiles*). Tacitus is deliberately heightening the emotional effect of the passage: there is no reason to doubt that his basic facts are true, but equally obviously the barbarians and the situation appeal to his imagination, and he gives us a fine piece of dramatic and descriptive writing, not merely a summary of facts.

truci sonore. This is probably the same as the *cantu truci* of *Hist.* II, 22, i.e. a war-chant. Here Tacitus, using *cantus* for the songs of merry-making, has to find another word for the war-chant, and finds it in the poetic *sonor.*

subiecta uallium. Introd. IV, 2 (iii).

resultantis. The adj. is proleptic, i.e. it expresses not a characteristic of the noun, but the result of the verb's action on the noun: 'filled the woods so that they echoed'. Cf. Virg. *Aen.* I, 69, *submersas obrue puppes.* The device is mainly poetical, and its use here is an illustration of the elaborate style of the chapter.

apud Romanos. The Romans are passive and helpless in contrast to the active and triumphant Germans. This is echoed in the structure of the sentence.

interruptae uoces. Probably not 'irregular challenges' as Furneaux takes it, but 'fitful murmurings', in contrast to the constant and exultant shouting of the Germans. *essent* is understood here and with *ignes.* See 7, 1 n.

tentoriis. See Introd. IV, 4 (iii *a*).

§ 2. **quies,** 'dream'. Cf. Stat. *Theb.* X, 324, *praesaga quies.*

paludibus. The abl. depends on the *e-* of *emersum.* See Introd. IV, 4, (i).

intendentis, 'stretching out' the hand, to invite Caecina also to his doom.

§ 3. **coepta luce.** *coeptus,* especially in contexts where, as here, it indicates time, often seems to be used as a deponent, with active meaning. Cf. *Ann.* II, 13, *nocte coepta.*

an. See 13, 6 n.

capto . . . campo. Introd. IV, 7 (iii).

ultra. For its position see 60, 3 n.

§ 4. **quamquam.** See 7, 3 n.

caeno fossisque, 'in the mud and the ditches'. The omission of *in* with the abl. is here made easier because the abls. are also in a sense instrumental abls. expressing cause. Cf. 68, 3. The *fossae* are not military ditches, but either ditches connected with the causeway or holes in the ground.

utque, 'and (as usual in such a crisis)'; the *-que* joins the clause to the three previous clauses under the government of *ut* = when, and the *ut tali in tempore* is parenthetical.

sibi, 'for him', i.e. 'about his own business'. The description of the confusion is vivid and poetical.

eodemque. That this, and not *et eodemque* is the correct reading has been convincingly demonstrated by Brink in *J.R.S.* 1951, pp. 47–48. The double conjunction is colloquial, and unlikely to have been used by Tacitus.

simul haec. *dicit* is understood. 'Saying this, he broke through the column.' Cf. Virg. *Aen.* XII, 268, *simul hoc.*

§ 5. **paludum.** Introd. IV, 2 (iii).

§ 6. **circumueniebatur ni . . . opposuisset.** See 23, 2 n.

solida. They had reached the other side of the marshland containing the *pontes longi.*

§ 7. **uallum . . . agger.** A camp site was formed by digging a ditch to form a square or oblong, inside which a rampart of earth was raised, strengthened by a palisade (*uallum*). *agger* is not here the rampart but the material to make it. This is the original meaning of the word. Cf. Caes. *B.G.* II, 20, *aggeris petendi causa*; ibid. VII, 79, *fossam . . . aggere explent.*

per quae egeritur. This is the occasion on which Tacitus notoriously fails to call a spade a spade. There seems to be no doubt about the meaning (special implements were required for digging, not carrying) and therefore about the reading of *egeritur* for M's *geritur.* Cf. Frontin. *Strat.* III, 7, 4, *fossam pariter et aggerem instituit, ut in usum eius existimarent hostes egeri terram.*

66. § 1. **decumana,** the rear gate of the camp, lying behind the legions and therefore farthest away from the danger point of enemy attack.

auersa hosti. *auersus* is used with *a* and the abl., or with a case which in most examples may be either dat. or abl. For another unequivocal dat. cf. Quint. VII, 1, 11, *iudex defensioni auersior.*

§ 2. **comperto.** Introd. IV, 4, (iv).

eundum erat. They 'would have had to go'. For the indic. see 42, 3 n.

67. § 1. **temporis ac necessitatis,** 'of the critical situation'. *moneo* in classical Latin is followed by *de* and the abl.; but *admoneo* and *commoneo* are found with the gen., and Tacitus here adapts that construction to the simple verb.

expugnandi hostis. *hostis* is the subject of *succederent* (44, 2 n.), *expugnandi* depends on *spe.* The normal order is deliberately distorted (see 28, 1 n.) to bring together the two operative words 'enemy' and 'attack'. Until the enemy attacked they could do nothing.

perueniri, 'and so to the Rhine'. The present tense is used for rhetorical emphasis, to encourage the belief in 'one rush—and then to headquarters with no further trouble'. Its motive is emotional, not temporal.

§ 2. **uictoribus.** This represents the protasis contrasting with *si fugerent.*

in castris honesta, their past victories—with 'dear ones at home', a stock theme for speeches before battle. Note that Tacitus here gives only the barest indication of the usual speech: the excitement lies in the rapid, vivid narrative, and a speech would spoil the effect.

aduersis, the reverses just suffered.

§ 3. **orsus a suis,** 'beginning with his own'. Caecina at least must have had more than one horse, because one had been killed the day before (65, 6). Other officers too may have had reserve horses, and these would help to replace those killed by Arminius in his first attack (65, 4).

nulla ambitione, 'without partiality', 'with no respect of persons'. Cf. *Ag.* 1, *sine gratia aut ambitione.*

68. § 1. agebat. See 50, 1 n.

sinerent. The simple subj. without *ut*, used with *suadeo* and similar verbs, is a relic of the original parataxis ('I advise: let them allow'). It is common in early Latin (Plaut. *Asin.* 644, *istuc quod faciamus nobis suades*) and not uncommon in the classical period, being nearer to the actual words of the adviser and therefore more vivid. Cf. Cic. *Fam.* VII, 7, 1, *essedum aliquod capias suadeo.*

atrociora, 'Inguiomerus advised more spirited action, of the kind that barbarians like'.

incorruptam, i.e. before it was damaged or lost, on the journey or in battle.

§ 2. proruunt fossas, 'overthrew the ditches', i.e. overthrew the earthworks round them so that the ditches were filled in, to make access easier. Cf. Livy, IX, 14, 9, *cum pars uellerent uallum atque in fossas proruerent.* This seems to be the correct explanation of the phrase, though Turnebus altered the text, complaining that such Latin made him sick (*nauseam mouet, cum hoc loquendi genus puteat*). The hurdles (*crates*) would act as bridges.

§ 3. munimentis, a mixture of local abl. and abl. of cause. See 65, 4 n. 'After they stuck at the rampart', i.e. 'as they were trying to cross the rampart'.

clamore. See 59, 1 n.

tergis. They came out of the gates and took the Germans in the rear.

aequis locis aequos deos, 'a fair fight (lit. fair gods) on a fair field'. For *locis* see 25, 1 n.

§ 4. quanto inopina. See 57, 1 n.

auidi . . . incauti, 'impetuous . . . improvident'. Latin, as usual, gains its emphasis by placing the comparative clause first: English says 'as lacking in resource in defeat as they had been impetuous in success'.

§ 5. post graue uulnus, 'after (suffering) a serious wound'.

deseruere. The use of a plural verb with two or more singular subjects is quite normal at all periods of Latin. Different writers show different preferences, and there are exceptions to all the rules, but the normal practice is this: (1) When the subjects, personal or abstract, form a single unit and precede the verb, the verb is usually plural. Cf. *Ann.* XIV, 5, *Agrippina et Acerronia protectae sunt*; *Ann.* I, 42, 1, *occisus Augusti pronepos, interfecta Tiberii nurus faciant*; 59, 1, *rapta uxor, subiectus uterus agebant.* (2) The singular verb, agreeing with the nearest subject, is normally used in the following circumstances:

(a) When the subjects are considered separately, e.g. Livy, XXV, 19, 6, *Fuluius in agrum Cumanum, Claudius in Lucanos abit*; *Ann.* XII, 45, *militum, quis Caelius Pollio praefectus, centurio Casperius praeerat.*

(b) When the verb precedes its subjects (*Ann.* XII, 65, *conuictam Messalinam et Silium*), or stands between them (Cic. *Tusc.* I, 3, *siquidem Homerus fuit et Hesiodus*).

(c) When it is desirable to emphasize one of the subjects—see 10, 2 n. on *abstulerat.*

Tacitus' particular preference is for the plural verb, even when the subjects are contrasted or separated. Cf. 42, 1, *non mihi uxor aut filius . . . sunt*; *Dial.* 42, *ego te poetis, Messalla autem antiquariis criminabimur.*

donec, 'as long as'. This meaning of *donec* (used most frequently, as here, with the indic.) seems to be confined to the poets and historians. Cf. *Ann.* XIV, 50, *libros conquisitos lectitatosque donec cum periculo parabantur*; Livy, I, 7, 13, *inde institutum mansit, donec Pinarium genus fuit.*

plus . . . eadem. Their physical condition was, if anything, worse: but their morale was infinitely improved by success.

ciborum. The gen. is objective and *egestas* means 'shortage', 'lack'; cf. Sall. *Cat.* 58, *frumenti egestas.*

69. § 1. circumuenti exercitus, 'of the army's being cut off'; for the use of the participle see 8, 6 n. *fama* can be used with a gen. expressing the subject-matter of the report (*fama crudelitatis*, Cic. *Cat.* IV, 12) and that can be extended by a participle to form a convenient alternative to an acc. and infin. clause. Cf. Livy, XXVII, 33, 3, *id inuentum famam interfecti regis uulgauit.*

ni . . . prohibuisset . . . erant. The real apodosis is suppressed— 23, 2 n. 'There were some who were for daring (and would have dared) that crime', i.e. 'there were some who, in their terror, would have dared to destroy the bridge, if A. had not prevented such an outrage'. Agrippina was last heard of (41) going for safety to the country of the Treviri. Her return is not recorded, but she is clearly here back at headquarters, awaiting the return of the main force.

pontem, probably the one built (49, 4) at the beginning of this series of campaigns.

solui. *prohibeo* is more commonly used with the acc. and infin. than with *ne* or *quominus.* Cf. Cic. *Tusc.* V, 103, *num ignobilitas sapientem beatum esse prohibebit?*

flagitium. The use of *audeo* with the acc. is mainly confined to the poets and historians, and is most common with nouns which mean 'outrage' (*scelus, nefas, flagitium*) or adjs. which describe such an action (*immania, multa*).

animi. Introd. IV, 2 (i).

munia . . . induit, 'assumed the duties of general'. Metaphors of clothing and stripping (see 2, 1 n. on *exuto*) are among Tacitus' favourite usages. This use of *induo* with an abstract obj. = 'assume', 'undertake' is classical.

ut quis. See 2, 1 n. and 27, 1 n.

uestem et fomenta, clothing to the *inops*, dressings to the *saucius*. See note on Double Zeugma, 55, 1.

§ 2. C. Plinius, the Elder Pliny. The reference here is to the twenty books *Bellorum Germaniae*, listed among his uncle's works by the Yr. Pliny in *Ep.* III, 5, 4. He states that his uncle began the work when he was serving in Germany, after Drusus had appeared to him in a dream and begged him to rescue him from oblivion. See Introd. II.

ponti. M has *poti*. The word required is obviously some part of *pons*, and the dat. should be retained. Tacitus is fond of the adnominal dat. (see Introd. IV, 3 (ii)) and such phrases as *paci firmator* (*Ann.* II, 46) and *causas bello* (*Ann.* II, 64) seem sufficient justification for the dat. here.

grates. The word is normally reserved for thanks to the gods, and normally governed by *agere*. But there are a few precedents for *habere*, usually in combination with *agere* (but cf. Plaut. *Stich.* 403, *Neptuno grates habeo*) and Tacitus will naturally turn to the unusual construction and the unusual application of the word.

§ 3. animum. For the acc. see Introd. IV, 1 (i). Cf. Lucr. V, 1262, *tum penetrabat eos, posse haec.*

non enim. The acc. and inf. represents Tiberius' thoughts, the thinking being expressed in a general way by *id . . . animum . . . penetrauit.*

simplicis, 'without ulterior motive'.

studia. M's *militum* requires something like *studia* to be supplied, preferably after *externos*, which ends a page.

§ 4. imperatoribus, 'generals'.

tamquam parum ambitiose, 'as if too little ambitiously she . . .', i.e. 'as if it were not pretentious enough to . . .'

ducis gregali, deliberately juxtaposed, as are *Caesarem* and *Caligulam* in the next phrase.

conpressam . . . seditionem. She had not, in fact, quelled the rebellion, but her departure (41) had been the thing which brought the soldiers to their senses—which letters written *nomine principis* (36, 3) had conspicuously failed to do.

There is no reason to doubt the *fact* that Agrippina's action irritated Tiberius—most of her actions did. But Tacitus adds to the effect by presenting that fact, not as a narrative statement, but dramatically. In the Or. Ob. we seem to hear Tiberius thinking. See Introd. II.

§ 5. Seianus. See 24, 2 n.

odia . . . iaciens, 'sowing the seeds of hatred for a distant future'.

quae reconderet. Tiberius is the subject of the final relative clause ('seeds of hatred for him to store away'), and the description is typical of Tacitus' view of Tiberius as a morose hypocrite. See Introd. II.

70. § 1. at Germanicus. This picks up and explains in detail the general reference in 63, 3.

uexerat, for *aduexerat.* Cf. 63, 3 and see 5, 1 n.

P. Vitellio. Uncle of the Emperor of 69, he spent some time in Gaul and Germany with Germanicus (*Ann.* II, 6), and was later one of those who accused Piso of complicity in the death of Germanicus (*Ann.* II, 74; III, 13). In 31 he was accused of embezzling public funds and committed suicide.

ducendas. For the plural see 33, 2 n.

quo leuior, lit. 'that the fleet might float more lightly on the shallow, and settle more lightly on the tidal, sea'. The sea between the mouth of the Ems and the Ijsselmeer, being shallow, has a very low ebb (Lipsius, the C16 Dutch scholar, says *ipsi nauigauimus atque experti sumus*); a lighter ship would be able to cross the shallows and, when left grounded by the ebb, would refloat more quickly. Cf. Pliny's description of the North African coast (*H.N.* V, 26) as *uadosum et reciprocum mare.*

§ 2. aestu. Vitellius was obviously to march near the shore, the intention perhaps being to keep the two halves of the force within sight of each other. The abls. are absolute, expressing cause.

sidere aequinoctii. This is the autumnal equinox, marking the end of the campaigning season. The use of *sidus* = 'season' is poetical. Cf. Virg. *Georg.* I, 1 and Ovid, *Pont.* II, iv, 25, *brumali sidere.* The whole passage shows poetic influence, both in structure (short, vivid, balanced phrases and deliberately rhythmical prose) and in vocabulary (cf. *freto, breuia*).

breuia. *breuis* 'shallow' and *breuia* 'shallows' are poetical usages which Tacitus appears to introduce into literary prose. Cf. Virg. *Aen.* V, 221, *breuibusque uadis* and *Aen.* I, 111, *in breuia et syrtis urget.* Tacitus uses the word also in *Ann.* VI, 33 and XIV, 29.

§ 3. sternuntur. *milites* or *homines* is understood from the context.

subtracto solo, 'the ground being taken from beneath them'— 'they lost their footing' or 'got out of their depth'.

non . . . et. See 4, 1 n. 'Shouts of mutual encouragement.'

nihil, adverbial acc., 'to no extent'; 'differed not at all'. See Introd. IV, 1 (iii).

inprudenti. This seems the obvious emendation for *prudenti* M, which makes no sense. M similarly shows *non prudentem* at *Ann.* IV, 70 where the sense requires *non inprudentem.*

§ 4. utensilibus, 'necessaries'. Col. XII, *praef.* 3 defines *utensilia* as *quibus aut alitur hominum genus aut etiam excolitur.* It clearly here means mainly 'food'.

quos hostis, '*an* army under siege'. The general nature of the comparison is shown by the present tense.

illic, 'for such men'. Cf. *Hist.* II, 47, *ciuile bellum a Vitellio coepit, et initium illic fuit*; and see note on 3, 3, *illuc. illic* here refers to the category just mentioned, *his* to the *miserabiles*: the 'rule' that *hic . . . ille* means 'the latter . . . the former' can, like many rules of idiom, be broken when sense and emphasis require it. Here the emphasis lies on the men in 'the situation we are describing' (*his*), and *illic* is conveniently joined to *quos . . . circumsidet* by an explanatory *quippe* (5, 1 n.) which makes its connexion with that phrase clear. 'Indeed worse: for in *that* case (*illic*) . . . while for *these* (men under discussion)' . . . For a similar use of *hic . . . ille*, cf. Claud. *Carm. Min.* LII, 21–2, *erret et extremos alter scrutetur Hiberos; plus habet hic uitae, plus habet ille uiae.*

§ 5. **lux.** Note the strong personification.

ad amnem. *Visurgin* (the Weser) is obviously wrong, as a glance at a map shows: Germanicus was on his way home. The mistake is not Tacitus', because his geography, though vague, is not wild, and he elsewhere knows where the Visurgis is (*Ann.* II, 9–17). The simplest explanation seems to be that *Visurgin* is a gloss, written in by someone who wrongly identified the *amnis*, and that it should be removed altogether from the text. *amnis* will then mean 'the river', i.e. the one which leads into the *lacus* (60, 2) and so home; the point, in fact, at which they leave the sea. It was only for the actual sea-passage that the force had to be divided (§ 1), and so when they reach 'the river' Caecina and his men are re-embarked (*inpositae legiones*). See Brink in *J.R.S.* 1952, pp. 39–42.

reducem. The nouns form a single unit and therefore one would expect the adj. to be plural (cf. *ducendas* § 1). But Caesar is the more important part of the unit and so the adj. agrees with him. For a similar use of the singular verb see 10, 2 n.

uidere. The subject is a general 'they'—probably Agrippina and the others waiting at headquarters (69).

71. § 1. **filium,** called Sesithacus, according to Strabo, VII, 292

§ 2. **ceterum.** See 3, 1 n.

quod cuique promptum, 'the thing which was ready to each', i.e. 'as their resources permitted'.

ad bellum . . . militem. He was willing to accept their help for the campaign, but the soldiers' welfare he considered his private concern.

§ 3. **saucios.** There is no certainty that regular military hospitals (*ualetudinaria*) existed at this time, although they did later. Some care of the sick and wounded there obviously was, and 69, 1 suggests that it was the responsibility of the officers and so ultimately of the general himself.

sibique et proelio, lit. 'secured for himself and for battle'. *sibi* is dat. of interest (Introd. IV, 3 (i)), *proelio* dat. of purpose (Introd. IV, 3 (v)). Tr. 'confirmed their fighting spirit and their loyalty to himself'.

72. § 1. triumphalia insignia. See 55, 1 n. The men awarded this distinction had certain privileges, notably that of wearing triumphal dress at festivals.

A. Caecinae sq. These were the officers next in seniority to Germanicus himself. He had been granted a regular triumph (55, 1); they are now given their appropriate honours.

patris patriae. Cicero seems to be the first Roman who was officially called *pater patriae* (Cic. *Pis.* 6). Augustus formally accepted the title in 2 B.C. (*R.G.* 35), but it had been used unofficially for some time before that; *E. and J.* 60, an inscription of 6 B.C., describes him by that title. Obviously something similar was happening with Tiberius (*saepius ingestum*), except that he never did accept the official title; but inscriptions exist which bear it (see *E. and J.* 102, a decree from Gytheion).

ingestum, 'pressed upon him'. Cf. Suet. *Hor., ne recusanti quidem amicitiam suam ingerere desiit.*

in acta sua iurari, 'the oath to uphold his enactments'. The magistrates of the Republic had on entering office taken oath to uphold the laws (Livy, XXXI, 50, 7, *magistratum autem plus quinque dies, nisi qui iurasset in leges, non licebat gerere*). With the appearance of a dictator and Princeps in *C* I B.C., some similar formula had to be devised to cover their enactments, not all of which were *leges*: for if their decrees and edicts were automatically rescinded at their death, constitutional chaos would follow. Emperors and magistrates swore accordingly to uphold the *acta* of previous Emperors (unless specifically excluded); Dio, LVII, 8, 5 records Tiberius' oath *in acta Augusti*. Normally the oath applied only to the *acta* of previous rulers, and not to the present holder of the office: but in 45 B.C. the magistrates swore to uphold the *acta* of Julius Caesar (Appian, *B.C.* II, 106) and in 29 and 24 B.C. those of Augustus (Dio, LI, 20, 1; LIII, 28, 1). It is this practice that Tiberius is prohibiting. But it gradually became the custom to take an annual oath *in acta principis*, thus pledging loyalty to future as well as to past enactments. Cf. *Ann.* XIII, 11; XVI, 22.

quamquam. See 7, 3 n.

permisit. The normal classical prose construction of *permitto* is *ut* with the subj. But there are a few exx. of the infin. (e.g. Cic. *Verr.* V, 22, *ut iam ipsis iudicibus coniecturam facere permittam*) and this becomes commoner from Livy on. The use of *permitto* in the impersonal passive with an infin. seems to be post-Augustan (cf. 15, 2, *curru uehi haud permissum*) as does this use of the acc. and inf. Cf. *Ann.* XIV, 12, *sepulcrum extrui permisit*.

§ 2. ciuilis animi, 'producing no confidence in his democratic intentions'. For other exx. of *ciuilis* see 8, 2; 33, 2; 54, 2.

legem maiestatis. The conception of high treason naturally changes with a changing constitution. An attempt to define it was made by

Saturninus in 103 B.C., in the *Lex Appuleia*, and that was followed by Sulla in one of the *Leges Corneliae*, which formulated some of the possible charges under this law. Anything which in any way 'diminished the majesty' of the state or her magistrates could be a *crimen maiestatis* (Cic. *Inv.* II, 53; *Pis.* 50). But with the establishment of the Principate difficulties arose, because 'the majesty of the state' was obviously closely connected with the person of the Princeps. Attacks on his life and safety were clearly treason; but what about libellous statements, defacing of his statues and attacks on his family? Some charges under these heads were admitted by Augustus (*Ann.* III, 24; *Ed. Cyr.* II—see *E. and J.* 311, II), with no very serious consequences. Tiberius revived the law, no doubt because he had not the prestige of Augustus to protect him: but the real misuse of it did not begin until Sejanus employed it to get rid of personal enemies. For Tacitus' emphasis on the law here see Introd. II.

    dicta. Claudia (Suet. *Tib.* 2) was in 246 B.C. tried for treason because she had audibly wished that her brother would lose another fleet, to make less of a crowd in Rome. But this was long before the *lex maiestatis* was framed, and is quoted as an extraordinary case. Tacitus' statement may stand as generally true.

    inpune, 'with safety' lit.; 'went unpunished'.

    § 3. primus Augustus. It appears that this statement may be true by convention rather than by law, i.e. that the definition of *maiestas* (*de dignitate aut amplitudine aut potestate populi aut eorum quibus populus potestatem dedit, aliquid derogare*, Cic. *Inv.* II, 53) can legally include libel of a magistrate, but that in fact that aspect of the law had fallen into abeyance. Augustus merely reminded people that it was possible to treat such charges as treason. See Smith in *C.Q.* 1951, pp. 177–9.

    cognitionem. See 75, 1 n.

    Cassii Seueri. His bitterness of style is mentioned by Tacitus (*Dial.* 26) and Quintilian (X, 1, 117). He is generally held to be one of those punished by Augustus in A.D. 12 (Dio, LVI, 27, 1). He was first exiled in Crete and then in A.D. 24 (*Ann.* IV, 21) as he persisted in his activities, formally banished to Seriphus.

    diffamauerat. The verb is poetical and post-Augustan. Cf. *Ann.* XV, 49, *Quintianus probroso carmine diffamatus.* Its use with the acc. of the person is like that of *differo* (4, 2 n.).

    Pompeio Macro. His suicide in A.D. 33 is recorded in *Ann.* VI, 18. The praetors, although declining in power, still retained some judicial functions.

    an. From the classical *haud scio an, dubito an*, in which *an* introduces clauses of doubt or uncertainty, its use is extended to other verbs of similar meaning. Cf. 79, 1, *actum . . . in senatu . . . an*; Livy, XLV, 20, 6, *consulti patres an locum darent.*

iudicia . . . redderentur, 'whether cases brought under the law of treason should be granted a trial'. For the phrase, cf. Cic. *Flacc.* 88, *iudicium ex edicto dedit.* It is used especially of the praetor granting a trial by allocating judges for it.

§ 4. **carmina,** scurrilous verses.

discordem . . . animum. Friction has already been suggested in c. 14. There probably was some irritation between two people, each of whom wanted power.

73. § 1. **in Falanio,** 'in the case of' lit. 'To mention the charges tried out on Falanius and Rubrius.' M gives *Falanio* here and *Faianio* in § 2; neither is a common name, neither seems impossible, and nothing further is known about either a Falanius or Faianius of this time. The evidence for the two names is given by Syme in *J.R.S.* 1949, p. 12; it is perhaps slightly, though not conclusively, in favour of Faianius.

modicis. The adj. indicates no formal distinction between these and other Equites, but merely that they were ordinary members of their order, of no great wealth or distinction.

inrepserit . . . corripuerit. All this must refer to *maiestas* trials during the reign of Tiberius only, otherwise *quanta Tiberii arte* has little meaning. That it could also describe the progress of such trials from Tiberius to Domitian is purely accidental. It is a perfectly good, if rather emotional, description of what happened during Tiberius' reign, but whether the process is correctly attributed to *ars Tiberii* is a different matter. See Introd. II.

repressum sit. Note that Tacitus, writing emotionally, is careful not to say that it was *Tiberius* who stopped them, although he records the fact casually in § 3.

§ 2. **cultores Augusti.** These are not the official *sodales Augustales* (54, 1), but a similar body connected with the worship of Augustus in private houses. The 'great houses' maintained men, organized on the analogy of the priestly colleges, to see to this cult. Any citizen could erect in his own grounds any shrine he chose, and such private worship existed during Augustus' lifetime (Ovid, *Pont.* IV, ix, 105 sq.), long before the official cult of his Genius (see 10, 6 n.) was established in Rome.

habebantur, 'were kept up'. Cf. *Ag.* 28, *qui exemplum et rectores habebantur.*

mimum, not the same type of performer as the *pantomimus* (54, 2). The mime as a dramatic performance was a short scene, farcical in character and usually indecent. Jugglers, acrobats and buffoons might take part in it, and the performance was probably largely improvization. It was a much older and lower and more 'popular' form of entertainment than the performance of the *pantomimi,* and the *mimi* were only too likely to be *corpore infames.* See Beare, *Roman Stage,* pp. 139 sq.

mancipasset, subj. of virtual oblique statement, representing the charge made.

uiolatum ... numen. He had sworn a false oath by the divinity of Augustus. Cf. Suet. *Gaius* 24, *per numen Drusillae deierauit*. The Genius of Augustus had been included in official oaths about 12 B.C. Note the change in construction from *Falanio obiciebat accusator quod* to *Rubrio crimini dabatur* with acc. and inf. The short sentence is also an effective contrast to the longer one preceding.

§ 3. **notuere.** *notesco* is a poetical word, apparently introduced into prose by Tacitus.

consulibus. This indicates that the charges were being brought before the Senate and not a praetor's court. Precisely when the Senate began to act as a judicial body is uncertain. *Ann.* IV, 21 implies that Cassius Severus (72, 3) had been tried and exiled by the Senate: and Volesus Messalla, proconsul of A.D. 12, had been dealt with by a Senatus Consultum (*Ann.* III, 68). It looks as if the Senatorial court came into being towards the end of Augustus' reign, and from that time on offences committed by Senators (and Equites) might come under its jurisdiction.

ludis, probably the *ludi Palatini* (Suet. *Gaius* 56). Dio, LVI, 46, 3 records that Livia 'held a private festival in his honour for three days in the Palatium' and that the festival was continued by successive Emperors.

§ 4. **perinde ... quam si.** Cic. uses (*Verr.* III, 48) *perinde ... quasi* and (*Rosc. Com.* 15) *perinde ac si*. Tacitus extends the use of *quam* (cf. 41, 3, *aeque quam*), and he alone seems to use *quam si* after *perinde*. Cf. *Ann.* XIII, 49. See also *perinde ... -que*, 76, 1 n.

deorum iniurias dis curae. The dry comment seems equally typical of Tiberius and of Tacitus himself.

74. § 1. **Granium Marcellum.** The name of M. Granius Marcellus appears on a tile found near Tifernum Tiberinum (Città di Castello) in Umbria.

praetorem Bithyniae, 'governor of Bithynia'. Marcellus *was* of praetorian rank, but it was customary to style all governors of Senatorial provinces (among which Bithynia was at this time included) proconsuls, though only the governors of Asia and Africa were of consular rank: a coin from his province (*B.C.H.* (1881) V, p. 120) actually describes Marcellus as GRANIUS MARCELLUS PROCOS. So *praetor* is not here used to indicate his rank, but in the general sense of 'man in charge'. Cf. Cic. *Fam.* II, 17, 6, *officio quaestorio te adductum reticere de praetore tuo non moleste ferebam*, where *praetor* = M. Bibulus, proconsul of Syria.

Bithynia was in Asia Minor, along the shore of the Black Sea, and was the province later governed by the Younger Pliny.

quaestor ipsius, 'his own quaestor'. The governor of a province was considered to stand to his young quaestor *parentis loco* (Cic. *Div. in Caec.* 61). This made any betrayal by the quaestor especially treacherous and impious; hence Tacitus' emphasis here. Cf. Cic. *Verr.* I, 11, *spoliatum a quaestore suo.*

Caepio Crispinus. A. Caepio Crispinus is mentioned on an inscription found in a tomb near the Tiber (*C.I.L.* VI, 31762) and is otherwise known only from this chapter.

maiestatis. For the gen. see Introd. IV, 2 (ii).

subscribente. The verb is used of 'signing an accusation', either as principal or second accuser. Here Caepio is clearly the prime mover and Hispo the seconder. Cf. Cic. Q. *Fr.* III, 3, 2, *Gabinium reum fecit P. Sulla, subscribente priuigno Memmio, fratre Caecilio, Sulla filio.*

Romanio Hispone. There seems to be little doubt that Romanius and not Romanus is the correct form of his name, and that it is the gentile name, Hispo the cognomen. He is mentioned several times by Seneca (e.g. *Contr.* II, 5, 20; IX, 3, 11) as Hispo Romanius, but such inversions are common (see 8, 3 n.). See Syme in *J.R.S.* 1949, p. 14; he suggests that Hispo came from Cisalpine Gaul.

qui. This must refer to Hispo. Doubts have been raised only because in § 3 the subject of *insimulabat* is obviously Crispinus, Hispo's share in the prosecution being indicated by *addidit Hispo*: and there is apparently no indication of a change of subject between the verbs following *qui*, and *insimulabat*. But the man described in § 2 as *egens, ignotus* can hardly be a Roman Senator (as Crispinus was); and it is very difficult to refer *qui* to any other name than the one it immediately follows. In fact, *subscribente . . . inuenere* is a parenthesis describing Hispo, and the return to the main statement (whose subject was Crispinus) is clearly indicated by *sed*; for a similar use of *sed* cf. Cic. *De Or.* II, 193; *Ann.* III, 62.

formam uitae, i.e. that of a *delator* (informer). Rome had no Public Prosecutor, and an accusation (*nominis delatio*) was made by any private citizen (as e.g. Cicero accused Verres), who was rewarded if the prosecution was successful and punished if it proved to be frivolous. Under the Republican criminal laws, where each crime was fairly clearly defined, this system worked quite well. But the importance and vagueness of crimes covered by the *lex maiestatis* (72, 2 n.) produced in the Empire a professional class of *delatores*, whose object was not the punishment of wrong-doers but self-aggrandizement and wealth. Tiberius had not the standing of Augustus, and needed the protection of the treason law; in spite of that, the early and obviously frivolous charges brought by the *delatores* he dismissed with scorn. But to Tacitus, knowing the terror inspired by the informers of Domitian's time, these first cases are the ominous shadow of evils to come. He therefore recounts them at length and with bitter comment; and to some extent he is justified, because the fact that such charges could be made at all indicates an insecurity of which unscrupulous men could take advantage.

celebrem, not 'often practised', as Furneaux takes it. *celeber* can mean 'infamous' as well as 'famous', and that seems clearly its meaning here. Cf. *Ann.* XIII, 47, *pons Muluius in eo tempore celebris nocturnis illecebris erat.*

miseriae . . . audaciae, 'the sufferings of the age and the villainous acts of men'. The plural of abstract nouns is often used in Latin to indicate separate exx. of the abstract quality or of acts inspired by it. Thus *laus* = 'praise' but *laudes* = 'expressions of praise'. Cf. 21, 2, *iras.*

§ 2. **nam.** This sentence is a good sketch of the career of the average professional informer of the first century A.D.

libellis. *libellus* originally means 'a little book' or 'pamphlet' and then any short piece of writing—diary, letter, memorandum, legal petition. From these meanings it developed the special sense of 'defamatory writing' from which our 'libel' comes. That meaning is clearly implied here.

saeuitiae. The dat. after *adrepo* ('creep into') is used by the Elder Pliny and Tacitus. Cicero uses *ad.* Cf. *Ann.* III, 50, *animis muliercularum adrepit*, and see Introd. IV, 3 (vi). The phrase means 'creep into the confidence of the cruel Emperor', but by using, instead of an adj. qualifying *princeps*, the abstract noun *saeuitia* with a defining gen., Tacitus emphasizes the quality and makes Tiberius almost an incarnation of cruelty ('the cruelty consisting of Tiberius'). The device is as old as literature, cf. Homer, *Il.* V, 781, βίην Διομήδεος; Plaut. *Mil.* 1434, *scelus uiri*; Cic. *Fam.* V, 8, 2, *pestes hominum.*

ex pauperibus, 'rich from being poor'. *ex* with the state from which one is changing is used in Latin as ἐκ is in Greek (cf. Dem. *De Cor.* 131, ἐλεύθερος ἐκ δούλου καὶ πλούσιος ἐκ πτωχοῦ γεγονώς). Cf. Sall. *Jug.* 10, *Romanos ex amicis amicissimos fecisti.*

postremum sibi. Most *delatores* did in fact eventually find themselves in the position of defendant, either through over-reaching themselves (*Ann.* IV, 31), or by living until there was a violent reaction against them (as after the death of Sejanus).

§ 3. **sed . . . insimulabat.** See note on *qui* § 1.

ineuitabile crimen, acc. in apposition to the phrase. See Introd. IV, 1 (iv).

credebantur, 'were believed to have been said' lit. *credo* in the meaning 'hold to be true' is found in a personal passive even in Cicero. Cf. *Rosc. Am.* 62, *res tam scelesta credi non potest.*

alia in statua. The odd use of *in* with the abl. after *indo* is explained by the fact that it does not depend entirely on *inditam.* 'And, on (almost 'in the case of') another statue, the head of Augustus had been cut off, and one of Tiberius placed (there).'

amputato capite. It was not an unheard of practice to substitute one head for another on a statue. Later Gaius (Suet. *Gaius* 22) ordered all the great statues of the ancient world, including that of Zeus at Olympia, to have their heads replaced by replicas of his own.

§ 4. **exarsit.** Tacitus does not make it clear whether Tiberius lost his temper at the charges or at their frivolity. But the consequent acquittal of Marcellus, and Tiberius' reaction to other similar charges at this time, make it fairly certain that it was their frivolity which angered him.

se quoque. He was perfectly entitled to vote in the Senate, but did not always do so on such occasions—presumably for the reasons given in § 5.

palam et iuratum, not by secret ballot but by open statement; and strengthened by an oath, that this was his true opinion. 'Openly and under oath.' For such an oath see 14, 4; and for the personal use of *iuratus,* cf. Cic. *Off.* III, 99, *Regulus iuratus missus est ad senatum.*

quo . . . fieret. This is not part of Tiberius' statement, but Tacitus' explanation of its significance. 'This would mean that everyone else would have to do the same.'

§ 5. **Piso.** See 13, 3 n.

quo . . . loco. Senators were asked for their opinion on the question before the House, in a fairly strict order of precedence. Under the Empire the Princeps usually spoke either first, so that his wishes were known, or last, when he could apply a veto if necessary. Piso's question is bold, because it shows clearly the absolute power of the Emperors— a fact which they preferred where possible to keep veiled.

§ 6. **patiens.** On the use of the positive adj. and the omission of *tanto* see 57, 1 n. 'Moved by this plea, and as patient in his change of heart as he had been ungoverned in his outburst of rage'; i.e. 'moved by this plea, he recovered himself, and showed a tolerance as great as had been his ungovernable outburst of rage'.

reciperatores. These were a board of jurymen who could take final hearings of civil cases, especially any involving damages. They offered a speedier and simpler method of settling such cases than did the permanent *quaestiones.* One of the Edicts of Cyrene (*E. and J.* 311, V) quotes a senatorial decree of 4 B.C., which provides for charges of extortion made by provincials against their governor to be dealt with in this way—the preliminary hearing to be in the Senate which will, when there appears to be a case, appoint a board to deal with it. Precisely this procedure seems to have been followed here.

75. § 1. **cognitionibus,** cf. 72, 3. *cognitio* = 'judicial investigation', 'trial' is classical and almost synonymous with *iudicium.* It was a perfectly legal procedure (Cic. *Att.* XVI, 16C, 11, *lex earum rerum consulibus cognitionem dedit*) but had more the nature of an *ad hoc* inquiry than of formal judicial proceedings. It is therefore suitably applied to distinguish the Senatorial or Imperial court from the Praetor's.

cornu. The meaning of 'corner' is not common, but classical. Cf. Cic. *Att.* IX, 14, 1, *ab utroque portus cornu moles iacimus.*

curuli, i.e. *sella curuli,* the chair which was the mark of his office as a senior magistrate. The use of the adj. alone in this meaning is post-Augustan. Cf. Pliny, *Pan.* 59, 2; Suet. *Nero* 13.

ambitum et potentium preces, 'intrigue and powerful personal influence'. The phrase is almost Hendiadys, a figure which emphatically co-ordinates two aspects of a statement instead of subordinating one to the other. Cf. the common *ui et armis* for *ui armorum.* The intrigues would consist mainly of the effect produced on the court by a defendant's powerful friends, who could aid a jury willing to please them, or ruin one which refused to do so.

ueritati . . . libertas. The presence of Tiberius ensured the preservation of the law's integrity (*ueritas;* cf. Cic. *Verr.* I, 3, *iudiciorum ueritas*) but underlined the existence of a Princeps who could interfere with the courts.

§ 2. **Pius Aurelius senator.** As no office is mentioned and his rank is here irrelevant, *senator* probably implies one who had not yet held curule office.

mole. Nipperdey seems to be right in taking this as 'construction' of the road, citing *Hist.* IV, 28, *machinas molemque operum Batauis delegat.* This fits the meaning and the structure more than does 'pressure', &c.

aerarii praetoribus. In *Ann.* XIII, 29, Tacitus describes the different systems of controlling the treasury (*uaria habita ac saepe mutata eius forma*). Since 23 B.C. (Dio, LIII, 32, 2) it had been in the charge of two praetors of the year, selected by lot. This lasted until A.D. 44, when Claudius gave it to specially selected quaestors.

erogandae . . . pecuniae. For the gen. see 64, 4 n. 'Ever anxious to spend money for a good cause.' Tacitus, in spite of his prejudice, here shows himself more generous and fair to Tiberius than does Suet. (*Tib.* 46–8), who calls him *pecuniae parcus et tenax.* As far as we can judge from the evidence, Tiberius was generous to real need, but neither extravagant nor a simpleton.

diu. *Ann.* VI, 45, records one such act very near the end of his life.

§ 3. **ueniam ordinis,** 'indulgence concerning his senatorial rank' lit. The gen. is a gen. of reference (Introd. IV, 2 (i)). 'Leave to renounce his rank as a Senator.' Augustus had established (Dio, LIV, 17, 3) first 400,000 sesterces as the minimum rating for a Senator, and later, as the country recovered from the civil wars and wealth increased, 1,000,000 sesterces—the sum given to Celer by Tiberius.

decies sestertium. See 8, 2 n.

conperto, impersonal abl. abs. See Introd. IV, 4 (iv).

paternas, 'inherited' and therefore not his fault. *Ann.* II, 48, records the expulsion from the Senate of five men *prodigos et ob flagitia egentis.*

§ 4. **causam.** *causa* M is clearly wrong, and this seems on the whole the best correction. Each man had one case, and their attempts were separate. In Suet. *Tib.* 47, *nisi senatui iustas necessitatium causas probassent,* the addition of the gen. and the adj. gives the phrase a different meaning, and *causas* = 'reasons'. It is not therefore a good parallel. There seems to be no difficulty in taking *causam probare* = 'prove their case'.

faceret, 'his austerity made him harsh even where he was acting rightly'. The subj. is caused by the indefinite antecedent. See 3, 7 n.

76. § 1. **stagnauerat,** 'had flooded'. The word is poetical and very rarely transitive. Cf. Ovid, *Met.* XV, 269, *quae stagnata paludibus ument.*

relabentem. It seems unnecessary to take this as = *cum relapsus esset.* Present participles are certainly used by the poets and later writers in the sense of a perfect active participle (see Introd. IV, 7 (i)), but here the present sense will stand. The damage would become obvious as soon as the waters began to subside. 'As it subsided, loss of life and property was apparent.'

Asinius Gallus. See 8, 3 n.

libri Sibyllini. One collection of oracular sayings was said to have been sold by a Sibyl to Tarquinius Priscus. It was entrusted to the *xvuiri sacris faciundis,* one of the priestly boards, and officially consulted in time of crisis. It was destroyed when the Capitol was burned during the Sullan disturbances, and various unofficial versions were current until Augustus had a new official collection made and copied (*Ann.* VI, 12; Suet. *Aug.* 31).

perinde . . . -que, a Tacitean variation on the classical *perinde . . . atque.* Cf. 73, 4 n.

obtegens, 'with his propensity for concealment'. It is much more likely that his motive was a desire to take more practical action.

coercendi fluminis, 'remedial measures consisting in the control of the river' lit. The gen. is one of definition or content (Introd. IV, 2 (iv)).

Ateio Capitoni. C. Ateius Capito, consul in A.D. 5, was a distinguished jurist. He had been *curator aquarum* since A.D. 13 (Front. *Aqu.* II, 102). His death in A.D. 22 is recorded by Tacitus (*Ann.* III, 75), who adds a brief account of his career.

L. Arruntio. See 8, 3 n.

§ 2. **onera.** The arrival of a new governor each year, with a larger staff than an imperial legate would have, caused the senatorial provinces heavier expenditure. Tiberius not only transferred Achaia and Macedonia to the imperial control, but attached them to the command of Moesia (80, 1), thereby making a further reduction in the staff. The provinces remained imperial until A.D. 44, when Claudius restored them to the Senate (Dio, LX, 24, 1; Suet. *Claud.* 25).

§ 3. **quamquam uili,** 'although cheap'. See 7, 3 n.

in uulgus. This stands in place of the commoner dat. There seems to be no other ex. of *in* and the acc. after *formidolosus,* but cf. the similar *grati in uulgus,* 28, 3.

et, 'even his father'—who was not, Tacitus implies, a squeamish man.

§ 4. **trahebant.** See 62, 2 n.

interfuisset. The subj. is virtual oblique, representing their suggested explanation.

crediderim, the potential subj. of mild assertion. 'I should incline to think.' Latin originally used the present subj. to express this meaning, but from Cicero on the perfect becomes increasingly common. Cf. the common *dixerit aliquis.*

Tacitus quite genuinely does not believe the rumour, but cannot resist quoting it, even in negative form.

77. § 1. **proximo priore,** 'the previous year' (see 54, 2). *priore anno* alone might simply mean '*a* previous year'; *proximo anno* can mean 'the previous year', but it can also mean 'the next (following) year'. The context usually makes the necessary meaning clear, but occasionally *prior* or *superior* is added to put it beyond doubt. Cf. Cic. *Fam.* I, 9, 20, *quem proximis superioribus diebus acerrime oppugnasset.*

occisis, 'with the deaths of . . .' The participle expresses not time but accompanying circumstances. See Introd. IV, 7 (iii).

e plebe, '(members of) the civilian population'.

set. Eriksson, pp. 82–5 defends *et* M. But all his exx. of *non modo* without *sed* have *etiam,* or *quoque,* or a verb which makes clear the beginning of the contrasting clause: and his interpretation of M's text depends on punctuation—always a dangerous prop. *set* seems the easiest and most obvious emendation.

praetoriae cohortis. All the soldiers mentioned probably belonged to this unit. That it was normally present to keep order at the games is clear from *Ann.* XIII, 24, *statio cohortis adsidere ludis solita.*

in magistratus. For the prepositional phrase attached to the noun see 8, 1 n.

§ 2. **ius uirgarum,** 'the right of flogging'—by means of the rods of the lictors who attended them.

§ 3. **intercessit.** With Augustus' appropriation of *tribunicia potestas* for the Princeps (2, 1 n.), the office of tribune had ceased to have any real power. It remained a possible step in an official career, but had few practical functions. Pliny (*Ep.* I, 23, 1) describes the usual conception of the office as *inanem umbram et sine honore nomen.*

Haterius Agrippa. D. Haterius Agrippa, consul of A.D. 22, was a relation of Germanicus (*Ann.* II, 51) and a man of loose morals (*Ann.* VI, 4).

simulacra. This exchange between Senators, without interference from Tiberius, looked like Republican freedom of speech. But it was only a shadow of the reality. This view is both true, and unfair to the Emperor. Genuine Republican *libertas* had led to administrative chaos: it was not possible to have the benefits of central control without the attendant restrictions. Tacitus knows this intellectually, but is emotionally bitter about it. Cf. his frequent use of *imago* to describe similar 'shadows' of the past (81, 2; *Ann*. III, 60).

praebebat, 'was accustomed to provide'.

immunis uerberum. Suet. *Aug*. 45 makes it clear that they could still be scourged on sentence for specific charges. What Augustus did was to deprive the magistrates of the right to order summary scourging of actors at any time and in any place.

neque fas . . . infringere. Tiberius lacked constructive imagination, and therefore foliowed faithfully the policies of Augustus. This did not always work, because the Principate was a living and changing force and required fresh decisions in the light of those changes.

§ 4. lucaris, 'pay'. *lucar* was said to have been so called because originally the money for the grant made for the production came from a forest (*lucus*)-tax.

fautorum. These are here obviously not only the hired *operae* (16, 3 n.), but supporters in general.

quis. See 8, 3 n.

spectarentur. There is no need to alter this, with Furneaux, to *sectarentur*. The subject is 'actors', who are prohibited from performing in private houses or grounds, where the state could exercise no control over them. The change of subject is made less awkward by the fact that the actors are the focal point of the previous two clauses, even though not their grammatical subject. For a similar change, cf. *Ann*. XIV, 31, *praecipui quique Icenorum, quasi cunctam regionem muneri accepissent* (sc. *centuriones et serui Romani), auitis bonis exuuntur.*

et . . . fieret. *ut* is understood with this clause, from the *ne* of the preceding ones. Cf. *Ann*. III, 51, *ne deferrentur idque spatium uitae damnatis prorogaretur.*

exilio, i.e. by means of penalties up to and including banishment. This would include imprisonment.

78. § 1. templum. There was already an altar to Augustus in Tarraco (Quint. VI, 3, 77). This temple is represented on coins from the mint of Tarraco (see Matt., Pl. LIII, 10), and was a cult-centre (cf. *ara Vbiorum*, 39, 1) for the whole of this Spanish province. Cf. *I.L.S.* 2714ᵃ, an inscription from Tarraco, *flam. Aug. prou. Hisp. citer.*

colonia Tarraconensi, the modern Tarragona, on the east coast of Spain, between the Ebro and Barcelona. Its loyalty to Julius Caesar during the Civil War gained for it the status of colony, and it became the chief city of Hispania Tarraconensis (or Citerior), the most important Spanish province.

exemplum. This was the first temple to Augustus alone, as an officially divine being, to be erected in the western provinces.

§ 2. **centesimam rerum uenalium,** a tax of 1 per cent. on sales, which, with the 5 per cent. payable as death-duties (*uicesima hereditatum*), was paid into the military treasury.

militare aerarium. This was founded by Augustus in A.D. 6, to provide a fund from which pensions might be paid to legionaries who had completed their term of service. He paid into it a large sum of his own money, and established the two new taxes mentioned in the previous note, to provide for its future income. See *R.G.* 17; Dio, LV, 25; Suet. *Aug.* 49. *post bella ciuilia* is used loosely, the point being that the taxes were Augustan and not Republican, and the length of time after the civil war being for this purpose unimportant.

uicesimo. This means a return to the original conditions of service (17, 2) and a cancellation of the concessions granted in the previous year (36, 3).

dimitterentur, i.e. transferred to special veteran companies, not finally discharged. Cf. 17, 3. Augustus' calculations when founding the *aerarium militare* had been based on a full-service term of twenty years.

male consulta, 'misguided concessions'.

sedecim stipendiorum, 'a term (limit) of sixteen years'. The gen. is one of definition or content (Introd. IV, 2 (iv)).

expresserant, 'had extorted'. Cf. 19, 5.

79. § 1. **Arruntio et Ateio.** See 76, 1.

an. See 72, 3 n.

exundationes, a rare word, found also in Seneca (*Ben.* IV, 5, 3) and Pliny (*H.N.* XIX, 37).

uerterentur, the simple verb for the commoner *auerto* (cf. Livy, XLI, 11, 3, *amnemque . . . auertit*). See 5, 1 n.

lacus, e.g. Lake Velinus § 3 and the lake near Clusium, through which the Clanis flowed.

augescit. This is indic. because it is an explanatory statement inserted by Tacitus, not part of their request.

municipiorum et coloniarum. H. J. Cunningham, in *C.Q.* 1914, p. 132 and 1915, p. 57 n., collected a number of exx. of this phrase, to show convincingly that when Tacitus uses it (as here) without qualification, he means by it the towns of Italy. Cf. *Ann.* III, 55, *noui homines e municipiis et coloniis atque etiam prouinciis in senatum adsumpti.* By this time the difference between *coloniae* (settlements of Roman citizens) and *municipia* (self-governing Italian towns in alliance with Rome) had largely disappeared; because the *coloniae* had a large measure of self-government and the *municipia* had the *ius suffragii* which gave them full Roman citizenship.

Florentinis, the inhabitants of Florentia, the modern Florence. Its early history is doubtful: it may have received a colony under the Triumvirs (*C.I.L.* XI, Suppl. 7030, calls it *colonia*), but it remained unimportant in Roman history.

Clanis, the Chiana. The diversion here suggested was actually made in 1782, and the waters carried into the Arno by the Canale di Chiana.

idque. The force of *ne* continues with this clause.

adferret, 'and that that should not bring destruction upon them', i.e. 'be permitted to bring'.

§ 2. **Interamnates,** the people of the Interamna which lay between the Nar (Nera) and the Tiber; now Terni.

parabatur. Like *augescit* in § 1, this is an explanation made by Tacitus.

superstagnauisset. The plup. subj. represents a fut. perf. indic. of the direct speech. The verb is found only here in Latin literature.

§ 3. **Reatini,** the inhabitants of Reate (Rieti). L. Velinus (Lago di Piediluco) lay just south of the Nar, and if its outlet there was blocked, flood waters would come up stream and inundate Reate.

obstrui. The acc. and inf. after *recuso* is post-classical. Cf. Plin. *H.N.* XXIX, 16, *quaestum esse recusabant.* It is probably influenced by the similar and much commoner construction with *prohibeo* (69, 1).

quippe . . . erupturum. The participle (Introd. IV, 7 (ii *b*)) = 'sure to'. For *quippe* see 5, 1 n. and 7, 3 n.

sua . . . suos, 'by allotting to rivers *their own* outlets'. For *suus* see 12, 3 n.

utque . . . ita. *-que* joins the whole phrase to *cursus. ut . . . ita* here mean little more than 'both . . . and', with the emphasis rather stronger on the word with *ita*.

sociorum. This is an odd use, for it was 100 years since the Italians ceased to be *socii* of Rome. But none of the suggested emendations really improves the sense. The rites go back to a time when these people were *socii*, and the old term may be used to remind Rome of her responsibility towards the Italians.

sacra. The worship of river-gods is very ancient, and representations of, e.g. the Tiber as a reclining male figure appear on Roman coins (cf. *R.I.C.* II, p. 217). A famous pair of statues of about Hadrian's time represent the Nile and the Tiber; the first is now in the Vatican Museum, the second in the Louvre.

patriis, 'native', not 'ancestral'; the adj. is here formed from *patria*, not from *pater*.

quin. See 23, 5 n.

§ 4. **seu . . . siue,** 'either . . . or'. *siue*, like *an* (13, 6 n.) develops into a disjunctive particle. Cf. Cic. *Sull.* 17, *eiecto siue emisso iam ex urbe Catilina.*

Pisonis. The omission of the *praenomen* need cause no difficulty, because Cn. Piso has recently been mentioned (74, 5) and no other has yet appeared in the Annals. This may therefore safely be taken as the same Piso as he of cc. 13 and 74.

80. § 1. Poppaeo Sabino. C. Poppaeus Sabinus, consul in A.D. 9 was grandfather of Poppaea Sabina, Nero's wife. He is mentioned again as governor of Moesia in A.D. 31 (*Ann.* V, 10) and apparently died in his province in A.D. 35. Tacitus, recording his death in *Ann.* VI, 39, says that he had been *maximis prouinciis per quattuor et uiginti annos impositus*, so we may assume that he was appointed governor of Moesia in A.D. 11, and from A.D. 15–35 governed Achaia and Macedonia too. His successful and prolonged tenure of this post is ascribed by Tacitus (*Ann.* VI, 39) to the fact that *par negotiis neque supra erat.*

prouincia Moesia. Moesia was bounded to the north by the Danube and to the east by the Black Sea, and occupied what is now east Yugoslavia and Bulgaria. It was subdued by Crassus (the consul of 30 B.C.) in 29 B.C., but precisely when it became a separate province is uncertain. It may for some time have been a 'military district', like the Germanies (31, 2 n.).

Achaia ac Macedonia. See 76, 2.

morum. See 56, 4 n. The plural here either makes the gen. more purely partitive—'it was one of the habits of Tiberius', or is a gen. of characteristic from *mores*—'it was a mark of the character of Tiberius'. The infins. are explanatory of *id.*

continuare imperia. The principle was Augustus' (see 2, 2 n. on *prouinciae*), but in practice governors of his time seem to have held office for 3–5 years. Many of Tiberius' governors had longer terms, e.g. L. Apronius in Lower Germany from A.D. 28 until at least 34 (*Ann.* IV, 73; VI, 30).

iurisdictionibus. This may refer to the more peaceful imperial provinces, or to the appointments of *procuratores*, etc. The phrase clearly means 'military and non-military commands'.

§ 2. causae. Other reasons still are given by Josephus (*Ant. Iud.* XVIII, 173–5) and Dio (LVIII, 23, 5). Some of the explanations contain a certain amount of truth: but the real reason was a desire for efficiency in the government of the provinces (2, 2 n.).

alii. *tradunt* is to be supplied from the preceding *traduntur.*

semel placita. *Ann.* IV, 6 records a similar policy in the arrangement of his household—*semelque adsumpti tenebantur prorsus sine modo, cum plerique isdem negotiis insenescerent.*

plures, 'too many'.

ut callidum, 'as his mind was subtle, so was his judgment hesitant' lit. Here *ut . . . ita* gives something of the effect of 'in proportion to'; the relationship is to some extent that of cause and effect. If one sees too many possibilities, one will end by taking no decisions at all. 'His subtlety of mind made it difficult for him to take any decisions.' This is not the whole truth about Tiberius, but there is some truth in it.

neque . . . et. See 6, 3 n.

sectabatur. For the indic. see 53, 6 n.

§ 3. quibusdam. L. Aelius Lamia was appointed governor of Syria some time after A.D. 21 but was never allowed to visit his province, though he apparently held the title for years. L. Arruntius, consul in A.D. 6, was similarly kept from Hispania Citerior. Quite why this happened is difficult to understand. Explanations of hesitancy or fear (*Hist.* II, 65) are not convincing. It may have been a genuine experiment in provincial government, or the result of the scheming of Sejanus. See Marsh, p. 191 and notes.

81. § 1. comitiis consularibus. On the elections under Tiberius see also 14, 4 and 15, 1.

tum primum. The consuls for A.D. 15 had been designated before Augustus died (14, 3).

deinceps. The context makes it clear that this means 'for the rest of his reign'. Tiberius' speeches would not furnish any information about the practice of his successors.

firmare¦ for *affirmare.* See 5, 1 n.

ausim. This is an old aorist optative form. Only *faxim* and *ausim* have survived in ordinary usage, and they are usually employed as potential subjs.

auctores, i.e. the literary sources for the period.

sed. For the omission of *etiam* see 60, 1 n.

orationibus. Someone may have collected and published the speeches of Tiberius, or Tacitus may have consulted them in the *acta senatus* (the Roman Hansard). The latter explanation is the more probable, because they were obviously speeches dealing with affairs of state and would therefore be delivered in the Senate. On Tacitus' use of such sources see Introd. II.

§ 2. modo sq. This passage is almost as vexed as the one dealing with praetorian elections (14, 4-15, 1), but the most probable explanation of it is this: Tacitus, accustomed to imperial *commendatio* for all the available places at the consular elections, is puzzled by his sources which do not seem to imply this for the reign of Tiberius. He records the procedures apparently used by that Emperor, as seen in his speeches made at election times. Tiberius either (*modo*) described the candidates without mentioning their names: or (*aliquando*) without either naming or describing them, urged the candidates not to canvass: or (*plerumque*) solemnly

stated that all names given in to him had been passed to the consuls—
who presided over elections—but that any other candidates who had
confidence in their powers could still give in their names. Tacitus
naturally sees this as typical Tiberian hypocrisy, but it more probably
indicates that the elections for the consulship were still openly com-
petitive.

These speeches were almost certainly made to the Senate, now the
effective controller of elections (see 15, 1 n.). Whatever the precise
rôle of the special *centuriae* mentioned in the *Tabula Hebana* (*E. and J*:
94a), the Senate's selection of candidates now clearly preceded theirs:
they remained part of the machinery of the elections, as the *Tabula*,
referring to A.D. 19, shows, but any real influence which they might
have exercised after their creation in A.D. 5, clearly ended in 14. See
A.J.P. 1954, pp. 225 sq.: *J.R.S.* 1955, pp. 9–21.

stipendia, 'military service'.

professos, 'given in their names'. Cf. Cic. *Arch.* 7, *si sexaginta diebus
apud praetorem essent professi.*

posse et alios. Theoretically, they could hand in their names to the
presiding consul. But it is not probable that candidates in practice ever
so ignored the Emperor.

speciosa, 'things which sounded well' lit. 'This sounded well, but
was in fact meaningless and misleading.' The adj. is acc. in apposition
to the phrase (Introd. IV, 1 (iv)). The bitter closing statement is very
characteristic of Tacitus. See Introd. III.

INDEX TO NOTES

officers of legion, 17, 1; 19, 4; 20, 1; 23, 3; *primi ordines*, 29, 2; *cohors ciuium Rom.*, 8, 2.

camps, 16, 2; 21, 1; 61, 2; 65, 7; 66, 1; 71, 3; conditions of service, 17, 2, 4; 20, 1; 36, 3; 37, 2; 78, 2; discharge, 17, 3; 78, 2.

standards, 17, 3; 18, 2; 20, 1; 30, 2; 34, 3; 37, 2; 38, 1; 39, 3, 4; 48, 2; 60, 3; military decorations, 24, 3; 44, 5.

augury, 62, 2.

aut, 8, 2; *aut . . . uel* for *aut . . . aut*, 13, 2.

benefactions of Augustus, 2, 1; by will, 8, 2; buildings, 9, 5.

cedo, imperat., 23, 3.

census, of Gaul, 31, 2.

ceterum, marking transition, 3, 1; 71, 2; = 'but in reality', 10, 1; 14, 2; 44, 4.

chiasmus, 2, 1; 29, 3.

colonia, used of German settlement, 59, 6; see also *municipium*.

commendatio, 15, 1.

comparatio compendiaria (shortened comparison), 28, 1.

comparative sentences, with positive adj. in one clause, 57, 1; 68, 4; with *tanto* omitted, 2, 1; 74, 6.

conditional sentences:
vivid apodosis in Or. Ob., 19, 5; 36, 2; suppressed apodosis, 23, 2; 35, 4; 63, 2; 65, 6; 69, 1; fut. partic. for apodosis, 36, 2; 45, 2; protasis expressed by noun, 67, 2.

consulship, origin of, 1, 1; consecutive, 3, 1; Augustus' use of, 2, 1; 9, 2; elections to, 81, 2.

dative:
of interest, 12, 2; 20, 1; 43, 1; 48, 2; 59, 3; 64, 3; 66, 1; 71, 3.
of possession, 11, 2; 13, 1; 24, 2; 29, 4; 53, 1; 69, 2.
point of view (ethic), 32, 3; 59, 1; agent, 1, 2; 10, 2; 17, 6; 42, 2; 57, 1; 62, 2.
purpose, 2, 1; 3, 1; 10, 1; 22, 1; 23, 5; 24, 2; 29, 4; 48, 3; 51, 2; 57, 5; with gerundive, 23, 4; 26, 2; 31, 2; 54, 1; 60, 2; 62, 1.
motion to a goal, 19, 1; 23, 1; 41, 1; 74, 2; with *nomen est*, 31, 2; form in -*u*, 10, 2.

death, expressions for, 3, 3.

decemuiri, 1, 1.

delatores, 74, 1; see also *maiestas*.

dictatorship, original use of, 1, 1; of Sulla, 1, 1.

diminutives, Latin use of, 59, 2.

dubium an, used adverbially, 5, 2.

eclipse, of moon in A.D. 14, 28, 1.
elections, 14, 4; 15, 1; 81, 2; see also *commendatio, nominatio*.
ellipse, of verb in subord. clause, 2, 1; of subj. verb, 7, 1; of *agebat*,
43, 1; of *dicit*, 65, 4.
et:
adding stronger adj., 1, 3; joining adjs. after neg., 4, 1; 29, 1; 70, 3;
= *etiam*, 4, 2; 76, 3; intensive, 4, 4; attaching last unit of series,
21, 2; 25, 2; = *et tamen*, 38, 2; with negs., 38, 2; distributive, 69, 1.
exile, 6, 2.

fleet, on Rhine, 45, 2.
forem, 8, 6.
frequentative verbs, Tac. use of, 4, 1.

genitive:
of reference: with nouns, 16, 1; 59, 4, 6; 75, 3; with adjs., 32, 2;
46, 2; 62, 2; 69, 1; with partics., 64, 4; 75, 2; gerund, 7, 3; 29, 1;
'legal', 3, 4; 21, 3; 74, 1.
partitive, 18, 2; 41, 1; 42, 1; 64, 3; *moris est*, 56, 4; 80, 1; with neut.
adjs., in oblique cases, 61, 1, 2; 65, 5; governed by a prep., 53, 5;
in pl., 9, 2; 17, 3; 50, 3; 61, 1; 65, 1; with positive adjs. 2, 1; 51, 2.
definition, 17, 3; 78, 2; with gerundive, 76, 1; with *nomen*, 2, 1;
9, 2; 58, 5.
purpose, 3, 6; objective, 14, 2; 27, 2; 53, 2; 58, 3; 67, 1; 68, 5; in
place of adj., 8, 1, 5; pl. of second declension archaic form, 8, 2.
Germany, not a province, 31, 2; Augustus' visits to, 46, 3; *Germania,
Germaniae*, 57, 2.
gladiators, kept by provincial governors, 22, 1.

hendiadys, 75, 1.
hexameter, in prose, 1, 1.
hic . . . ille, 70, 4.

iam, adding emphasis, 21, 3; *iam iamque*, 47, 3.
igitur, position of, 4, 1.
illic, illuc, used personally, 3, 3; 70, 4.
imperator, 3, 1; 9, 2; 31, 5; 58, 5.
imperfect tense, denoting 'begin to', 18, 3; 21, 1; 'was for', 20, 2; 56, 3;
habitual action, 23, 3; 'endeavour', 39, 4.
imperial cult:
worship of living Emperor, 10, 6; *ludi Augustales*, 15, 2; 54, 2; *sodales
Augustales*, 54, 1; *cultores Augusti*, 73, 2; temple at Tarraco, 78, 1;
oath by Genius, 73, 2.
imperium, 2, 1; 14, 3.

indicative:

with exprs. of suitability and fitness, 42, 3; 66, 2; in Or. Ob., 10, 2,
5; 28, 3; 35, 1; 36, 3; 39, 2; 44, 5; 57, 1; 58, 4; 79, 1, 2; used to
suggest statement of fact, 53, 6; 80, 2.

infinitive:

with *agitare*, 18, 2; *animus est*, 56, 5; *tendere*, 19, 3; *subigere*, 39, 3;
monere, 63, 1; *niti*, 64, 1; *permittere*, 72, 1.

historic, Introd. IV, 6 (ii); inf. explaining a noun, 43, 2; passive inf.
with *imperare*, 39, 5; with *desino, coepi*, 13, 5; 34, 2.

with acc. after *metus*, 39, 2; *prohibere*, 69, 1; *recusare*, 79, 3.

in subord. clauses in Or. Ob., 5, 2; 12, 1.

iurare, in uerba, 7, 2; 34, 1; *in acta*, 72, 1; *iuratus* = 'under oath', 74, 4.

kings, at Rome, 1, 1.

legati, meaning of, 42, 4; 59, 3.
limes, meaning of, 50, 1.
lot, used in election, 54, 1.

maiestas, law of, 72, 2–3; trials in reign of Tiberius, 73, 1; see also
delatores.
municipium, with *colonia*, 79, 1.

names, order reversed, 8, 3; repeated, for emphasis, 13, 1.
negatives:

non + jussive subj., 11, 1; *neque* + jussive subj., 43, 2; *neque . . . et*,
6, 3; 80, 2; *neque . . . sed (uerum)*, 58, 1.

nominatio, 14, 4.
non modo . . . sed, 60, 1; 77, 1; 81, 1.

opening sentence, significance of, 6, 1.
operae, 16, 3.
oratio obliqua, use of, 41, 1; rhet. questions in, 17, 1; 17, 6; 40, 2; 46, 3.
order, interwoven, 28, 1; 67, 1.

participles:

present: forming periphrastic tense, 14, 3; with gen., 64, 4; 75, 2;
used aoristically, 76, 1; Introd. IV, 7 (i); *ut . . . cupientibus erat*, 59, 1.

future: expressing intention, 31, 1; 33, 2; 79, 3; purpose, 24, 1; =
hypothetical clause, 36, 2; 45, 2; 46, 2.

perfect: circumstantial, 65, 3; 77, 1; + noun = abstract noun and
gen., 3, 6; 8, 6; 16, 1; 42, 1; 59, 1; Introd. IV, 7 (iv).

deponent, used passively, 7, 5; with *tamquam, quamquam, ut, quippe*
see *tamquam*, &c.

river gods, 79, 3.

sed, indicating return to main statement, 74, 1.

senate, servility of, 7, 1; 12, 1; as court of justice, 73, 3; procedure, 74, 5; census required for, 75, 3.

sesterces, 8, 2; 75, 3.

si, clause = explanatory clause, 11, 3; 49, 3; with subj. = 'in the hope that', 48, 1.

Sibylline books, 76, 1.

singular, collective, 50, 1; verb, with sing. and pl. subjects, 10, 2; 56, 2; adj., with two sing. nouns, 70, 5.

siue = 'or', 79, 4; = *siue quod*, 62, 2.

sponte, without *sua*, 8, 4.

subject, changed within sentence, 77, 4.

subjunctive:
   potential, 28, 5; 32, 3; 43, 1; 64, 4; 76, 4; repeated action, 7, 5; 15, 3; 27, 1; 44, 5; with *donec*, 1, 2; 13, 6; 32, 2; with *tamquam*, 12, 4; virtual oblique, 6, 1, 3; 9, 1; 11, 3; 32, 3; 36, 2; 40, 1; 46, 1; 52, 1; 73, 2; 76, 4; generic, 3, 7; 11, 2; 35, 5; 75, 4; with *potius quam*, 35, 4; with *magis quam ut*, 52, 2; tenses in consec. clauses, 3, 4; simple tense for periphrastic, 19, 5; representing vivid apodosis in Or. Ob., 19, 5; indirect jussive without *ut*, 68, 1; Repraesentatio, Introd. IV, 5 (iv); 17, 5; 19, 3.

substantives, used adjectivally, 9, 5.

supine, second, 35, 5.

suus = 'one's own', 10, 2; 12, 3; 41, 1; 79, 3.

tamquam, with subj., 12, 4; with partic., 7, 3, 5.

taxes: *tributum* and *uectigalia*, 11, 4; *centesima rerum uenalium*, 78, 2.

templum, of Augustus, 10, 7; used as bank, 8, 1; = 'sacred grove', 51, 1.

text: 4, 4; 8, 1, 2, 3; 9, 4; 10, 5; 13, 2; 15, 3; 19, 1; 20, 2; 21, 2; 27, 2; 28, 1, 3; 32, 1; 34, 1; 35, 3; 36, 2; 38, 1; 41, 1; 42, 1; 47, 2; 49, 1; 51, 2; 56, 2; 57, 4; 59, 4; 63, 3; 65, 4, 7; 68, 2; 69, 2, 3; 70, 3, 5; 73, 1; 74, 1; 75, 4; 77, 1, 4; 79, 3, 4.

Titii sodales, 54, 1.

toga, praetexta, 3, 2; = 'civil life', 12, 3.

-tor, -trix, 4, 4; 10, 2; 24, 2; 30, 1; 49, 2; 55, 2; 58, 3.

tribuni, militum consulari potestate, 1, 1; *populi*, 77, 3; of legion, 19, 4.

tribunicia potestas, 2, 1.

triumph, under the Principate, 55, 1; triumphal dress, 15, 2; insignia, 72, 1.

triumuiri, 1, 1; 2, 1.

uel = *aut*, 13, 2.

uocabulum = 'nickname', 23, 3; = 'title', 3, 7.
ut, with partics., 47, 3; with *sino*, 43, 2; with subj. after *magis*, 52, 2;
supplied from *ne*, 77, 4; *ut . . . ita*, 12, 1; 42, 3; 79, 3; 80, 2.
utinam, elliptical use of, 58, 2.

verb, simple for compound, 5, 1; compound for simple, 4, 1; periphrastic form, 14, 3.

zeugma, 17, 4; 49, 1; 58, 1; double zeugma, 55, 1; 69, 1.

INDEX OF PROPER NAMES

Romans are generally listed under the gentile name (e.g. Sempronius Gracchus, *s.v.* Sempronius), except when they are more commonly known by another name (e.g. Augustus). Paragraph references are omitted when the name occurs more than once in a chapter.

VOCABULARY

Long vowels are marked ‾, unless double consonants make the syllable necessarily long: diphthongs and final *i, o, u* are long, if unmarked.

Verbs are indicated as transitive or intransitive, and parts of speech (e.g. adv., conj.) indicated, only where doubt seems reasonable.

Words enclosed in square brackets are unattested forms.

Hyphens are used for convenience of abbreviation only, and have no etymological significance.

ā, ab (prep. w. abl.), *from, by*

ab-do, -didi, -ditum, 3 (tr.), *hide*

ab-dūco, -duxi, -ductum, 3, *take away*

ab-eo, -ii, -itum, -īre, *go away*

abhorreo, 2 (no sup.), *be averse to*

ab-icio, -iēci, -iectum, 3, *throw away*

abn-uo, -ui, -uitum, 3, *deny, reject, refuse*

abol-eo, -ēui, -itum, 2, *destroy, efface*

ab-rumpo, -rūpi, -ruptum, 3 (tr.), *break*

abs-cēdo, -cessi, -cessum, 3, *depart*

ab-soluo, -solui, -solūtum, 3, *acquit*

abs-tineo, -tinui, -tentum, 2, *abstain from*

abstrūs-us, -a, -um, *reserved*

ab-sum, āfui, -esse, *be away from*

ac-cēdo, -cessi, -cessum, 3, *come near, be added*

ac-cendo, -cendi, -censum, 3, *kindle, inflame*

ac-cido, -cidi, 3, *happen*

ac-cīdo, -cīdi, -cīsum, 3, *cut down, weaken*

accio, 4, *summon*

ac-cipio, -cēpi, -ceptum, 3, *receive, accept, hear, interpret*

accol-a, -ae (c.), *neighbour*

ac-colo, -colui, -cultum, 3, *live near*

accūsāt-or, -ōris (m.), *prosecutor*

āc-er, -ris, -re, *sharp, strict*

acerb-us, -a, -um, *harsh*

aci-ēs, -ēi (f.), *battle-line, battle*

Actiac-us, -a, -um, *relating to Actium*

act-um, -i (n.), *enactment*

acūt-us, -a, -um, *sharp*

ad (prep. w. acc.), *to, for, as regards*

adaequo, 1, *make equal to*

adcelero, 1 (tr.), *hasten, accelerate*

adclāmo, 1, *shout*

adclīu-is, -e, *sloping upwards*

ad-cresco, -crēui, -crētum, 3, *grow*

ad-curro, -curri, -cursum, 3, *run to*

adcurs-us, -ūs (m.), *a running to, rush up*

ad-do, -didi, -ditum, 3, *add*

ad-dūco, -duxi, -ductum, 3, *bring to, induce*

adeo (adv.), *so far, so much, so*

ad-eo, -ii, -itum, -īre, *approach*

adfero, attuli, adlātum, adferre, *bring to, announce*

ad-ficio, -fēci, -fectum, 3, *affect*

adfīnit-as, -ātis (f.), *relationship*

ad-fundo, -fūdi, -fūsum, 3, *pour into*

225

adgest-us, -ūs (m.), *collection*

adhibeo, 2, *apply, use*

adhuc (adv.), *still, yet*

adiaceo, 2 (no sup.), *lie near*

ad-icio, -iēci, -iectum, 3, *add, apply*

ad-igo, -ēgi, -actum, 3, *bind (w. an oath), bring to, inflict on*

ad-imo, -ēmi, -emptum, 3, *take away*

ad-ipiscor, -eptus sum, 3 (dep.), *obtain*

ad-lābor, -lapsus sum, 3 (dep.), *flow*

adleuo, 1, *lift up, mitigate*

adloqui-um, -i (n.), *encouragement*

admodum (adv.), *to the limit, very*

admoneo, 2, *mention, speak of*

adopti-o, -ōnis (f.), *adoption*

adorno, 1, *equip, adorn*

ad-pōno, -posui, -positum, 3, *appoint*

adprobo, 1, *approve, confirm*

ad-rēpo, -repsi, -reptum, 3, *creep to*

adrogan-s (arrogans), -tis, *arrogant*

adroganti-a, -ae (f.), *arrogance*

adscio, 4, *receive, admit*

ad-scisco, -scīui, -scītum, 3, *admit*

ad-scrībo, -scripsi, -scriptum, 3, *add to*

ad-sideo, -sēdi, -sessum, 2, *attend, assist*

adsimulo, 1, *liken to, compare*

adsisto, astiti, 3, *stand at or near*

adsol-eo, -ēre, *be accustomed*

adstrep-o, -ere, *applaud noisily*

adsuetūd-o, -inis (f.), *habit*

adsulto, 1, *attack*

ad-sum, -fui, -esse, *be present*

ad-sūmo, -sumpsi, -sumptum, 3, *receive, adopt*

adtrecto, 1, *touch, handle*

ad-ueho, -uexi, -uectum, 3, *convey to; (pass. ride to)*

ad-uenio, -uēni, -iuentum, 4, *arrive*

aduent-us, -ūs (m.), *arrival*

aduersor, 1 (dep.), *oppose, resist*

aduersus, aduersum (prep. w. acc.), *against*

aduers-us, -a, -um, *unfavourable, unsuccessful, contrary, hostile;* perf. part. of *aduerto*

aduer-to, -ti, -sum, 3, *turn to*

adūlāti-o, -ōnis (f.), *flattery, adulation*

adulescen-s, -tis, *young;* as noun, *young man*

adulescentul-us, -i (m.), *mere youth*

adult-er, -eri (m.), *adulterer*

adult-us, -a, -um, *adult, mature*

adūlor, 1 (dep.), *flatter*

ad-uoluo, -uolui, -uolūtum, 3 (tr.), *roll towards;* (pass. *grovel at*)

aed-es, -ium (f. pl.), *house*

aedifici-um, -i (n.), *building*

aedīlit-as, -ātis (f.), *aedileship*

aeg-er, -ra, -rum *sick;* aegrē (adv.), *with difficulty*

aemulāti-o, -ōnis (f.), *jealousy*

aequālit-as, -ātis (f.), *equality, political equality, uniformity*

aequinocti-um, -i (n.), *equinox*

aequ-us, -a, -um, *equal;* aequē (adv.), *equally*

aequo, 1, *make equal, level*

aerāri-um, -i (n.), *public treasury*

aes, aeris (n.), *bronze*

aest-as, -ātis (f.), *summer*

aestimo, 1, *value*

aestīu-us, -a, -um, *of summer;* aestīu-a, -ōrum (n. pl.), *summer camp*

aest-us, -ūs (m.), *tide*

aet-as, -ātis (f.), *age*

aetern-us, -a, -um, *eternal*

Afric-us, -a, -um, *African*

ag-er, -ri (m.), *field, land*

agg-er, -eris (m.), *causeway, material for rampart*

aggero, 1, *heap up*

ag-gero, -gessi, -gestum, 3, *bring to*

agito, 1, *consider, meditate upon, do, behave*

agm-en, -inis (n.), *army troop, army, column*

ago, ēgi, actum, 3, *act the part of, do, drive, deal with*; agere de, *bring up (of a proposition)*

āio, ait (def. vb.), *say*

āl-a, -ae (f.), *wing, squadron*

alb-eo, -ēre, *be white*

aliās (adv.), *on another occasion*

alibi (adv.), *elsewhere*

aliēn-us, -a, -um, *belonging to another*

alio (adv.), *to another place*

aliquandŏ, *sometimes*

aliqu-is, -id, *someone*

aliter, *otherwise*

ali-us, -a, -ud, *other*; alii . . . alii, *some . . . others*

altār-ia, -ium (n. pl.), *altar*

alte, *deeply, highly*

alt-er, -era, -erum, *other (of two), second*

alue-us, -i (m.), *channel*

alumn-us, -i (m.), *nursling*

amanter, *affectionately*

ambig-o, -ere, *doubt*

ambigu-us, -a, -um, *doubtful*

ambio, 4, *encompass, surround*

ambiti-o, -ōnis (f.), *partiality*

ambitiōse, *ostentatiously*

ambit-us, -ūs (m.), *going round, canvassing, corruption, circuit*

ambulo, 1, *walk*

amīciti-a, -ae (f.), *friendship*

amīc-us, -i (m.), *friend*

ā-mitto, -mīsi, -missum, 3, *lose*

amn-is, -is (m.), *river*

āmōlior, 4 (dep.), *remove*

am-or, -ōris (m.), *love*

ā-moueo, -mōui, -mōtum, 2, *remove*

am-plector, -plexus sum, 3 (dep.), *embrace*

amputo, 1, *cut off*

an (conj.), *or, whether*

anc-eps, -ipitis (n.), *danger*

an-go, -xi, -ctum, 3, *vex, trouble*

angusti-ae, -ārum (f. pl.), *scarcity*

angust-us, -a, -um, *narrow*

anim-a, -ae (f.), *soul, breath*

anim-us, -i (m.), *mind, spirit, intention*

annōn-a, -ae (f.), *provisions, corn-supply*

ann-us, -i (m.), *year*

annu-us, -a, -um, *annual*

antĕ, anteā (adv.), *before*; antĕ (prep., w. acc.), *before*

ante-eo, -ii, -itum, -īre, *go ahead, go before*

ante-fero, -tuli, -lātum, -ferre, *carry before, give preference to*

antefix-us, -a, -um, *fastened in front of, nailed to*

antehab-eo, -ēre, *prefer*

ante-pono, -posui, -positum, 3, *place, set before, prefer*

antequam (conj.), *before*

ante-uenio, -uēni, -uentum, 4, *come before, anticipate*

antīqu-us, -a, -um, *old*

anxi-us, -a, -um, *uneasy, hesitant*

aper-io, -ui, -tum, 4 (tr.), *open, reveal*

appello, 1, *call, name*

apud, aput (prep. w. acc.), *near, at, in, with*

aqu-a, -ae (f.), *water*

aquil-a, -ae (f.), *eagle, legionary standard*

aquilif-er, -eri (m.), *standard-bearer*

aquil-o, -ōnis (m.), *north wind*

ār-a, -ae (f.), *altar, monument*

arbit-er, -ri (m.), *controller*

arbitri-um, -ī (n.), *authority, decision*

arb-or, -oris (f.), *tree*

arcān-us, -a, -um, *secret*

arc-eo, -ui, -tum, 2, *ward off, prevent*

ardesco, arsi, 3, *become violent*

ard-or, -ōris (m.), *eagerness*

ardu-us, -a, -um, *difficult*

arg-uo, -ui, -ūtum, 3, *censure, provoke* ?

arm-a, -ōrum (n. pl.), *arms, military power, warfare*

armo, 1, *arm*

ar-s, -tis (f.), *art, stratagem, way of life, conduct*

art-us, -ūs (m.), *limb*

as, assis (m.), *as (copper coin)*

aspecto, 1, *look at attentively, pay attention to, look to*

aspect-us,-ūs (m.), *aspect, appearance*

asp-er, -era, -erum, *harsh*

asperit-as, -ātis (f.), *harshness*

aspernor, 1 (dep.), *reject, despise*

aspero, 1, *exasperate*

a-spicio, -spexi, -spectum, 3, *look at, see*

ast-us, -ūs (m.), *cunning*

at, *but*

at-tineo, -tinui, -tentum, 2, *hold back*

at-tingo, -tigi, -tactum, 3, *touch on, mention*

attonit-us, -a, -um, *stupefied*

atque, ac, *and*

atr-ox, -ōcis, *savage, spirited*

auāriti-a, -ae (f.), *greed*

auct-or, -ōris (c.), *instigator, author*

auctōrit-as, -ātis (f.), *influence, decree*

auct-us, -ūs (m.), *increase, rise*

audāci-a, -ae (f.), *boldness*

audeo, ausus sum, 2 (semi-dep.), *dare*

audio, 4, *hear*

ā-ueho, -uexi, -uectum, 3, *carry off*

ā-uello, -uelli (-uulsi), -uulsum, 3, *remove*

āuersor, 1 (dep.), *turn away from*

āuers-us, -a, -um, *turned away*

aufero, abstuli, ablātum, auferre, *take away, remove*

augeo, auxi, auctum, 2 (tr.), *increase, exalt*

augesc-o, -ere (intr.), *increase*

augurāt-us, -ūs (m.), *office of augur*

Augustāl-is, -e, *Augustan*

aui-a, -ae (f.), *grandmother*

āui-a, -ōrum (n. pl.), *remote or trackless places*

auidit-as, -ātis (f.), *greed*

auid-us, -a, -um, *eager*

aul-a, -ae (f.), *court*

aur-is, -is (f.), *ear*

aur-um, -i (n.), *gold*

aut, *or*

au-us, -i (m.), *grandfather*

auxiliār-is, -e, *of auxiliary troops*;

auxiliār-es, -ium (m. pl.), *auxiliary troops*

auxiliāri-us, -a, -um, *of auxiliary troops*

auxili-um, -i (n.), *help, assistance*

auxili-a, -ōrum (n. pl.), *auxiliary forces*

barbar-us, -a, -um, *barbarian*

bellāt-or, -ōris (m.), *soldier, warrior*

bell-or, -āri, *fight*

bellic-us, -a, -um, *of war, military*

bell-um, -i (n.), *war*

bene (adv.), *well*; bene facere, *benefit*

benefici-um, -i (n.), *benefaction, kindness*

benignē (adv.), *with kindness*

bienni-um, -i (n.), *period of two years*

bīn-i, -ae, -a, *two each*

bon-us, -a, -um, *good, capable*; bon-um, -i (n.), *benefit, advantage, blessing*

breu-is, -e, *short*; breu-ia, -ium (n. pl.), *shallows*

Brundisin-us, -a, -um, *Brundisian*

cadāu-er, -eris (n.), *corpse*

cado, occidi, cāsum, 3, *fall, die*

caed-es, -is (f.), *murder*

caedo, cecīdi, caesum, 3, *cut, kill*

caelest-is, -e, *heavenly*

cael-um, -i (n.), *sky, heaven, climate*

caen-um, -i (n.), *mud*

caerimōni-a, -ae (f.), *religious ceremony or rite*

caesp-es, -itis (m.), *turf*

callid-us, -a, -um, *subtle*

camp-us, -i (m.), *field, courtyard or camp*

candidāt-us, -i (m.), *candidate*

cāniti-es, [-ēi] (f.), *grey hair*

cant-us, -ūs (m.), *singing*

cap-ax, -ācis, *capable of*

capess-o, -ii, -itum, 3, *administer*

capio, cēpi, captum, 3, *capture, take*

capitāl-is, -e, *capital*

captīu-us, -i (m.), *captive*

cap-ut, -itis (n.), *head, capital*

carc-er, -eris (m.), *prison*

cārit-as, -ātis (f.), *affection*

carm-en, -inis (n.), *poem*

cār-us, -a, -um, *dear*

cass-us, -a, -um, *empty*; in cassum (adv.), *in vain*

castell-um, -i (n.), *fort*

castit-as, -ātis (f.), *chastity*

castr-a, -ōrum (n. pl.), *camp*

cās-us, -ūs (m.), *opportunity, mishap, chance*; cāsū, *by chance*

catēn-a, -ae (f.), *chain, bond*

cateru-a, -ae (f.), *squadron*

cauillor, 1 (dep.), *criticize*

caus-a, -ae (f.), *reason, cause, case*; causā + gen., *for the sake of*

causor, 1 (dep.), *give as a reason*

-ce (demonstr. particle), *this, here*

cedo (old imperat.), *give!*

cēdo, cessi, cessum, 3, *pass to, turn out, yield, withdraw*

celeb-er, -ris, -re, *much frequented, celebrated, infamous*

celebrāti-o, -ōnis (f.), *festival*

celebro, 1, *praise*

cens-eo, -ui, -um, 2, *propose, move, think*

cens-us, -ūs (m.), *census*

centēsim-a, -ae (f.), *tax of 1 per cent*

centuri-a, -ae (f.), *company of soldiers, century*

centuri-o, -ōnis (m.), *centurion*

centuriōnāt-us, -ūs (m.), *centurionate, office of centurion*

cerno, crēui, crētum, 3, *see*

certām-en, -inis (n.), *contest, struggle, strife*

certē (adv.), *at least*

certo, 1, *struggle, contend, fight*

cert-us, -a, -um, *fixed, certain*

ceru-ix, -īcis (f.), *neck*

cēter-us, -a, -um, *the rest of*; cēterum (adv.), *meanwhile, however, but in reality*

cib-us, -i (m.), *food*

cicātr-ix, -īcis (f.), *scar*

cieo, cīui, citum, 2, *call to, excite*

cingo, cinxi, cinctum, 3, *surround, accompany*

circā (prep. w. acc.), *round*

circum (adv.), *round about*

circum-do, -dedi, -datum, 1, *place around, surround*

circum-eo,-ii,-itum,-īre, *surround, go round*

circum-fero, -tuli, -lātum, -ferre, *carry round*

circum-fundo, -fūdi, -fūsum, 3, *pour round*

circum-gredior, -gressus sum, 3 (dep.), *walk round*

circumiect-us, -a,-um, *surrounding (of districts)*

circum-sedeo (-sideo), -sēdi, -sessum, 2, *besiege, invest*

circum-sisto, -steti, 3, *stand around*

circum-sto, -steti, 1, *stand around*

circum-uenio, -uēni, -uentum, 4, *encompass, overthrow, surround*

circ-us, -i (m.), *stadium*

cis (prep. w. acc.), *on this side of*

cito, *quickly, soon*

cito, 1, *summon*

cit-us, -a, -um, *quick*

ciuīl-is, -e, *belonging to a citizen, civil, unassuming, democratic*

cīu-is, -is (m.), *citizen*

cīuit-as, -ātis (f.), *state, citizenship*

clād-es, -is (f.), *disaster*

clāmito, 1, *cry out*

clam-or, -ōris (m.), *shout, shouting*

clāritūd-o, -inis (f.), *brightness, renown*

clār-us, -a, -um, *brilliant, clear, famous*

class-is, -is (f.), *fleet*

claudo, clausi, clausum, 3, *close, imprison*

clēmen-s, -tis, *merciful, indulgent*

clēmenti-a, -ae (f.), *mercy*

clien-s, -tis (m.), *dependant, retainer*

cōdicill-i, -ōrum (m. pl.), *note, official note*

coep-i, -isse (def. vb.), *begin*

coepto, 1, *begin, undertake*

coerceo, 2, *confine, restrain*

coet-us, -ūs (m.), *crowd*

cōgito, 1, *imagine, think*

cogniti-o, -ōnis (f.), *inquiry, trial*

cognōment-um, -i (n.), *name*

cog-nosco, -nōui, -nitum, 3, *get to know*

cohibeo, 2, *repress, check*

cohor-s, -tis (f.), *cohort, retinue*

collēg-a, -ae (m.), *colleague*

collēgi-um, -i (n.), *college (priestly)*

col-ligo, -lēgi, -lectum, 3 (tr.), *collect*

colo, colui, cultum, 3, *cultivate, worship, inhabit*

colōni-a, -ae (f.), *colony*

com-es, -itis (c.), *companion*

cōmit-as, -ātis (f.), *kindness, affability*

comitāt-us, -ūs (m.), *retinue*

cōmiter, *cheerfully*

comiti- a -ōrum (n. pl.), *assemblies for elections, elections*

comitor, 1 (dep.), *accompany*

commaculo, 1, *stain*

commendo, 1, *recommend*

commeo, 1, *visit often*

commīliti-um, -i (n.), *military companionship*

commīlit-o, -ōnis (m.), *fellow-soldier*

commod-um, -i (n.), *profit, benefit*

com-moueo, -mōui, -mōtum, 2, *move, excite*

commūnio, 4, *fortify*

commūn-is, -e, *common, general*

comparāti-o (conparāti-o), -ōnis (f.), *comparison*

compendi-um, -i (n.), *short way*

com-perio (con-perio), -peri, -pertum, 4, *discover, detect*

com-pesco, -pescui, 3, *repress, check*

com-plector, -plexus sum, 3 (dep.), *embrace*

com-pleo, -plēui, -plētum, 2, *fill*

com-pōno, -posui, -positum, 3, put together, compose

com-primo (con-primo), -pressi -pressum, 3 check, repress, fold (the hands)

concaed-es, -ium (f. pl.), barricade

con-cēdo, -cessi, -cessum, 3, depart from, concede, allow, assent to

concent-us, -ūs (m.), harmony

con-cieo, -ciui, -citum, 2, assemble, collect, excite

conciliāt-or, -ōris (m.), agent

concilio, 1, win over

con-cino, -cinui, 3, sound together

con-cipio, -cēpi, -ceptum, 3, conceive

conclāmo, 1, exclaim together

concor-s, -dis, agreeing, of the same mind

concubi-us, -a, -um, of the time of sleep; nocte concubiā, early in the night

concurs-us, -ūs (m.), concerted rush

condici-o, -ōnis (f.), condition, term

con-do, -didi, -ditum, 3, hide, bury

con-dūco, -duxi, -ductum, 3, be profitable

cō-necto, -nexui, -nexum, 3, connect

confessi-o, -ōnis (f.), confession, admission

con-ficio, -fēci, -fectum, 3, finish, kill

con-fīdo, -fisus sum, 3 (semi-dep.), trust in, rely on

con-fingo, -finxi, -fictum, 3, fabricate

conflicto, 1, strike, torment

con-gero, -gessi, -gestum, 3, accumulate, heap upon

conglobo, 1 (tr.), gather together

con-gredior, -gressus sum, 3 (dep.), contend with, fight

congrego, 1 (tr.), collect together

congruen-s, -tis, agreeing

coniecto, 1, guess

coniunct-us, -a, -um, kindred

con-iunx, -iugis (c.), spouse, wife

conloqui-um, -i (n.), conversation

con-quīro, -quīsīui, -quīsītum, 3, search for, collect

consanguine-us, -a, -um, related

conscienti-a, -ae (f.), conscience, guilty conscience

consci-us, -a, -um, privy to; as noun, accomplice, confidant

consens-us, -ūs (m.), unanimity

con-sentio, -sensi, -sensum, 4, agree

con-sīdo, -sēdi, -sessum, 3 (intr.), settle

consili-um, -i (n.), plan, intention, judgment

consor-s, -tis (c.), sharer, partner

conspicu-us, -a, -um, conspicuous, striking

constanti-a, -ae (f.), firmness, self-possession

consternāti-o, -ōnis (f.), alarm

con-stituo, -stitui, -stitūtum, 3 establish, decide

con-sto, -stiti, -stātum, 1, agree; ratio constat, the account balances; constat, it is well known

cons-ul, -ulis (m.), consul

consulār-is, -e, of a consul, consular

consulāt-us, -ūs (m.), consulship

con-sulo, -sului, -sultum, 3, consult, deliberate; w. dat., take care of

consulto, 1, deliberate, take counsel

consult-um, -i (n.), decree, plan

contact-us, -ūs (m.), contact, infection

contāmino, 1, defile

con-temno, -tempsi, -temptum, 3, despise

con-tendo, -tendi, -tentum, 3, *go*

contermin-us, -a, -um, *neighbour-ing*

con-tineo, -tinui, -tentum, 2, *contain*; perf. part. content-us, -a, -um, *content, satisfied*

con-tingo, -tigi, -tactum, 3, *touch*

continuo, 1, *connect uninterruptedly, continue*

continu-us, -a, -um, *continuous*

conti-o, -ōnis (f.), *assembly, meeting*

contiōnābund-us, -a, -um, *speaking in a public assembly*

contiōnor, 1 (dep.), *harangue*

contrā (adv.), *on the other side, in opposition, on the contrary*; (prep. w. acc.), *against*

con-traho, -traxi, -tractum, 3, *scrape together, bring together, unite*

contuberni-um, -i (n.), *common tent, tent-companionship*

contueor, 2 (dep.), *gaze upon*

contumāci-a, -ae (f.), *obstinacy, arrogance*

contumēli-a, -ae (f.), *insult*

con-uello, -uelli, -uulsum, 3, *pick up, shake, break*

con-uenio, -uēni, -uentum, 4, *meet*

con-uerto, -uerti, -uersum, 3, *change, transform, turn round*

conuīui-um, -i (n.), *feast, banquet*

cōpi-a, -ae (f.), *opportunity, access, plenty*; in pl., *forces*

cōram (prep. w. abl.), *in the presence of*

corn-u, -ūs (n.), *horn, corner*

corp-us, -oris (n.), *body*

cor-ripio, -ripui, -reptum, 3, *sweep away*

cor-rumpo, -rūpi, -ruptum, 3, *corrupt, seduce*

crāt-is, -is (f.), *hurdle*

crēdibil-is, -e, *credible*

crē-do, -didi, -ditum, 3, *believe*

cremo, 1, *burn, cremate*

creo, 1, *choose, elect*

crīm-en, -inis (n.), *charge, crime, guilt*

cruciāt-us, -ūs (m.), *torture*

crūdēlit-as, -ātis (f.), *cruelty*

crūd-us, -a, -um, *raw*

cruent-us, -a, -um, *bloody*

cru-or, -ōris (m.), *blood*

cubicul-um, -i (n.), *bedroom*

cubīl-e, -is (n.), *bed*

culp-a, -ae (f.), *blame*

cult-or, -ōris (m.), *priest*

cult-us, -ūs (m.), *style of dress*

cum (prep. w. abl.), *with*

cum (conj.), *when, since*

cumulo, 1, *heap up*

cunctābund-us, -a, -um, *dilatory*

cunctanter, *slowly, reluctantly*

cunctāti-o, -ōnis (f.), *delay, hesitation*

cunctor, 1 (dep.), *delay, hesitate*

cunct-us, -a, -um, *all*

cune-us, -i (m.), *wedge, army column*

cupīd-o, -inis (f.), *wish, desire*

cup-io, -īui, -ītum, 3, *wish, desire*

cūr, *why?*

cūr-a, -ae (f.), *concern, care*; in pl., *cares of state*

cūri-a, -ae (f.), *Senate House*

cūro, 1, *have charge of*; perf. part. cūrāt-us, -a, -um, *urgent*

curr-us, -ūs (m.), *chariot*

curs-us, -ūs (m.), *course*

curūl-is, -e, *entitled to a sella curulis, curule*; as noun, curūl-is, -is (f.), *curule chair*

curuo, 1 (tr.), *bend*

custōdi-a, -ae (f.), *guard*

cust-os, -ōdis (m.), *guard*

damno, 1, *condemn*

damn-um, -i (n.), *loss*

dē (prep. w. abl.), *about, concerning, from*

de-a, -ae (f.), *goddess*

dēbeo, 2, *be bound (I ought)*

dē-cēdo, -cessi, -cessum, 3, *leave, depart*

decemuirāl-is, -e, *belonging to the decemuiri, decemviral*

dē-cerno, -crēui, -crētum, 3, *decree*

deciēs, *ten times*

dē-cipio, -cēpi, -ceptum, 3, *deceive*

decōr-us, -a, -um, *suitable, fine*

dēcrēt-um, -i (n.), *decree*

decumān-us, -a, -um, *of the tenth part* or *cohort*; porta decumāna, *the main gate of a camp*

decum-us, -a, -um, *tenth*

dec-us, -oris (n.), *glory*

dēdec-us, -oris (n.), *disgrace*

dēditi-o, -ōnis (f.), *surrender*

dē-do, -didi, -ditum, 3 (tr.), *surrender*

dēfecti-o, -ōnis (f.), *failure*

dēfect-or, -ōris (m.), *rebel*

dē-fendo, -fendi, -fensum, 3, *defend*

dē-fero, -tuli, -lātum, -ferre, *confer, bring down*

dē-figo, -fixi, -fixum, 3, *stupefy, transfix*

dē-fleo, -flēui, -flētum, 2, *weep over*

dēform-is, -e, *disgusting, unsightly*

dē-fungor, -functus sum, 3 (dep.), *finish with, die*

dēgen-er, -eris, *degenerate*

dēgenero, 1, *degenerate*

dehinc, *next, then*

dē-icio, -iēci, -iectum, 3, *cast down*

dein, deinde, *then*

deinceps (adv.), *thereafter*

dē-lābor, -lapsus sum, 3 (dep.), *fall down*

dē-ligo, -lēgi, -lectum, 3, *choose*

dēminūti-o, -ōnis (f.), *decrease*

dē-mitto, -mīsi, -missum, 3, *send down*

dē-moueo, -mōui, -mōtum, 2, *remove*

dēmum (adv.), *at last*

dēnāri-us, -i (m.), *denarius (silver coin)*

dēn-i, ae, a, *ten each*

dēnique, *finally, in short*

den-s, -tis (m.), *tooth*

dens-us, -a, -um, *thick*

dē-pello, -puli, -pulsum, 3, *divert, drive away*

dē-posco, -poposci, 3, *demand*

dēprecor, 1 (dep.), *apologize, ask to have removed*

dē-ripio, -ripui, -reptum, 3, *pull down*

dē-scisco, -scīui, -scītum, 3, *revolt*

dē-scribo, -scripsi, -scriptum, 3, *describe*

dē-sero, -serui, -sertum, 3, *desert*

dēsert-or, -ōris (m.), *deserter*

dēsīderi-um, -i (n.), *wish*

dēsigno, 1, *nominate, elect*

dē-silio, -silui, -sultum, 4, *jump down*

dē-sino, -sii, -situm, 3, *cease*

dēsōlo, 1, *abandon*

dēstino, 1, *design, destine*

dē-stringo, -strinxi, -strictum, 3, *unsheathe, draw*

dē-sum, -fui, -esse, *be wanting, be lacking*

dēteri-or, -us, *worse*; in dēterius, *unfavourably*

dē-tero, -trīui, -trītum, 3 (tr.), *wear out*

dēterreo, 2, *deter, discourage*

dēterrim-us, -a, -um, *worst*

dē-torqueo, -torsi, -tortum, 2,
   twist
dē-traho, -traxi, -tractum, 3, *take*
   away
dētrecto, 1, *refuse*
dē-uinco, -uīci, -uictum, 3, *subdue*
de-us, -i (m.), *god*
dext-er, -ra, -rum, *right*; dexter-a,
   -ae (f.), *right hand*
dico, 1, *proclaim, dedicate*
dī-co, -xi, -ctum, 3, *say, relate*
dictāt-or, -ōris (m.), *dictator*
dictātūr-a, -ae (f.), *dictatorship*
dictito, 1, *say repeatedly, say*
dict-um, -i (n.), *word*
dī-dūco, -duxi, -ductum, 3 (tr.),
   separate
di-es, -ēi (m. & f.), *day*
diffāmo, 1, *defame*
differo, distuli, dilātum, differre,
   separate, spread abroad, defame,
   defer, differ
difficult-as, -ātis (f.), *difficulty*
digit-us, -i (m.), *finger*
dignit-as, -ātis (f.), *grandeur, dignity*
dign-us, -a, -um, *worthy*
dī-gredior, -gressus sum, 3 (dep.),
   depart
dī-lābor, -lapsus sum, 3 (dep.),
   (intr.), *scatter, disperse*
dīlargior, 4 (dep.), *bestow*
dīlect-us, -ūs (m.), *levy*
dī-mētior, -mensus sum, 4 (dep.),
   measure out
dī-mitto, -mīsi, -missum, 3, *dis-*
   charge, send away
dīrepti-o, -ōnis (f.), *plundering*
dī-ripio, -ripui, -reptum, 3, *plun-*
   der, snatch away
dīr-us, -a, -um, *awful*
dis-cēdo, -cessi, -cessum, 3, *sepa-*
   rate, depart
dis-cerno, -crēui, -crētum, 3 (tr.),
   separate

discessi-o, -ōnis (f.), *departure*
disciplīn-a, -ae (f.), *discipline*
disco, didici, 3, *learn*
discordi-a, -ae (f.), *dissension, dis-*
   cord, strife
discord-o, -āre, *quarrel*
discor-s, -dis, *discordant, disagreeing*
discrep-o, -ui, 1, *differ*
dis-curro, -curri, -cursum, 3, *rush*
   in different directions
dīs-icio, -iēci, -iectum, 3 (tr.),
   scatter
di-spergo, -spersi, -spersum, 3 (tr.),
   scatter
dispertio, 4, *divide*
dissensi-o, -ōnis (f.), *discord*
dis-sentio, -sensi, -sensum, 4,
   disagree
dis-sero, -serui, -sertum, 3, *discuss,*
   discourse on
dis-sideo, -sēdi, -sessum, 2, *disagree,*
   be disaffected
dissocio, 1 (tr.), *separate*
disson-us, -a, -um, *confused*
dis-traho, -traxi, -tractum, 3, *tear*
   apart, distract
diu, *for a long time*
dīuers-us, -a, -um, *different, distant*
dīu-es, -itis, *rich*
dī-uido, -uīsi, -uīsum, 3 (tr.),
   divide
dīuīn-us, -a, -um, *divine*
dīuīsi-o, -ōnis (f.), *distribution*
diurn-us, -a, -um, *daily*
dīu-us, -a, -um, *deified, divine*
do, dedi, datum, 1, *give*
doc-eo, -ui, -tum, 2, *teach*
document-um, -i (n.), *proof*
dol-or, -ōris (m.), *grief*
dol-us, -i (m.), *trick, treachery*
domestic-us, -a, -um, *domestic*
domināti-o, -ōnis, (f.), *absolute*
   power, despotism
dominor, 1 (dep.), *be master*

domin-us, -i (m.), *master*

dom-us, -ūs (f.), *house, home, household, family*; domi, *at home*

dōnec, *until, as long as*

dōno, 1, *present, grant*

dōn-um, -i (n.), *gift, award*

dubitāti-o, -ōnis (f.), *hesitancy*

dubito, 1, *hesitate*

dubi-us, -a, -um, *doubtful*

dūco, duxi, ductum, 3, *lead, draw*

duct-us, -ūs (m.), *bringing, conducting*; ductus aquārum, *aqueduct*

dulcēd-o, -inis (f.), *pleasantness, charm*

dum, *while, as long as, provided that*

du-o, -ae, -o, *two*

duodecim, *twelve*

dupl-ex, -icis, *double*

duplico, 1, *double*

dūriti-a, -ae (f.), *harshness*

dūro, 1, *be hard, be callous, continue*

dūr-us, -a, -um, *hard, harsh*

dux, ducis (m.), *leader, general*

ē, ex (prep. w. abl.), *out of, from, in consequence of*

ē-dīco, -dixi, -dictum, 3, *declare*

ēdict-um, -i (n.), *edict*

ē-do, -didi, -ditum, 3, *bring forth, produce*; perf. part. ēdit-us, -a, -um, *high*

ēduco, 1, *rear, educate*

ē-dūco, -duxi, -ductum, 3, *bring up, rear*

effero, extuli, ēlātum, efferre, *raise, exalt*

ef-feruesco, -ferui, 3, *rage*

ef-ficio, -fēci, -fectum, 3, *complete, finish*

effigi-es, -ēi (f.), *image*

ef-fringo, -frēgi, -fractum, 3, *break open*

ef-fundo, -fūdi, -fūsum, 3, *pour out*; in pass., *indulge in, rush out*

egen-s, -tis, *poor, needy*

egēn-us, -a, -um, *destitute*

ē-gero, -gessi, -gestum, 3, *bring out, dig*

egest-as, -ātis (f.), *need, shortage*

ego, mei, *I*

ē-gredior, -gressus sum, 3 (dep.), *go out*

ēgregi-us, -a, -um, *excellent*; ēgregie (adv.), *outstandingly, excellently*

ē-icio, -iēci, -iectum, 3, *throw out*

ē-lābor, -lapsus sum, 3 (dep.), *escape*

ē-ligo, -lēgi, -lectum, 3, *choose*

ē-luo, -lui, -lūtum, 3, *cleanse*

ē-mergo, -mersi, -mersum, 3, *arise, come forth*

ēmerit-us, -a, -um, *veteran*

ēminen-s, -tis, *distinguished*

ēn (interj.), *see! see there!*

enim, *for*

enimuēro, *certainly*

ē-nītor, -nīsus (-nixus) sum, 3 (dep.), *struggle out*

eo, īui, itum, īre, *go*

eo (adv.), *to that point, for that reason*

eōdem, *to the same place*

epistul-a, -ae (f.), *letter*

epul-ae, -ārum (f. pl.), *banquet*

equ-es, -itis (m.), *horseman, knight*

equ-us, -i (m.), *horse*

ergā (prep. w. acc.), *towards*

ergo, *therefore*

ē-ripio, -ripui, -reptum, 3, *snatch away, rescue*

ērogo, 1, *spend*

err-or, -ōris (m.), *mistake*

ē-rumpo, -rūpi, -ruptum, 3, *break out, burst forth*

ērupti-o, -ōnis (f.), *sally*

et, *and, also, even*

etenim, *for*

etiam, *even, also*

etsi, *although*

ē-uādo, -uāsi, -uāsum, 3, *emerge, come out*

ē-ueho, -uexi, -uectum, 3, *convey out*; in pass., *advance*

ē-uenio, -uēni, -uentum, 4, *happen, fall to one's lot*

ē-uinco, -uīci, -uictum, 3, *overcome*

ēuīto, 1, *avoid*

exanim-is, -e, *dead*

exanim-us, -a, -um, *dead*

ex-ardesco, -arsi, -arsum, 3, *be inflamed*

exauctōro, 1, *discharge early or conditionally*

ex-cēdo, -cessi, -cessum, 3, *depart, die, exceed*

excess-us, -ūs (m.), *death*

excidi-um, -i (n.), *destruction*

ex-cīdo, -cīdi, -cīsum, 3, *cut out*

excio, 4, *bring out*

ex-cipio, -cēpi, -ceptum, 3, *accept, receive*

excubi-ae, -ārum (f. pl.), *guard*

excurs-us, -ūs (m.), *sally, invasion*

excūso, 1, *excuse*; perf. part. ex-cūsāt-us, -a, -um, *excusable*

ex-cutio, -cussi, -cussum, 3, *shake off*

exempl-um, -i (n.), *example*

exerceo, 2, *exercise*; perf. part. exercit-us, -a, -um, *severe*

exercit-us, -ūs (m.), *army*

ex-igo, -ēgi, -actum, 3, *drive out*

exili-um, -i (n.), *exile*

exim (adv.), *then*

ex-ino, -ēmi, -emptum, 3, *take away, rescue*

existimo, 1, *think, consider*

exiti-um, -i (n.), *ruin, death*

exit-us, -ūs (m.), *death, outcome*

exosculor, 1 (dep.), *kiss fondly*

expedīt-us, -a, -um, *light-armed*

experienti-a, -ae (f.), *experience*

ex-perior, -pertus sum, 4 (dep.), *experience*

exper-s, -tis, *having no share in*

ex-pleo, -plēui, -plētum, 2, *fulfil*

explōrāt-or, -ōris (m.), *scout, spy*

ex-posco, -poposci, 3, *request, demand*

expostulāti-o, -ōnis (f.), *remonstrance*

expostulo, 1, *demand*

ex-primo, -pressi, -pressum, 3, *extort*

exprobro, 1, *criticize, point indignantly to*

expugnāti-o, -ōnis (f.), *storming*

expugno, 1, *take by storm*

ex-sequor, -secūtus sum, 3 (dep.), *perform, accomplish*

ex-soluo, -solui, -solūtum, 3, *pay, release*

exspecto, 1, *expect, await*

ex-struo (-truo), -struxi, -structum, 3, *heap up, construct*

extern-us, -a, -um, *foreign*

exterreo, 2, *strike with terror*

ex-tinguo, -stinxi, -stinctum, 3, *extinguish, kill*

ext-o, -are, *stand out*

extoll-o, -ere, *elevate, exalt, praise*

ex-torqueo, -torsi, -tortum, 2, *extort*

extorr-is, -e, *exiled*

extrā (prep. w. acc.), *outside*

ex-traho, -traxi, -tractum, 3, *drag out*

extrēm-us, -a, -um, *last, extreme*

ex-trūdo, -trūsi, -trūsum, 3, *drive out*

ex-ul, -ulis (c.), *an exile*

exundāti-o, -ōnis (f.), *overflowing*

ex-uo, -ui, -ūtum, 3, *strip off, shed*

facess-o, -i, -ītum, 3, *create, cause*

facēti-ae, -ārum (f. pl.), *wit*

faci-es, -ēi (f.), *appearance*

facil-is, -e, *easy*; facile, *easily*

facin-us, -oris (n.), *deed, crime*

facio, fēci, factum, 3, *do, make*

facti-o, -ōnis (f.), *party, faction*

fact-um, -i (n.), *deed*

fācund-us, -a, -um, *eloquent*; fācunde, *eloquently*

fall-ax, -ācis, *treacherous*

fallo, fefelli, falsum, 3, *deceive*; perf. part. fals-us, -a, -um, *false, deceitful*

fām-a, -ae (f.), *report, public opinion, reputation*

famili-a, -ae (f.), *household*

fāmōs-us, -a, -um, *slanderous*

fās (n., indecl.), *right*

fasc-es, -ium (m. pl.), *lictor's rods*

fast-i, -ōrum (m. pl.), *calendar*

fastīgi-um, -i (n.), *high rank*

fātāl-is, -e, *dangerous, deadly*

fateor, fassus sum, 2 (dep.), *acknowledge*

fatīgo, 1, *weary, tire*

fāt-um, -i (n.), *fate*

fau-or, -ōris (m.), *favour, popularity*

faust-us, -a, -um, *lucky*

faut-or, -ōris (m.), *supporter*

fēcundit-as, -ātis (f.), *fertility*

fēcund-us, -a, -um, *fertile*

fēmin-a, -ae (f.), *woman*

fērāl-is, -e, *connected with the dead*

fer-io, -īre (tr.), *strike*

fermē, *almost*

fero, tuli, lātum, ferre, *bear, support, set up, bring, pass (a law), carry*

ferōci-a, -ae (f.), *savagery*

fer-ox, -ōcis, *spirited, savage*

ferr-um, -i (n.), *weapon, arms, sword*

fess-us, -a, -um, *wearied, tired*

festīno, 1, *hasten*

fest-us, -a, -um, *festal, of a festival*

fict-um, -i (n.), *fiction*

fict-us, -a, -um, *false, feigned*

fid-es, -ēi (f.), *honesty, loyalty, trust, protection, confidence*

fīdo, fīsus sum, 3 (semi-dep.), *trust*

fīdūci-a, -ae (f.), *confidence*

fīd-us, -a, -um, *trustworthy, reliable*

fī-go, -xi, -xum, 3, *fix*; perf. part. fix-us, -a, -um, *immovable*

fīli-a, -ae (f.), *daughter*

fīli-us, -i (m.), *son*

fīnio, 4, *finish*

fīn-is, -is (m.), *end, limit*; in pl., *territory*

fio, factus sum, fieri, *be done, happen*

firmo, 1, *fortify, strengthen, affirm*

fisc-us, -i (m.), *money-bag*

flāgitiōs-us, -a, -um, *criminal, disgraceful*

flāgiti-um, -i (n.), *scandal, crime*

flāgito, 1, *demand*

flagran-s, -tis, *passionate*; flagranter, *ardently, eagerly*

flām-en, -inis (m.), *priest, flamen*

flamm-a, -ae (f.), *flame*

flēbil-is, -e, *tearful*

fle-cto, -xi, -xum, 3, *bend, turn*

flēt-us, -ūs (m.), *weeping*

flor-eo, -ui, 2, *flourish, be in prime, be successful*

fluct-us, -ūs (m.), *wave*

flūm-en, -inis (n.), *river*

flu-o, -xi, -xum, 3, *flow*

fluui-us, -i (m.), *river*

foed-us, -eris (n.), *treaty*

foed-us, -a, -um, *base, vile*

fōment-um, -i (n.), *poultice, lenitive, dressing*

for-es, -um (f. pl.), *double doors*

form-a, -ae (f.), *manner, kind*

formīd-o, -inis (f.), *fear*
formīdolōs-us, -a, -um, *fearful*
for-s, -tis (f.), *chance, fortune*
fortē, *accidentally, by chance*
fort-is, -e, *brave, strong*
fortūn-a, -ae (f.), *fortune*
for-um, -i (n.), *Forum*
foss-a, -ae (f.), *trench*
fragm-en, -inis (n.), *fragment*
frango, frēgi, fractum, 3 (tr.), *break*
frāt-er, -ris (m.), *brother*
fret-um, -i (n.), *strait, channel, sea*
fron-s, -tis (f.), *front*
fruor, fructus sum, 3 (dep.), *enjoy, benefit*
frustrā, *in vain*
frustror, 1 (dep.), *frustrate, disappoint*
fug-a, -ae (f.), *flight*
fugio, fūgi, fugitum, 3, *flee*
fulgeo, fulsi, 2, *glitter*
fulg-or, -ōris (m.), *splendour*
fundo, fūdi, fūsum, 3, *rout*
fūnest-us, -a, -um, *dismal*
fungor, functus sum, 3 (dep.), *perform, carry out*
fūn-us, -eris (n.), *funeral*
fur-o, -ui, 3, *be mad, rage*
fur-or, -ōris (m.), *fury, frenzy*

Gallic-us, -a, -um, *Gallic*
gaudeo, gāuīsus sum, 2 (semi-dep.), *rejoice*
gaudi-um, -i (n.), *joy*
gemino, 1, *double*
gemit-us, -ūs (m.), *lamentation*
gen-er, -eri (m.), *son-in-law*
gen-s, -tis (f.), *tribe, nation*
gen-u, -ūs (n.), *knee*
Germānic-us, -a, -um, *German*
gero, gessi, gestum, 3, *carry, manage*; res gestae, *exploits*

gigno, genui, genitum, 3, *beget, bring forth*; in pass., *be born*
gladiāt-or, -ōris (m.), *gladiator*
gladi-us, -i (m.), *sword*
glisc-o, -ere, *grow, increase*
glob-us, -i (m.), *crowd, group*
glōri-a, -ae (f.), *glory, desire for glory*
gnār-us, -a, -um, *known, knowing*
grad-us, -ūs (m.), *step, degree*
grātes (def. noun, f.), *thanks*
grāti-a, -ae (f.), *friendship, support, favour*
grāt-us, -a, -um, *pleasing*
grauesc-o, -ere, *grow worse*
grauid-us, -a, -um, *pregnant*
grau-is, -e, *serious, disastrous, heavy, troublesome*; grauiter, *seriously*
grauo, 1, *weigh down*
gregāl-is, -e, *common, ordinary*
gregāri-us, -a, -um, *ordinary*
gurg-es, -itis (m.), *whirlpool*

habeo, 2, *have, hold, keep, consider, handle*
habit-us, -ūs (m.), *deportment, dress*
haereo, haesi, haesum, 2, *stick, cling to*
haesitāti-o, -ōnis (f.), *irresolution*
hast-a, -ae (f.), *spear*
haud, *not*
haurio, hausi, haustum, 4, *suck in*
hebesc-o, -ere, *grow dim*
hercule, (*by Hercules!*) *certainly, assuredly*
hēr-es, -ēdis (c.), *heir*
hīberno, 1, *pass the winter, winter*
hībern-us, -a, -um, *of winter*; hībern-a, -ōrum (n. pl.), *winter quarters*
hīc, haec, hōc, *this*
hīc (adv.), *here*

hiemo, 1, *pass the winter, winter*

hiem-s, -is (f.), *winter*

hinc (adv.), *from here, after this*

Hispāniens-is, -e, *Spanish*

histri-o, -ōnis (m.), *actor*

histriōnāl-is, -e, *concerning an actor*

hom-o, -inis (c.), *human being, man*

honest-us, -a, -um, *honourable*

hon-or, -ōris (m.), *honour, public office*

honōr-us, -a, -um, *honorific*

horrid-us, -a, -um, *savage*

hortāt-us, -ūs (m.), *encouragement, exhortation*

hortor, 1 (dep.), *encourage, urge*

hort-us, -i (m.), *garden*

host-is, -is (m.), *enemy*

huc (adv.), *to this place;* huc illuc, *hither and thither, in all directions*

hūmān-us, -a, -um, *human*

humil-is, -e, *low, shallow*

hum-us, -i (f.), *ground*

iaceo, 2, *lie, have fallen*

iacio, iēci, iactum, 3, *throw, mention*

iactanti-a, -ae (f.), *ostentation*

iam, *now;* iam iamque, *at any moment*

iānu-a, -ae (f.), *door*

ibi, *there*

ict-us, -ūs (m.), *blow*

idcirco (adv.), *for that reason*

īdem, eadem, idem, *the same*

ideo (adv.), *for that reason, therefore*

idōne-us, -a, -um, *suitable*

igitur, *therefore*

ignār-us, -a, -um, *ignorant*

ignāui-a, -ae (f.), *cowardice, listlessness*

ignāu-us, -a, -um, *lazy, cowardly*

ign-is, -is (m.), *fire*

ignōbil-is, -e, *obscure, of low birth*

ignōmini-a, -ae (f.), *disgrace*

ignōranti-a, -ae (f.), *ignorance*

ig-nosco, -nōui, -nōtum, 3, *pardon*

ignōt-us, -a, -um, *unknown*

ill-e, -a, -ud, *that*

illic, *there*

illuc, (adv.), *to that place, to that person*

imāg-o, -inis (f.), *idea, vision, thought, appearance*

imbēcill-us, -a, -um, *weak*

imb-er, -ris (m.), *rain*

imb-uo, -ui, -ūtum, 3, *stain*

imitor, 1 (dep.), *portray, imitate*

immens-us, -a, -um, *enormous*

immerit-us, -a, -um, *undeserved*

immin-eo, -ēre, *overhang, impend, threaten*

immodesti-a, -ae (f.), *intemperate conduct*

immōt-us, -a, -um, *unmoved, motionless*

impediment-a, -ōrum (n. pl.), *luggage*

impensē, *eagerly*

imperāt-or (inperator), iōris (m.), *commander-in-chief, general*

imperātōri-us, -a, -um, *belonging to a general*

imperito, 1, *command*

imperīt-us (inperītus), -a, -um, *inexperienced*

imperi-um, -i (n.), *right of commanding, authority, order, empire*

impero, 1, *order*

impet-us, -ūs (m.), *attack*

impi-us, -a, -um, *wicked, unrighteous*

impl-eo (inpleo), -ēui, -ētum, 2, *fill up, fulfil*

implico, 1, *entangle*

impudīciti-a, -ae (f.), *immorality*

impūne (inpūne), *with impunity, safely*

in (prep. w. acc.), *into, towards, to, against*; (prep. w. abl.), *in, on*

inān-is, -e, *empty*

inaus-us, -a, -um, *unattempted*

incautē, *incautiously*

incaut-us, -a, -um, *unguarded*

in-cēdo, -cessi, -cessum, 3, *appear, occur, be spread about, happen to, go, press forward*

incen-do, -di, -sum, 3, *inflame, burn*

incept-um, -i (n.), *attempt, undertaking*

incert-us, -a, -um, *uncertain*

in-cipio, -cēpi, -ceptum, 3, *begin*

incitāment-um, -i (n.), *inducement, incentive*

inclīnāti-o, -ōnis (f.), *tendency*

inclīno, 1, *bend, sink*

inclū-do, -si, -sum, 3, *shut in, imprison*

incolum-is, -e, *safe*

incolumit-as, -ātis (f.), *safety*

incorrupt-us, -a, -um, *unspoiled*

increp-o, -ui, -itum, 1, *rebuke*

incult-us, -a, -um, *uncultivated*

incūri-a, -ae (f.), *carelessness*

in-curro, -curri, -cursum, 3, *rush on, attack*

incurs-us, -ūs (m.), *attack*

incūso, 1, *blame*

inde, *for that reason, then, from there*

indēfess-us, -a, -um, *indefatigable*

indici-um, -i (n.), *sign*

in-dīco, -dixi, -dictum, 3, *inflict, impose, announce*

indign-us, -a, -um, *unworthy*

indiscrēt-us, -a, -um, *indistinguishable*

in-do, -didi, -ditum, 3, *give to, apply*

indomit-us, -a, -um, *ungovernable*

in-dūco, -duxi, -ductum, 3, *bring into, introduce, exhibit*

in-dulgeo, -dulsi, -dultum, 2, *concede, indulge*

ind-uo, -ui, -ūtum, 3, *clothe, dress, assume*

industri-a, -ae (f.), *diligence*

in-eo, -ii, -itum, -īre, *enter upon, begin*

inerm-is, -e, *unarmed*

inerm-us, -a, -um, *unarmed*

inēuītābil-is, -e, *unavoidable*

inexpert-us, -a, -um, *untried*

infāmi-a, -ae (f.), *disgrace*

infām-is, -e, *notorious, infamous*

infan-s, -tis (c.), *infant, child*

infanti-a, -ae (f.), *infancy*

infaust-us, -a, -um, *unlucky*

infect-us, -a, -um, *stained, polluted*

infēl-ix, -īcis, *unfortunate*

infens-us, -a, -um, *hostile, oppressive*

inferi-or, -us, *lower*

in-fero, -tuli, -lātum, -ferre, *inflict, bring in*

infest-us, -a, -um, *hostile*

in-fīgo, -fixi, -fixum, 3, *drive in*

infim-us, -a, -um, *lowest*

in-fringo, -frēgi, -fractum, 3 (tr.), *break*

infructuōs-us, -a, -um, *unprofitable*

ingenit-us, -a, -um, *inborn*

ingeni-um, -i (n.), *genius, disposition*; in pl., *men of genius*

ingen-s, -tis, *huge, great*

in-gero, -gessi, -gestum, 3, *heap upon, thrust into*

inglōri-us, -a, -um, *inglorious*

in-gredior, -gressus sum, 3 (dep.), *enter*

ingru-o, -i, 3, *rush upon, attack*

in-icio, -iēci, -iectum, 3, *put on*

inimīciti-ae, -ārum (f. pl.), *quarrel*

inimīc-us, -a, -um, *hostile*; as noun, *enemy*

inīqu-us, -a, -um, *unjust, unreasonable, unfavourable*

initi-um, -i (n.), *beginning*

iniūri-a, -ae (f.), *injury, wrong*

in-licio, -lexi, -lectum, 3, *entice*

in-lūdo, -lūsi, -lūsum, 3, *mock, violate*

inlustr-is, -e, *distinguished, famous, bright*

inluui-es, -ēi (f.), *dirt*

inmin-eo (immineo), -ēre, *threaten, be near at hand*

inmīt-is, -e, *harsh*

inmūn-is (immūnis), -e, *exempt*

inno, 1, *float on*

innocen-s, -tis, *innocent*

innocenti-a, -ae (f.), *innocence*

innoxi-us, -a, -um, *innocent*

inoffens-us, -a, -um, *without hindrance, without obstacle*

inopi-a, -ae (f.), *want*

inopīn-us, -a, -um, *unexpected*

inop-s, -is, *needy*

in-par (impar), -paris, *unequal, inferior*

inpauid-us, -a, -um, *fearless*

inpedio (impedio), 4, *hinder*; perf. part. inpedīt-us, -a, -um, *obstructed, difficult*

in-pello (impello), -puli, -pulsum, 3, *break into, incite*

inplācābil-is, -e, *implacable*

in-pōno, -posui, -positum, 3, *set over, put in, put on*

inpotenti-a, -ae (f.), *lack of restraint, violence*

inprosperē, *unfortunately*

inprōuid-us, -a, -um, *improvident*

inprōuīs-us, -a, -um, *unexpected*

inprūden-s, -tis, *inadvertent*

inpuls-us, -ūs (m.), *pressure, striking*

inpūnīt-us, -a, -um, *unpunished*

inquam, inquit (def. vb.), *say*

inqui-es, -ētis, *restless*

in-repo, -repsi, -reptum, 3, *creep in*

in-rīdeo, -rīsi, -rīsum, 2, *mock, jeer*

inrīs-us, -ūs (m.), *derision*

inrit-us, -a, -um, *vain, useless, frustrated*

in-rumpo, -rūpi, -ruptum, 3, *break into*

insectāti-o, -ōnis (f.), *insulting, censuring*

insector, 1 (dep.), *pursue*

insepult-us, -a, -um, *unburied*

in-sero, -sēui, -situm, 3, *plant in, insert*; perf. part. insit-us, -a, -um, *inborn, natural*

in-sero, -serui, -sertum, 3, *put into*

in-sideo, -sēdi, -sessum, 2, *sit on, take possession of*

insign-is, -e, *outstanding, distinguished*; as noun, insign-e, -is (n.), *decoration, badge*

insimulo, 1, *accuse*

in-sisto, -stiti, 3, *press upon, stand upon*

insomn-is, -e, *sleepless*

instabil-is, -e, *unstable*

instar (n., indecl.), *image, likeness*

instinct-us, -ūs (m.), *instigation*

instit-uo, -ui, -ūtum, 3, *establish, found*

institūt-um, -i (n.), *way of life, habit*

in-struo, -struxi, -structum, 3, *draw up*

insul-a, -ae (f.), *island*

in-sum, -fui, -esse, *be in*

insuper (adv.), *over and above*

in-surgo, -surrexi, -surrectum, 3, *rise up, grow in power*

integ-er, -ra, -rum, *unimpaired, sound*

intelle-go, -xi, -ctum, 3, *understand*

intemerāt-us, -a, -um, *undefiled*

intemptāt-us, -a, -um, *unattempted, untouched*

inten-do, -di, -tum, 3, *threaten with, stretch out*; perf. part. intent-us, -a, -um, *strict, eager, intent on*

intento, 1, *stretch out threateningly*

inter (prep. w. acc.), *between, during, among*

inter-cēdo, -cessi, -cessum, 3, *veto*

intercessi-o, -ōnis (f.), *intervention, veto*

interdum, *sometimes, from time to time*

intereā, *meanwhile*

interfect-or, -ōris (m.), *murderer*

inter-ficio, -fēci, -fectum, 3, *kill*

inter-fluo, -fluxi, 3, *flow between*

inter-iicio, -iēci, -iectum, 3, *put between, add to*

interim, *meanwhile*

inter-mitto, -mīsi, -missum, 3, *remit for a time*

interrit-us, -a, -um, *unafraid*

interrogāti-o, -ōnis (f.), *interrogation, question*

interrogo, 1, *ask*

inter-rumpo, -rūpi, -ruptum, 3, *interrupt*

inter-sum, -fui, -esse, *take part in*

interuall-um, -i (n.), *interval*

inter-uīso, -uīsi, -uīsum, 3, *inspect*

intim-us, -a, -um, *inmost, fundamental*

intoleran-s, -tis, *intolerant*

intrā (prep. w. acc.), *within*

intro, 1, *enter, pierce into*

intro-eo, -ii, -itum, -īre, *enter*

intro-spicio, -spexi, -spectum, 3, *inspect, examine*

intueor, 2 (dep.), *gaze at*

intum-esco, -ui, 3, *swell, increase*

intūt-us, -a, -um, *unsafe*

in-uādo, -uāsi, -uāsum, 3, *invade, take possession of*

inualid-us, -a, -um, *weak*

in-ueho, -uexi, -uectum, 3, *carry into*; in pass., *inveigh against*

in-uenio, -uēni, -uentum, 4, *find*

in-uideo, -uīdi, -uīsum, 2, *grudge, envy*; perf. part. inuīs-us, -a, -um, *hated*

inuidi-a, -ae (f.), *jealousy, unpopularity*

inuīt-us, -a, -um, *against one's will, unwilling*

inuoco, 1, *invoke, implore*

inuolo, 1, *seize*

inuol-uo, -ui, -ūtum, 3, *involve, roll round*

ips-e, -a, -um, -*self, he himself*

īr-a, -ae (f.), *anger, bitterness*

īrascor, īrātus sum, 3 (dep.), *be angry with*

is, ea, id, *that*

ist-e, -a, -ud, *that of yours*

ita, *so, thus*

it-er, -ineris (n.), *journey, road, march*

iubeo, iussi, iussum, 2, *order*

iūdici-um, -i (n.), *justice, judgment, trial*

iugulo, 1, *cut the throat, kill*

iug-um, -i (n.), *ridge*

iūment-um, -i (n.), *pack animal*

iungo, iunxi, iunctum 3 (tr.), *join, attach*

iūrisdicti-o, -ōnis (f.), *jurisdiction*

iūro, 1, *swear*; perf. part. iūrāt-us, -a, -um, *under oath*

iūs, iūris (n.), *right, legal right, authority*

iusiūrandum, iūrisiūrandi (n.), *oath*

iuss-um, -i (n.), *order*

iuss-us, -ūs (m.), *order, decree*

iustiti-um, -i (n.), *public mourning*

iuuen-is, -is, *young*; as noun, *young man*; comp., iunior, *younger*

iuuent-a, -ae (f.), *youth*

iuuent-us, -ūtis (f.), *youth, young people*

iuuo, iūui, iūtum, 1, *help*

iuxtā, *equally*

labe-facio, -fēci, -factum, 3, *shake, loosen*

lābor, lapsus sum, 3 (dep.), *fall, slip*

lab-or, -ōris (m.), *labour, work, suffering, exertion*

lacess-o, -īui, -ītum, 3, *attack*

lacrim-a, -ae (f.), *tear*

lac-us, -ūs (m.), *lake*

laetiti-a, -ae (f.), *delight*

laetor, 1 (dep.), *rejoice*

laet-us, -a, -um, *cheerful, pleasing*

laeu-us, -a, -um, *left*

lāmentor, 1 (dep.), *lament*

lan-guesco, -gui, 3, *decline, grow faint*

languid-us, -a, -um, *languid, sluggish*

lanio, 1, *tear in pieces*

lap-is, -idis (m.), *stone, milestone*

laps-o, -āre, *slip, fall*

largior, 4 (dep.), *bestow*

largīti-o, -ōnis (f.), *bribery, largess*

larg-us, -a, -um, *plentiful*

lascīui-a, -ae (f.), *licence, licentiousness*

lascīuio, 4, *take licence*

latebr-a, -ae (f.), *hiding place*

lāt-us, -a, -um, *wide*

lat-us, -eris (n.), *side, flank*

laudo, 1, *praise*

laus, laudis (f.), *praise*

lēgāti-o, -ōnis (f.), *office of envoy, mission, embassy*

lēgāt-um, -i (n.), *legacy*

lēgāt-us, -i (m.), *envoy, legionary commander*

legi-o, -ōnis (f.), *legion*

legiōnāri-us, -a, -um, *legionary*

lēgo, 1, *leave as a legacy, bequeath*

lego, lēgi, lectum, 3, *choose*

lēnio, 4, *mollify, assuage*

lent-us, -a, -um, *slow*

leuāment-um, -i (n.), *alleviation*

leu-is, -e, *light*

leuo, 1, *take away*

lex, lēgis (f.), *law, condition*

libell-us, -i (m.), *little book, document, pamphlet*

liben-s, -tis, *willing*; libenter (adv.), *willingly*

līber, -a, -um, *free*

lib-er, -ri (m.), *book*

līber-i, -ōrum (m. pl.), *children*

lībert-as, -ātis (f.), *freedom*

libīd-o, -inis (f.), *passion, lust*

lībro, 1, *poise*

licenti-a, -ae (f.), *licence, freedom*

lict-or, -ōris (m.), *attendant*

lign-a, -ōrum (n. pl.), *firewood*

līm-en, -inis (n.), *threshold*

līm-es, -itis (m.), *path, military road*

līmōs-us, -a, -um, *slimy, muddy*

lingu-a, -ae (f.), *tongue*

linquo, līqui, 3 (tr.), *leave*

litter-ae, -ārum (f. pl.), *letter*

līt-us, -oris (n.), *shore*

loco, 1, *place, put, establish*

loc-us, -i (m.), *place, position, rank*

Lolliān-us, -a, -um, *of Lollius*

longinquit-as, -ātis (f.), *duration*

longinqu-us, -a, -um, *distant*; ē longinquo, *from a distance*

long-us, -a, -um, *long*

loquor, locūtus sum, 3 (dep.), *speak*

lōrīc-a, -ae (f.), *breastplate*

lūbric-us, -a, -um, *slippery*; lūbric-um, -i (n.), *slippery place*

lūc-ar, -āris (n.), *pay*

luct-us, -ūs (m.), *grief*

lūc-us, -i (m.), *grove*

lūdibri-um, -i (n.), *mockery*

lūdic-er, -ra, -rum, *sportive, theatrical*; lūdicr-um, -i (n.), *show*

lūdificor, 1 (dep.), *deceive*

lūd-us, -i (m.), *game*

lūn-a, -ae (f.), *moon*

lux, lūcis (f.), *light, daylight*

lux-us, -ūs (m.), *extravagance, debauchery*

lymphāt-us, -a, -um, *mad*

māchināt-or, -ōris (m.), *contriver*

macto, 1, *sacrifice*

macul-a, -ae (f.), *stain*

maer-eo, -ēre, *be sorrowful*

maestiti-a, -ae (f.), *sorrow*

maest-us, -a, -um, *melancholy*

magis (adv.), *more*

magistrāt-us, -ūs (m.), *magistrate*

magnific-us, -a, -um, *splendid*

magnitūd-o, -inis (f.), *greatness, extent*

magn-us, -a, -um, *great*

maiest-as, -ātis (f.), *majesty, high treason*

mai-or, -us, *greater*

male, *wrongly*

mālo, mālui, malle, *prefer*

mal-um, -i (n.), *evil*

mal-us, -a, -um, *wicked*

mancipo, 1, *sell*

mandāt-um, -i (n.), *order, instruction, commission*

mando, 1, *order, entrust*

man-eo, -si, -sum, 2, *remain*

mān-es, -ium m. pl.), *souls of the dead*

manipulār-is, -is (m.), *ordinary soldier*

manipul-us, -i (m.), *company of soldiers, maniple*

man-us, -ūs (f.), *hand, power, armed band, band*

mar-e, -is (n.), *sea*

marīt-us, -i (m.), *husband*

māt-er, -ris (f.), *mother*

māteri-es, -ēi (māteri-a, -ae) (f.), *material, opportunity, timber*

matrimōni-um, -i (n.), *marriage*

mātūrē, *quickly*

mātūro, 1 (tr.), *hurry on, accelerate*

mātūr-us, -a, -um, *ripe, mature, timely*

maxim-us, -a, -um, *greatest*; maxime, *most, especially*

medeor, 2 (dep.), *relieve, heal*

medicīn-a, -ae (f.), *remedy*

meditor, 1 (dep.), *think of*

medi-us, -a, -um, *middle*; medi-um, -i (n.), *middle*

meli-or, -us, *better*

membr-um, -i (n.), *limb*

memori-a, -ae (f.), *remembrance*

memoro, 1, *recount, relate, mention*

men-s, -tis (f.), *mind*

mens-a, -ae (f.), *table*

mens-is, -is (m.), *month*

mereo(r), 2, *deserve, earn*

mer-go, -si, -sum, 3 (tr.), *submerge*

merit-um, -i (n.), *merit, desert*

mēt-o, -ātum, 1, *measure*

met-uo, -ui, -ūtum, 3, *fear*

met-us, -ūs (m.), *fear*

me-us, -a, -um, *my, mine*

mīl-es, -itis (m.), *soldier*

mīlitār-is, -e, *military*

mīliti-a, -ae (f.), *warfare, military service*

mille (indecl. adj.), *thousand*; mille passuum, *mile*; in pl. mīli-a, -ium (n. pl.), *thousands* mīm-us, -i (m.), *mimic actor*

min-ae, -ārum (f. pl.), *threats*

min-ax, -ācis, *threatening*

minist-er, -ri (m.), *helper*

ministeri-um, -i (m.), *service*

minitor, 1 (dep.), *threaten*

min-or, -us, *less, inferior*

min-uo, -ui, -ūtum, 3, *reduce, violate*

mīror, 1 (dep.), *wonder*

mīr-us, -a, -um, *wonderful*

misc-eo, -ui, mixtum, 2, *mix, stir up*

miser, -a, -um, *wretched, miserable*

miserābil-is, -e, *pitiable*

miserāti-o, -ōnis (f.), *pity*

miseri-a, -ae (f.), *misery*

misericordi-a, -ae (f.), *pity*

miseror, 1 (dep.), *deplore*

missi-o, -ōnis (f.), *discharge*

miss-us, -ūs (m.), *sending*

mītigo, 1, *pacify, appease*

mitto, mīsi, missum, 3, *send, discharge*

mōbil-is, -e, *easily moved*

moderāti-o, -ōnis (f.), *moderation*

moderāt-or, -ōris (m.), *controller*

moderor, 1 (dep.), *restrain, set bounds, govern, command*

modesti-a, -ae (f.), *moderation, diffidence, sobriety, good conduct*

modic-us, -a, -um, *moderate*; modicē, *slightly*

modo, *only*; modo . . . modo, *now . . . again*

mod-us, -i (m.), *measure, due measure, limit, manner*

mōl-es, -is (f.), *mass weight, trouble, construction*

mōlior, 4 (dep.), *struggle, remove*

moll-is, -e, *mild, soft*; molliter, *gently*

moneo, 2, *warn*

mon-s, -tis (m.), *mountain*

morior, mortuus sum, 3 (dep.), *die*

mor-s, -tis (f.), *death*

mortāl-is, -e, *mortal, of man*

mōs, mōris (m.), *fashion, custom*; in pl., *character*

mōt-us, -ūs (m.), *emotion, tumult*

moueo, mōui, mōtum, 2 (tr.), *move, disturb*

mox, *later on, presently*

mulco, 1, *beat*

muliebr-is, -e, *of a woman*

mulier, -is (f.), *woman*

muliercul-a, -ae (f.), *mere woman, helpless woman*

multiplico, 1, *multiply*

multitūd-o, -inis (f.), *crowd, multitude*

multo, 1, *punish*

mult-us, -a, -um, *much*; in pl., *many*

mūni-a, -ōrum (n. pl.), *official duties*

mūnicipi-um, -i (n.), *town*

mūnificenti-a, -ae (f.), *liberality, generosity*

mūniment-um, -i (n.), *defence, protection*

mūnio, 4, *fortify*

mūnīti-o, -ōnis (f.), *fortification*

mūnīt-or, -ōris (m.), *fortifier*

mūn-us, -eris (n.), *duty, office*

murm-ur, -uris (n.), *murmur, grumbling*

mūto, 1, *change*

mūtuor, 1 (dep.), *borrow*

mūtu-us, -a, -um, *mutual*

nam, *for*; namque, *for*; -nam (intens. particle), *-ever*

nascor, nātus sum, 3 (dep.), *be born*

nātūr-a, -ae (f.), *nature*

nāu-is, -is (f.), *ship*

nē, *that . . . not, lest*; nēue (neu),
  and that . . . not; nē . . . quidem,
  not even

-ne (interrog. particle)

necdum, *not yet, and not yet*

necessit-as, -ātis (f.), *necessity,
  force*; in pl., *necessary expenses*

necessitūd-o, -inis (f.), *need*

nego, 1, *deny, refuse*

negōti-um, -i (n.), *business*

nep-os, -ōtis (m.), *grandson*

nept-is, -is (f.), *granddaughter*

nēquāquam (adv.), *by no means*

neque, nec, *nor, and not*; neque
  . . . neque, *neither . . . nor*

nequ-eo, -ii, -itum, -īre, *be unable*

nesci-us, -a, -um, *unknown, un-
  knowing*

nex, necis (f.), *murder*

ni, *unless*

nihil (nīl) (n., indecl.), *nothing*; as
  adv., *not at all*

nihilō minus (adv.), *none the less*

nimis (adv.), *too much, excessively*

nimi-us, -a, -um, *excessive*

nisi, *unless, except*

nītor, nīsus (nixus) sum, 3 (dep.),
  strive, make an effort, depend on

no, nāui, 1, *swim*

nōbil-is, -e, *noble*

nōbilit-as, -ātis (f.), *nobility*

nocen-s, -tis, *guilty*

nocturn-us, -a, -um, *nocturnal*

nōlo, nōlui, nolle, *be unwilling, refuse*

nōm-en, -inis (n.), *name, title*

nōmino, 1, *nominate*

nōn, *not*

nōnān-us, -a, -um, *of the ninth
  legion*

nondum (adv.), *not yet*

nōs, nostri (nostrum), *we*

nosco, nōui, nōtum, 3, *get to know,
  know*

not-a, -ae (f.), *mark*

nōtesco, nōtui, 3, *become known*

nouerc-a, -ae (f.), *step-mother*

nouercāl-is, -e, *of a step-mother*

nou-us, -a, -um, *new, strange*; rēs
  nouae, *revolution*; nouissim-us,
  -a, -um, *last*

nox, noctis (f.), *night*

noxi-us, -a, -um, *guilty*

nūb-es, -is (f.), *cloud*

nūbo, nupsi, nuptum, 3, *marry (oj
  the woman)*

nūdo, 1, *strip*

nūd-us, -a, -um, *bare*

null-us, -a, -um, *no, none*

num, *if, whether*

nūm-en, -inis (n.), *divinity, deity*

numero, 1, *count*

numer-us, -i (m.), *number*

numm-us, -i (m.), *coin, sesterce*

numquam, *never*

nunc, *now*

nuntio, 1, *announce*

nunti-us, -i (m.), *news*

nūper, *recently*

nupti-ae, -ārum (f. pl.), *marriage*

nur-us, -ūs (f.), *daughter-in-law*

nusquam, *nowhere*

nūto, 1, *nod, falter*

O (excl.), *O*

ob (prep. w. ac.), *on account oj*

ob-eo, -ii, -itum, -īre, *come to*

oberro, 1, *wander about*

ob-icio, -iēci, -iectum, 3, *reproach,
  charge*

obiecto, 1, *charge*

ob-lino, -lēui, -litum, 3, *smear*

oblittero, 1, *wipe out*

oblīuiscor, oblītus sum, 3 (dep.),
  forget

ob-nītor, -nīsus (-nixus) sum, 3
  (dep.), *push against*

oboedio, 4, *obey*

ob-ruo, -rui, -rutum, 3, *strike down, overwhelm*

obscūr-us, -a, -um, *hidden, secret, dark*

obsequi-um, -i (n.), *obedience*

ob-sequor, -secūtus sum, 3 (dep.), *obey, yield to*

obs-es, -idis (m.), *hostage*

ob-sideo, -sēdi, -sessum, 2, *besiege*

ob-sisto, -stiti, 3, *stand in the way of, block the way*

ob-sto, -stiti, -stātum, 1, *oppose, resist*

ob-stringo, -strinxi, -strictum, 3, *bind (by oath)*

obstru-o, -xi, -ctum, 3, *block*

ob-tego, -texi, -tectum, 3, *conceal*

obtempero, 1, *obey, comply with*

obten-do, -di, -tum, 3, *plead as an excuse*

obtent-us, -ūs (m.), *pretext*

obtestāti-o, -ōnis (f.), *earnest entreaty*

obtestor, 1 (dep.), *call as witness*

ob-tineo, -tinui, -tentum, 2, *obtain, acquire*

obtrecto, 1, *disparage*

obturbo, 1, *throw into confusion*

obuiam (adv.), *in the way, to meet, against*

obui-us, -a, -um, *in the way, to meet*

oc-cido, -cidi, -cāsum, 3, *fall down, die*

oc-cīdo, -cīdi, -cīsum, 3, *kill*

oc-cipio, -cēpi, -ceptum, 3, *begin*

oc-culo, -cului, -cultum, 3, *conceal*; in occulto, *secretly*; occultē, *secretly*

occulto, 1, *conceal, hide*

occupo, 1, *seize*

oc-curro, -curri, -cursum, 3, *meet*

occurso, 1, *run to meet*

octāu-us, -a, -um, *eighth*

octŏ, *eight*

ocul-us, -i (m.), *eye*

ōd-i, -isse (def. vb.), *hate*

odi-um, -i (n.), *hatred*

offen-do, -di, -sum, 3, *offend, displease*

offensi-o, -ōnis (f.), *offence, dislike*

offero, obtuli, oblātum, offerre, *offer, present*

of-ficio, -fēci, -fectum, 3, *obstruct*

offici-um, -i (n.), *duty*; in officio, *loyal*

of-fundo, -fūdi, -fūsum, 3, *spread around*

ōlim, *once, formerly*

ōm-en, -inis (n.), *omen*

o-mitto, -mīsi, -missum, 3, *give up, neglect*

omn-is, -e, *all, every*

onero, 1, *burden, oppress, load*

on-us, -eris (n.), *burden*

onust-us, -a, -um, *loaded*

oper-ae, -ārum (f. pl.), *hired supporters, claque*

operor, 1 (dep.), *work*

opperior, 4 (dep.), *wait*

oppid-um, -i (n.), *town*

oppl-eo, -ēui, -ētum, 2, *fill, flood*

op-pōno, -posui, -positum, 3, *put against*

op-primo, -pressi, -pressum, 3, *press down, check, subdue*

[ops], opis (f.), *power*; summā opē, *with full strength*; in pl., *wealth, power*

optim-us, -a, -um, *best*; optumē (adv.), *best*

op-us, -eris (n.), *work*

ōrāti-o, -ōnis (f.), *speech*

ōrāt-or, -ōris (m.), *speaker*

orbo, 1, *bereave*

ordior, orsus sum, 4 (dep.), *begin*

ord-o, -inis (m.), *rank, order*

oríg-o, -inis (f.), *source, birth*

orior, ortus sum, 4 (dep.), *rise arise, begin, be descended from*

ornát-us, -ús (m.), *decoration*

óro, 1, *beg, entreat*

ós, óris (n.), *mouth, face*

os, ossis (n.), *bone*

oscul-um, -i (n.), *kiss*

osten-do, -di, -sum, 3, *show*

ostentát-or, -óris (m.), *exhibitor*

ostento, 1, *show, exhibit*

ostent-us, -ús (m.), *display*

óti-um, -i (n.), *leisure, peace*

pábul-um, -i (n.), *fodder*

pact-us, -a, -um, *betrothed*

paenitenti-a, -ae (f.), *repentance*

pág-us, -i (m.), *district*

palam, *openly*

pálor, 1 (dep.), *wander*

pal-us, -údis (f.), *swamp*

Pannonic-us, -a, -um, *Pannonian*

pantomím-us, -i (m.), *ballet-dancer*

pár, paris, *equal*; pár est, *it is proper*

paren-s, -tis (c.), *parent*

páreo, 2, *obey*

pario, peperi, partum, 3, *acquire*

pariter, *equally, together*

paro, 1, *procure, contrive, prepare*

par-s, -tis (f.), *part, share*; in pl. *party, faction*

partic-eps, -ipis (c.), *sharer*

partim, *partly*

partior, 4 (dep.), *distribute*

part-us, -ús (m.), *offspring, birth*

paruul-us, -a, -um, *very small*

parum (adv.), *too little, not at all*

passim (adv.), *without order, in every direction, indiscriminately*

pate-facio, -féci, -factum, 3, *lay open*

pat-er, -ris (m.), *father*; in pl., *senators*

patern-us, -a, -um, *belonging to a father, inherited*

patibul-um, -i (n.), *gibbet*

patien-s, -tis, *patient* (pres. part. of patior)

patior, passus sum, 3 (dep.), *allow suffer*

patri-a, -ae (f.), *native country*

patri-us, -a, -um, *ancestral, native*

patro, 1, *perform, perpetrate*

patru-us, -i (m.), *uncle*

pauc-i, -ae, -a, *few*

paueo, páui, 2, *tremble, fear*

pauesc-o, -ere, *begin to fear, fear*

pauid-us, -a, -um, *terrified*

paulátim, *gradually, little by little*

paulo, paulum (adv.), *a little*

pau-or, -óris (m.), *terror*

pauper, -is, *poor*

paupert-as, -átis (f.), *poverty*

pax, pácis (f.), *peace*

pecco, 1, *do wrong*

pect-us, -oris (n.), *breast*

pecúni-a, -ae (f.), *money*

ped-es, -itis (m.), *foot-soldier, infantryman*

pel-licio, -lexi, -lectum, 3, *entice, coax*

pello, pepuli, pulsum, 3, *drive back*

penát-es, -ium (m.), *household gods, home*

penes (prep. w. acc.), *in the power of, under the control of*

penetro, 1, *pierce, penetrate*

penitus, *deeply*

per (prep. w. acc.), *through, throughout, by means of*

per-cello, -culi, -culsum, 3, *strike*

percuss-or, -óris (m.), *murderer*

per-dúco, -duxi, -ductum, 3, *bring*

peregrín-us, -i (m.), *foreigner*

per-fero, -tuli, -látum, -ferre, *endure, carry out*

per-ficio, -fēci, -fectum, 3, *achieve, accomplish*

perfidi-a, -ae (f.), *treachery*

per-fringo, -frēgi, -fractum, 3, *break through*

per-fugio, -fūgi, 3, *fly for refuge*

per-go, -rexi, -rectum, 3, *go, advance*

perīclitor, 1 (dep.), *be in danger*

perīculōs-us, -a, -um, *dangerous*

perīcul-um, -i (n.), *danger*

per-imo, -ēmi, -emptum, 3, *destroy*

perinde, *equally*

perīti-a, -ae (f.), *experience*

periūri-um, -i (n.), *perjury*

permeo, 1, *cross*

per-misceo, -miscui, -mixtum, 2, *mix together*

per-mitto, -mīsi, -missum, 3, *allow*

permodest-us, -a, -um, *very modest*

per-moueo, -mōui, -mōtum, 2, *move, excite*

per-mulceo, -mulsi, -mulsum, 2, *appease*

pernici-es, -ēi (f.), *destruction*

pernocto, 1 (no sup.), *pass the night*

pernōt-esco, -ui, 3, *become known*

per-pello, -puli, -pulsum, 3, *drive compel*

perpetior, -pessus sum, 3 (dep.), *endure*

per-rumpo, -rūpi, -ruptum, 3, *break through*

per-scrībo, -scripsi, -scriptum, 3, *write in full*

persol-uo, -ui, -ūtum, 3, *pay*

per-stringo, -strinxi, -strictum, 3, *graze, grate upon*

pertim-esco, -ui, 3, *fear greatly*

pertin-eo, -ui, 2, *concern, relate to*

peruā-do, -si, -sum, 3, *spread abroad*

peruasto, 1, *lay waste, devastate*

per-uenio, -uēni, -uentum, 4, *reach, arrive at*

peruicāci-a, -ae (f.), *firmness*

peruic-ax, -ācis, *determined*

peruigil, is, *watchful*

pēs, pedis (m.), *foot*

pessim-us, -a, -um, *worst*

pessum (adv.), *down*; pessum dare, *ruin*; pessum īre, *be ruined*

pet-o, -īui, -ītum, 3, *seek, ask for*

piācul-um, -i (n.), *sin, propitiatory sacrifice*

piet-as, -ātis (f.), *dutiful affection*

piget, piguit (pigitum est), 2, *it displeases*

pīl-um, -i (n.), *javelin*

pio, 1, *atone for, appease*

placeo, 2, *be pleasing*; placuit, placitum est, *it was decided*

plāco, 1, *appease*

planct-us, -ūs (m.), *wailing*

plānē, *clearly, certainly*

plāniti-es, -ēi (f.), *plain*

plān-um, -i (n.), *level ground*

pleb-ēs, -ēi (f.), *common people*

plebs, plebis (f.), *common people, plebeians*

plēr-ique, -aeque, -aque, *most, the majority, many*

plērumque, *generally, very often*

plūrim-us, -a, -um, *most*; in pl., *very many*

plūs, plūris, *more*; in pl., *the majority, the mass, several, too many*

poen-a, -ae (f.), *punishment, penalty*

polliceor, 2 (dep.), *promise*

Pompēiān-us, -a, -um, *of Pompey, Pompeian*

pō-no, -sui, -situm, 3, *place, lay, set aside, put forward*

pon-s, -tis (m.), *bridge*

pontif-ex, -icis (m.), *pontiff, priest*

pontificāt-us, -ūs (m.), *office of pontiff, pontificate*

populār-is, -is (m.), *fellow-country-man*

populāti-o, -ōnis (f.), *ravaging, devastation*

populor, I (dep.), *plunder*

popul-us, -i (m.), *people*

por-rigo, -rexi, -rectum, 3, *stretch out, extend*

port-a, -ae (f.), *gate*

porten-do, -di, -tum, 3, *foretell, predict*

posco, poposci, 3, *demand*

possum, potui, posse, *be able*

post (prep. w. acc.), *after*

post, posteā (adv.), *afterwards*

poster-us, -a, -um, *next*; in post-erum, *for the future*; poster-i, -ōrum (m.), *posterity*

post-pōno, -posui, -positum, 3, *put after, neglect*

postquam (conj.), *after*

postrēmo, postrēmum (adv.), *finally*

postulāt-um, -i (n.), *demand*

postulo, I, *ask, accuse*

poten-s, -tis, *powerful*

potenti-a, -ae (f.), *might, power, political influence*

potest-as, -ātis (f.), *power, authority*

poti-or, -us, *preferable, more powerful*; potius (adv.), *rather*

potior, 4 (dep.), *gain possession of*

potissim-us, -a, -um, *most important*

praebeo, 2, *offer, provide*

praec-eps, -ipitis, *headlong*

prae-cipio, -cēpi, -ceptum, 3, *anticipate*

praecipu-us, -a, -um, *particular, special*

praeclār-us, -a, -um, *remarkable, famous*

praed-a, -ae (f.), *booty, spoil*

praedict-us, -a, -um, *aforementioned*

praedit-us, -a, -um, *endowed with*

prae-eo, -īui, -itum, -īre, *go before*

praefect-us, -i (m.), *commander*

prae-fero, -tuli, -lātum, -ferre, *carry in front*

praemātūr-us, -a, -um, *too early*

prae-mitto, -mīsi, -missum, 3, *send forward*

praemi-um, -i (n.), *prize, reward*

prae-pōno, -posui, -positum, 3, *prefer*

prae-scrībo, -scripsi, -scriptum, 3, *write beforehand, prescribe*

praescripti-o, -ōnis (f.), *title*

praesen-s, -tis, *present, immediate*; in praesens, *for the present*

prae-sideo, -sēdi, 2, *preside over, command*

praesidi-um, -i (n.), *guard, garrison, protection, fortification*

prae-sūmo, -sumpsi, -sumptum, 3, *take beforehand*

praetempto, I, *try out*

praeter (prep. w. acc.), *except*

praetext-a, -ae (f.), *toga praetexta, purple-bordered toga*

praet-or, -ōris (m.), *praetor*

praetōriān-us, -a, -um, *praetorian*

praetōri-um, -i (n.), *praetorian guard*

praetōri-us, -a, -um, *belonging to a general*; praetōria cohors, *praetorian cohort*

praetōri-us, -i (m.), *ex-praetor*

praetūr-a, -ae (f.), *praetorship*

praeualeo, 2 (no sup.), *have greater power, be more important*

prāuē, *improperly, wrongly*

prae-uenio, -uēni, -uentum, 4, *anticipate*

precāri-us, -a, -um, *precarious*

precor, 1 (dep.), *beg*

premo, pressi, pressum, 3, *repress*

pren-do, -di, -sum, 3, *catch*

prenso, 1, *catch*

preti-um, -i (n.), *price*; pretium est, *it is worth while*

prex, precis (f.), *prayer, entreaty*

prīdem (adv.), *long ago*

prīmān-i, -ōrum (m. pl.), *soldiers of the first legion*

prīmordi-um, -i (n.), *beginning*

prīmōr-es, -um (m. pl.), *chief men*

prīm-us, -a, -um, *first*; prīmo, prīmum (adv.), *at first*

princ-eps, -ipis, *first, chief*; as noun, *leader, chief man, Emperor*

principāt-us, -ūs (m.), *reign, rule*

principi-um, -i (n.), *beginning*; in pl., *headquarters*

pri-or, -us, *former*

prisc-us, -a, -um, *old, of former times*

prīuātim, *privately*

prīuāt-us, -a, -um, *private*

prīuign-us, -i (m.), *step-son*

pro (prep. w. abl.), *for, in place of*

probo, 1, *approve, prove*

probr-um, -i (n.), *insult, abuse*

proc-ax, -ācis, *pert, impudent*

prō-cēdo, -cessi, -cessum, 3, *advance*

proc-er, -eris (m.), *chief man, noble*

prōcēr-us, -a, -um, *tall*

prō-cido, -cidi, 3, *fall prostrate*

proclāmo, 1, *shout*

prōconsulār-is, -e, *proconsular*

procul, *far off*

prō-cumbo, -cubui, -cubitum, 3, *prostrate oneself, sink*

prōditi-o, -ōnis (f.), *treachery*

prōdit-or, -ōris (m.), *traitor*

prō-dūco, -duxi, -ductum, 3, *bring forward*

proeli-um, -i (n.), *battle*

profān-us, -a, -um, *secular, common*

prō-fero, -tuli, -lātum, -ferre, *extend, enlarge, bring forward*

proficiscor, profectus sum, 3 (dep.), *set out*

pro-fiteor, -fessus sum, 2 (dep.), *declare, give in one's name*

profug-us, -a, -um, *fugitive*

profund-us, -a, -um, *deep*

prō-gredior, -gressus sum, 3, (dep.), *come forward*

prohibeo, 2, *prohibit, forbid*

prō-icio, -iēci, -iectum, 3, *drive out, exile, throw out, throw down*

proindē, *therefore*

prō-lābor, -lapsus sum, 3 (dep.), *sink*

prōminen-s, -tis (n.), *prominent part, promontory*

prōmisc-us, -a, -um, *indiscriminate*

prōmo, prompsi, promptum, 3, *produce*; perf. part. prompt-us, -a, -um, *ready, prepared*

pronep-os, -ōtis (m.), *great-grandson*

prope, *near, nearly*

properē, *quickly*

propero, 1, *hurry*

proper-us, -a, -um, *quick, speedy*

propinquo, 1, *approach*

propinqu-us, -a, -um, *near*; as noun, *relative*

propi-or, -us, *nearer*

propri-us, -a, -um, *one's own*

propter (prep. w. acc.), *beside*

prōpulso, 1, *ward off, drive back*

prōrogo, 1, *extend*

prorsus, *absolutely*

prō-rumpo, -rūpi, -ruptum, 3, *rush out*

prō-ruo, -rui, -rutum, 3, *overthrow, demolish*

proscripti-o, -ōnis (f.), *proscription, confiscation*

prosper-us, -a, -um, *fortunate, successful*; prosperē, *successfully*

prō-spicio, -spexi, -spectum, 3, *provide for*

prō-sterno, -strāui, -strātum, 3, *throw down*

protē-go, -xi, -ctum, 3, *protect*

prō-tero, -trīui, -trītum, 3, *trample underfoot*

prō-ueho, -euxi, -uectum, 3, *carry forward*; perf. part. prōuect-us, -a, -um, *advanced*

prō-uenio, -uēni, -uentum, 4, *succeed*

prō-uideo, -uīdi, -uīsum, 2, *make provision for*

prōuinci-a, -ae (f.), *province*

[prōuīs-us, -ūs] (m.), *foreseeing*

prout, *in proportion as*

proxim-us, -a, -um, *next, nearest, last*

prūden-s, -tis, *experienced, intelligent*

pūblic-us, -a, -um, *belonging to the state, public*; pūblicē, *in a public capacity*

pudīciti-a, -ae (f.), *virtue*

pud-or, -ōris (m.), *modesty, shame*

pu-er, -eri (m.), *boy*

puerīl-is, -e, *childish, youthful*

pugn-a, -ae (f.), *fight, battle*

pugno, 1, *fight*

pulch-er, -ra, -rum, *fine*

pūnio, 4, *punish*

quā (adv.), *where*

quadrāgēn-i, -ae, -a, *forty each*

quadrāgēsim-us, -a, -um, *fortieth*

quadrāgintā, *forty*

quadringenties, *four hundred times*

quae-ro, -sīui, -sītum, 3, *seek*

quam, *than, how*

quaest-or, -ōris (m.), *quaestor*

quamquam, *although*

quamuīs, *however much, although*

quando, *when?, since*

quandōque, *some day, at what time soever*

quant-us, -a, -um, *how great*

quartadecumān-i, -ōrum (m. pl.), *soldiers of the fourteenth legion*

quart-us, -a, -um, *fourth*

quasi, *as if*

quattuor, *four*

quattuordecim, *fourteen*

-que, *and*

qu-eo, -īui, -itum, -īre, *be able*

queror, questus sum, 3 (dep.), *complain*

quest-us, -ūs (m.), *complaint*

qui, quae, quod (rel. pro.), *who, which*; (interr. adj.), *which? what?*; (indef. adj.), *any*

quia, *because*

quīcumque, quaecumque, quodcumque, *whoever, whatever*

quīdam, quaedam, quoddam, *a certain one, someone*

quidem, *indeed*

qui-es, -ētis (f.), *peace, quiet, rest, dream*

quiēt-us, -a, -um, *quiet, peaceful*

quīn, *indeed, why not?*

quingēn-i, -ae, -a, *five hundred each*

quinquāginta, *fifty*

quinque, *five*

quinquies, *five times*

quintadecumān-i, -ōrum (m. pl.), *soldiers of the fifteenth legion*

quintān-i, -ōrum (m. pl.), *soldiers of the fifth legion*

quint-us, -a, -um, *fifth*

quippe (adv. and conj.), *indeed, inasmuch as*

Quirīt-es, -ium (m. pl.), *Roman citizens*

quis, quid (indef. pro.), *anyone, anything*; (interr. pro.), *who? what?*

quisquam, quaequam, quicquam, *anyone, anything*

quisque, quaeque, quodque, *each*

quisquis, quidquid, *whoever, whatever*

quo, *in order that, to what point or place?*

quod, *because*

quōminus, *that . . . not, but that*

quondam, *formerly, once*

quoniam, *since*

quoque, *also*

quot (indecl. adj.), *how many?*

quoties, quotiens, *as often as*

quotus quisque, quota quaeque, quotum quodque, *how few*

rabi-es, [-ēi] (f.), *madness*

rap-io, -ui, -tum, 3, *carry off, seize*

raptim, *hurriedly*

rapto, 1, *carry off*

rapt-or, -ōris (m.), *abductor*

rār-us, -a, -um, *rare, scanty*

rati-o, -ōnis (f.), *account, reason plan*

rebell-es, -ium (m. pl.), *rebels*

rebelli-o, -ōnis (f.), *rebellion*

recen-s, -tis, *fresh, recent*

reciperāt-or, -ōris (m.), *recoverer (member of a judicial board)*

re-cipio, -cēpi, -ceptum, 3, *receive*

reciproc-us, -a, -um, *tidal, receding*

recito, 1, *read aloud*

recon-do, -didi, -ditum, 3, *hoard*

rect-or, -ōris (m.), *guide, tutor, rider*

recūso, 1, *refuse*

red-do, -didi, -ditum, 3, *restore, render*

red-eo, -īui, -itum, -īre, *return*

red-igo, -ēgi, -actum, 3, *drive back*

red-imo, -ēmi, -emptum, 3, *buy, buy off*

redintegro, 1, *renew*

redit-us, -ūs (m.), *return*

re-dūco, -duxi, -ductum, 3, *lead or bring back*

red-ux, -ucis, *returned*

re-fero, -ttuli, -lātum, -ferre, *bring back, revive, repay, report, mention*

regim-en, -inis (n.), *direction, control*

regnātr-ix, -īcis (adj. f.), *reigning, ruling*

regn-um, -i (n.), *kingdom*

rego, rexi, rectum, 3, *rule*

re-gredior, -gressus sum, 3 (dep.), *return*

regress-us, -ūs (m.), *return*

re-icio, -iēci, -iectum, 3, *refer*

re-lābor, -lapsus sum, 3 (dep.), *subside*

relāti-o, -ōnis (f.), *proposition, motion*

religi-o, -ōnis (f.), *religion, religious rite*

re-linquo, -līqui, -lictum, 3, *leave behind*

reliqui-ae, -ārum (f. pl.), *remains*

reliqu-us, -a, -um, *left, remaining*

remedi-um, -i (n.), *cure, remedy*

remeo, 1 (no sup.), *come back, return*

re-mitto, -mīsi, -missum, 3, *relax, excuse, sacrifice*

renouo, 1, *renew*

renuo, renui, 3, *refuse*

reor, ratus sum, 2 (dep.), *think*

reppello, reppuli, repulsum, 3, *reject*

repentē, *suddenly*

repentīn-us, -a, -um, *unexpected*

reperio, repperi, repertum, 4, *find*

repet-o, -īui, -ītum, 3, *seek again*; pecūniae repetundae, *money extorted, extortion*

re-pōno, -posui, -positum, 3, *restore, replace*

reporto, 1, *take back, bring back*

reposc-o, -ere, *claim*

re-primo, -pressi, -pressum, 3, *check*

repudio, 1, *refuse*

repuls-a, -ae (f.), *rejection*

requi-es, -ētis (f.), *rest*

requi-esco, -ēui, -ētum, 3, *rest, take consolation*

rēs, rei (f.), *thing, affair, history, fact*; respublica, reipublicae (f.), *state, republic*; rēs Romāna, *Roman state, power of Rome*

re-sisto, -stiti, 3, *resist*

resol-uo, -ui, -ūtum, 3, *loosen, destroy*

re-spicio, -spexi, -spectum, 3, *see behind*

re-spondeo, -spondi, -sponsum, 2, *reply*

respons-um, -i (n.), *answer*

result-o, -ātum, 1, *resound, echo*

resur-go, -rexi, -rectum, 3, *appear again*

retic-eo, -ui, 2, *keep silence*

re-tineo, -tinui, -tentum, 2, *keep, preserve, maintain, hold back*

reuerenti-a, -ae (f.), *respect*

re-uerto, -uerti, -uersum, 3, *turn back*

reuoco, 1, *recall, revive*

re-us, -i (m.), *defendant*

rex, rēgis (m.), *king*

rīp-a, -ae (f.), *bank*

rīte, *duly, properly*

rīu-us, -i (m.), *stream*

rōb-ur, -oris (n.), *hardness, strength*

rogito, 1, *ask*

rogo, 1, *ask*

rog-us, -i (m.), *funeral pyre*

rud-is, -e, *rough, ignorant, unskilled*

rūm-or, -ōris (m.), *rumour, talk*

rumpo, rūpi, ruptum, 3 (tr.), *break*

ruo, rui, rutum, 3, *rush down*

rursum, rursus, *again*

sac-er, -ra, -rum, *holy*; sacr-um, -i (n.), *holy thing, sacred rite*

sacerd-os, -ōtis (m.), *priest*

sacerdōti-um, -i (n.), *priesthood*

sacrāment-um, -i (n.), *oath*

sacro, 1, *dedicate*

saepe, *often*

saep-io, -si, -tum, 4, *surround, fence in*

saeuio, 4, *rage, be angry*

saeuiti-a, -ae (f.), *cruelty*

saeu-us, -a, -um, *cruel, severe*

sagitt-a, -ae (f.), *arrow*

saltem, *at least*

salt-us, -ūs (m.), *woodland, wood*

sal-ūs, -ūtis (f.), *safety*

salu-us, -a, -um, *preserved, safe*

san-cio, -xi, -ctum, 4, *decree, ordain*

sānē, *certainly, indeed*

sangu-is, -inis (m.), *blood*

sānit-as, -ātis (f.), *health*

sapien-s, -tis, *wise*

sapienti-a, -ae (f.), *wisdom, good sense*

sarcin-a, -ae (f.), *pack, baggage*

satiet-as, -ātis (f.), *satiety*

satio, 1, *satisfy*

satis, *enough, sufficiently*

sauci-us, -a, -um, *wounded*

sax-um, -i (n.), *stone*

scel-us, -eris (n.), *crime*

scīlicet, *of course*

scindo, scidi, scissum, 3, *cut*

scio, 4, *know*

scrībo, scripsi, scriptum, 3, *write*

script-or, -ōris (m.), *writer*

script-um, -i (n.), *composition*

scrob-is, -is (f.), *trench, grave*

scrūtor, 1 (dep.), *explore*

sē *or* sēsē, sui, *himself, themselves, &c.*; sēmet, *strengthened form of* se

sēcess-us, -ūs (m.), *retirement*

sēcrēt-us, -a, -um, *secret*; sēcrēt-um, -i (n.), *a secret*

sector, 1 (dep.), *chase, run after*

secund-us, -a, -um, *second, favourable, successful*

secūr-is, -is (f.), *axe*

sēcūrit-as, -ātis (f.), *safety*

sed, set, *but*

sēdecim, *sixteen*

sedeo, sēdi, sessum, 2, *sit*

sēd-es, -is (f.), *site*

sēditi-o, -ōnis (f.), *mutiny*

sēditiōs-us, -a, -um, *mutinous*

segniti-a, -ae (f.), *slowness, sloth*

semel, *once*

sēmerm-us, -a, -um, *half-armed, badly armed*

sēmirut-us, -a, -um, *half-demolished*

sēmisomn-us, -a, -um, *half asleep*

semper, *always*

sempitern-us, -a, -um, *eternal*

senāt-or, -ōris (m.), *senator*

senāt-us, -ūs (m.), *senate*

senect-ūs, -ūtis (f.), *old age*

senesco, senui, 3, *grow old*

sen-ex, -is, *old*; as noun, *old man*

sēn-i, -ae, -a, *six each*

senīl-is, -e, *belonging to an old man*

seni-um, -i (n.), *old age, debility*

sens-us, -ūs (m.), *feeling, sentiment*

sententi-a, -ae (f.), *opinion*; dē sententiā, *to suit one's self, according to one's wish*

sen-tio, -si, -sum, 4, *perceive, feel*

sēparo, 1 (tr.), *separate*

sep-elio, -elīui, -ultum, 4, *bury*

septem, *seven*

sepultūr-a, -ae (f.), *burial*

sequor, secūtus sum, 3 (dep.), *follow*

serm-o, -ōnis (m.), *talk*

seruio, 4, *serve*

seruiti-um, -i (n.), *slavery, slave*

seruit-ūs, -ūtis (f.), *slavery*

seruo, 1, *keep*

seru-us, -i (m.), *slave*

sesterti-um, -i (n.), 100,000 *sesterces*

seuērit-as, -ātis (f.), *strictness*

sex, *six*

sexāgēn-i, -ae, -a, *sixty each*

sexāgēsim-us, -a, -um, *sixtieth*

sext-us, -a, -um, *sixth*

sex-us, -ūs (m.), *sex*

si, *if*

Sibyllin-us, -a, -um, *Sibylline*

siccit-as, -ātis (f.), *drought*

sicc-us, -a, -um, *dry*

Sicul-us, -a, -um, *Sicilian*

sī-do, -di, 3 (intr.), *settle*

sīd-us, -eris (n.), *star, heavenly body, season*

signif-er, -eri (m.), *standard-bearer*

significāti-o, -ōnis (f.), *indication*

sign-um, -i (n.), *sign, password, standard, signal*

silenti-um, -i (n.), *silence*

sil-eo, -ui, 2, *be silent*

silu-a, -ae (f.), *forest*

simpl-ex, -icis, *simple*

simul, *at the same time*

simulācr-um, -i (n.), *image, statue*

simulāti-o, -ōnis (f.), *pretence, hypocrisy*

simulo, 1, *pretend*

sincēr-us, -a, -um, *genuine, reliable*

sine (prep. w. abl.), *without*

singul-i, -ae, -a, *one to each, individuals*

sinist-er, -ra, -rum, *left, improper*

sino, sīui, situm, 3, *allow*; perf.
part. sit-us, -a, -um, *placed*

sin-us, -us (m.), *bosom*

sīue (seu), *or if*; sīue . . . sīue,
whether . . . or, either . . . or

soc-er, -eri (m.), *father-in-law*

societ-as, -ātis (f.), *alliance*

socio, 1 (tr.), *share*

soci-us, -a, -um, *sharing, allied*; as
noun, soci-us, -i (m.), *partner,
companion, ally*

sōcordi-a, -ae (f.), *indolence*

sodāl-is, -is (m.), *companion (member of priestly college)*

soleo, solitus sum, 2 (semi-dep.),
be accustomed; perf. part. solitus, -a, -um, *customary*

solid-us, -a, -um, *solid*

sollemn-is, -e, *statutory*

soller-s, -tis, *clever*

sōlor, 1 (dep.), *comfort*

sol-um, -i (n.), *ground*

sol-uo, -ui, -ūtum, 3, *pay, loosen,
relax, release, dismiss*

sōl-us, -a, -um, *alone, only*

son-or, -ōris (m.), *din*

son-us, -i (m.), *noise*

sordid-us, -a, -um, *sordid, mean*

sor-or, -ōris (f.), *sister*

sors, sortis (f.), *lot*

spati-um, -i (n.), *interval, space*

speci-es, -ēi (f.), *appearance, form,
pretext*

speciōs-us, -a, -um, *plausible*

spectācul-um, -i (n.), *show*

specto, 1, *watch, examine, test*

speculor, 1 (dep.), *watch*

sperno, sprēui, sprētum, 3, *despise,
scorn*

spēro, 1, *hope*

spes, -ei (f.), *hope*

spīrit-us, -ūs (m.), *breath of life,
spirit*

spīro, 1, *breathe*

splendid-us, -a, -um, *bright*

spoli-a, -ōrum (n. pl.), *spoil, booty*

sponte, *of one's own free will*

stabil-is, -e, *firm*

stagno, 1, *flood*

statim, *immediately*

stati-o, -ōnis (f.), *guard*

statu-a, -ae (f.), *statue*

stat-uo, -ui, -ūtum, 3, *appoint, fix*

stat-us, -ūs (m.), *state, condition*

steril-is, -e, *barren, empty*

sterno, strāui, strātum, 3, *stretch
out, fling down*

stimul-us, -i (m.), *sting, torment*

stīpendi-um, -i (n.), *pay, service*

stirps, stirpis (f.), *offspring*

sto, steti, statum, 1, *stand*

stolidē, *stupidly*

strāg-es, -is (f.), *massacre*

strēnu-us, -a, -um, *vigorous, nim-
ble*; strēnuē, *actively, energetically*

strep-o, -ui, 3, *roar, make a noise*

stringo, strinxi, strictum, 3, *unsheathe, draw*

stru-o, -xi, -ctum, 3, *contrive, erect*

studi-um, -i (n.), *enthusiasm, parti-
san zeal, inclination, profession,
pursuit*

suā-deo, -si, -sum, 2, *advise*

sub (prep. w. acc. and abl.), *under*

sub-do, -didi, -ditum, 3, *substitute*

subdol-us, -a, -um, *deceptive*

sub-dūco, -duxi, -ductum, 3, *lead
up*

sub-icio, -iēci, -iectum, 3, *subject*;

subiect-a, -ōrum (n. pl.), *lower
ground*

sub-igo, -ēgi, -actum, 3, *tame,
compel*

submer-go, -si, -sum, 3 (tr.),
drown

subnix-us, -a, -um, *relying on*

sub-scrībo, -scripsi, -scriptum, 3,
sign an acccusation

subsidiāri-us, -a, -um, *reserve*
subsidi-um, -i (n.), *aid, support*
subtra-ho, -xi, -ctum, 3, *take from beneath, suppress*
sub-uenio, -uēni, -uentum, 4, *help*
suc-cēdo, -cessi, -cessum, 3, *advance*
success-or, -ōris (m.), *successor*
suēt-us, -a, -um, *accustomed, customary*
suf-ficio, -fēci, -fectum, 3, *be sufficient*
suf-fodio, -fōdi, -fossum, 3, *pierce under* or *through*
suggest-us, -ūs (m.), *platform*
sum, fui, esse, *be*
sum-moueo, -mōui, -mōtum, 2, *remove*
summ-us, -a, -um, *most important, highest*
sūm-o, -psi, -ptum, 3, *take, assume*
sumpt-us, -ūs (m.), *expense*
super (adv.), *above*; (prep. w. acc.), *on top of, on*
superbi-a, -ae (f.), *pride, arrogance*
superbi-o, -īre, *be proud*
superi-or, -us, *upper*
supero, 1, *surmount, overcome, pass over*
superstagn-o, -āui, 1 (intr.), *spread out*
superst-es, -itis (c.), *survivor*
superstiti-o, -ōnis (f.), *superstition*
super-sum, -fui, -esse, *be left over, remain*
suppl-eo, -ēui, -ētum, 2, *make good, make up*
suppl-ex, -icis, *humble, submissive*
supplici-um, -i (n.), *punishment*
suprā (adv.), *over*; (prep. w. acc.), *above, over*
suprēm-us, -a, -um, *last*; suprēm-a, -ōrum (n. pl.), *last rites*
sur-go, -rexi, -rectum, 3, *rise*

sus-cipio, -cēpi, -ceptum, 3, *undertake*
suspecto, 1, *suspect*
suspen-do, -di, -sum, 3 (tr.), *hang up*; perf. part. suspens-us, -a, -um, *hesitant*
suspic-ax, -ācis, *suspicious*
su-spicio, -spexi, -spectum, 3, *look at askance, suspect (these meanings perhaps only in participles)*
sustento, 1, *support, maintain*
sus-tineo, -tinui, -tentum, 2, *hold up, support*
su-us, -a, -um, *his, her, its, their (own)*

tabernācul-um, -i (n.), *tent*
tāb-es, -is (f.), *wasting away*
taciturnit-as, -ātis (f.), *taciturnity*
taedi-um, -i (n.), *weariness*
tāl-is, -e, *such*
tam, *so*
tamen, *however, nevertheless*
tamquam, *as if, on the ground that*
tandem, *at last*
tant-us, -a, -um, *so great, so much*; tantum, *only*
tardo, 1, *make slow, delay*
tard-us, -a, -um, *slow*; tardē, *slowly*
Tarentīn-us, -a, -um, *Tarentine*
Tarracōnens-is, -e, *belonging to Tarraco*
tegm-en, -inis (n.), *covering, clothing*
te-go, -xi, -ctum, 3, *cover, hide*
tēl-um, -i (n.), *weapon*
temero, 1, *defile, dishonour*
temperanti-a, -ae (f.), *restraint*
tempero, 1, *refrain, regulate*
tempest-as, -ātis (f.), *time, season, storm*
templ-um, -i (n.), *temple, sanctuary*

tempto, 1, *try*

temp-us, -oris (n.), *time, season*;
in tempore, *opportunely*; tem-
por-a, -um (n. pl.), *crisis*

tēmulent-us, -a, -um, *drunken*

ten-ax, -ācis, *holding fast, tenacious*

tendo, tetendi, tentum, 3, *stretch
out, encamp, be quartered, aim, go*

tenebr-ae, -ārum (f.), *darkness*

ten-eo, -ui, -tum, 2, *hold, possess*

tentōri-um, -i (n.), *tent*

tenu-is, -e, *thin*

tenus (prep. w. abl.), *up to*

terg-um, -i (n.), *back, rear*

termin-us, -i (m.), *boundary*

terr-a, -ae (f.), *country, land, ground*

terreo, 2, *frighten*

terrestr-is, -e, *of the land*

terr-or, -ōris (m.), *fear, terror*

terti-us, -a, -um, *third*

testāment-um, -i (n.), *will*

test-is, -is (m.), *witness*

testor, 1 (dep.), *testify*

Teutoburgiens-is, -e, *Teutoburgen-
sian*

theātrāl-is, -e, *of the theatre, theatrical*

theātr-um, -i (n.), *theatre*

tim-or, -ōris (m.), *fear*

tīr-o, -ōnis (m.), *new recruit, inexperienced soldier*

Titi-us, -a, -um, *Titian*

titul-us, -i (m.), *title*

tog-a, -ae (f.), *toga, civil life*

tolero, 1, *endure*

tollo, sustuli, sublātum, 3, *remove*

torment-um, -i (n.), *engine*

tot (indecl. adj.), *so many*

totidem (indecl. adj.), *just as many*

totiens, *so often*

tōt-us, -a, -um, *whole*

tracto, 1, *treat, discuss, practise*

trā-do, -didi, -ditum, 3, *relate,
record, hand down, hand over*

tra-ho, -xi, -ctum, 3, *draw, drag,
appropriate, interpret*

trām-es, -itis (m.), *path*

trā-mitto, -mīsi, -missum, 3, *pass
over, send across*

tranquill-us, -a, -um, *quiet, peaceful*

trans-fero, -tuli, -lātum, -ferre,
transfer

trecēn-i, -ae, -a, *three hundred each*

trepido, 1, *be alarmed*

trepid-us, -a, -um, *anxious*

tr-ēs, -ia, *three*

tribūn-al, -ālis (n.), *platform*

tribūnici-us, -a, -um, *belonging to
a tribune*

tribūn-us, -i (m.), *tribune*

trib-uo, -ui, -ūtum, 3, *bestow*

trib-us, -ūs (m.), *tribe (political)*

tribūt-um, -i (n.), *tribute*

trīcēn-i, -ae, -a, *thirty each*

trīcies, *thirty times*

trīginta, *thirty*

trist-is, -e, *sad*

tristiti-a, -ae (f.), *moroseness*

triumphāl-is, -e, *triumphal*

triumph-us, -i (m.), *triumph*

triumuir, -i (m.), *one of a board of
three, triumvir*

trucīdo, 1, *murder*

truculent-us, -a, -um, *savage*

trū-do, -si, -sum, 3, *push*

truncāt-us, -a, -um, *mutilated*

trunc-us, -i (m.), *trunk*

trux, trucis, *fierce, savage*

tu, tui, *you (sing.)*

tub-a, -ae (f.), *trumpet*

tueor, 2 (dep.), *look upon, watch,
protect*

tum, *then*

tum-esco, -ui, 3, *swell*

tumultuāri-us, -a, -um, *hastily
raised*

tumult-us, -ūs (m.), *uproar*

tumul-us, -i (m.), *sepulchral mound,*
barrow
tunc, *then*
turb-a, -ae (f.), *mob rioting*
turbāt-or, -ōris (m.), *agitator, dis‑*
turber
turbid-us, -a, -um, *violent*
turbo, 1, *disturb, agitate*
turb-o, -inis (m.), *storm*
turp-is, -e, *shameful, disgraceful*
tūtēl-a, -ae (f.), *care, charge*
tūtor, 1 (dep.), *protect*
tūt-us, -a, -um, *safe*
tu-us, -a, -um, *your (sing.)*

uacāti-o, -ōnis (f.), *exemption*
uacu-us, -a, -um, *empty*
uadōs-us, -a, -um, *shallow*
uaecordi-a, -ae (f.), *madness*
uaecor-s, -dis, *mad, frenzied*
uagor, 1 (dep.), *go about, wander*
uag-us, -a, -um, *wandering*
ualeo, 2, *be strong, have strength*
ualētūd-o, -inis (f.), *state of health,*
ill health
ualid-us, -a, -um, *strong, vigorous,*
powerful
uall-es, -is (f.), *valley*
uall-um, -i (n.), *palisade, fortifica‑*
tion
uān-us, -a, -um, *empty, unmeaning*
Variān-us, -a, -um, *of Varus,*
Varian
uari-us, -a, -um, *various, different;*
uariē, *in different ways*
uasto, 1, *devastate*
uast-us, -a, -um, *enormous*
ubi, *where?, where (rel.), when*
-ue, *or*
uectīg-al, -ālis (n.), *tax*
uehicul-um, -i (n.), *carriage*
ue-ho, -xi, -ctum, 3, *convey, carry;*
in pass., drive, travel

uel, *or*
uelut, *as if*
uēnāl-is, -e, *for sale*
uenditi-o, -ōnis (f.), *sale*
uen-do, -didi, -ditum, 3, *sell*
uenēn-um, -i (n.), *poison*
uenerāti-o, -ōnis (f.), *respect*
ueni-a, -ae (f.), *pardon, indulgence*
uenio, uēni, uentum, 4, *come*
uēr, -is (n.), *spring*
uerb-er, -eris (n.), *whip;* in pl.
flogging
uerbero, 1, *beat*
uerb-um, -i (n.), *word*
uereor, 2 (dep.), *fear*
uerg-o, -ere, *bend, incline*
uērit-as, -ātis (f.), *truth*
uernācul-us, -a, -um, *of slaves*
uer-to, -ti, -sum, 3, *turn, overturn,*
change
uēr-us, -a, -um, *true;* uēr-um, -i
(n.), *truth;* uērum, uēro (adv.),
indeed
uesc-or, -i, *feed, eat*
uesper-a, -ae (f.), *evening*
uesper-asco, -āui, 3, *become evening*
uest-er, -ra, -rum, *your (pl.)*
uestīgi-um, -i (n.), *footstep, track,*
trace
uest-is, -is (f.), *clothing, dress*
ueterān-us, -a, -um, *veteran*
uet-us, -eris, *old, earlier*
uetust-as, -ātis (f.), *old age*
uetust-us, -a, -um, *ancient*
uexillāri-i, -ōrum (m. pl.), *army*
units
uexill-um, -i (n.), *standard*
ui-a, -ae (f.), *road, street, way*
uiātic-um, -i (n.), *travelling money*
uīcēn-i, -ae, -a, *twenty each*
uīcēsimān-us, -a, -um, *belonging to*
the twentieth legion; uīcēsimān-i,
-ōrum (m. pl.), *soldiers of the*
twentieth legion

uīcēsim-us, -a, -um, *twentieth*

uīcies, *twenty times*

uict-or, -ōris (m.), *victor*

uictōri-a, -ae (f.), *victory*

uīc-us, -i (m.), *village*

uideo, uīdi, uīsum, 2, *see; in pass., seem*

uig-eo, -ēre, *be vigorous*

uigili-ae, -ārum (f. pl.), *watchmen, watch*

uīginti, *twenty*

uīl-is, -e, *cheap*

uin-cio, -xi, -ctum, 4, *bind*

uinco, uīci, uictum, 3, *conquer*

uincul-um, -i (n.), *chain, bond*

uiolāt-or, -ōris (m.), *violator*

uiolenter, *violently*

uiolenti-a, -ae (f.), *violence*

uiolo, 1, *injure, dishonour*

uir, -i (m.), *man*

uirg-a, -ae (f.), *rod*

uirg-o, -inis (f.), *virgin*

uirīl-is, -e, *male*

uirītim, *individually*

uirt-ūs, -ūtis (f.), *worth, courage, quality*

uīs (def. noun) (f.), *violence, force, power*

uī-so, -si, -sum, 3, *visit*

uīs-us, -ūs (m.), *sight*

uīt-a, -ae (f.), *life*

uīt-is, -is (f.), *staff*

uiti-um, -i (n.), *vice, fault*

uitt-a, -ae (f.), *priest's fillet, chaplet*

uix, *scarcely*

uixdum, *scarcely*

ulciscor, ultus sum, 3 (dep.), *avenge*

ūlīg-o, -inis (f.), *moisture*

ull-us, -a, -um, *any*

ultim-us, -a, -um, *farthest*

ulti-o, -ōnis (f.), *vengeance*

ultrā (adv.), *farther;* (prep. w. acc.), *beyond*

ūmen-s, -tis, *damp*

umer-us, -i (m.), *shoulder*

ūmid-um, -i (n.), *damp place*

umquam, *ever*

ūnā (adv.), *together*

und-a, -ae (f.), *water, wave*

unde, *from where, from whom*

undēuīcēsim-us, -a, -um, *nineteenth*

undique, *on all sides*

ūnetuīcēsimān-i, -ōrum (m. pl.), *soldiers of the twenty-first legion*

ūnetuīcēsim-us, -a, -um, *twenty-first*

ūnic-us, -a, -um, *sole, single*

ūniuers-us, -a, -um, *general;* in pl., *all together;* in ūniuersum, *all together*

ūn-us, -a, -um, *one, only*

uocābul-um, -i (n.), *name, nickname*

uoco, 1, *call, summon, put*

uolito, 1, *rush about*

uolo, uolui, uelle, *wish, want*

uolunt-as, -ātis (f.), *inclination, good-will*

uol-uo, -ui, -ūtum, 3, *turn over, consider*

uolupt-as, -ātis (f.), *pleasure*

uolūto, 1, *turn over, consider*

uōs, uestri (uestrum), *you* (pl.)

uōt-um, -i (n.), *prayer*

uox, uōcis (f.), *voice*

urbān-us, -a, -um, *belonging to the city*

urbs, urbis (f.), *city*

urgeo, ursi, 2, *drive, urge*

ūro, ussi, ustum, 3 (tr.), *burn*

usque, *all the way to*

usquam, *anywhere*

ūsurpo, 1, *use, employ*

ūs-us, -ūs (m.), *employment, necessity*

ut, uti, *when, as, that, so that, how*

utcumque, *however*

ūtensili-a, -um (n. pl.), *neces-saries*

ut-erque, -raque, -rumque, *each*

uter-us, -i (m.), *womb*

ūtilit-as, -ātis (f.), *benefit, profit*

utinam (particle of wishing), *I wish that . . .!*

ūtor, ūsus sum, 3 (dep.), *use*

utrimque, *on both sides*

utrum, *whether*; utrum . . . an, *whether . . . or*

uulgo, 1, *publish*

uulg-us, -i (n.), *mob, public*

uulnero, 1, *wound*

uuln-us, -eris (n.), *wound*

uult-us, -ūs (m.), *facial expression*

ux-or, -ōris (f.), *wife*

uxōri-us, -a, -um, *belonging to a wife*